Date Due

JE 18 69	AG 25'72	AP 27'85
JY 16 69	CORRESPONDENCE STUDY	CORRESPONDENCE STUDY
AG 1 69		
AG 5'80	JA 08'74	
OC 09'69	JA 29'74	SE 09 '85
MAR 18 71	MY 07'74	
AP 09'71	JY 24'74	
AP 23'71	CORRESPONDENCE STUDY	
MY 07'71	OC 8 74	
	DE 9 74	
	CORRESPONDENCE STUDY	
MY 30'71	JE 10'76	
	AG 24'77	
JE 4'71	SE 06'76	
OC 13'71	CORRESPONDENCE STUDY	
JAN 8 72		
AG 03'72	AG 03'81	

Demco 38-297

William Boyd Allison

WILLIAM BOYD ALLISON

A Study in Practical Politics

By LELAND L. SAGE

STATE HISTORICAL SOCIETY OF IOWA

IOWA CITY 1956

**PRINTED IN THE UNITED STATES OF AMERICA
BY THE TORCH PRESS, CEDAR RAPIDS, IOWA**

To

MARGARET
CAROLYN
AND ALL OUR FAMILIES

Editor's Foreword

THIS life of one of Iowa's most distinguished citizens is the eighteenth full-length volume published by the State Historical Society of Iowa in its Biographical Series. It is the story of a man who represented Iowa longer in the halls of Congress than any other Iowan. It is the story of a long legislative career rarely equaled in the annals of American congressional history.

William Boyd Allison represented Iowa for forty-three years in Washington — eight years in the House of Representatives (1863-1871) and thirty-five years in the United States Senate (1873-1908). He was nominated for an unprecedented seventh term in the Senate and, had he lived, his service would have extended over forty-two years. His career ended an era which had seen a handful of Senators (Allison, Aldrich, Hale, Platt, and Spooner) virtually write the laws of this Nation. Such men as Robert M. La Follette, Charles Curtis, William E. Borah, and John H. Bankhead, were just beginning their senatorial careers when Allison died in 1908.

Only a man of magnetic personality and unimpeachable integrity could have endeared himself for so many years to Iowans. Although quiet, dignified, and unassuming, Allison commanded attention and respect whenever he appeared on an Iowa political platform or on the floor of the United States Senate. His audience invariably listened, learned, and went away impressed. The "capricious moods" of the Senate never baffled him. "His patience was never exhausted, the serenity of his temper never ruffled. He could grant to an adversary an amendment with such grace and deference to superior judgment

vii

that the flattered enemy accepted a few suggestions from the master as a tribute to his talents. The post-mortem revealed his mistake."

Allison liked people and people liked him. He was elected a member of Alpha Delta Phi at Western Reserve. He was a charter member of Mosaic Lodge No. 125, A.F. & A.M. at Dubuque and was present when his young secretary, Lee McNeely, received his Third Degree. When Dubuque high school won the state football championship in 1906, Senator Allison was invited to attend and respond to the toast "Our Boys." His great interest in young people probably endeared him to older ones. A young man once came to thank him for a position he had received through Allison and asked what he could do in return. Allison's reply was characteristic: "Yes, my boy, you can do much for me by doing well for yourself; be industrious and be honest." This advice epitomized Allison's own life: "Start right, keep right, end right."

Although Allison was deeply immersed in national politics for over forty years, he never lost contact with the home folks. His neighbors in Dubuque always rejoiced when Allison returned home and resumed his favorite post on the side porch at 1134 Locust Street. Looking back over a vista of ninety years, Mrs. Harriett Tredway Peaslee, who lived next door to Allison as a girl, remembers vividly that Senator Allison would call out "How's Hattie this morning," whenever she appeared in her garden. And when Hattie's husband returned from his Cascade lumber yards Allison would always inquire "How are the pigs coming." According to Mrs. Peaslee, Allison felt every Iowan ought to be concerned with crops and livestock.

Although austere in appearance, Allison was never severe. A correspondent of the Boston *Daily Advertiser* wrote in 1887 that Allison was "very approachable" in his comfortable Washington home.

It is a house which newspaper man, clerk, or searcher after aid or information never fears to enter. The reception is always frank, unaffected and thoroughly sincere. The visitor is sure to learn the first time just what can and just what cannot be done. He is made to feel at once that whatever is said is meant, that he has done right in speaking frankly and will be answered in that way. The man he faces carries the stamp of thorough fairness and honesty, even in the smallest things, in his face and eyes.

Allison could generally be found in one of two places — his home at 1124 Vermont Avenue, or his committee room. His favorite room at home was his sitting room and study, just back of the parlor and separated from it only by folding doors and portiers. Here, surrounded by his books, magazines, and Congressional Directories, and well supplied with long slender dark cigars "quite as likely to be chewed to pieces as smoked," Allison spent the hours from five to eleven o'clock at night poring over the work of Congress for that day and preparing for the morrow. He could always be found in his committee room at 9 a. m. "as owlish as Beck, Hoar or McMillan, and often more so than they. He is a very rapid writer, and in his correspondence he establishes the rule that every letter he receives shall be answered."

Despite his prodigious labors, Allison always found time to greet young people. "The small boy who ventures into the room when Mr. Allison is at liberty is sure to enjoy himself. For, while Mr. Allison has no children of his own, he has a great admiration for those of others, and especially for boys."

The high regard with which Allison was held in the Senate is recalled by his secretary — Lee McNeely of Dubuque. In 1907 all Senators were requested to send in their nominations for a new Reading Clerk to Senator Nelson W. Aldrich. Allison accepted McNeely's suggestion of John C. Crockett, a young man with a rich bass voice who had thrilled all attending the Republican state convention in Des Moines. After gaining the approval of Congressman Benjamin P. Birdsall of the Third District and the entire Iowa delegation, Allison recommended him. Competition for Reading Clerk finally narrowed down to John C. Crockett of Iowa and William Tyler Page of Virginia, who had served in the House Clerk's office since 1881. At this point Senator Aldrich called on McNeely and told him the choice lay between his own candidate (Page) and Crockett, but that he would defer in favor of Allison's candidate if it would help the elder statesman in Iowa. McNeely said Crockett's appointment would be highly beneficial to Allison, and John C. Crockett received the appointment, which he held for forty years, retiring to Eldora in 1947 at the age of eighty-three.

Allison's library of approximately fifteen hundred volumes is housed in the Allison Room in the Dubuque Public Library. In addition to hundreds of books on government, economics, history, banking, finance, and the tariff, the library contained volumes of American and English literature. An omnivorous reader, Allison doubtless read most of these volumes, if only for relaxation from the strain that accompanied his efforts to solve the many problems facing the Nation. Alexander Hamilton was his guidepost in finance, Robert Burns his favorite poet, and "The Cotter's Saturday Night" his favorite poem. The Allison Room and the Allison-Henderson Memorial Park in Dubuque pay tribute to this great statesman.

Seventeen Senators and thirteen Representatives eulogized Allison in memorial services in Washington. Senator Hale declared Allison brought to the task of legislation "unbounded good sense, fidelity of purpose," and a matchless "capacity for sustained labor." Senator Aldrich extolled him as an "acknowledged leader" whose "irresistible charm" made him unique in the Senate, where he was the "oldest in service, wisest in counsel, the friend and mentor of all." Champ Clark asserted Allison had achieved the "widest and most enduring fame" of any Iowan. Chauncey Depew closed his eulogy as follows:

If, as I believe, those who meet in the activities of this life are reunited hereafter, it was a wonderful band of immortals who greeted Allison. . . . When he first obtained the floor in Congress, he addressed Speaker Schuyler Colfax, and when he spoke last, forty-five years afterwards, Vice-President Fairbanks in the chair recognized the Senator from Iowa. Seward, Chase, and Stanton, John Sherman, James G. Blaine, and Thaddeus Stevens were his associates and intimates. When the future historian writes the story of this remarkable period and portrays the actors in that great national drama who contributed to its distinction, he will place among the few in the front rank the name of William B. Allison.

In the following pages Professor Leland Sage has faithfully covered the highlights of Allison's career, his many political battles, and his services to Iowa and to the Nation. Representing a dozen years of painstaking research, the book will stand as a monument to the memory of perhaps the greatest statesman ever to serve Iowa in the Nation's capitol. As the "Sage of Dubuque" was laid to rest in Dubuque an admirer declared: "Like the majestic river, bluff and forest crowned, that washes her eastern border, the influence of his life will flow on and on, a blessing to all mankind."

WILLIAM J. PETERSEN

OFFICE OF THE SUPERINTENDENT
STATE HISTORICAL SOCIETY OF IOWA
IOWA CITY, IOWA

Acknowledgments

My DEBT TO many scholars is great. Edward Younger of the University of Virginia, author of the biography, *John A. Kasson*, published by the State Historical Society in 1955, has been a never-failing source of information, guidance, and friendly encouragement. Ralph M. Sayre, formerly of Parsons College, now dean of the College of Idaho, who is writing a biography of Albert B. Cummins, has been most generous in sharing his notes and his ideas with me. The Reverend Harry J. Sievers, S.J., whose exhaustive study of Benjamin Harrison is far advanced, has kindly furnished many pertinent items. My colleague, Wallace D. Farnham, read the manuscript in rough draft.

I am especially grateful to officials of the Newberry Library, Chicago, for a Fellowship in Midwestern Studies, and to President James W. Maucker and Dean Martin J. Nelson of Iowa State Teachers College for grants from the faculty research funds.

Curators of manuscript collections have been most kind and generous. Claude R. Cook and Emory H. English of the Iowa State Department of History and Archives at Des Moines have assisted me in more ways than I can enumerate here. I have been privileged to draw on their personal knowledge of Iowa political history as well as on the archival riches in their keeping. David C. Mearns, Chief, and C. Percy Powell of the Division of Manuscripts, Library of Congress; Stanley Pargellis of the Newberry Library; Jay Monaghan and the late Harry E. Pratt, Illinois State Historical Library; Richard C. Overton, trustee of the Cunningham-Overton Collection of Charles E. Perkins Letterbooks; Watt P. Marchman, Rutherford B. Hayes

Memorial Library, Fremont, Ohio; and Stephen T. Riley, Massachusetts Historical Society, Boston, gave access to their materials.

Librarians in many places have complied with my requests for assistance: Marybelle McClelland and Donald O. Rod, and staff members Evelyn Mullins and Mary Dieterich, at Iowa State Teachers College; the librarians of the State University of Iowa, Indiana University, Ohio State Museum, Western Reserve Historical Society, Princeton University, New York Public Library; at the municipal public libraries at Wooster, Ashland, and Hudson, Ohio, and at Cedar Falls, Burlington, Cedar Rapids, Des Moines, Charles City, and Dubuque, Iowa. The Waterloo *Courier* allowed the use of its volumes.

Abram Garfield granted the use of certain restricted papers of President James A. Garfield; Winthrop W. Aldrich made a similar dispensation for a portion of the Nelson W. Aldrich papers; Frederick Sheffield of New York City, Mrs. Donald Metcalf (Elizabeth Clarkson Zwart) of Des Moines, Mrs. L. L. J. Howe of Highland Park, Illinois, and Fred H. Allison of Belmond, Iowa, kindly allowed me the use of family papers in their possession. Lee McNeely of Dubuque, Allison's last secretary, has been helpful in supplying information and reminiscences; so have been F. E. Bissell, John R. Wallis, Martha Baker, Elsie Datisman, and Ethel Linehan.

Others whom I wish to thank for various forms of assistance are Carolyn S. Robinson, Mary Gantt Stinnett, Patricia Sage, William C. Lang, Irving H. Hart, Alison Aitchison, James Hearst, Wallace Anderson, Edward Nehls, Fred and Lois Wellborn, Frances P. Dolliver, Mrs. Adelaide Seemuth, George S. May, Ardis S. Mork, and Carolyn S. Rowray.

William J. Petersen, genial superintendent of the State Historical Society of Iowa, has encouraged me steadily from the day I first broached the subject of a biography of Senator Allison. Mildred Throne, associate editor for the Society, who was particularly charged with the oversight of this book and the tedious details of seeing the manuscript through the press, will always be gratefully remembered for her contributions toward its improvement and its completion.

Finally, I am grateful to my wife, Margaret Pearson Sage, for her long hours of library work, note-taking, and discerning criticism.

LELAND L. SAGE

Iowa State Teachers College,
Cedar Falls, Iowa

Contents

Illustrations

☆ I ☆

The Ohio Years

ON A HOT August day in 1908 they brought the old man home to die. For more than a year he had suffered from a glandular trouble common to advanced age — he good-naturedly referred to it as his "local trouble" — but only recently had the disease become acute, weakening him in body and mind. Two months before, on the assumption that he could serve another term, the Conservative Republicans of Iowa had fought off the challenge of a brilliant spokesman of the younger Progressives and had nominated the venerable statesman for a seventh term in the United States Senate. But now the hand of death could no longer be stayed. So they brought him in from the country estate of an old friend, whence he had been taken to escape the intense heat of Dubuque, to let him die in the familiar surroundings of the modest home that had been his for half a century. The long public career of William Boyd Allison had come to a close.

As a lawyer-politician, transplanted from Ohio, Allison had bought that home shortly before Lincoln's first inaugural. As one of the faithful, he had been present in Washington to hear Lincoln say: "A majority held in restraint by constitutional checks and limitations, and always changing easily with deliberate changes of popular opinions and sentiments, is the only true sovereign of a people." By this principle, implemented as it was in his day, Allison had been willing to live his life. By it he had lost several bids for office, including one that furnished a vision of the White House; by it he had won

1

ten elections and was in line for an inevitable eleventh victory when the end came.

In 1863 William Boyd Allison had been sworn in as a Republican member of the lower house of Congress. Now, in 1908, not one man who had held high national office in that year was still serving his nation — he had outlived and outrun most of his early rivals in the intervening races for place, power, and fame. But at last he was ready to join them in final retirement. Never a professing believer, he had made his peace with his God. He slept.

From far and wide they came to do him honor. For a day the roll call of the political leaders of Washington would have to be made in Dubuque. President Theodore Roosevelt, whom Allison had served so well, could not come, but Vice President Charles W. Fairbanks was there. Senators, Representatives, Governor Albert B. Cummins of Iowa (whose effort to unseat him he had recently repulsed), state legislators by the score, friends from the worlds of politics, business, journalism, agriculture, education, labor — all were there, so many that it would be hopeless to attempt a definitive enumeration. At the hour of his funeral all Iowa paused in silent tribute; in Dubuque businessmen closed their doors. A few days later an old friend wrote of him: "Iowa is nearly an orphan in these days. . . . It seems as though we had lost a point of the compass." Later he would be honored by a monument erected on the grounds of the State Capitol, the only one of her citizens that Iowa has honored in this fashion.

Such, in brief, was the career of Senator William Boyd Allison of Iowa. We would like to know as much of his origins, but only a few forebears can be named. This would be a matter of greater regret but for the fact that he himself did not make much of his family — he was not a "family man" by profession. Allison was born March 2, 1829, the second son of John and Margaret (Williams) Allison, in Perry Township, Wayne (now Ashland) County, Ohio. His father was born in 1798 near Bellefonte, Pennsylvania, the son of a certain Matthew Allison, born in the north of Ireland in 1750. There are no records of this Matthew Allison, but he is referred to as a veteran of the Revolutionary War who settled in Centre County, Pennsylvania. His wife's name is not known.

John's wife and her family are likewise shrouded in obscurity. A propertied family by the name of Williams, presumably hers, lived in Bellefonte in 1824, the year of the marriage of John and Margaret.

The *Book of Marriages* of Wayne County, Ohio, gives December 2, 1824, as the date of the marriage; the inference is that John Allison preceded Margaret Williams to the Ohio frontier and that she followed later for the wedding. According to the headstone over her grave in the cemetery of the hamlet of Rowsburg, Ohio, Margaret died on October 10, 1861, aged sixty-two years, two months, and two days. This would make her birth date August 8, 1799.

Allison told friends in later years that his middle name, Boyd, came from his mother's relatives and that the forebears on both sides of his family were Scotch-Irish. One of Allison's friends, in a short sketch of his life, wrote of Margaret Allison: "She was a fine specimen of the matrons of those days, and her strong mind, quick apprehension, and executive capacity was inherited by her son." [1]

John Allison acquired a farm in Wayne County and settled down to the frontiersman's life of clearing the forest. The farm was on good level land of at least average fertility.[2] The Allisons seem to have lived a life comparable to that of their neighbors. Three children were born to them: Matthew, born October 20, 1827; William Boyd, born March 2, 1829; James Harrison, born July 27, 1835.[3] Father John was for many terms a justice of the peace, a staunch Whig,[4] and a member of the Mount Hope Presbyterian Church, where the family attended services regularly.[5] In short, the Allisons were typically honest, God-fearing people who were inconspicuous members of the great migratory forces that quickly transformed the state of Ohio from the wilderness of the 1790's to the well-developed, widely populated state of 1850.[6]

Three separate waves of migrants swept across Ohio almost simultaneously, initiating historical forces which still exert their influence. A New England wave washed across New York and northwestern Pennsylvania, finally depositing its burden in the northeast corner of Ohio. Many of the pioneers came from Connecticut and settled down in the lands reserved by that state — the famous "Western Reserve." Bringing with them their ideas on religion, education, and architecture, they stamped the whole region with the New England character.[7] Up to 1850 the Industrial Revolution had not affected this area extensively. "As Quebec was, in a sense, more like Old France than France itself, the Western Reserve was in some respects more like the land of the old-time Puritan than the region east of the Hudson." [8]

Another wave of migration was mostly made up of Scotch-Irish settlers who came to Ohio by way of Pennsylvania, New York, New Jersey, Delaware, and Maryland.[9] Very obviously, the Allisons belonged to this wave. These migrants settled in the central and southern tiers of counties and tended to move farther west than had the New Englanders, who waited some time before they sent settlers on to the other western states. It has been claimed that these Scotch-Irish were the most valuable element in the make-up of the American people.[10] "The Irish who came to Ohio before 1825 were largely Scotch-Irish, many of whom had lived for a time in the Middle States or in Virginia or Kentucky. Most of them were Ulster Protestants like James Wilson, who became a Steubenville editor, and was destined to be the grandfather of [Woodrow Wilson]." [11] By virtue of his family connections and residence in Wayne and Ashland counties, William Boyd Allison enjoyed to the highest degree the legacy of these people. At the same time, because of proximity to the Western Reserve and by schooling in that area, he benefited from the New England influence.

A third wave of settlers came from the South, principally from the vast state of Virginia, as it was then organized, and from Kentucky. These people, too, brought their culture with them — their manners, their architecture, their ideas pro and con slavery. A few of them were abolitionists, many of them were voluntary emancipators of their slaves, some believed in gradual emancipation and colonization of the Negro, and many, especially in and near Cincinnati, were still proslavery or at least states' rights people. The Allisons were far removed from them both in residence and in ideas.

William Boyd Allison left virtually no accounts of his boyhood and early manhood.[12] The story has to be pieced together from many widely divergent sources. A few facts and impressions can be gained by a study of the career of one of his well-known boyhood companions and schoolmates, Clement (Clem) Studebaker, of wagon and automobile fame. Clem and his four brothers and their father, John, lived only a mile or so from the Allison farm.[13] In 1897, on the occasion of a civic reunion, Studebaker returned to Ashland as a hero of the Industrial Revolution. He made a rather affecting reminiscent speech and then toured the surrounding country to revisit the scenes of his childhood, in his remarks coupling himself in memory with Senator William B. Allison, then at the height of his fame and power.

The Studebakers, like the Allisons, had come from Pennsylvania; hard times forced their father to put some of the boys out to work. Young Allison, who also "worked out," doubtless knew the same people and had the same boyhood experiences as young Clem Studebaker. Two items stand out in Clem's reminiscences. While driving through the Ohio countryside, he pointed out the site of the schoolhouse, where he and Allison had first attended school. The next stop was at the Daniel Carter farm on the Wooster road, where he had worked fifty years before at $4.00 a month. "He helped the girls churn butter, milked the cows, helped with the washing, did all kinds of work on the farm, and spent some of the happiest days of his life at this place. Mrs. Carter was a remarkable woman. Daniel Carter was one of the active movers in getting the new county, Ashland, formed." [14] This family was important in the life of Bill Allison also; he married one of the Carter girls.

Young William had better than average cultural opportunities for his day. In his home, as in most of the other Presbyterian homes of the frontier, churchgoing was virtually as much an educational program as a religious interest. The Presbyterians, like the Congregationalists and Episcopalians, were more concerned over an educated ministry than some other denominations of the developing frontier; they also were concerned over the education of the rank-and-file membership. "The net result of this emphasis was to make almost every Presbyterian preacher in the West, a school master." [15]

After attendance in the country school, Allison went to the village of Wooster, some twenty miles away, for tuition in Professor Parrot's Academy. Diligent inquiry and research have turned up no information regarding such an academy, but Allison mentioned it prominently and apparently with pride in the short biographical sketches written or authorized by him. The farm boy did not cut a very fine figure among his friends, judging from a description written by a former schoolmate:

At school he was somewhat familiarly known as "Big-Eyed Bill," and the girls of those days about Wooster, Ohio, used to laugh at the awkward and overgrown youngster, who took it good humoredly, however, and soon showed that he had good stuff in him. A lady who was in school with him says:

"Little did any of us think that boy would ever amount to anything. He was at the foot of our class and the butt of all, he was such a greenhorn. He lived on a farm, and walked into Wooster every day to school. He never wore any suspenders, and was always hitching up his trousers like a sailor. When we girls made fun of him he would run after us, and if he caught one that girl was sure to be kissed. And he had a horrible tobacco breath. I believe that boy chewed tobacco from the time he put on boy's clothes. But he was kind hearted and would never tell the teacher, no matter what we put on him. Yes, 'Big-Eyed Bill' was patient as an ox." [16]

Following his schooling at Wooster, Allison was persuaded by Wooster friends to attend Allegheny College at Meadville, Pennsylvania. The centennial history of the college refers to him as a member of the class of 1852, coming from "Perry, Ohio" in 1848. Actually he was enrolled in the preparatory academy that was conducted in conjunction with the college. [17] Among Allison's contemporaries at Allegheny was Cyrus K. Holliday, with whom he kept house and "got up" meals. Holliday later helped found the city of Topeka and organize the Republican party in Kansas and was the first president of the Santa Fe Railway.

The effect of the Allegheny experience on Allison can only be a subject of speculation. His attendance there fell during the thirteen-year regime of President John Barker, one of the brighter periods during the early days of struggle for survival so common to all frontier or "fresh-water" colleges. The academy and college students were treated much alike. As one of approximately 175 academy students, the young Ohioan could have joined with the others to hear the sparkling debates between Allegheny's professor of mathematics, Calvin Kingsley (later a Methodist bishop), and President Rufus P. Stebbins of the newly founded rival, the Meadville Theological Seminary — champions, respectively, of orthodox Trinitarianism and questionable Unitarianism. If these debates did not attract Allison's Presbyterian ears, surely there were hot discussions of the issues arising from the war with Mexico. The all-important literary societies would also furnish ample outlets for his interests and energies. [18]

Allegheny College, founded in 1817 by a Presbyterian minister who hoped to reproduce his beloved alma mater, Harvard College, in the West, had been lost by the Presbyterians to the Methodists, who took over the institution in 1833; yet the school was not narrowly sectarian. "Boys of many creeds came freely to the halls of Bentley [the original college building]." [19] Allison himself left no record of his own religious convictions; he was never the kind to talk freely about a thing so personal.

The record is furthermore blank as to Allison's failure to return to the halls of Bentley after only one year of attendance. Perhaps a lack of funds affected the decision, although the outlay was small in view of the housekeeping arrangements he shared with Cyrus Holliday. It seems to have been a common experience for many boys to attend only a brief period.[20] Allison interrupted his course to follow the familiar pattern of so many lawyer-politicians in the making — he became a schoolteacher. The fact is mentioned only casually in the biographical sketches and in but a few letters of all the thousands he preserved. In January, 1866, Sadie A. Cook of Coupeville in Washington Territory wrote to ask him if he were her "well beloved teacher of early childhood days . . . the W. B. Allison who taught school in Cambridge, Ohio." [21] A letter from Rev. David A. Cunningham asserts that both he and Allison taught school in the Perry Township neighborhood and that they attended old-fashioned spelling bees together. "When you and I were young school teachers I never forget [sic] the spelling school or match we had one night at the Jones School house." [22]

After this interlude of schoolteaching came what was surely the most exciting year of Allison's life to that date — a year at Western Reserve College at Hudson in the very heart of the New England of the West. Twenty-one years old and out in the world more than the average young man of his community, he was in a fair way toward learning something of real importance. The issues of the day, culminating in the Compromise of 1850, were very much in the air. The Allisons were Whigs, and Father John was something of a local leader, so it is quite reasonable to assume that a young man with a normal interest in public affairs would be alive to the question of the extension and expansion of the South's "peculiar institution." In going to Western Reserve, Allison was entering a hotbed of interest in the subject.

It was Allison's misfortune to matriculate in this "Yale of the West" at a time when the college's affairs were in a state of crisis and its very continuance doubtful. Financial difficulties, the bane of the existence of all such small denominational colleges, were no less present at Western Reserve than anywhere else. Allison, one of but fifty-three students, was admitted to membership in the Alpha Delta Phi fraternity, a group well known for its high scholastic standing.

The faculty consisted of President George Edward Pierce, one professor, and one tutor.[23]

Allison lived and studied only one year among the Presbyterians of the Western Reserve in their educational capital at Hudson. This year put him into close contact with the most pronounced religious background for antislavery agitation [24] and gave him a chance to learn to work with people of this persuasion, even though his own personal traits would never allow him to express himself in their manner.[25] Most of this antislavery feeling and action eventually came to be channeled into the Republican party, whose early history owed much to the leadership of the churches and the church colleges.[26] A short time later the people of the Reserve became famous for their thoroughgoing Republicanism, so much so that when an Iowan wanted to report to an Ohioan on the enthusiastic Republicanism of northern Iowa, he knowingly compared it to the Western Reserve.[27] A Democratic editor in Cleveland, suffering under Republican zeal and recognizing its true source, broke out with a veritable rage: "These old blue law, blue bellied Presbyterians that hung the witches and banished the Quakers, are determined to convert the people of this region into a race of psalm singers, using the degenerate dregs of the old puritans remaining here to drive the Democracy out." [28]

Sometime in 1850 or 1851 Allison returned to Wooster, the scene of his previous study in Professor Parrot's Academy, this time to read law in the office of Hemphill and Turner.[29] The fact that his older brother Matthew had located there as a drygoods merchant may have influenced William's choice of Wooster.[30] His law study probably followed the usual custom of acting as office boy and messenger, all the while absorbing scraps of legal learning more by osmosis than by cerebration. He was admitted to the bar after less than a year's study, a much less significant accomplishment at that time than would now be the case.[31]

Allison chose Ashland as the place to hang out his first shingle. There would seem to be several good reasons for this move. In 1846 his township, Perry, and three others in the same range had been joined to other townships for the creation of Ashland County. Ashland, a new and growing county seat, might offer legal business to the young lawyer back from his travels and his studies. It was a flourishing small town, only three or four miles from the scenes of his boyhood and from his father's home. Old family friends and neighbors would be potential clients. Furthermore, a friend of the family, Jacob O. Jennings, the county clerk, could offer clerical work on conveyancing and other legal routines which would add to his legal learning and at the same time eke out his purse.[32] Since Allison's practice was admittedly small, he spent most of his time in reading works on government, economics, and history. There were three partnerships in four years: first with a J. W. Smith; second, with Bolivar W. Kellogg; and finally with one William Osborn.[33] In 1852 Allison took a small local part in the losing Whig campaign for Winfield Scott against Franklin Pierce.

In spite of partnership troubles and a meager income, Allison made a secure place for himself in his community in a remarkably short time. He acquired property in a good section of the town, joined the Masonic Lodge, and quickly became an officer in it.[34] In 1854 he married into the county's first family, the Daniel Carters, who were from Maryland and Pennsylvania. Daniel Carter, who built the first cabin in the township that contains the present city of Ashland,[35] was the employer of Clem Studebaker and, most likely, of William ("Big-Eyed Bill") Allison. Anna Carter was the lady's name, although it was frequently written as Anne or Ann. The one printed enumeration of the members of the Carter family would indicate that the bride was sixteen years older than the groom,[36] a statement that may have been an error. Even so, it surely was a stroke of good fortune for an impecunious young lawyer to contract a marriage alliance with the first family of the town and county.

William B. Allison, now attorney at law and solicitor in chancery, came into the professional arena at a momentous time. A fledgling lawyer could not have begun his career when state and national politics were in a greater state of flux. The Compromise of 1850 had provided a temporary pacification of the basic quarrel between proslavery and antislavery groups; but slowly and surely the forces that were leading up to a crisis were doing their work. Eventually a man would have to take his stand. Several years later Lincoln would say unequivocally that the nation could not survive half-free and half-slave, but already men were beginning to make up their minds and announce their decisions, pro and con. Some drifted into one camp or the other as the years went by, while others could not decide finally and definitely until forced to do so by the opening of hostilities in 1861.

In later life Allison acquired the reputation of a cautious and non-controversial man, but in these early days of decision and action he was among the first to line up with the men who eventually made up the Republican party. There was no compromise here, unless one regards the entire Republican position itself as a compromise between abolitionism and tolerance. Regardless of what later uses this party was put to, and regardless of Allison's motivation then or later, the credit for helping form an antislavery party is his and cannot be denied him. The antislavery influence encountered at Western Reserve College undoubtedly was one explanation for his attitude. His was a modest part, for there is not a single known copy of any burning message or stirring appeal from him, but he made his way from Whiggism into Republicanism, with only a slight and possibly calculated detour into Know-Nothingism, and never left the slightest doubt as to his basic decision to go along with the new movement — all of this in the face of the fact that the two counties he drew business from were Democratic.

Many diverse elements had to be brought together to form the political amalgamation which within two years of its first formal meetings would take its place as a major party and within six years win a presidential contest. In the words of John R. Commons, "Its members came together by a magic attraction, as crystals appear in a chilled solution. Not one man nor one set of men formed the party. . . . The fluid solution was there, and when the chill came the crystals formed." [37]

Every state had its own story and its own leaders. In Allison's home state, the blending of the various elements is most importantly shown in the series of events that led to the formation at Columbus in 1855 of a Fusion (Republican) party which nominated and later elected Salmon Portland Chase as Governor of the state on an antislavery platform. In fact, the story of this formative stage of Ohio Republican politics almost takes the form of a biography of Chase. This is fortunate, because Allison was a Chase man at the time and also at the 1860 convention in Chicago. Thus, in studying Chase, we indirectly study Allison.

Chase well illustrates the difficulties which beset the politicians of his time. He began his career as a Whig, but in 1849 went over to the Free Soilers. As such, he was elected to the United States Senate in 1849 by an Ohio legislature that was a mixture of uncertain Democrats, Whig remnants, and Free Soilers. In 1851 Chase deserted the Free Soilers for the Democrats, but he continued to classify himself along with Senator Benjamin F. Wade, a Whig, as an antislavery man. Chase's purpose in going over to the old party was to work for its conversion into a Free Democratic party, but his efforts were a decided failure. In 1852 the proslavery Franklin Pierce was elected President, and in 1856 Chase's own state elected a state legislature with a clear Democratic majority which would in time replace him as Senator with George E. Pugh, a proslavery man.[38] In spite of this, Chase remained firm in his antislavery convictions. In 1854 he became a recognized leader of the opposition to the Kansas-Nebraska Act, and his "Appeal of the Independent Democrats in Congress to the People of the United States," which was endorsed by Senator Charles Sumner and four abolitionists in the House, "set off the explosion" that produced the Republican party.[39]

All over the Midwest and in scattered places elsewhere men were meeting to discuss the issue brought up by the passage of the Kansas-Nebraska Act. Their sacred purpose was the prevention of the extension of slavery into the territories; many of them approached the problem with Christian consciences and Christian determination to stamp out the whole institution of slavery. It was distinctly not an abolitionist movement in the Garrisonian sense, but there were many abolitionists in it, and the antislavery impulse owes much to them. Congregationalists, Methodists, and Baptists from New England, Presbyterians of New York and Pennsylvania, Quakers of Pennsylvania, and their children of the frontier states, a myriad of people such as the Allisons, furnished the backbone of the new and rapidly growing movement.[40] It was not a movement of people of great wealth or high social station. Small farmers like the Allisons and laboring people and small merchants in the cities formed the rank and file of the party.[41]

Many towns vie for the the honor of being the birthplace of the Republican party. Ripon in Wisconsin, Jackson in Michigan, and other places claim the distinction. As one historian has put it, "Many a Republican has made his pilgrimage and stood in devout reverence on the spot pointed out to him as the birthplace of his party. Not all of them, however, have stood at the same place." [42] There were dozens of birthplaces because everywhere throughout the Middle West and in many places in the East, in schools, churches, public buildings, and shaded groves, under a variety of titles, people were meeting to form an opposition to Stephen A. Douglas and the Democracy.

Such a meeting was held in Ashland, Ohio, on May 11, 1854, and three Allisons — John, J. B. [W. B.?], and Alexander — were present and prominent enough to warrant special notice.[43] The Allisons had been staunch Whigs, but many a Whig now cast in his lot with the new movement. These anti-Nebraska meetings were taking place all over the Midwest. In Iowa they were held under the leadership of James W. Grimes, the father of Republicanism in that state, and Allison's future mentor. Others active in Iowa were James Harlan, educator, politician, Methodist leader, and Allison's great rival in days yet to come; Josiah B. Grinnell, who would later be Allison's colleague in the convention of 1860 and in the House of Representatives; James F. Wilson, ex-Ohioan and colleague-to-be in both houses of the national legislature and also a business associate. Some day Allison would meet these men and others such as Samuel J. Kirkwood, William Peters Hepburn, Aylett R. Cotton, and William Loughridge, all Ohio-Iowans, and be able to compare the Iowa and Ohio stories.

In Ohio the supreme leader was Salmon Portland Chase. Anti-Nebraska Democrats, ex-Whigs, Free Soilers, Know-Nothings, and Independents must all be fused into one united party. The leaders, practical politicians who were aware of the need for a vote-getting organization, knew all the tricks of building one. The first and most important job was to bring about a victory for the antislavery over the antiforeigner element of the Know-Nothing party. No less a man than Chase himself cooperated with the Know-Nothings.[44] In view of Allison's devotion to Chase it is not surprising to find that the young Ashland lawyer at one time "carried a dark lantern." [45]

Months went by while personal and political forces were at work to bring about fusion. To change the figure, the ordeal of birth was long drawn out, and there were many moments of uncertainty over the outcome. On July 13, 1854, a fusion convention met in Columbus in the City Hall but had to move into a larger building, because a thousand delegates had swarmed into the city for this meeting. Among the thousand was William Boyd Allison, a delegate from Ashland County.[46]

The convention adopted seven resolutions as a platform, the main plank being one that promised to nullify the Kansas-Nebraska Act wherever it affected territory that had been made free by the Missouri Compromise. The platform further promised to oppose by lawful means any additional increase in either slave states or slave territory.[47] This momentous action was followed by the nomination of candidates for state offices. An illustration of the confusion of the times is seen in the uncertainty over a name for the new group. One paper called them the "Republicans," but names such as "People's Movement" and "Anti-Nebraska Movement" also appeared. Some used the name "Know-Nothings" because of the close affiliation. Whatever its name, the ticket was victorious, but the fight was not over.

After much persuasion, the antislavery, anti-Douglas forces took another long step forward on July 13, 1855, the exact anniversary of the first meeting, a date originally chosen on sentimental grounds as the anniversary of the passage of the Northwest Ordinance in 1787. Allison was there to take a part. "On Friday, the thirteenth of July, in the Town Street Methodist Church at Columbus, the Ohio Republican party shed the outworn garments of fusion."[48] John Sherman, the permanent chairman of the convention, has left his own description of the meeting and of Allison's official part in it. The convention, Sherman wrote, was "composed of heterogeneous elements, every shade of political opinion being represented." The first problem, that of choosing a chairman who had not been "offensively conspicuous in one of the old parties," was resolved by the election of Sherman himself. His comment, "I was selected, much to my surprise, and, for a time, much to my chagrin," is understandable: at this time Lincoln himself would not have publicly joined in a meeting with such a party. "Mr. Allison, since a distinguished Member of the United States Senate," Sherman concluded, "was elected secretary of the convention."[49]

If John Sherman, the Mansfield lawyer and Congressman, had not been found "offensively conspicuous," it is pretty safe to assume that young William B. Allison, the Ashland attorney of some three years' standing, also escaped this characterization. But if not offensively conspicuous, nevertheless he was there as a founder and an officer. Since this was one of the major events of his early life, it would be interesting to know in detail the alignment of forces that made him secretary of the convention. In politics even a minor office such as this has some significance. To bestow it on someone is to win that person's influence and support and maybe that of a faction to which he belongs. Of more importance to Allison himself, however, would be the friendships and acquaintances to be followed up in years to come. To be able to boast in the future that one had been a charter member of the Republican party, especially in a key state such as Ohio, would mean a favored position in the small and select group that initiated and won a revolution and received as their reward the power to run the country for many years to come.

But it is not enough to account for Allison as a Republican, even as a founder, in 1855. In the confused politics of the times, that new party had as yet no national organization and, indeed, none at all in some of the states — Iowa, for example. Even the name was not yet a certain one, and survival was only a probability. Like a new religion, it had to draw off both members and doctrine from some of its predecessors and its current rivals if it were to endure and prosper. Specifically, it must replace the old Whig party in the North and it must contain its rival of almost identical age, the American party, better known as the "Know-Nothings." [50] There was a real doubt as to which party would absorb the other. Some of the Northern state branches of the Know-Nothing party had antislavery sentiments similar to the Republicans, while the Southern branches were strongly proslavery.

A prolonged period of doubtful relationships between the Republicans and the Know-Nothings marks the political history of 1855-1856. Some men found it possible, probably expedient, to join both groups and wait to see which one triumphed. For instance, Lieutenant Governor Thomas H. Ford of Ohio, who led that state's delegation to the Know-Nothing convention in February of 1856, was one of the candidates for Vice President on the Frémont ticket at the Republican convention in June of the same year.[51] There was nothing inconsistent in such a dual membership, in the one supporting the Republican gospel of opposition to the extension of slavery into the territories, in the other the Know-Nothing "nativist" doctrine of "America for Americans." But the Republicans could not absorb the anti-Catholic and antiforeign doctrines of the Know-Nothings without antagonizing some of the very groups they hoped to attract to their banner, such as the German immigrants. Conversely, the Know-Nothings thought of themselves as a safe, unionist, middle group between the extremists on the slavery question, both of whom were dis-unionist in tendency.[52]

Like many other ex-Whigs, Allison played along with both groups. He was one of the twenty-three Ohio delegates to the Know-Nothing convention at Philadelphia in February, 1856. This implies that he had previously been a leader of that party on the local level in his home state, as charged by an opposition newspaper when it asserted that he was a charter member of the first Know-Nothing lodge in Ashland County. Very likely this was true.

The Philadelphia meeting of the Know-Nothings took place on February 19-21, 1856.[53] The delegates were torn by battles over the platform, over the admission of certain delegations — especially those from Louisiana and Pennsylvania — and by mutual recriminations.[54] Governor Ford of Ohio was accused at least twice on the floor of being a "Black Republican" trying to disrupt the convention — an accusation which was promptly denied but would seem to have had some basis in fact. Ford led the Northern bolters who left the convention when the proslavery members seemed to be gaining the upper hand, and, as already mentioned, was later considered for the vice-presidential nomination by the Republicans in June. After the bolt of the Northern, antislavery men — including Allison — the remaining members of the convention nominated Millard Fillmore and Andrew Jackson Donelson as the Know-Nothing standard-bearers.[55] But the split caused by the Ohio men had damaged the party beyond repair.

Nothing daunted, the proslavery Know-Nothings met again at Philadelphia on June 12 and made a public announcement of Fillmore's acceptance. On the same day the antislavery "North Americans" — the seceders of the February meeting — met in New York. After a hard fight on the part of some for John C. Frémont, the convention nominated Nathaniel P. Banks of Massachusetts to head their ticket. This strategy was dictated by those who favored cooperation with the Republicans in their forthcoming convention and was based on a desire not to give Frémont the "kiss of death" by an endorsement, but to nominate a pro-Frémont man such as Banks, who would easily defer to the California hero at the proper time. To make confusion confounded, certain dissenters among the bolters now bolted the New York meeting and nominated Admiral Robert Field

Stockton, another hero with a glamorous reputation based on California exploits.[56]

The published list of the delegates at the New York meeting of Know-Nothings does not include Allison's name, although he may well have been present; he was entitled to be there. Nor was he a member of the Ohio delegation to the Republican national convention that met at Philadelphia on June 17 and nominated John C. Frémont and William L. Dayton as the first ticket of the infant party. This move reduced the intraparty tensions in Ohio and elsewhere, since now all factions could unite behind Frémont against the Democratic nominee, James Buchanan.

Back in Ohio, Allison sought the office most suited to his situation. He became the Republican candidate for prosecuting attorney in Ashland County and made a good fight. Not only was he up against an able opponent but also an opposition newspaper that spared him not in the least. Consider the following as a sample of the journalistic style and ethics of the times. The piece is about a Fourth of July Republican meeting held in a "grove west of town" to ratify the nominees of the Philadelphia convention. After belittling the presiding officers and even the minister who prayed, the writer treated Allison in this vein:

Wm. B. Allison, Esq., a Charter member of the first Know-Nothing lodge ever organized in Ashland County, had the hardihood to read the Declaration of Independence. We suppose mother earth never flew up and struck William a harder lick in the face while in any of his mellow moods than did the following passage from this same Declaration, which was one of the gravest charges preferred against George the Third, the father of Know Nothingism in America: "He has endeavored to prevent the Population of these States; for that purpose obstructing the Laws for Naturalization of Foreigners. . . ." A live Know Nothing, reading the Declaration of Independence to a crowd of Black Republican Sectionalists, on the 4th of July! Oh Liberty, how many crimes are committed in thy name.[57]

Some six weeks later the satirical editor indulged in another great display of lampooning the candidates, again ending up with Allison:

For Prosecuting Attorney we have Wm. B. Allison, Esq. William is rather a singular specimen of humanity — a sort of political joker — a kind of "now you see him and now you don't" sort of man. At first it was hard for him to support the nomination of Frémont. Whether this nomination [his own] will increase his ardor remains to be seen. He was a charter member of the first Know Nothing lodge in Ashland, and was a delegate to the

Philadelphia Convention which nominated Fillmore!!! He was born and raised a Whig, and stumped this county for Scott in 1852. We presume he has no hopes of being elected. The Democracy have a little "mustang" in reserve who will surely distance him in the race.[58]

The "Little Mustang," who opposed Allison, was the very able Thomas J. Kenny of Ashland. The Ashland *Times* reported that Allison made "able speeches" and that the "cause . . . is onward," [59] but the final result was a bitter disappointment. The opposition paper carried banner headlines on October 15, reporting a "glorious victory in Ashland County! . . . Thomas J. Kenny, the fearless young Democratic orator whose efforts during the campaign have been so effective, leads his Know Nothing opponent, Mr. Allison by 188 votes. Verily, William, 'Jordan am a hard road to trabble.' "

Defeat by a margin of 188 votes — 2,056 to 1,868 — was not bad for one's first race against a strong opponent in a county habitually Democratic. How large were these 188 votes? Did they send the young attorney westward in search of greener fields? Perhaps so. Not only did his county go Democratic in 1856, but the prospect looked no better for the future. If this were his prediction, Allison proved himself a good prophet. The next year Chase barely carried the state for Governor and did not carry Ashland County. In 1859 the Republican candidate, William Dennison, did better in the state but lost both Ashland and Wayne counties.[60] Allison's congressional district, the Fourteenth, elected Philemon Bliss as a Republican in 1856 and likewise Cyrus Spink of Wooster in 1858, and, after Spink's death, Harrison Gray Otis Blake of Medina,[61] but the margins were small and due to the inclusion of Western Reserve precincts in the district. Even in the crucial election of 1860, Wayne County went for Douglas rather than Lincoln.

All these facts seem to support the theory that Allison left Ashland County in search of a new location both politically and professionally. Truly his lines had fallen in unpleasant places. Only moderately successful at the law, with three different partners in four years; member of a struggling party whose leader, Chase, was involved in many factional disputes; who could blame Allison for wanting a change of location? Ben: Perley Poore explained it this way: in the campaign of 1856 Allison strongly supported Frémont. "He saw, however, that if he remained at Ashland there was not much prospect of his realizing more than a competency, and having married a daughter of

Daniel Carter, in 1854, he made up his mind to go West." [62] The
author of the Campaign Biography of 1896 explained it a little more
romantically: Allison was not very prosperous in Ashland but in
spite of this he married Anna Carter. "It was this extra responsibility
which soon thereafter turned his thoughts westward."

There is not much point in making Allison's decision a complex
matter. His story illustrates the winning of the West as well as any
other in the sagas of the millions of people who migrated from the
East and the South to find new beginnings in a country that was not
quite all staked out and nailed down.[63] From time immemorial men
have gone out into the great wide world in search of fame and fortune
which have eluded them at home. Nothing could be more commonplace; nothing could be more exciting.

☆ II ☆

From Buckeye to Hawkeye

ALLISON WAS now a young man in search of a home. Any one who has ever been through the trying experience of choosing a location for his life's work can well imagine the soul-searching and the cautious investigations that occupied the young lawyer in looking for a spot where he could send down his roots, build up a practice, and make his permanent home. Allison gave this problem all the attention and care that one would expect of a cautious and conservative man of Scotch-Irish lineage. Now twenty-eight years of age, with three years of married life behind him, and five years of legal practice to his credit, the choice was for him a critical one. He could hardly afford to make a mistake.

Late in 1856 or early in 1857, Allison spent a week examining the possibilities of Chicago. Apparently not satisfied with the prospects, he followed the new Rock Island Railroad out to Davenport but soon rejected it as a potential location and returned to Chicago for further investigation. But something was lacking in the charms of the lake city which then had about fifty thousand inhabitants. Next he visited Galena, Illinois. Still he was not satisfied.

At last, in January or February of 1857, he rode the Dubuque ferry, or perhaps a cutter or bobsled, across the Mississippi from Dunleith, a name that must have pleased his Scotch tastes. His mind was filled with the facts, figures, and impressions he had just gained from a comparative study of the merits and demerits of Chicago, Davenport, and Galena. How would Dubuque compare with them?

After a short stay in Dubuque, Allison made up his mind to settle in that booming Iowa town. He returned to Ohio, closed out his affairs, brought his wife out to live among the alien corn, and plunged at once into professional practice, business, and politics.[1] Referring many years later to his fortunate choice of Iowa, he made the typical politician's gesture. He had chosen Iowa, he said, because it was one of the empire states of the West. Then, more candidly, he added: "It was largely accidental but I like to think that there is Providence even in accidents."[2]

As usual, Providence was assisted by good hardheaded business sense. Dubuque was well located. It was the best traffic point on the Mississippi between St. Louis and St. Paul. East and west rail traffic to and from Chicago crossed the river there (by ferry) and unloaded cargoes for shipment on the river north and south, in areas where as yet the rails had not been laid. For a long time to come Dubuque would be a great milling center, devouring the logs that were rafted down the Mississippi.[3] But the basic and all-important reason for Allison's choice of Dubuque was not in his analysis of its business prospects. Providential or otherwise, there was another reason.

In the Dubuque *Daily Express and Herald* for May 1, 1857, an advertisement appears for "M. Allison's Insurance Agency." This "M. Allison" of the advertisement was none other than William's older brother, Matthew, the very same who had lived in Wooster at the time of William's law study there. Matthew, already well established in business in Dubuque, would be able to tide the younger brother over a few lean months and at the same time introduce him into the business and political circles of a booming little city. He had come to Dubuque in 1855 and by his own advertised admission had done well in these two years. In 1856 the local newspaper listed him as a "leader" in the newly founded Republican party, along with many of the prominent businessmen of the city.[4] A helpful brother under these circumstances was an asset beyond price which Allison gratefully acknowledged many years later.[5]

Within the year the younger Allison moved to a rented house, where he lived until 1861, when he was able to purchase a home of his own. The City Directory of 1857-1858 lists him as a "boarder" on Julien Avenue; there is no mention of his wife. The next year's Directory again listed him as a boarder at the corner of 11th and Locust (near the site of the home he later purchased at 1134 Locust

Street). One possible inference from these references to him as a boarder is that Mrs. Allison was spending much of her time elsewhere, very likely in Ohio with relatives.

Dubuque, as Allison found it in April of 1857, was in an era of great expansion. The farsighted hinted at a panic, but it had not come as yet. The city was beginning to draw away from its hearty rival, Galena. Sprawling along the Mississippi, the business district was forced into a longitudinal rather than a lateral growth by a magnificent bluff that runs parallel to the river. Dubuque's leaders were awake to the possibilities, but time and capital were necessary before full realization of these possibilities could be attained. To capitalize on the arterial advantages of the great river, considerable dredging of sloughs was necessary, and docking and warehouse facilities must be provided. The local taxpayer did not as yet have the vision to see that these things should come out of the municipal purse, and no serious effort had been made to secure federal largess for such projects. Dubuque needed a Congressman who could get federal funds for river and harbor improvements and for a bridge over the Mississippi. In 1855 the rails from Chicago had reached Dunleith, just across the river, and some day a railroad bridge must replace the ferry (or bobsled) that had brought Allison across the river on his first visit. Railroads were already pushing westward from Dubuque, and the two sets of rails must be linked by a bridge. But these things would require time.

Meanwhile, the city did well. Originally settled by Julien Dubuque, the site early attracted notice because of its trade and its favorable setting on the river.[6] Its permanent settlement as a village and its growth date from 1833. Prominent among Dubuque's first settlers were many people of Southern background, but Ohio, Pennsylvania, New York, and the New England states contributed more, just as they did to the state of Iowa as a whole, with Ohio in the lead.[7]

Most pronounced of all in positive and enduring but rather localized influence on Dubuque were the settlers from Germany and Ireland. The Germans, coming in great numbers after the revolutionary days of 1848,[8] had settled all over the "Old Northwest"; just why so many came to Dubuque and its hinterland would make an interesting study. Their numerical and group importance in the affairs of Dubuque was such that in the hectic days of rallying support for the Union in April, 1861, all mass meetings had to be addressed twice — once in

English and once in German. The Irish were perhaps not so distinc-
tive, but they were just as positive an element in the heterogeneous
population of the city. In religion as well as in politics they made a
powerful impression on the life of the city as they helped some of the
Germans to swell the membership of the Catholic churches. These
Irish and German people so regularly gave their votes to the Democrats that Dubuque earned the title of the "Gibraltar of Iowa Democracy."

Allison's permanent residence in Dubuque began in April, 1857,
luckily at a time when the city seemed to be at a peak of its progress.
Its boosters were almost ecstatic over the prospects for growth. In
April, 1855, one newspaper had said: "It Opens Well. — The spring
business never before opened with such flattering prospects as it does
this season. Dubuque is unmistakably going ahead. It is as much as
we can do to keep posted on the progress of the place." Some two
years later, just two months before Allison's arrival, the same newspaper asserted that the once small village had undergone such a remarkable development in real estate values that 64-foot lots that had
sold in 1844 for $100 or $200 would now bring $400 a front foot,[9]
a positive though not spectacular increase in value.

To be sure, there were those who foresaw trouble. Horace Greeley,
on an observation trip in Iowa in February, 1857, "feared that speculation was rife and that disaster was inevitable. In Iowa City he
observed that 'almost every one here who isn't drunk is getting rich,
or thinks he is'." [10] A little later, on May 19, the Dubuque *Daily
Express and Herald* published an editorial warning that rents were
too high and must come down or businessmen would leave the city.
But two days later confidence returned. Taking note of a piece in the
Albany, New York, *Journal*, which said that a panic was impending
and that the West would suffer more than the East, the editor reassured his readers: "Now there never was less prospect of a 'crash' in
the west than at the present time. . . . Such a thing as a general crash
at the West is simply ridiculous." Within three months the crash had
come.

Neither Allison nor the editor could be expected to foresee the
panic that would break in August and temporarily set business back.
Even so, what other city would not suffer in the same way? By all
known standards, Allison made a good choice when he decided to
settle in Dubuque. With a well-established older brother to introduce

him and help him along with bed and board, what could look more promising? The City Directory of 1858, which credited Dubuque with a population of 15,957 people, promised a field for both business and politics. Although Allison was probably more interested in business opportunities than in the political picture at that time, the official voting figures showed that Dubuque had the largest urban vote in all of Iowa, an important factor for a prospective politician. Among the counties, Dubuque had 4,005 votes, a close second to Lee County (containing Keokuk and Fort Madison) with 4,588.[11]

As April was the date of Allison's arrival, the new citizen must be congratulated on the speed with which he entered a business partnership. The matter had probably been arranged during his visit of inspection. On May 1, 1857, a new card appeared in the Dubuque *Daily Express and Herald*, at the top of the column devoted to advertisements of the legal firms of the city:

Ben M. Samuels   D. N. Cooley   Wm. B. Landerson [*sic*]

SAMUELS, COOLEY AND ALLISON

Attorneys at Law

and

Solicitors in Chancery

Will give their undivided attention to the practice of their profession in Dubuque and adjoining counties. Office Nos. 1 and 2, Rebman's Block, corner of 8th and Main Streets.

It was unfortunate that Allison's name should have been misspelled the first time it appeared professionally in the paper. The next day the advertisement was printed with the correct spelling, however, and ran steadily for several months. Since the personnel of the partnership shows men of a rather queer juxtaposition of views, illustrating the political difficulties of the times, it is important to become acquainted with each of Allison's partners.

Benjamin M. Samuels was Dubuque's leading Democrat of the late fifties, and Iowa's also, as proved by his frequent nomination for United States Senator, Representative, and Governor. He was a shining example of the Southern influence projected into Dubuque and Iowa. A native of Parkersburg, Virginia (now West Virginia), where he was born on December 20, 1823, he had been trained by his father, one of the most eminent lawyers of his day in Virginia. He came to

Dubuque in 1848 for the practice of law; in 1849 he was elected city attorney; in 1850 he became a member of the county central committee of his party; and in 1854 he successfully ran for the lower house of the Iowa General Assembly. By this time Samuels had gained local fame as an orator. When the great Whig-Republican candidate for Governor, James W. Grimes, spoke in Dubuque in 1854, it was Allison's future partner who was put up to answer him. Although Samuels carried Dubuque County by about 450 votes on a platform endorsing the Kansas-Nebraska Act, the state as a whole went to Grimes and the Whig-Republicans. In later years Samuels became almost a perennial candidate for the Democrats whenever a high office was to be filled.[12]

Dennis N. Cooley represents the other extreme of background and beliefs. Born in Lisbon, New Hampshire, in 1825, educated there and in Vermont, he came to Iowa in 1854, after finishing his law studies. In 1855 he and Samuels formed a partnership. Cooley, who achieved great success as lawyer, businessman, and public servant, was the sort of man who makes money in his law practice, becomes president of the First National Bank and president of the Board of Trustees of a college (Cornell College, Mount Vernon, Iowa), is a prominent churchman (Methodist), and whose wife is the inevitable president of the women's club of the city.[13] One need hardly add that he was a Republican. A leading Republican editor later testified that Cooley's campaign oratory matched that of the "brilliant and fascinating Samuels." [14]

This strangely matched firm of Samuels and Cooley now admitted the lawyer from Ohio. This partnership, being just two years old, hardly deserved the description later given by Ben: Perley Poore, "an old, established law firm," unless this be an indication of the raw youthfulness and fluidity of a boom town on the Mississippi. Now Allison, a Republican, joined Cooley to make it two against one in the firm; what would be the effect?

The answer was not long in coming. The newly made threesome lasted less than four months. This must have grieved Allison's brother and alarmed his wife; was this the herald of a repetition of his professional experience at Ashland? Would there be three partnerships made and broken in the next four years in Dubuque?

At the time of Allison's admission to the firm of Samuels and Cooley, both men had publicly taken different stands and were actually opponents pitted against each other in the mounting political combat. For once Allison did not play the role of peacemaker. Cooley broke with Samuels; the one remaining question is about Allison. Did he stay with Samuels or go with Cooley?

Somewhat surprisingly, Allison stayed with the Democrat, probably because he had no other choice. He and Cooley had clashed from the very first; their incompatability, both personal and political in nature, would assert itself repeatedly for many years to come.[15]

Allison had arrived in Dubuque pretty much as a soldier of fortune, a man on the make, with two roads to success opening before him. One was the road of steady, unremitting application to his chosen profession, accompanied by a frugal, careful type of living in which venturesome business risks would be avoided and a strictly local mark would be made by becoming the servant and counselor of others. Such a career does not seem out of reason to expect from one of Allison's rather limited background and achievements. It was the kind of career he would later preach to others, as his younger brother and nephews could well testify. The other road began with an easy and casual law practice, gradually leading to business associations with large risks involved, and simultaneously branching off into politics. If successful in politics he could serve and promote the business ventures of himself and his associates. This, of course, was the road that he chose.

The most striking fact about Allison at this stage is the rapidity with which he impressed himself upon his new fellow-citizens at Dubuque and upon the Republican party of Iowa. He was a man of fairly good education and of somewhat more than average intellectual ability but certainly not brilliant. His success seemed to be due to his ability to impress people with his "safeness." Somehow he inspired a sense of confidence in his judgment. There is hardly any other available explanation for his choice as a director of the Dubuque Branch of the Iowa State Bank less than two years after settling in the city.[16] He was not yet a property owner and almost certainly not a large stockholder,[17] but he measured up to his opportunity. The friends he made now remained his for years to come. Among the directors was Rufus E. Graves, a successful banker and promoter, a loyal friend to Allison and, with his brother Julius K. Graves, long dependent upon him for business counsel and political favors. Other acquaintances who almost overnight developed into close business associates were

Henry L. Stout, C. H. Booth, J. L. Waller, and P. B. Bradley, leading businessmen of Dubuque. Stout and J. K. Graves were especially outstanding, and Allison was soon on as intimate terms with them as if he had been a long-time resident of the city instead of a newcomer.

In Allison's law practice, the story is much the same. In his first three years at Dubuque, he enjoyed some success as a practicing attorney. All the manuscript biographies for which he furnished the facts stress his devotion to a successful legal business during these years.[18] Part of this business was no doubt due to the Panic of 1857 and its aftermath. In fiduciary cases involving financial embarrassment, a lawyer who can inspire trust and who can extend friendship as well as legal advice enjoys a great advantage. Undoubtedly much of his practice consisted in serving as legal adviser and personal representative for his business associates. His most notable retainer as a lawyer was as counsel in the case of Gelpcke *v.* The City of Dubuque,[19] well known to all students of constitutional law.

In the area of politics there is the greatest amount of evidence demonstrating the ex-Ohioan's rapid advancement. He was soon accepted as a member in full standing of the Republican party of Iowa. After barely two years of residence Allison served as delegate to the state convention held in Des Moines on June 22, 1859, where he helped to nominate the former Ohioan, Samuel Jordan Kirkwood, for Governor. A year later Allison was a delegate to the national convention that nominated Lincoln, and still a year after that he was chairman of the resolutions committee at the state convention.

To understand Allison's rapid development, it is helpful to assay some factors other than his personality. Most important of all was the newness of the party in Iowa. Allison did not have to edge his way into an old and well-established party and elbow aside veteran placeholders or spokesmen for vested interests. The party was less than a year old when Allison made his first visit to the state. As a charter member of the Ohio branch, he would have heard with the greatest interest the brief history of the Iowa party in which fellow immigrants from Ohio had played such a prominent part.

In general the stories in Ohio and Iowa run along the same lines. There was the same multiplicity of splinter-parties — Seward Whigs, strongly antislavery; Silver Grey Whigs, who did not want to interfere with slavery; Free Soilers and Free Democrats; "Hunkers," the Democrats who favored the Southern views on slavery; and Know-

Nothings.[20] On the side of the opposition, Allison's new home town, Dubuque, was the capital of Iowa Democracy; quite logically, many of the leaders of that party lived there. The Douglas Democrats defended their doctrine of popular sovereignty under the leadership of the very Ben M. Samuels who was Allison's law partner; the Buchanan Democrats or Hunkers were led by one Dennis A. Mahony, the chief Democratic editor of the state, and eventually by Mahony's partner and co-editor, Stilson Hutchins, both of whom were bitterly opposed to the current developments in the formation of an anti-slavery, nationalist party.[21]

As in Ohio, the mechanics of decision in antislavery politics called for a quick stab at the Whigs to put an end to a party already dying a slow death, and a subtle absorption of the Know-Nothings, arranged in such a way as to get their votes without accepting their principles. The other splinter parties did not pose a serious problem, since they were all looking for a successful antislavery party to tie to. The Iowa leader who played the role of Chase in Ohio was a Whig lawyer turned politician, James Wilson Grimes of Burlington. A New Hampshireman, he had come west in Iowa's territorial days, gained experience as a civil service employee and amassed a comfortable fortune as a lawyer and real estate owner. In religion he was a strong Congregationalist; in politics he was among the first in Iowa to subscribe to the doctrine of nonextension of slavery into the territories.[22] In August, 1854, he ran successfully for the governorship of Iowa on a Whig ticket with a Free Soil endorsement, a combination arranged at a convention held on March 28 at Crawfordsville, Iowa — one of the many Midwestern towns that claim to have been the birthplace of the Republican party.[23]

The campaign was strenuous and exciting, and Grimes's opponent, Curtis Bates, was a foe worthy of his best efforts. "The combination supporting Grimes was in reality a Republican party though not so named." [24] As Grimes himself later reported to Chase, "The southern half of our State is strongly pro-slavery, but I think we will carry a majority for free principles, and for a disconnection with slavery. . . . The north third of our State will be to Iowa, politically, what the Western Reserve is to the State of Ohio." [25] Grimes not only secured the endorsement of the Free Soilers, but he personally persuaded the leaders of the Abolitionists, Dr. Curtis Shedd, George F. Magoun, and Rev. Asa Turner of Denmark, Iowa, to withdraw their ticket.[26]

In his personal platform, contained in campaign literature, Grimes announced on April 8, 1854, that he favored an amendment of the state constitution to permit banks; that he supported prohibition laws and a federal homestead act; and that he opposed the extension of slavery.[27] For many years to come no Republican in the West would improve on this platform, although it was issued by a nominal Whig. Its author won by a statewide margin of 2,120 votes. Dubuque County was sufficiently satisfied with Ben M. Samuels' rebuttal of Grimes to give its customary Democratic majority to Bates and to elect Democrats to both houses of the state legislature.

This was a "Republican" rather than a Whig campaign and victory. So it seemed to Horace Greeley, who was watching the results closely. The victory was achieved, said Greeley, "by a fusion of all honest parties, — by the combination of men previously entertaining different or antagonistic sentiments on political questions, who came together on the common ground of Slavery Restriction and Liquor Prohibition, and fought the glorious battle of Freedom as one man." Greeley was at pains to correct a sub-editor who had written in his absence of the Grimes election as a Whig victory.[28]

For some time after the 1854 campaign most of the energies of the leaders of the new antislavery movement went into organizational activities. An interesting coincidence and perhaps a significant one is that Grimes of Iowa and young Allison of Ohio, completely unknown to each other, were supporting the same man, Salmon P. Chase. In April, 1855, Grimes wrote to Chase: "What is going to be done in 1856? How are we going to bring the antislavery forces into the field, and under whose standard? I believe a very large part of the friends of freedom in Iowa would be glad to see you a candidate for the presidency. I am one of the number. How do you feel on the subject, and are your aspirations that way inclined at present?" [29] A few months later Grimes wrote Chase to congratulate him on his election in October, 1855, as Governor of Ohio.[30] Allison had worked for Chase in that campaign.

The first recorded effort to summon an Iowa convention of those in the new movement was made by the Fairfield *Ledger* in September, 1855, when that paper proposed a meeting in conjunction with their agricultural fair.[31] There seems no reason to doubt that James Falconer Wilson, recently arrived from Newark, Ohio (in 1852 or 1853), had a hand in this, as he was actively associated with the paper in the capacity of guest editorial writer.[32] Wilson undoubtedly would have been in close touch with the Ohio movement and under its influence. The Fairfield proposal was not carried out, but it led to other suggestions for a Republican convention.

Finally came the "call" that brought results. Dated January 3, 1856, it appeared early in January in the Burlington *Daily Hawk-Eye and Telegraph* and the Mount Pleasant *Observer* and was widely copied. These locations were not accidental. Burlington was the home of Governor Grimes; Mount Pleasant was the home of Senator James Harlan, definitely a leader in the movement against the extension of slavery. Probably in an effort to create a feeling of confidence, the call was signed "Many Citizens." Grimes has been considered the "probable author," but Harlan might well have had a hand in it. He later claimed, in campaign speeches against Allison and others, that he had been the first to editorialize in favor of a Republican party in Iowa.[33] Samuel J. Kirkwood made the first "Republican" speech in the state as early as 1855, according to a well-informed participant in these early developments,[34] so he, too, should be credited with the honor of being one of the founding fathers.

The convention met in Iowa City on February 22, 1856, the same day as one that met in Pittsburgh to arrange for a full national convention. Four hundred delegates from thirty-nine counties were present at Iowa City; others, such as William Penn Clarke, might have been there but for the conflict with the Pittsburgh meeting. The body of resolutions finally agreed upon contained thirty-nine articles or paragraphs all on one subject: opposition to the extension of slavery. Delegates were selected for the Republican national convention already called for the following June, and nominees were named for the various state offices. Governor Grimes headed the Iowa delegation to the Philadelphia convention that chose John C. Frémont as the first Republican presidential candidate.[35] In Dubuque, Matthew Allison joined such men as Oliver P. Shiras, Lewis A. Thomas, M. Mobley, and others in crying "free soil, free speech, free schools and Frémont," or variations on that theme,[36] while his brother William was, as we have seen, bolting from the Know-Nothing convention in Philadelphia because of opposition to the proslavery domination of that gathering.

Iowa, as Allison found it in 1857, was only eleven years old as an organized state, the twenty-ninth in order of admission to the Union, having come in in 1846 as the partner of Florida in the balancing of free and slave states so vital to the politics of that day. The new party, with logical consistency, now advocated a new constitution for Iowa. A constitutional convention was called and sessions held in Iowa City from January to April, 1857, the very months when Allison was clearing up his affairs in Ohio and preparing for his new location. Since it was a convention dominated by his own party and since it was preparing a framework of government under which he would have to live, it is very likely that he followed its sessions with great interest. So it might be said that Allison arrived in Iowa in the Year One of the present state government. It may well be that the first political action witnessed by him in his newly adopted residence was the vote of ratification which took place in August.

Years later an older friend wrote that he had supported Allison, not for favors done, but because he believed that from his first days in Dubuque he had always tried to do his duty.[37] This faithfulness to the job set before him characterizes Allison's first years in Dubuque. His political activities were first noticed by the newspapers in the 1859 campaign. In that year he was a delegate to the Republican state convention, held in Des Moines on June 22, where he helped to nominate for Governor one whom he may have known a few years earlier in Ohio — Samuel Jordan Kirkwood.[38]

In the campaign that followed Allison made his first formal appearance as a Republican party worker. As a warm supporter of Kirkwood in this race against a distinguished opponent — Augustus Caesar Dodge of Burlington, former Senator and former Minister to Spain — Allison was in a good position to work in a critical area where every vote taken away from the Democracy was a bonus for the Republicans. Kirkwood won the race in which his plain exterior, homespun virtues, and superiority at rough-and-tumble debating were asserted at the expense of the aristocratic Dodge. Undoubtedly the victorious Kirkwood was not only grateful to Allison but politically obligated as well. This is one of the truly important personal and political associations in Allison's life. Years later a mutual friend of the two men wrote to Allison: "The Grand Old 'War Governor' of our noble State of Iowa claims the honor (to me personally) of being the first one at the 'commencement of the War' and while or when Governor, to have brought Senator Allison into public notice — for which he says 'he has always been justly and personally proud of'." [39] Indeed, Kirkwood's friendship and patronage were crucial and invaluable factors in Allison's career.

The most outstanding evidence of Allison's rapid progress in winning recognition and acceptance in his new state was his selection as a delegate to the Republican national convention of 1860 in Chicago. It was an honor which touched him deeply and which he gratefully acknowledged on later occasions. Yet he came by the honor only because the state convention went to ridiculous lengths in passing out the delegacies. The state was entitled to eight votes in the national convention; the Iowa convention ultimately decided to send thirty-two delegates, each with one-fourth vote, a manifestation of democracy which later brought forth snickers from the members of the national convention when the Iowa delegation was presented.[40] The delegates were selected at a state convention at Des Moines in January. After choosing nine delegates-at-large, the convention yielded to pressure for further recognition of the faithful and allowed each of the eleven state judicial districts two delegates. After these district delegates were elected the convention wound up the farce by choosing two more delegates-at-large, making a grand total of thirty-three! Since each delegate had only one-fourth vote, it is obvious that one of the thirty-three would have to be content with a silent membership in the delegation.[41] Luckily for Allison, he was one of the two men selected by the Ninth Judicial District, the other being State Senator A. J. Brown of Cedar Falls.

One more reason for Allison's quick success in Iowa must be mentioned. The keynote is given in Chase's letter wherein he refers to Iowa as "our young sister." Both quality and quantity considered, no state contributed so much to Iowa in these formative years as Ohio.[42] The Buckeye State was the birthplace or the former residence of a large number of Iowa's leading citizens. For example, in the Senate of the Iowa General Assembly of 1858, Ohio was the state of origin of nine members out of thirty-three. Kentucky and Pennsylvania were in a tie for second place with six members each. When an authority on Iowa drew up a list of the ten outstanding men in the state's history, Ohio could claim three — Allison, Kirkwood, and James B. Weaver — and the list had omitted James F. Wilson.[43] Colonel Grenville M. Dodge checked on the state of nativity of the men in his regiment in 1861, a regiment recruited in western Iowa, and found 261 were from Ohio, 243 from Indiana, 202 from Pennsylvania, 65 from New York, 45 from Virginia, and 35 from Kentucky.[44]

Thus the "old Ohio tie" eased the way for Allison's introduction into Iowa politics and gave him a bond of union with many of the state's leaders around 1860. Samuel J. Kirkwood leads the list, of course, if we pass lightly over his Maryland birth and Washington youth and claim him as a Buckeye for his adult career in Ohio. He had lived with relatives in Hanover Township, Ashland County, before moving to John Sherman's city of Mansfield, where he had risen to considerable success as a lawyer. A member of the Ohio Constitutional Convention of 1850, Kirkwood moved to Iowa in 1855 and so quickly showed his ability that he was pressed into service in the Iowa Constitutional Convention of 1857 and then elected Governor in 1859.[45]

Such a friend could work wonders in pushing along the political progress of an apt pupil such as Allison. It is not possible to say exactly how or when Allison met Kirkwood, but it is likely that the two men had known each other in Ohio circles and in social gatherings of lawyers on the circuit.[46] Tales of this able and straightforward barrister, whose slight eccentricities and indifference to appearance and toilet endeared him to his friends and provided talking points for his superficial critics, were common in Ohio and followed him to Iowa and dogged him for the remainder of his life. They had mostly to do with a disinclination to a frequent change of linen and a refusal to adopt the technique of the handkerchief. Apparently such things made no difference in Allison's attitude. Early in 1861 we find an exchange of letters between the two in terms of profound mutual trust based on old friendship. The bonds of Masonic brotherhood furnished another basis for their desire to aid each other.

Second place on the list would certainly go to James Falconer Wilson of Fairfield, already referred to as one of the founding fathers of Iowa Republicanism. Wilson has been shortchanged in the Iowa hall of fame. Only a brief sketch here and there perpetuates his name, while many others less deserving have been honored by full-length biographies.[47] He and his bride came out from Newark, Ohio, where he had studied law in the offices of Judge William Burnham Woods, later a member of the Supreme Court of the United States. Wilson helped to form the Iowa Republican party, represented his district in the state senate, was a delegate to the convention that nominated

Lincoln, and was elected to the national House of Representatives in 1861 when Samuel R. Curtis resigned to go off to war. The exact moment of the beginning of the Wilson-Allison partnership has not been found. Their acquaintance could well have begun at the Republican state convention in June, 1859, if not sooner. Whenever it was, a political friendship was formed which would not end until Wilson's death in 1895.

Other ex-Ohioans were now influential in Iowa. Aylett R. Cotton, of Lyons, formerly of Austinburg, Ohio, and an alumnus of Allegheny College, was a member of the Iowa Constitutional Convention. William Peters Hepburn, once of Wellsville, Columbiana County, now a lawyer at Marshalltown and sometime clerk of the Iowa House of Representatives, was a prominent delegate at many political conventions.[48] William Loughridge of Oskaloosa, formerly of Youngstown and Mansfield, was a member of the state senate. Clark Dunham of Burlington, editor of the Burlington *Hawk-Eye*, was probably the most influential Republican journalist in the state just before and after 1860. A Vermonter by birth, he had spent his boyhood and young manhood in Ohio, where he studied at Granville College, now Denison University.[49] Samuel Ryan Curtis, born in New York, but soon taken to Ohio (eventually settling in Wooster where conceivably he could have known Allison), came to Keokuk and was elected to Congress in 1856. He served until 1861, resigning to enter the Union Army as a colonel, later becoming one of Lincoln's political major generals.[50] Addison H. Sanders, a Cincinnatian, came to Davenport in 1856 and soon established himself as a powerful Republican editor of the *Daily Gazette*. Others who ought to be mentioned are William F. Sapp of Council Bluffs; Sylvester Bagg of Waterloo; Frank T. Campbell of Newton; Hoyt Sherman of Des Moines; Ralph P. Lowe of Keokuk (from Warren County, Ohio; Governor of Iowa, 1857-1859); John H. Charles of Sioux City; Cyrus Bussey of Bloomfield; John Teesdale of Iowa City and later Des Moines, a well-known editor; John A. T. Hull; Jackson Orr; S. S. Farwell, and many more.

All of these men could help Allison's career; most of them did in one way or another. As a founding father of their common party in Ohio, he had a ready point of contact with them and a claim on their political friendship and assistance.[51] He entered the lists later than the men just mentioned, but in a few years he was their peer or superior.

However true this may have been, it was not apparent in the year 1860 at the Chicago convention in the Wigwam. Here Allison was just one among many; others in the delegation stood head and shoulders above him in prominence and influence. Outstanding by any kind of measurement was a gentleman from Des Moines by the name of John Adam Kasson, as lately arrived in the state as was Allison, but even more quickly accepted and promoted. Originally from Vermont, Kasson had moved first to Massachusetts, where he had attained some success in the practice of law and had married into the famous Eliot family, and then to St. Louis, where he was notably successful at the bar, and where he became friendly with such notables as B. Gratz Brown and Judge Edward Bates. For a variety of reasons Kasson decided to abandon these lucrative professional connections and move westward to Des Moines.[52] This village had just been chosen as the state's capital, but had little else to recommend it at the time. Kasson immediately joined forces with the infant Republican party, and his abilities were recognized in his election to the chairmanship of the state central committee in 1859. His managerial talents were quickly and successfully demonstrated in his direction of the first campaign of Samuel J. Kirkwood for Governor.[53] Tremendous energy and enthusiasm and much political know-how were poured into his work as chairman. There were those, however, who dissented from the leadership of this brilliant man despite his meteoric rise to power, thinking him to be too urbane, impractical, and overly ambitious.[54]

Such was the man who received the coveted honor of being Iowa's representative on the Committee on Resolutions in 1860. As others milled around the Wigwam and bargained for votes in hotel rooms, and as still others looked on as spectator-members of the convention, Kasson was among those who stayed by the unspectacular job of reducing to written English the steadfast convictions and vague aspirations of the party. His yeoman labors in this matter were acknowledged by no less an authority than Horace Greeley, the chairman of the Resolutions Committee.[55]

Aside from Kasson's service in helping to write the platform, the Iowa delegation's part in the convention was not noteworthy. Allison was given the post of assistant secretary, every state furnishing one such official.[56] The delegation went into the convention without official instructions but not without special favorites. Some were for Seward, probably the favorite of more Iowa delegates than any other man; Kasson, partly because of his former St. Louis connections, was in favor of Edward Bates; and Chase was preferred by some, including Allison.[57] Lincoln's support from Iowa was at first very small, a fact which was of course soon translated into a myth to the opposite effect. The greatest Lincoln support among Iowans was furnished by unofficial observers who took a great interest in the results. Outstanding in this respect was Governor Kirkwood, who apparently was in close alliance with Norman B. Judd and Henry Farnam of Illinois, Nathaniel B. Baker of Clinton, and Grenville M. Dodge of Council Bluffs, spokesmen for the railroad interests that did so much to make Lincoln's victory possible. Among other contributions, Kirkwood helped Greeley kill the Seward boom by the doubtful assertion that Seward could not carry Iowa.[58] Coker F. Clarkson of Grundy County contributed a more obvious asset to the Lincoln cause by helping to organize demonstrations of the rail-splitters.[59]

Kirkwood had difficulty in lining up the Iowa delegation for Lincoln. On the first ballot Iowa voted as follows, each delegate having one-fourth of one vote: Seward, two; Bates, one; Chase, one; Lincoln, two; Simon Cameron, one; John McLean, one. On the second ballot the Iowa vote stood: Seward, two; McLean, one-half; Chase, one-half; Lincoln, five. The third ballot produced two Iowa votes for Seward, one-half vote for Chase, and five and one-half for Lincoln. It was on this ballot that Lincoln came within one and one-half votes of victory. As soon as this was discovered, but before the vote was announced, David K. Cartter of Ohio arose, mounted a chair, secured recognition ahead of all others and announced a change of four votes to Lincoln.[60]

One can easily imagine the confusion which attended this development, adding to an already tense situation. In the tumult that followed, "one of the secretaries, with a tally sheet in his hands, shouted, — 'Fire the salute! Abe Lincoln is nominated!' " [61] This announcement to the convention chairman was also a cue to a watcher stationed in the skylight, who was to pass the word to his assistants outside, whereupon a cannon was fired as a signal to the waiting throngs.[62] No published account mentions the name of this secretary, but Ben: Perley Poore asserted flatly that Allison was the "first" to announce to the convention chairman that Lincoln had been nominated. Poore received most of his data from Allison, and it fits in nicely with the story as given by observers who tell all but the name of the secretary.[63]

After the convention had finished its work, some five hundred members took an excursion to Dubuque, undoubtedly a clever public relations stunt by the railroads. The party was royally welcomed by a committee which put aside all partisan politics and entertained the visitors as guests of the city. A committee of eleven members was set up by a mass meeting over which Allison presided. He was made a member of the main committee and also of the subcommittee that crossed the Mississippi to Dunleith and met the delegation.[64] During their stay in Dubuque the Chicago Light Guard Band serenaded Mayor Henry L. Stout and the city's honored citizen who had been a delegate to the convention, William B. Allison, as gestures of recognition of their official positions.[65] After an outing on the Mississippi the delegates departed for Clinton on the *Fanny Harris* and the *Alhambra.*[66] Such activity on Allison's part in hastening home from the convention and arranging the hospitality on such short notice indicates his talent for getting things done, a talent that in a later day would have surely earned for him the title of "expediter."

Allison was now thoroughly initiated as an Iowan. He had been given a chance to serve the party and had succeeded as well as could be expected. It seems valid to assume that a glow of satisfaction could now come over him as he contemplated his position as a businessman, lawyer, and politician of statewide and even nationwide connections and acquaintances. From this time forward he could discount his political failure at Ashland. It would be too much to call him a power in Iowa politics, but he was a factor. Now a new problem confronted him. Would politics or business claim his first allegiance? To phrase it more accurately, would he be a businessman in politics or a politician in business?

☆ III ☆

Allison Joins "Dodge & Co."

HOWEVER IMPORTANT the election of 1860 may appear in retrospect, for Allison and for millions of others the slogans of the day were "business as usual" and "politics as usual." The probable truth is that people were far more concerned over hard times than over the issue of slavery in 1860 — the long arm of the Panic of 1857 was still upon them. The theme of hard times, poor crops, bad weather, and heavy indebtedness runs constantly through the letters of that year. The success of the Republican party in Iowa was in part due to the belief that that party would do more than the Democrats in providing government assistance in pulling the economy out of the trough of the great depression that had characterized most of the 1850's.[1]

Allison was caught in this situation as much as any other average man. During the late fifties he must be seen not only as a politician but as a busy, hard working lawyer and family man. Furthermore, his business and political life was complicated in 1860 by the death of his wife. The exact date of her death has not been determined; a conspiracy of silence seems to hang over the entire married life of William B. and Anna Carter Allison. The cause of her death was a pulmonary disease; [2] there is no evidence as to the length of her illness or the inroads into her husband's time and resources.

In spite of personal tragedy, however, Allison took part in the activities connected with the Republican campaign of 1860. His senior partner, Benjamin M. Samuels, was even more prominently involved in the presidential politics of the Democrats. In April the former

Virginian had been the leader of the Iowa delegation to the Charleston convention that ended so disastrously in the disruption of the Democratic party. As a Douglas Democrat, Samuels had fought for the adoption of the minority report of the resolutions committee as against the majority report favored by William L. Yancey of Alabama. The success of the Douglas group in securing the adoption of their report, with its provision for endorsement of the Douglas theory of popular sovereignty, drove Yancey, Robert Barnwell Rhett, and other implacable proslavery men from the convention hall. And the man who made the major speech introducing and championing the minority report was Benjamin M. Samuels.[3] A few weeks later he again led the Iowa Democrats to join with other Democrats at Baltimore in the nomination of Stephen A. Douglas. The anti-Douglas members of the party nominated John C. Breckinridge, while the remnants of the Whig party nominated John Bell, thus ensuring the success of the young Republican party at the polls in November.

Probably few law firms in America that year saw their business disrupted as did the partnership of Samuels and Allison, with one member a delegate to the Republican convention, the other to the Democratic. Fortunately, the firm had admitted a junior partner, George B. Crane, who stayed on the job at home and attended to the firm's affairs while Samuels and Allison were out politicking and looking after personal business. Not only did the conventions take Allison and Samuels away from their law office: Allison actively campaigned for the Lincoln-Hamlin ticket and his fellow-townsman, William Vandever, candidate for Congress, and in so doing worked for the defeat of his own law partner, Samuels, the perennial candidate for the Democrats during these years, who was campaigning for Douglas and for himself as Vandever's opponent.[4]

As a campaigner, whether for himself or for others, Allison was always a pessimist. He could never be accused of laziness or indifference; with favorable majorities almost certain for his side, he still advocated work, work, work. This attitude, combined with his willingness to carry his share of the load of routine party management, is well illustrated in a letter to William Penn Clarke.

I have had it in my mind many times to write you upon the subject of expenses of our Del[egation] at Chicago. You must have been at some expense there, which should be shared by the Delegation. Please give me my proportion of such expense and I will forward you [the amount] at once. Would be glad to hear from you, how the skies look in your locality, the Democracy of the State are making great efforts. I fear we are not sufficiently organized.[5]

Allison's most conspicuous service during the campaign undoubtedly was membership on the committee that handled the arrangements for the visit to Dubuque of Senator William H. Seward and party, including the Charles Francis Adamses, Sr. and Jr.[6] The committee of five members was headed by Edward C. David, a prominent insurance man and politician; Allison's name came second; the final name on the list was Oliver P. Shiras. An imposing printed circular was sent far and wide announcing the meeting for September 20, 1860, in the very "Gibraltar of Iowa Democracy." The committee hoped the gathering would be the biggest political meeting ever held west of the Mississippi. "If there is a Wide-Awake Company in your town, we should be pleased to see all its members present in uniform. On the evening of the 20th, there will be a grand Torch-Light Procession of Wide-Awakes." Half-fare tickets were available on the Dubuque & Sioux City and the Dubuque Western railroads. A covering letter sent to Governor Kirkwood invited the chief executive of Iowa to be present and emphasized that this was to be Seward's only speech in Iowa.[7] The event proved to be as colorful and grand as the committee had predicted.

The work of Allison and the Republicans was crowned with complete success. Their efforts were facilitated by the national disruption within the Democratic party, which was epitomized in Iowa, even in Dubuque alone. Benjamin Samuels and the Douglas faction were opposed by another Dubuquer, General George Wallace Jones, whose followers hotly favored Breckinridge. As if this were not enough, Jones and Douglas had been enemies for years because of a trivial dispute over a railroad matter. The intensity of the factionalism, which was frequently compared to that between the Capulets and the Montagues, can be gauged by a letter from General Jones during the campaign to Buchanan's Attorney General:

Mr. Samuels is the same gentleman who went to the Charleston Convention from this State and as such drew up the minority report. Before and since his return home from the Convention he has been the *unscrupulous and bitter reviler* of Mr. Buchanan and his Adm. and is, besides, almost the idolizer of the most corrupt of all politicians S. A. Douglas whose election to the Presidency he is now warmly espousing as well as his own to Congress from this District.[8]

Even without the Democratic split, Lincoln and the Republican ticket would have carried Iowa. The popular vote ran 70,118 for Lincoln, 55,639 for Douglas, 1,763 for Bell, and 1,034 for Breckinridge. The Republican candidates for the state offices all won handily, while Republicans Samuel R. Curtis and William Vandever were returned to Congress.

Politicians, of course, are interested in power — in the appointments that can be secured or in the business contracts that can be made by virtue of influence with the winners in any given election. The men who were the leaders of Iowa Republicanism were no exception to this rule. Even Herbert M. Hoxie, one of the worst in this respect, was shocked at the clamor for office: "I am in receipt of letters every mail asking me to aid the writers in getting offices. Such a scramble for place I had not dreamed of. I did suppose that some men were working for principle and not for pay but I find that I am mistaken." [9] Leaders such as Grenville M. Dodge, Hoxie, and their friend, P. R. Reed of Moline, Illinois, were interested in bigger game than offices, however. They wanted contracts for supplying goods to the Indian reservations, western forts, and railroad construction crews. Their idea was to get the Iowa delegation in Congress to help them and to make use of the "pull" that their associate, John A. Kasson, had with Judge Edward Bates, the probable Attorney General in the incoming Lincoln administration.[10]

Allison, who soon joined these men in their frantic search for business favors from the government, was at the moment pulling all possible wires in an effort to secure an appointment from Lincoln as United States District Attorney for Iowa. The position would not be filled until the new administration was well under way, but all the recommendations had to be rounded up and filed with Judge Bates before the inauguration of Lincoln as President on March 4. This was the juiciest plum on the federal patronage tree in Iowa, and Allison lost little time after the November election in going after it. On December 16 he wrote to the influential William Penn Clarke of Iowa City, who had been chairman of the state's delegation to the Chicago convention, and disclosed his candidacy in a somewhat awkward statement of his ambition:

> I have it in mind to be an applicant for the office of U. S. D Atty for this State under the adm of Mr. Lincoln & write you to know whether I can rely upon the Chairman of the Iowa Del at Chicago & my *friend*, for aid in

this laudable aspiration. If any Gentleman more prominent in the profession or party is urged of course, my humble claims will be withdrawn.

I would be glad to hear from you on this or any other subject. I will say to you that I have the encouragement from all the leading Republicans, whose influence I care for in this part of the State.[11]

On the back of this letter there is the endorsement, "ans. Dec. 25/60." Unfortunately, Clarke's reply to Allison is not available.

The only person competing against Allison for the prize was William H. F. Gurley of Davenport. Apparently Allison did not consider him to be "more prominent" in either the profession or the party, and he battled him to the end for the position. Although Gurley had a claim on Lincoln's affections going back to the time when he had been a page boy for a committee on which Lincoln had served during his one term in Congress,[12] this was not his only qualification for the office. He had made a good record as a party worker since coming to Iowa in 1856, a year earlier than Allison; he had attained some prominence as a member of the ways and means committee in the Iowa House of Representatives; and he had gained fame as a stump speaker at party rallies. His greatest assets, however, were strong endorsements [13] from seventeen party leaders, including Senators Grimes and Harlan, Representatives Curtis and Vandever, Judge John F. Dillon,[14] and John A. Kasson. Judge Dillon's recommendation referred to Gurley as a man of "high and unblemished character," devoted to Republican principles. He was a "sound and able lawyer," wrote the Judge, and his appointment would be "received by the people, the bar, and the party of the State" with "signal favor." [15] Almost the only Republicans of importance not on Gurley's list of references were Kirkwood, Dodge, William Penn Clarke, and Fitz Henry Warren. Unfortunately, they were not on Allison's list either.

Allison's one recommender, Timothy Davis, a former member of Congress and a fellow-Dubuquer, gave Allison a letter of introduction to Bates which did no more than damn him with faint praise. Allison wanted to be appointed district attorney for Iowa, wrote Davis. "Mr. A. is by profession a lawyer of high standing at the bar, of unexceptional moral character, and was a delegate to the Chicago nominating convention. I can but think his appointment would be highly gratifying [sic] and satisfactory to the Republican party of the State — Permit me to recommend him to your attention." [16]

The scene now shifted to Washington. At last Allison met the up-

and-coming Grenville M. Dodge. This brilliant young engineer, with one railroad to his credit and others to come, had discovered some of the possible connections between business and government, especially the Interior Department's power to let contracts to furnish supplies to the Indians, and the power of Congress to make land grants to railroads. Massachusetts-born and Vermont-educated as an engineer at Norwich University, Dodge already had had more business and professional experience at the age of twenty-nine than most men would accumulate in a lifetime. After a brief apprenticeship served in Illinois, he had moved on to Iowa, where he had surveyed the route for the Iowa link in the Rock Island system from Davenport to Council Bluffs, the Mississippi & Missouri Railroad, popularly known as the "M. & M." Dodge had picked Council Bluffs for his home and the capital of a financial empire that soon came to include rail stocks, real estate holdings in many towns and future towns along the M. & M., a bank in Council Bluffs, bank stock in Omaha, and a freighting and trading business that ran all the way to Denver. His brother Nathan P. Dodge and the firm of Baldwin and Pegram (made up of John T. Baldwin and Benjamin P. Pegram) looked after the details but always under the watchful eye and driving energy of "Gren." Partly due to the Panic of 1857 and partly due to an overeager expansion of his far-reaching activities, he was now on the verge of financial ruin.

No one could have had a keener interest than Dodge in the new administration or more hopes that somehow there would be a new climate for businessmen willing to undergo the real dangers and grueling hardships of opening up and bringing about the settlement of the vast areas beyond the wide Missouri. He was ready to pay the price in terms of discomfort, exposure to the elements, fighting off Indian raids, and risk of capital: all he asked from the government was a beneficent Congress, an interested President, and friendly courts; the same attitudes on the state level would be helpful. Besides his brother and the firm of Baldwin and Pegram, Dodge's friends and followers included Judge Caleb Baldwin of the Iowa Supreme Court, a fellow-townsman and brother of his partner, John T. Baldwin; Herbert M. Hoxie of Des Moines, energetic, faithful, knowing, a perfect "front man," manager, and lobbyist; and John A. Kasson of Des Moines, lawyer and politician, soon to be a statesman. Dodge had worked with some of these men at the Chicago Republican convention, where he had been summoned by his superiors in the railroad world who desperately wanted Lincoln as the Republican candidate. He had worked to elect not only Lincoln but also Samuel R. Curtis of Keokuk as Congressman from Iowa's First District. Soon it would be true that Grenville M. Dodge was the man to know if you wanted to get ahead in Iowa politics.[17]

Allison's first contact with Dodge and his go-getting friends, who may well be called "Dodge & Co.," came about under the most favorable circumstances. Nearly everyone who had come to Washington was after something for himself or a friend, and the common objectives of job-hunting drew them together. Dodge and Hoxie took charge of the campaign of the Iowans. For living quarters and a base of operations, they rented half a house at 854 C Street, near the National Hotel, one of the popular hostelries of the time, and they took their meals at Gautier's, the most famous restaurant in the city. Besides Dodge and Hoxie, the group included at least six others — Allison; Kasson; E. C. David of Dubuque; Gurley, Allison's rival for the district attorneyship; C. H. Eldridge of Davenport; and John I. Blair of New Jersey, a railroad promoter largely instrumental in building the North Western lines through Iowa.[18] Hoxie's reward, as a member of Dodge & Co., was the post of United States Marshal for Iowa.

Many years later (1888), Allison recalled his first meeting with Dodge and made the startling assertion that neither of them was interested in getting an office for himself at the time. This was true enough for Dodge, but obviously a convenient fiction in Allison's case.[19] He wanted the district attorneyship, and he pulled every wire he knew in the hopes of getting the plum. In spite of his extensive efforts, however, he lost it to Gurley, who probably deserved it more than did Allison. Unfortunately, Gurley soon was forced to resign on account of ill health; he died a few years later, having made practically no ripple on the surface of Iowa politics after 1861.

The defeat was a bitter disappointment to Allison. In his own explanation, which he poured out to Governor Kirkwood as his confidant, Allison blamed it all on the "cupidity and treachery" of William Vandever, who at first told Allison that the Iowa delegation was unanimous for him, but "within 24 hours changed front and forced Mr. Gurley upon the delegation." According to Allison's story, Grimes and Harlan held out for a week, refusing to yield to Vandever's "caprice"; at last, in order to avoid a rupture in the party, the Senators withdrew Allison's name. "Mr. Vandever aspires to the Senate," Allison concluded, "& I think he became satisfied that I would not further his ambitious pretensions in that direction & he therefore took occasion to throttle me. Such however is the fate of many more deserving than myself, which enables me to endure it with the fortitude of a Christian." [20] At the same time Allison wrote to John Sherman, a friend of the old Ohio days, and congratulated him on his recent election as United States Senator from Ohio as a just reward to a faithful servant. "Republics are not so ungrateful as I supposed when I was defeated for Dist. Atty." [21]

Allison's natural chagrin at the time is understandable, but he hardly looked the matter squarely in the face. Representative Vandever and Senators Grimes and Harlan had all written strong recommendations for Gurley before the state's delegation could have met and taken action. Perhaps Grimes and Harlan changed their minds and held out for Allison, as Allison says, but it seems unlikely that the two powerful Senators would have surrendered to Vandever, a fledgling Representative.

Still another disappointment was in store for Allison. In his letter to Kirkwood, he made some very involved references to a possible vacancy on the state supreme court. The main point of his remarks was that he was interested in a place on the court but doubted his fitness for the post; he had sounded out a possible appointee, F. E. Bissell of Dubuque, who indicated no interest in such a place. In short, Allison was hinting broadly to Kirkwood that he would like to be appointed if Judge George G. Wright should resign.[22]

Attorney Bissell played his part in the little drama to perfection. On March 26 he wrote to Governor Kirkwood that Judge John F. Dillon had been recommended for the place, that he was "eminently qualified," but that his appointment would "break up the courts in his district." If Dillon were not appointed, Allison would do very well, wrote Bissell. "He is a young man of promise in the profession, has good habits, is willing to devote himself to hard labor, and he has a good discriminating legal mind." [23] Kirkwood, however, did not fall in with the scheme. His letter to Allison is not available, but Allison's reply indicates that the Governor had spoken his mind freely. In an outburst running nearly a thousand words, Allison gave assurance after assurance that he had not really sought the place, that he knew he was not fitted for it, that others were better fitted, especially Judge

Dillon. He had originally recommended F. E. Bissell mainly "to remove from competition a good lawyer." After reading the letter, one
is definitely ready to say that the gentleman "doth protest too much."
In his eagerness to get ahead, Allison had gone too far. As time went
on he would learn to be more subtle.

One interesting sidelight in the same letter is Allison's appraisal of
other possible appointees for the post. "We all have a high opinion of
Mr. Miller of Keokuk, but suppose from his locality he could not be
selected." (It would be only a matter of weeks before Samuel F.
Miller of Keokuk would be appointed to the Supreme Court of the
United States, where for many years he would serve with great distinction.[24]) Also, in this letter Allison included further but incon-
clusive discussion of Vandever's motives in opposing him for the
district attorneyship and closed with an expression of the hope that
Kirkwood would run again in the fall; "we may need all the strength
possible if the administration continues in its present do-nothing
policy. . . . The dispatches . . . seem to indicate that our friends at
Washington will do nothing to Stem the tide of Dissolution & save
us if not from ruin, from demoralization in the Estimation of our
loyal people & from absolute disgrace in the eyes of the civilized world.
We must have a policy of some kind soon, or our party and our country
will go down together."[25]

This letter was written on April 7; already President Lincoln had
settled upon a definite enough policy that in a few more days would
bring about the showdown at Fort Sumter. In the meantime, Allison
had almost guaranteed the success of his future by the friendship and
alliance he had established with Grenville M. Dodge of Council Bluffs.
The effectiveness of that alliance was demonstrated when Allison came
to the rescue of the sagging Dodge fortunes by persuading the Dubuque Branch Bank, of which he was a director, to make a left-handed
loan to Dodge. On April 2 he wired Dodge: "Will let Bluff's Branch
have $5000 to loan you. Have written you & Branch." [26] Before the
matter could be closed, however, the country was thrown into the
long-dreaded but poorly-anticipated war, and the whole deal had to
be called off.[27]

On April 12 came the first shot of the Civil War, and on the 14th
came the surrender of Fort Sumter. In the mix-up over the judgeship,
Allison had told Kirkwood, "I am well satisfied to bide my time."
He would not have to wait much longer.

☆ IV ☆

Allison and the Civil War

THE NEWS OF Fort Sumter plunged Dubuque into feverish excitement. People gathered in groups at street corners and elsewhere to discuss the situation, while mass meetings stirred up enthusiasm and support for the war. The first mass meeting in Dubuque was held at the corner of Main and Eighth streets, near Allison's office, and speeches were made by Oliver P. Shiras, D. N. Cooley, Benjamin M. Samuels, Frank W. Palmer (the new editor of the Dubuque *Times*), S. P. Adams, and others.[1] Under Lincoln's call for 75,000 volunteers, Dubuque's social-military organizations of long standing, the Governor's Grays, the Washington Guards, and the Jackson Guards, hurriedly recruited up to maximum company strength and waited for marching orders.

Allison took a prominent part in the promotion of war activities. At one mass meeting a committee was set up on his motion for the purpose of receiving and distributing funds for the families of volunteers. Henry L. Stout, Dubuque's wealthiest citizen and one of Allison's closest friends, was made president of the committee, and Allison's brother Matthew was named director for the Fourth Ward. William Allison subscribed $50, the second largest amount reported.[2] On April 25 the *Weekly Times* reported that Allison had also donated $50 to the Governor's Grays "to be spent by them as their pleasure might dictate. It is needless to say that Mr. Allison stands high in the estimation of the Grays." On May 1, Allison and a group visited the Dubuque troops stationed at Davenport.

46

Perhaps Allison, now thirty-two years of age, in the prime of life, a childless widower with absolutely no family obligations, gave some thought to enlistment. On this the record is bare, except for sarcastic allusions to it in the opposition press. But the record is all too complete that he and his new associates in "Dodge & Co." at first regarded the war merely as a great opportunity for making some money. Their letters speak for themselves.

Herbert M. Hoxie, temporarily sojourning in Dubuque because of illness, wrote to Dodge excitedly, two days after the fall of Sumter: "Now is the time for war contracts. Had you better not write Kasson at once. . . . We ought to supply the Northwest forts with provisions, etc. 'Bully' for Lincoln." [3] A few days later Allison wrote Dodge in the same vein. "Can't we arrange together to make something out of this *rebellion* or war. I will be in Davenport next week and will look the field over. Hoxie and myself have had a talk on the subject. I hope I may meet you at the rendezvous at Davenport. Business here is substantially suspended and all are on the qui vive for the war." [4] A further example of opportunism came in another letter from Hoxie to Dodge:

There must be money in this war some place and we ought to have our share. How shall we go to work on it? That is the question. All other things failing let not this golden opportunity slip through your hands. . . . Don't you enlist or take command of a company. There will be plenty of men that will want to go. Keep clear of that.[5]

Since no one, in April of 1861, had any notion of the nature or the duration of the war, it was only natural for businessmen to expect to make a quick profit. But Dodge, whose patriotism was unassailable, was immune to Hoxie's advice about enlistment; his friends were left to fend for themselves for the time being. He utilized a mission to St. Louis and Washington on behalf of Governor Kirkwood as a chance to present his application for a commission in person. First rejecting a captaincy in the regular army, he ultimately accepted a colonelcy in the Fourth Iowa Infantry, to be mustered in at Council Bluffs.[6]

Allison did not have long to wait for a recognition of his abilities as an expediter of public projects. Late in May the General Assembly, meeting in special session, passed a new militia law that provided, among other things, for a Governor's staff of four aides with the rank of lieutenant colonel of cavalry. A day or so later another act pro-

vided for four additional "special aides" with the same rank.[7] Among
those appointed under these acts, Allison was Governor Kirkwood's
logical choice for Dubuque, and there can be no doubt as to the value
of his services.[8] The appointment came in June, but the greatest
activity in Dubuque, as everywhere else, came after the Confederate
victory at Bull Run on July 21. New calls for volunteers meant that
passes had to be issued on the railroads leading into Dubuque, a camp
with barracks erected as a receiving depot, blankets secured, and a
thousand and one details looked after. In August the wounded soldiers
who began to return from the fronts required assistance on their
leaves of absence or their return to civilian life.

Allison looked after all of these things efficiently.[9] On October 26
the Dubuque *Herald*, an anti-war newspaper, admitted that "Colonel
Allison is justly entitled to the praise of being the most energetic and
popular officer in this part of the State." [10] He gave valuable aid to
Colonel Addison H. Sanders of Davenport, one of Kirkwood's aides,
in getting a camp laid out in Dubuque.[11] As one of Kirkwood's special
aides, "Mr." Allison now became "Colonel" Allison, a title that clung
to him for many years. His closest friends and eventually a large public
seem to have been satisfied with his managerial-promotional contribution to the war at Dubuque in lieu of active military service.

A post of civilian recruiting and enrolling officer gave Allison a
chance to meet a large number of people, and some of these cursory
meetings developed into permanent friendships. One such case was
that of his meeting with David Bremner Henderson of Fayette County.
This young man, until then a serious student at Upper Iowa University,
presented himself at Dubuque to offer his services and those of a
company he would raise if desired. Most accounts of Henderson's
life say he was encouraged by an unnamed "enrolling officer" to go
home and raise his company if he could. The enrolling officer was
Allison. In a short time Henderson returned with students from
the college and others from his county; he himself had been elected a
lieutenant after declining the captaincy. Soon Lieutenant David B.
Henderson and his men were formally enrolled as Company C of the
Twelfth Iowa Infantry, Colonel Joseph Jackson Woods commanding.[12]

As the months of 1861 went by, the fortunes of battle and the
gradual clarification of the issues forced men to make up their minds
about the war. The first great wave of enthusiasm and its accompany-

ing spirit of unity [13] gave way to sober reflection and to a bitter disunity that produced lasting scars on Northern society. Americans have
never yet fought a war as a completely united people, never less so
than during the Civil War. The people of the North did not all agree
that preservation of the Union, the official reason for the war as de-
fined by Congress, was the real reason.[14] Likewise, the people of the
South were far from united in the belief that secession was justified
and that a war was necessary as a means of upholding the doctrine of
states' rights. Hence the efforts of the "war party" in each section
were impeded to some extent by the divisions among the people.

The minority party in the North made a very real effort to establish some kind of "Union" party. Certainly there could be no complaint in Iowa during the early months of the war on the attitude of
such Democratic leaders as John F. Duncombe of Fort Dodge, W. W.
Belknap of Keokuk, W. H. M. Pusey of Council Bluffs, Benjamin M.
Samuels of Dubuque, or his notable fellow-townsman, Dennis A.
Mahony.[15] But all advances made by the Democrats were uncere-
moniously rejected by the Republicans and by none more so than by
Allison and his kind, who clustered around the second-term candidacy
of Samuel J. Kirkwood.[16] Allison worked hard for the renomination
of Kirkwood in 1861 and for the creation of a partisan platform with
a strong appeal to the voters. As chairman of the committee on resolutions at the state convention, the highest post he had yet received
from his party, he helped to prepare a document which, though unanimously adopted, had no originality; it merely repeated the shibboleths
of the day.[17]

Probably no one was more distressed by the sordid aspects of "politics as usual" than President Lincoln. Preoccupied as he was with the
war and the effort to prove that the unity of the country could not be
broken, he nevertheless could not escape from petty politicians who
could never rise to his exalted views.[18] He found that there was not
only disunity among the American people; there was even a division
within his own party, which soon developed radical and conservative
wings, and among the northern Democrats, who divided on the issue
of support of the war.

This disunity is dramatically illustrated in the political aspirations
and operations of Allison and his rivals in the congressional race of
1862. By virtue of the growth of population as revealed in the census
of 1860 and a certain amount of political jugglery, Iowa's quota in

the national House of Representatives was raised from two to six. A mild gerrymander by the Republican General Assembly made it possible for the Democratic votes in Dubuque County to be overcome by a preponderance of Republican strength in several other counties of the newly created Third District.[19] This quite naturally quickened the interest of many potential Republican candidates.

As for Allison, it is impossible to say with finality just when he began to entertain the idea of running for Congress. One unsupported story has it that when he was passed over for Gurley as District Attorney, Mrs. Harlan, wife of the senior Senator from Iowa, comforted the disappointed candidate with the advice to go home and run for Congress.[20] The first solid evidence of his interest is found in a letter to Governor Kirkwood in June of 1862, regarding a possible opponent, Shubael P. Adams:

I write you today to ask you a special favor which if granted will be or may be of much service, viz — That you will hold in *abeyance* until after our Congressional nomination the appointment of Shubail [*sic*] P. Adams as Swamp Land Agent. If you give him that appointment now it will wield a power in my district that may defeat me for nomination. I think my chances are now good, but if he has this appointment he can use it in some of the northern counties to great advantage, as that is to them an important consideration. As you have already indicated that you would probably appoint him I cannot ask you to appoint another. But you will if you have any interest in my success greatly serve me by allowing the matter to rest until after the nomination. I beg of you to do this favor for me now. . . . The interests of the State cannot suffer by postponement. Please answer me with reference to this.[21]

This plea for help against Adams was based on a well-founded fear. The gentleman in question was able in every respect. During the campaign of 1861, when both Adams and Allison were speaking for Kirkwood, such a seasoned and expert judge as Jacob Rich, soon to become the dean of Iowa politicians and political journalists, readily praised Adams far more than Allison for the excellence of his oratory and the value of his arguments. Kirkwood was under special obligation to Adams for his assistance in that campaign, probably as much as to Allison. The latter already had an appointment — the post of special aide to the Governor; now it might be Adams' turn to receive the Governor's favor.[22] Adams represented the abolitionist element out of which would soon come a Radical wing of the party. Such members were dissatisfied even as early as 1861-1862 with the pace of the war and with the reluctance to deal immediately with the question of emancipation. The difference between Allison and Adams was only a difference of degree; by his own later admission, Allison was not as "radical" in 1862 as his party rival,[23] but he was closer to this wing than to the other, soon to be known as "conservative" Republicans.

Another strong aspirant for the congressional nomination was Lieutenant Governor Oran Faville of Mitchell County. He was openly favored by the New Hampton *Courier* and by one of the outstanding editors in the state, the learned A. B. F. Hildreth of the Charles City *Intelligencer*. The great point with these editors was their jealousy of Dubuque, which was charged with wanting a "perpetual lease" on the congressional position. Both William Vandever and Timothy Davis, preceding Representatives, had been Dubuquers. In the opinion of Hildreth, Adams and Allison had no merits for the position other than being from Dubuque, a "secession-polluted city." [24] Faville's ability was attested by his selection as chairman of the committee on permanent organization and membership on the committee on resolutions of the state convention held at Des Moines on July 30, just a few days before the Third District convention met at West Union on August 6.

When the great day finally came, the little town was alive with excitement, and its hotel taxed to capacity by the visiting delegates. Judging by their later editorials, both Hildreth and Rich seemed to have been as much impressed by the surprisingly high "quality" of the delegates, evidenced by the absence of drinking and brawling, as they were by the virtues of the candidates and the principles of the party. There were 133 delegates present. One informal and three formal ballots were necessary to reach a decision. On the informal ballot, the traditional test of strength in nominating conventions, five candidates received votes: Allison and Adams were tied with 31 each; F. A. Brush received 29; Oran Faville, 22; and S. Murdock, 16; four delegates evidently not voting. Adams then withdrew, probably because the Dubuque delegation of 21 members was unanimously for Allison. The first formal ballot gave Allison 49½ and Faville 48, while the remainder was divided among Brush, Murdock, and a newcomer, Reuben Noble. On the second formal ballot Allison climbed to 60, Faville reached 53, and Brush, the remaining runnerup, 19. Brush then withdrew, and the nomination went to Allison on the third ballot, when he received 75 and Faville 58.[25] On the motion of an opponent, Judge E. H. Williams of Elkader, the vote was made unanimous.[26]

Jacob Rich, who saw the convention from his post as secretary, reported to his paper the impressive fact that Allison came to the convention supported by a unanimous Dubuque delegation.

Col. Allison has become well known throughout the district, by his connection with the Governor's staff, and his indefatigable exertions to promote the comfort and convenience of the soldiers have made for him a favorable name. As a man he possesses superior social qualities; is courteous and affable, and as a consequence very popular. As a lawyer he is greatly esteemed by the Dubuque bar, and there occupies a promising position. He makes a good argument, reasons closely, is analytical and logical. He talks readily, but attacks the judgment, not the fancy, of his auditors. With practice, as was the case with Col. Vandever, he will become a forcible and effective stumper.[27]

The Dubuque *Herald*, a Democratic paper, gave the opposition point of view:

Abolitionists and Republicans of this the Third Congressional District, after considerable travail, nominated Wm. B. Allison, Esq. as their candidate for Congress. Mr. Allison, it is fair to presume, was thought by his political friends to be their strongest candidate, although a large minority of them thought otherwise, and so do we. From our point of view, Mr. Allison is the very man for us to beat the easiest. . . . As a neighbor and fellow-citizen we respect Mr. Allison, but as a politician, we look upon him as one of those who have brought our country to its perilous condition.[28]

The author of this rather moderate appraisal — the *Herald's* editor — was Allison's probable opponent in the contest, Dennis Aloysius Mahony, better known as D. A. Mahony. If not the Democrats' nominee, certainly Mahony would at least be their outstanding spokesman. Through the editorials in his paper, he spoke for the whole party in the "Northwest," not for Dubuque or Iowa alone. And by 1862 he had come to be recognized as the keenest, sharpest, most damaging critic of the "war party" in the region. His paper deserves to be classed with the Chicago *Times*, the St. Louis *Times*, and the Columbus *Crisis* as a medium for the point of view of the "Peace Democrats."

Mahony, an Irishman who had come to Iowa by way of Philadelphia, where he was educated, was a man of deep convictions. A devout Catholic, he came to the West to serve as a teacher and lay missionary; for some years he taught school at a small Irish community named Garry Owen in Jackson County. Then he moved to Dubuque and became a successful real estate and insurance man; later he added newspaper work to his busy career. His depth of feeling and his sense of self-assurance are proved by his courage in occasionally standing against the famous Bishop Loras.[29] Before the war he had become one of Dubuque's, even Iowa's, first citizens.

At the first of the war Mahony appears to have been as loyal as anyone else; he added to his editorials and his attendance at mass meetings by offering to raise a company of Irishmen if authorized by Governor Kirkwood, an offer that was not accepted. On April 30, 1861, Mahony wrote to Kirkwood, whom he had known as a member of the state legislature, criticizing the Governor's choice for recruiting agents in Dubuque and offering the constructive advice that Kirkwood should have a military aide and a staff "so that some system and order would be observed in the military organization."[30] But gradually Mahony turned from constructive criticism to fierce denunciation of the motives of the supporters of the war and to dire predictions of the ultimate results. It was an abolitionist's war, said he, not a war to preserve the Union. The war would create far more problems than it would solve, especially in the field of race relations; in his view, it was an "unnecessary" war, a costly, wasteful war. His motto was, "The Constitution as it is and the Union as it was."[31]

Such views drove Radical Republican editors to frenzied attacks; Jacob Rich wrote of Mahony:

The Dubuque *Herald*, edited by that old sinner D. A. Mahony, is daily filled with articles intended to cast odium upon the government authorities from the President down, and with others directly intended to give aid and comfort to the Southern Rebels. The *Herald* while it is not as bold and manly as the Charleston *Mercury*, is filled with treason as rank and vile in every issue. Out upon the hoary-headed old Traitor, and let not Iowa be longer disgraced with his miserable carcass.[32]

Thus can be seen the emergence of the point of view that led to the labeling, and libeling, of the Democratic party as the "party of treason." Many Democrats, who supported the war as loyally as the Republicans and who earned for themselves the title of "War Democrats," hated the Peace Democrats as fiercely as did the Radicals, but when election time came around the Republicans conveniently forgot this, and all Iowa Democrats became "Secesh" or "Copperheads."[33]

Therefore, there seems to be something more than casual coincidence in the fact that on August 14, just eight days after Allison's nomination and six days before the Democrats were scheduled to hold their district convention, Allison's friend, United States Marshal Herbert

M. ("Hub") Hoxie, appeared in Dubuque and with his deputies awakened Mahony from his slumbers, arrested him, put him on a steamboat for Burlington, and from there took him to Washington, where he was lodged in Old Capitol Prison and thus effectively removed from personal participation in the campaign.[34] Allison did not, so far as we know, request the arrest of the Democratic leader, but it is hard to believe that he did not know of the plan.

Mahony later asserted that the arrest was made without warrant, inasmuch as Marshal Hoxie refused to show him an alleged order from Secretary of War Stanton, and that he was never given the trial to which he was entitled.[35] The Republican newspapers that briefly reported the incident merely said that the charge was interference with enlistments.[36] It is certainly true that Mahony's editorials could have discouraged enlistments, and recent writers have accepted this as the "charge." [37] As a matter of fact, a Republican editor and historian, a contemporary of the event, later wrote: "He was never brought to trial, which he repeatedly demanded, and it is not known what the charges were upon which he was arrested." [38] Mahony himself wrote two friendly letters to Governor Kirkwood while the party was resting in Davenport, contending that he had never intended to embarrass the government but rather to admonish it for its error.[39]

Editor Jacob Rich, who may be depended upon to give the fairest statement of any of Mahony's opponents, said he believed the arrest to be in accordance with the wishes of the soldiers, the people, and the loyal press, and that the government was justified in seeing that Mahony's work was stopped. Still, Rich felt not "exaltation but regret" at the necessity of the action. Mahony he conceded to be a man of talent and potentially of great service to the government, possessing much influence over the Irish Catholics in the state; unfortunately, instead of serving his government he had merely helped to sow disloyalty.[40]

Allison and other opponents of Mahony were not interested in splitting hairs over constitutional arguments. They had the power to have Mahony put away for the time being, and they used it. The same thing was done to other opponents of the war: David Sheward of Fairfield, editor of the *Constitution and Union*; Dr. Edson B. Olds of Ohio; and many others.[41] Hoxie was again the "law" in the Sheward case; someone furnished a special train for the trip from Burlington to Fairfield, and Sheward was taken to Washington as a companion prisoner with Mahony. After his departure, Sheward's work was carried on with impunity by the banker, Charles Negus, while Mahony's successor was Stilson Hutchins, a man whose pen was dipped in a more venomous brand of poison than had ever been Mahony's.[42]

As to Mahony, the sequel reads like a storybook rather than sober history. As a "prisoner of state," as he called himself, languishing on the third floor of Old Capitol Prison in Washington, the unfortunate editor was somehow able to send messages to the faithful at home in the Third District.[43] On August 20 the Democrats met at West Union and defied the captors of their hero by nominating him to be Allison's opponent, not however without a struggle with the milder wing of the party; Mahony won over Senator G. W. Gray of Allamakee County by the narrowest of margins: 52-2/3 to 51-1/3.[44]

To Stilson Hutchins, the nomination of his colleague was more important as a "vindication of a principle than as a personal triumph," [45] but to the Republican papers it was an act both infamous and suicidal. "The Democrats . . . have placed the capsheaf to their infamy and consigned their party in Iowa to perdition," wrote one editor. "These fellows seem to be determined to show the people of Iowa how low in infamy they can sink," wrote another. "They are lost to all sense of shame or decency." [46]

The Cedar Falls *Gazette* was even more vehement:

The Democratic party of this State cut its own throat when it nominated D. A. Mahony . . . for Congress. . . . Nothing that its opponents could say, will as fully and conclusively prove to the masses that treason lurks in Iowa Democracy, as the nominating of a man who for a long time has openly and boldly acted the part of a traitor, and who, at the time he was nominated, was under arrest on the charge of treason. . . . Think of it, a traitor under arrest for his openly displayed hostility to the Government, nominated for one of the highest and most important offices in the gift of the people. Such loyalty is a cheat and a lie, and every honest man will repudiate it.[47]

So now the people of Iowa and the nation were treated to the strange spectacle of two gentlemen from Dubuque running for the same seat in Congress, each one claiming a monopoly on the title of patriot; one, Mahony, prematurely patriarchal in appearance, manner, and tone; the other, Allison, young and energetic, with bristling hair and beard, hopeful that at last he was on the way to political success.

As a nominee of the war party, Allison took full advantage of his party's claims to patriotism, and he smeared his opponent without mercy. In this he was aided by the best speaking talent that the party could produce. Probably the most pretentious meeting held during the campaign was one at Independence, then the largest town in the district west of Dubuque. Editor Jacob Rich in the *Buchanan County Guardian* of September 23, 1862, urged the friends of the Union to attend.

> Let every hater of treason and rebellion come to Independence on Wednesday, September 24, at 2 o'clock P. M. and hear Iowa's distinguished Senator, James W. Grimes, discuss the great issues of the hour. Col. W. B. Allison and S. P. Adams, Esq., of Dubuque will also be present and address the meeting.
>
> This will be a great occasion. Let every man and woman be present and listen to loyalty and truth as expounded by eloquent tongues.

The same paper, on the 30th, gave a full report of the meeting, which had proved to be a gala occasion with hundreds in attendance. Allison opened the afternoon with a speech of three quarters of an hour, wherein he asserted that although there used to be several great party questions — slavery, the tariff, public lands — now there was only one — the preservation of the Union and the Constitution. Unfortunately, said Allison, with heavy sarcasm, his opponent could not discuss this question in person, but his views could be found day after day in the columns of the Dubuque *Herald*. Allison then read a number of excerpts showing that Mahony had "labored for recognition of the Southern Confederacy, declared for the right of rebellion, argued that the interests of the West were with the South, denounced the measures of the government for its own protection, defended rebellion, and justified the South." He showed that Mahony as a Vallandigham follower could not be counted on to vote support for the government. As for himself, said Allison, he would use any measures for crushing rebellion; the provisions, the horses and cattle, the slaves of the rebels should be seized; Negroes should not be exempt from service. "Mr. Allison spoke effectively, and was listened to attentively, and greeted repeatedly with applause." The speeches of the other orators were reviewed, the one by Shubael P. Adams receiving even more space than the speech of Senator Grimes.

Hutchins, Mahony's substitute in the editorial chair of his newspaper, did not fail to strike out for him and against Allison at every opportunity. Mahony had merely correctly prophesied the horrors and expense of war to suppress the rebellion, Hutchins averred, and he wanted the President to use constitutional means. He declared that after force was determined upon, Mahony had offered to raise a full regiment of Irishmen, but the offer had been refused by the Governor, *"through the interference of William B. Allison"* on the ground that the political effect would damage the Republican cause.[48]

The same issue carried an editorial that demonstrated the feeling of the time:

We understand that W. B. Allison with well affected horror, is in the habit of asking Democrats if they intend to vote for D. A. Mahony, "the traitor." We can tell Mr. Allison one thing which though it may be wounding to his self-pride, is nevertheless about as true as anything he is in the habit of uttering, that when he is known only on war claim reports, and possibly upon the lists of Congressional Delegations, Mr. Mahony's name, rising higher in the esteem of the people as the years go by, shall be known as that of a man who dared to go to a political bastile [*sic*] in penalty of holding opinions which could neither be bought by gold nor silenced by threats. He may be a traitor, as Mr. Allison generously and felicitously declares, but it is a treachery to those sentiments, and to that creed which ten years hence it will be the shame of any decent man to have ever holden. As for us, we would sooner be Mr. Mahony, in prison, with his consciousness of duty well performed, than Mr. Allison in Congress, the representative of a party which has effected the ruin of the country.

Hutchins returned to the charge on October 1, asserting that Allison used his expense money while serving as Governor's aide partly in traveling around the district and getting acquainted politically. He had not been in the state long and would not be so far advanced in politics if he had not used this military method for building up friendships in the right places.

On leaving his native State of Ohio, it is said he abandoned the dark lantern party, whose proscriptive principles aimed at disfranchising a large portion of good American citizens; and on becoming a resident of this State, he affiliated with the Abolitionists, whose standard-bearer he now is in this Congressional District. He is a fortunate man, so far as being a political adventurer is concerned; for there are many older men in the District, longer residents of the State, men of ability and large experience, who have entertained conservative principles and uniform political tenets, any one of whom in ordinary times would have been nominated over him. But will the *conservative* people of the district allow him to be elected?[49]

The answer was in the affirmative. Iowa won for herself a place in the vanguard of the Republican party by her staunch support of the Lincoln ticket in 1862, a place which assured recognition for years to come in the distribution of Cabinet honors and other places at the disposal of the party leaders. While other states were giving distress to the Republicans, Iowa was rolling up majorities for all six of the congressional candidates of that year.

Allison's victory would not have been impressive if only the "home" vote had been counted. His margin over Mahony was only 1,357 in a vote of 9,684 to 8,327. But in addition, he won 2,248 votes from the soldiers in the field, with only 125 from the boys in blue for Mahony.[50] No other Iowa Democratic candidate received so few soldier votes, although Mahony had predicted several days before the election that he would receive a heavy soldier vote because the "Abolitionists brought on the war and left the Democrats to fight it out." [51]

The soldier vote having proved to be of so much importance, a considerable contest developed among those seeking credit for the innovation of sending ballots to the men at the front. Allison later definitely claimed a part in urging the idea upon Governor Kirkwood, first having secured the endorsement of Senator Grimes. A year later a man in a good position to know about such things gave the credit for authorship to Judge John F. Dillon of Davenport, but he may have been referring only to the legal drafting of the bill.[52] The enabling act was passed in a special session of the legislature called by Governor Kirkwood in September, 1862. The method of voting provided for was complex, but the principal agents in the matter were voting commissioners who went to the camps to distribute the ballots to the men in service and to supervise the voting. The party leaders were almost frantic in their desire to secure a favorable return from this source. More than one letter from officers to the political leaders back home testifies to the pressure brought to bear to get them to use their influence on their men.[53]

At long last Allison could breathe the sweet air of victory. Now he had thirteen months to prepare for his duties in Washington. How did a Congressman-elect spend his time in the long interval between election and induction into office? Allison is on record for only one action of any note. In March, 1863, he joined with others to put some fear into the hearts of the local opponents of the war. Mahony, after his release, had not moderated the tone of his writing; the pages of the *Herald* demonstrate the reason for that paper's popularity among the anti-war people of the Northwest. For example, on January 6, 1863, Lincoln was described as "a brainless tyrant, a perjured public servant, a blundering partisan, a buffoon President." The answer of men like

Allison was to organize a chapter of the Loyal League, or Union League as it came to be known, a newly instituted movement to build up Northern morale and to further the interests of the Republican party. A reporter for the *Herald* wrote that one night he saw "Bissell, Conger, Allison, Blocklinger, Shiras, Adams, and others" steal out one by one from a secret meeting in the old Turner Hall. The *Herald* editor added that "these midnight gatherings of a lawless confraternity have no worthy object for a stimulus." [54]

Meanwhile, the Iowa political pot was boiling. Merit was the last thing looked for; the object was to win the elections. Iowa during these years followed the practice of electing the Governor, certain lesser state officers, and members of the General Assembly in the odd-numbered years. Representatives in Congress and certain other state officers were elected in the even-numbered years, while United States Senators were elected by the state legislature in January of the even-numbered years. Consequently, what with annual county, district, and state nominating conventions in addition to these elections, Iowa politicians and voters were hardly ever free from the shadow of some impending political event. As a seasoned campaigner of later years described it, "We work through one campaign, take a bath and start in on the next." [55] Politics was a full-time occupation, and one wonders at the hardihood of the campaigners of that day, canvassing by horseback or buggy, with only an occasional trip by train.

Allison, now a professional politician, undoubtedly assisted in the campaign of 1863, but apparently not as a speaker. His name does not appear in the lists of the advertised spellbinders. He was not an effective man on the hustings, and he had not yet acquired the prestige that guaranteed him a hearing for his calm and rational approach to the problems of the day.

His party hardly needed him, however. Relying on their reputation as the "party of patriotism," they named a wounded soldier, Colonel William Milo Stone of Knoxville, for Governor.[56] The Democrats lived up to expectations and put at the head of their ticket another soldier, Democratic General James M. Tuttle of Des Moines, a man with an excellent war record and an unassailable reputation. The Republican ticket came through nicely, and the politicians could now relax for a few weeks until the General Assembly would meet in January, 1864, and begin the session by electing, inevitably, Senator Grimes to succeed himself.

☆ V ☆

Congressman Allison Joins the Radicals

WHEN WILLIAM BOYD ALLISON took his seat in the Thirty-eighth Congress on December 7, 1863, he was thirty-four years of age, a widower without children or home cares to absorb his attention and give him solace. He could devote his entire time to his own interests and the causes of his friends, his party, and his country. He was ambitious and obviously enjoyed and sought out the company of influential people; he aggressively looked for opportunities to work with and serve people who were doing things. Bankers, railroad builders, political leaders, and editors made up the circle of his friends and associates.

A discerning journalist from Iowa, whose articles from Washington appeared in several Hawkeye newspapers under the pseudonym of "Linkensale," had this to say about Allison shortly after the new session began:

Mr. Allison of the Third District is the youngest man of the Delegation. He looks like a man of brain, energy and backbone. If he be not a clever fellow, in the best and highest sense of that phrase, there is no sense in looks. He has so much of the milk of human kindness in his nature that if one had lost his reckoning in a great city and should see Allison in a crowd of a dozen men, he would walk straight up to him and tell him of his perplexity — so good natured is the very phiz of the member from the Dubuque District. He is almost always smoking, and evidently enjoys his Havana hugely. The only unmarried man of the delegation, he is, of course, the best dressed man.

He is a good speaker, a fine lawyer, an entertaining conversationalist, an indefatigable worker, and an adroit politician. He will do honor to his District, and the State.[1]

There would be plenty for the "indefatigable worker" to do in his freshman term. With Gettysburg and Vicksburg behind and the emancipation policy established, the Union forces might safely anticipate eventual victory, if only the will to win were not weakened. The Congress which Allison entered was first of all obligated to put through the necessary supply bills in support of the men in service. This was mostly routine business by this time, however; the major attention of the members was soon absorbed by a fight between the executive and legislative branches of the government for control of readmission of the defeated Southern states, some of which had already been brought under federal military control. This issue had not been before the people when they voted for members of the Congress in 1862, but it became the dominant subject of debate and decision before the term was up.

The lower house of this Congress was made up of 186 members: 102 Republicans, 75 Democrats, and 9 Border State men.[2] There were 50 members in the Senate, of whom 37 were Republicans, 12 Democrats, and one an old-line Whig. Something of the spirit of an exclusive club prevailed in each house. The personnel of the lower house was indeed outstanding, perhaps more so than its members realized at the time. For many of them it was the beginning of a sweepstakes in which the prizes sometimes would go to unexpected places. Among the members was a future President: but who, on that December day or for many a year to come, would have put his money on James A. Garfield? One would be a Vice President, and seventeen would advance to the Senate; five would be Cabinet members; any number would aspire to a presidential nomination, including Allison; and one would be an "also ran" in a presidential race — James Gillespie Blaine.[3] Truly this was a better than average assemblage of men thrown together by the chances of American politics. Add the names of such distinguished Senators as Iowa's own Grimes and Harlan, and one can see that Allison was privileged to rub shoulders with the best. He could always look back with pride and say that his freshman term of Congress was a training school with excellent instructors and brilliant fellow-students.

The Iowa delegation itself was a notable one. James F. Wilson of

Fairfield and John A. Kasson of Des Moines were by far the ablest members of the group and also the most experienced. Wilson had a small running start on the others, since he had been selected in 1861 to fill out the term of Samuel R. Curtis, who had resigned to enter the army.[4] Wilson was already the chairman of the Committee on the Judiciary. Kasson had been rewarded for his work in the convention of 1860 with the post of First Assistant Postmaster General and now had the prestige of having completed a successful mission to Paris, where he had been the American delegate at the first international postal conference.[5] Through his acquaintance with Attorney General Edward Bates and the influential Blair family of St. Louis,[6] Kasson had a more direct contact with President Lincoln than any of the others. As Herbert M. Hoxie commented significantly to Grenville M. Dodge in regard to efforts to secure the latter's promotion: "Kasson has been indefatigable, worked every day, and he is a tower of strength. He is about the only Lincoln man in our delegation and could do therefore more than all else." A few months later Hoxie wrote again on the subject of the promotion and made this acute observation, at Allison's expense to be sure: "Grimes, Kasson and Allison all promised to look after the matter and I believe Grimes is in earnest. Kasson will do everything in his power for you. Allison also — but he don't amount to much in that way."[7] Allison's other three colleagues were Hiram Price, a man of considerable wealth and distinction in his home city of Davenport; Josiah Bushnell ("J. B." to all concerned) Grinnell of Grinnell, minister, educator, real estate and railroad promoter; and Judge Asahel W. Hubbard, soon to return to the practice of law and the promotion of railroads at Sioux City.[8] In such company as this Allison was neither the best nor the worst, neither first nor last, and the phenomenal thing is that he soon outran the whole group in the game of politics.

Iowa's Senators at the time were truly outstanding. James Wilson Grimes was without doubt Iowa's most powerful and acceptable spokesman, from the year of his election as Governor in 1854 until his vote against the conviction of Andrew Johnson in the impeachment proceedings of 1868. It is hardly to be doubted that he is the greatest statesman in Iowa's history. His influence on Allison was beyond measure. Their close association is attested by the fact that during some part of Allison's eight years in the House he roomed at the home of Senator and Mrs. Grimes,[9] where he undoubtedly met

Mary Nealley, Mrs. Grimes's beautiful and charming niece, whom Senator Grimes had legally adopted as his daughter. Allison's indebtedness to and gratitude for the great Senator's influence were expressed in a letter to Mrs. Grimes a short time after Grimes's death in 1872:

I feel more indebted to Mr. Grimes than any one for the little success I have achieved. His early friendly recognition of me at Washington gave me a position and companionship that would otherwise have required years of patient labor [to achieve]. To enjoy his friendship was to secure the confidence of the truest and best men of the country. The inducements to temptation and folly are so great at Washington that, but for his friendly counsel and guidance, I might have yielded to them. In his death the State and the country have suffered a great loss, and the young men who enjoyed his confidence, and looked to him for guidance in the future, will look in vain to find one suited to take his place.[10]

Allison's dependence upon Grimes appeared one thing to a friendly observer, another to a hostile critic. Jacob Rich's letters indicate approvingly that Allison had become a member of the Grimes-Kirkwood political camp with Rich himself as a kind of manager and clerk who maintained harmony. By contrast, a cynical and unfriendly Iowa Republican, after a period of observation in Washington, summed up his feelings toward Allison bluntly in these words: "I found that what Grimes told him to do he did." Whatever the correctness of these appraisals, each one clearly indicates that Allison had made a place for himself in the entourage of the great and powerful Senator from Burlington, evidence of Allison's genius for quickly ingratiating himself with men of influence and power.[11]

Iowa's other Senator was the redoubtable James Harlan of Mount Pleasant, the erstwhile president of Iowa Wesleyan College in that city and so much a leader, spokesman, and defender of the Methodist Church that he was frequently referred to as the "Reverend James Harlan," perhaps sometimes in irony but often in honest error.[12] He could make as much claim upon the sentiments of Iowa Republicans as Grimes. As a young teacher he had come to Iowa in 1846 after exposure to the antislavery beliefs of President Matthew Simpson of Indiana Asbury College at Greencastle. He wrote editorials for an Iowa City newspaper called the *Republican* eight years before the Republican party was organized in Iowa.[13] He surely must be counted among the founders of the party, even though not present at the meeting at Iowa City on February 22, 1856, when formal organization took place. In Allison's first two terms in Congress, Harlan was at the peak of his power as a Senator, as a Cabinet member, and as an intimate friend of the Lincoln family.[14] He was a great booster for railroad construction, and his name is attached to many pieces of railroad legislation.[15] Only the exigencies of intraparty politics could ever make Allison and Harlan rivals.

It would be rewarding to find evidence to sustain the claims of Allison's eulogists that he received rapid recognition in Congress and made valuable contributions to the war when translated to this "higher realm" of activity. It has not been found. Allison could be counted upon for a regular vote, but in the main his record was undistinguished. Speaker Schuyler Colfax assigned him to the Committee on Public Lands and the Committee on Roads and Canals.[16] His first public act in Congress occurred on December 17, 1863, when he voted for a resolution sponsored by his colleague, Hiram Price, calling for a canal connecting the Mississippi River, the Great Lakes, and the Hudson River.[17] On the same day he made his first legislative proposal, a resolution "That the Committee on Roads and Canals be instructed to inquire into the expediency and necessity of improving the upper rapids of the Mississippi River by a canal commencing at Davenport, at the foot of such rapids, with leave to report by bill or otherwise." [18] Nothing came of this resolution during this session of Congress, but Allison's career as a legislator was fully launched with an effort to do something for all those interested in river commerce, including Dubuquers.

A more important phase of his career — that of a "railroad" Congressman — began a short time later when, on January 20, 1864, he introduced a bill for a grant of land to aid in the construction of two new railroads in Iowa — the McGregor Western and the Cedar Falls & Minnesota.[19] Senator Harlan introduced and guided a similar bill through the Senate. On referral to Allison's committee in the House, a Sioux City-Minnesota road replaced the Cedar Falls-Minnesota line in the terms of the bill. In this form it passed the House and won acceptance from Harlan — who again guided it through the Senate.[20]

Allison's own opinion on his bill is seen in a letter to Editor Hildreth of Charles City, a town on the projected route of the McGregor Western.

I have succeeded in getting through the House for you my McGregor land grant bill. It will also pass the Senate; probably to-day. . . . Mr. Harlan will accept the proposition. Judge Hubbard, from Sioux City, has faithfully stood by me in the matter, although seemingly against his interest. But he believes with me that it is better to give the Company immediate aid so as to insure the completion of the road, at least to the Cedar river valley, without delay.[21]

The road from McGregor westward, provided for in Allison's and Harlan's combined bill, eventually became a link in the "Milwaukee System" serving northeastern Iowa, with Mason City as its headquarters. Allison frequently made political capital out of his part in the undertaking, more than once citing it as an example of service when asked "What has Allison done for Iowa?"[22]

Meanwhile, Allison had been serving the railroad interests with another bill, introduced on February 17, 1864. This was an amendment to the original Iowa railroad land grant act of May 15, 1856, and incorporated, among other things, a provision sponsored by James F. Wilson that the Mississippi & Missouri Railroad must run through the cities of Des Moines and Council Bluffs. General Dodge, not too busy winning the war to keep up with the proceedings in Washington when railroads were at stake, sent an inquiry to Kasson, asking why Allison, and not Wilson, had introduced the bill. His query was answered by the ubiquitous Herbert M. Hoxie, who had come to Washington in connection with this legislation. Hoxie explained to Dodge that "Allison introduced the bill for two reasons. One that he was on the Land Committee, the other that we wanted to commit him by its provisions." Hoxie also gave a hint as to the reason for Dodge's interest in the bill by explaining that Cedar Rapids promoters were trying to bypass both Des Moines and Council Bluffs and to build the road westward across the Missouri at De Soto, Nebraska, rather than at Council Bluffs.[23] Rumors of a possible merger of the Mississippi & Missouri, building through central Iowa, with the Cedar Rapids & Missouri River, located one tier of counties to the north, may have speeded passage of this legislation.[24] Whatever the motivation, an act of service had been performed for General Dodge and Council Bluffs by William Boyd Allison, and the ties of partnership were strengthened.

Further actions of Allison in the area of railroad interests in the Thirty-eighth Congress were rather limited. He secured an amendment to H. R. No. 438 which was itself an effort to amend the Union Pacific Railroad Act of 1862 giving aid to a railroad from the Missouri River to the Pacific. Allison's amendment, obviously designed to protect the interests of Iowa and of his Iowa friends, read: "Provided, that no bonds shall be issued or land certified by the United States to any person or company for the construction of any part of the main trunk line of said railroad west of the hundredth meridian of longitude and east of the Rocky mountains until said road shall be completed *from or near Omaha* [italics added] . . . to the said one hundredth meridian of longitude."[25]

But such matters as river improvements and aid to railroads were mere routine. The great issue of the times was the question of control of the restoration of the seceded states to the Union, a process known as "Reconstruction." This important issue was formally opened on December 8, 1863, just one day after Allison began his service in Congress, when the President issued a proclamation announcing his plan for use in Louisiana, Arkansas, Tennessee, and part of Virginia — in short, those areas which had already been brought under control by Union troops.[26] Lincoln here acted under authority assumed to be his by virtue of his powers as commander-in-chief of all military forces. Presumably Allison at first approved of this presidential move, and practically everyone else also accepted it without protest. For example, both the outgoing and incoming Governors of Iowa endorsed it in their messages to the General Assembly, and editorial opinion was generally favorable.[27]

A division of sentiment among Republicans in Congress was not long in showing up, however. Those Republicans who were most relentless in the prosecution of the war (and who regarded this as a virtue which must be self-advertised); those who were most contemptuous of their fellow-Republicans whose measures were cautious and considerate of the rights of others, even the enemy; and those who were most certain that all truth and virtue were on the side of the Union opposed the President. These have come down in history as the "Radical Republicans," also known as "Vindictives," "Unconditionals," and "Jacobins." After the President's proclamation of December 8, this group gradually advanced into open conflict with him and with anyone who differed with them. They heaped their sneers of "treason" on War and Peace Democrats alike and on opponents within their own party, whom they called "Conservatives" as a badge of shame.

The Radicals have been described recently as follows:

A more unlovely knot of politicians would be hard to find. Self important, humorless, itching for power, and scornful of ethical scruple, they sold their wares at their own valuation and paraded behind a front of crusading zeal. Unmerciful in their pressure upon Lincoln, they used the stratagems of patronage, party trickery, and propaganda to impose their pattern upon all phases of war effort. With a technique of intimidation that moderates found hard to resist, they made it their business to take over problems of army command, conduct of campaigns, composition of the Cabinet, formulation of war aims, and reconstruction of a shattered nation in proscriptive and punitive terms.[28]

Who were some of these Radical Republicans with whom Allison now joined and to whom he gave an increasing allegiance? Thaddeus Stevens was the acknowledged leader; Henry Winter Davis of Maryland, Schuyler Colfax and George W. Julian of Indiana, James M. Ashley and John A. Bingham of Ohio, Roscoe Conkling of New York, and John Covode of Pennsylvania were prominent examples of the species in the House; all except Stevens were overshadowed by the brilliancy of Charles Sumner, Zachariah Chandler, Lyman Trumbull, and Benjamin ("Old Ben") Wade in the Senate.[29] There were also great figures out of Congress who expressed the Radical point of view: Edwin M. Stanton in the Cabinet, Benjamin F. ("Stormy Ben") Butler in the Army, and Horace Greeley and Joseph Medill of the press.

To all these names can be added those of the entire Iowa delegation, both Senators and Representatives,[30] although certain reservations must be made about Senator Grimes and Congressmen Kasson and Grinnell. The conservatism of these three developed slowly and cautiously; this is understandable when it is remembered that they were going against a strong current of opinion in Iowa, an overwhelmingly Radical state. It is impossible to imagine stronger expressions of the Radical point of view than those found consistently in the leading Republican journals of Iowa in late 1864 and after, or those in the campaign speeches of most of the candidates.[31]

The first great test regarding Reconstruction came on the proposal to confiscate the lands of those in rebellion. The bill, subsequently known as the "Homesteads on Forfeited Estates Act," was chiefly the handiwork of Senator Lyman Trumbull of Illinois. Nothing could better illustrate the extremities to which the war as a revolution, not as a conflict to restore the Union, had been driven. By the terms of this proposal, confiscated estates in the insurrectionary areas would be awarded as homesteads to those who had been in the military or naval service of the United States. Allison passed this first test of Radicalism with flying colors by voting for it twice, once as H. R. No. 18 and again as H. R. No. 276, his speech for the latter being his maiden effort and one that was long remembered by his friends as a strong statement worthy of use as campaign literature.[32] N. C. Deering of Osage, an Iowan of some standing and not many years later a Congressman in his own right, reported on Allison's speech: "Our Representative Col. Allison, made an able and appropriate speech in the House last evening. I happened to be present and heard it. The speech and the manner of delivery were creditable both to himself and to our District. When will our Congressional Convention be held, and will there be any opposition to Mr. Allison's renomination?"[33]

But it was too early to ask about Allison's renomination. Other matters of greater importance had to be settled first. Republican party fortunes seemed at a low ebb in 1864. In spite of the victories of 1863, the war continued to make vast demands, and there was a great deal of dissatisfaction within the party over President Lincoln's policies. Without waiting to see what the Republican convention at Baltimore would do, some of the more Radical members went off on a tangent and nominated General John C. Frémont for President in a meeting at Cleveland on May 31; others flirted strongly with the idea of nominating the Secretary of the Treasury, Salmon P. Chase. It would be interesting to know how much attention Allison gave to this idea; as an old Chase man, he probably favored Chase, as did others, including Senator Grimes.[34] As for the Democrats, their leaders were in favor of cessation of hostilities, but they nominated General George B. McClellan, who was strongly in favor of going on with the war.

The great majority of the Republicans never seriously considered the possibility of nominating anyone except Lincoln, however. To do so would have been to confess both failure and insincerity of purpose. This is not to say that he was a popular candidate in 1864. Iowa supported him, and Governor William M. Stone was one of the nominators. Allison was not a delegate to the national convention at Baltimore that dutifully but unenthusiastically renominated Lincoln. As least one if not more of the Iowa delegation called on Allison at Washington en route to Baltimore, and the entire delegation, accompanied by the Iowa members of Congress, visited Secretary Chase, a not altogether insignificant fact.[35] Shortly after the convention, Allison joined Senator Grimes and Representatives Grinnell and Hubbard in urging ex-Governor Kirkwood to allow himself to be placed at the head of the state ticket as a presidential elector, not only because it would help the party, but because it would also fit in with their plans to keep Kirkwood before the people as a prospect for the Senate race in 1866. Allison was particularly interested in Kirkwood's senatorial candidacy.[36]

The Republican leaders' enthusiasm for Lincoln dimmed almost to the point of invisibility in July and early August. In spite of the convention's endorsement of the President, his enemies invented a much greater test of Radicalism than the Trumbull bill on confiscation of estates: this was the Wade-Davis bill, under consideration since March 22 and finally passed on July 2, 1864. On this measure, which completely and harshly denied the executive's right to a part in the Reconstruction process, the Iowa delegation, with Allison near the top of the alphabet heading the list, was one vote short of unanimity. John A. Kasson chose not to vote and thus dared to resist the orthodox point of view. Congressmen Grinnell and Hubbard voted with the majority but "under protest." Senators Grimes and Harlan added their votes and their prestige in support of the bill in the Senate. Lincoln used a pocket veto on the measure, and the sponsors had to content themselves with a public manifesto restating the Radical position. Now the fat was in the fire; "Old Ben" Wade was the antithesis of Lincoln, and there seemed to be no compromise between their views. Many Republicans who up to this time had cautiously avoided a decision between the President and the Radicals now crossed the line into the Radical camp; others drew back as they contemplated the extremities of the Radical position.

The air was thick with rumors; it is impossible to track down all of them and assay their real truth and meaning. The only valid conclusion is that they indicate the unpopularity of the President with the Radical majority of his own party. In this readiness to pillory Lincoln, Allison is not on record beyond the fact that his reputation was that of an undeviating Radical. If he subscribed to the plan to call on Lincoln to resign the nomination in favor of some one else, the fact is not known; if any other Iowan was positively implicated in that dangerous stratagem, the fact is equally well hidden from history.[37] Fortunately for Lincoln and for the country, a turn in the military fortunes of the Union forces temporarily lessened the Radical pressure on the President.

Allison's own renomination in 1864 was a foregone conclusion. At the district nominating convention held at West Union on August 24, he was nominated by acclamation and accepted the honor in a "neat and pertinent speech." [38] His Democratic opponent was Benjamin Billings Richards, a Dubuquer of more patriotic sentiments than his predecessor of 1862. It seems impossible that the Union men should have felt any qualms about the results, but Allison displayed here the caution that marked his entire career, as witness the following appeal to Kirkwood:

I have been renominated and the Peace Men have presented their candidates and platform. My own judgment is from what I have seen that the present condition of affairs requires a vigorous canvass on our part. The Copperheads here & most of the War Democrats here are jubilant for McLellan [sic]. I mean those War Democrats who have never formally acted with us. At the Congressional Convention most of the leading men in my District expressed an earnest desire that you should canvass this part of the State. I think owing to the local prejudices in the North against some men in the South & Central, that you are one of the few who can satisfy all, and do good. . . . I therefore wish . . . that you can spend at least two weeks in my District. I think it will be not only bread cast upon the waters, but result in immediate good to us all, & our cause. I am quite anxious on this subject.

Kirkwood sent this letter to Hiram Price, with a pencil notation on the back: "Please read the enclosed — I must go up and help Allison. So you must go on without me." Price replied: "All right Gov. I am glad you can & will help Allison. My competitor is Geo. H. Parker, as bitter a Cop, as they make these days." [39]

Allison's campaign was not an exciting one. Even the Dubuque *Herald*, the Democratic organ, paid little attention to the race. There was some joshing of Allison to the effect that he had promised to volunteer for military service but had backed down and employed a substitute.[40] All this may have amused the readers, but it changed nothing as to the final results. True to form, Democrat Richards carried Dubuque by 3,316 to 1,753, almost identical with the figures on the presidential race (McClellan, 3,317, Lincoln, 1,742). Even Allison's own township went to Richards, 1,345 to 1,007. But the other counties in the district easily overcame this disadvantage, and Allison triumphed, along with all the other Republican members of the Iowa delegation. Lincoln carried the state and enough of the country to win, partly due to the heroic work of Senator Zachariah Chandler of Michigan in securing the withdrawal of Frémont as a rival candidate and in placating the Radicals by obtaining the dismissal of Montgomery Blair from the Cabinet.[41]

The remainder of Allison's first congressional term was uneventful as far as his own activity was concerned. He sponsored resolutions, introduced amendments to various bills, some of which were accepted, some rejected. When Congress adjourned on March 3, 1865, he returned to Iowa. The final victory and tragedy of the Civil War were near at hand.

Allison reached Dubuque in good time to take part in the celebration of the glorious news from Appomattox and to make a "most eloquent" speech at the victory rally, but in less than a week rejoicing turned to mourning over the assassination of President Lincoln. At the memorial services held by the clergy on April 19, Allison was the only layman to speak, and he made a moving and effective speech in which he eulogized Lincoln and urged the people to "sustain the new President. . . . He is a man of ability, he is honest, he is a patriot." [42] These were the first and probably the last kind words Allison would have to say about Andrew Johnson.

As a freshman Congressman, Allison had had little occasion to know Lincoln well. His growing Radicalism had forced him to oppose the President on many issues, but the two had been on good terms. In an interview given many years later, Allison told of his first meeting with Lincoln. The President asked him if he had read Petroleum V. Nasby's book. Allison, unaware that Nasby's "Confederit X Roads" letters, serialized in many newspapers, had been published in book form, replied in the negative. Lincoln, whose admiration for such humorists as Nasby and Artemus Ward was well known, promptly declared, "Not to have read Nasby proclaims a man an ignoramus." Allison explained that he had read Nasby's letters in the newspapers; Lincoln was pleased, and Allison was at once "acquitted of being an ignoramus." [43] Following Lincoln's death, Allison took no part in the efforts to apotheosize the martyred President, nor did he try to make capital out of some presumed special friendship with him.

After the climactic events of April, Allison plunged into a summer filled with politics. The political pot had begun to boil in Iowa just before the war ended, which may explain Allison's haste in returning home as soon as Congress adjourned. In March of 1865 Senator Harlan,

whose term would expire in 1867, had announced that he would resign from the Senate to accept appointment by President Lincoln as
Secretary of the Interior.[44] The obvious sequel would have been for
Governor William M. Stone to appoint Samuel J. Kirkwood to serve
until the January, 1866, session of the General Assembly could elect
a successor. This would have given Kirkwood an advantage in the
contest for the remainder of the "short term," as the unfinished period
was always called, and for the succeeding full term as well. Governor Stone at first gave every indication that the appointment would
be forthcoming as a matter of course, but days lengthened into weeks,
and the long-expected announcement did not materialize.

Kirkwood was not alone in the field by any means. Harlan's announcement in March was followed immediately by suggestions for
many possible successors. Allison's name was mentioned almost at
once by his home town paper, the Dubuque *Times*, and by several
other Iowa papers, including Senator Grimes's editorial spokesman,
the Burlington *Hawk-Eye*.[45] John A. Kasson also had support for
the office, and William Vandever, a prewar Congressman, informed his
friends that he was willing to be a Senator. Fitz Henry Warren of
Burlington, Grenville M. Dodge of Council Bluffs, and others were
mentioned as the contest grew hotter.[46]

The whole picture of Iowa Republican factional politics in the
postwar period comes into focus during this senatorial contest. Grimes,
Kirkwood, Wilson, Allison, Dodge, and Rich went into one camp of
Republicanism and were soon joined by new men whose names would
become prominent. David B. Henderson, who had emerged from the
war as a colonel, now began his career as a lawyer-politician by reporting to Kirkwood on one of his minor rivals, F. A. Brush.[47] Ken-
tucky-born George Cartie Tichenor of Des Moines, another Civil
War colonel, had been a War Democrat who had come over into the
Republican party "with flaming sword," to use his own flamboyant
phrase that so perfectly fits his personality. He now appeared as the
special champion of General Dodge, on whose staff he had served, and
in so doing began his long career as a scout, reporter, and manager for
the Grimes-Kirkwood-Allison wing of the party — the wing soon to
be taken over by Dodge.

For a while, after the victory at Appomattox and the tragedy at
Washington, the senatorial fight was pushed into the background,
only to resume in intensity through the summer months. Fortunately

for Allison's future career, any senatorial ambitions he might have had in 1865 were restrained by his mentor, Jacob Rich, recently retired editor of the Independence *Buchanan County Guardian*, and now chief strategist for Kirkwood and his faction of the Radical Republicans. Rich assured Kirkwood in several letters that Allison had no intention of allowing his name to be used in the contest. Azro B. F. Hildreth, editor of the Charles City *Intelligencer*, also talked to Allison and then assured Kirkwood that he need fear no opposition from the Dubuque Congressman.[48]

Rich, who was loyal both to Kirkwood and to Allison, wrote to the former in April, assuring him of support and also indirectly describing Allison. Kirkwood had suggested that he might concede the short term to Allison; Rich disagreed with him.

I did not see, Governor, how we could concede the short term without conceding away all our arguments. We did not argue your claims because you were a cleverer, more social, more companionable fellow than Allison, for we dont think you are. Nor because we liked you personally any better than the Colonel [Allison], for we dont. Nor because our interests, disconnected with the general interest, would be better served by you than him. You know the Colonel's social characteristics, and know, also, that we could depend upon him for having our local interests subserved. But the ground we took, the only ground that we could take, the ground that it was our pride and strength to take, was that your selection was best for the public interest, for the State, and for the Nation.

The "prompt and active efforts made by your friends," said Rich, had kept Allison "out of the field," thus simplifying the contest and ensuring Kirkwood's success.[49]

On June 2, Governor Stone wrote his famous "virtual promise" letter to Kirkwood. He would make the appointment, he claimed, but not until after the gubernatorial convention at which Stone hoped to be renominated. "I do not think it advisable for you to be at the State convention, as it would help to give color to the assumption that there is a bargain and sale between us, and sway the friends of *other* gentlemen against me. . . . You will be Senator, and I Governor again, if our friends understand each other, and are *prudent* and *discreet* in their management." [50]

But soon a new factor entered the picture. Rumors were rife that Harlan, unhappy in Johnson's Cabinet, might want to return to the Senate.[51] In July he wrote candidly to Kirkwood, giving a guarded assurance of support but not specifying whether for the long or short

term. He then jocularly proposed a swap of offices, after Kirkwood
had tired of the Senate.[52]

In September, Rich reported to Kirkwood that he and Allison had
seen Harlan and that both now believed that Harlan wanted the long
term. Senator Grimes wrote to the same effect a few days later.[53]
Meanwhile, Stone had won renomination at the June convention but
had not lived up to his promise of appointing Kirkwood. Even after
his re-election in October, Stone made no move in the senatorial contest, and it became apparent that both the short and long terms would
be left to the General Assembly. As early as November, Allison expressed the belief that Harlan was Kirkwood's only formidable rival.
Harlan himself was not idle during these months. He even turned to
his patron, Bishop Matthew Simpson, and asked for a word from him
to two Methodist preachers then active in Iowa politics on the grounds
that such intervention might well bring him the nomination for the
long term.[54]

Kirkwood's chances for the long term now declined. In spite of
this, however, he received assurances from no less a person than Senator Grimes himself. In a series of letters from Washington, Grimes
reported on the pro-Harlan efforts being made there and furnished
some damaging facts for use in the campaign. Coming from such a
source as the incorruptible Senator Grimes, the charges against Harlan
cannot be lightly dismissed. They boil down to two main points:
Harlan had been spending large sums — more than his salary would
justify — for a new house in Washington, a fact which aroused sus-
picions as to the source of Harlan's wealth; and, secondly, he was
working heavily on the Methodists to secure their votes. Grimes
ridiculed the efforts made to have Harlan appear as an unambitious
man being drafted for office by his friends, and he asserted flatly that
the entire Iowa delegation in Congress preferred Kirkwood.[55]

The Harlan faction, as opposed to the Kirkwood-Grimes-Allison
group, included Fitz Henry Warren, William Penn Clarke, D. N.
Cooley, Elijah Sells, and others. Kasson, in many ways the ablest of
the Iowa Republicans at this time, was never wholly accepted by
either faction, but usually was forced to favor the Harlan group because ultimately he was totally repudiated by the other camp, now
gradually coming under the control of Grenville M. Dodge.[56]

On the eve of the election in January, 1866, the anti-Harlan people
still hoped for some turn of fortune that would enable Kirkwood or

a pro-Kirkwood man to emerge as the winner,[57] but such was not to be the case. After two ballots, Harlan was chosen by a majority of the members of the Republican caucus for the long term; Kirkwood and his friends had to be consoled with the short term.[58]

The important thing about this Harlan-Kirkwood contest was its role as a divisive factor in Iowa Republicanism. From this time forward there was to be a struggle unto the death, politically speaking, until one faction or the other had triumphed. Kirkwood was only a symbol; the real contest was between the Harlan men and the group that will have to be called the Grimes-Kirkwood-Allison-Dodge faction, with Dodge quickly developing as the "boss," with Jacob Rich and George C. Tichenor as the managers, and with William B. Allison as the standard-bearer. The contest was not a Conservative-Radical fight within the Republican party, for the Conservatives counted for little in Iowa politics, but rather a struggle for power within the Radical ranks themselves. Allison's future, unclouded by a struggle with Kirkwood for the senatorship in this year, was now assured.

☆ VI ☆

Politics, Legislation, and Business

WHEN THE THIRTY-NINTH Congress opened its session in December, 1865, Allison received a rich reward: he was appointed to a post on the Committee on Ways and Means, by common consent the highest ranking committee in the House. The chairman, Justin S. Morrill, was already well established as one of the leading members of the House, for whom a long tenure could be predicted, hailing as he did from the safe Republican state of Vermont. Others on the committee were Samuel Hooper of Massachusetts, a wealthy Boston banker and investor in railroad stocks, who was a helpful friend to Allison; James Brooks of New York; James A. Garfield of Ohio, with whom Allison developed an intimate friendship; John Wentworth of Illinois; Roscoe Conkling of New York, a redoubtable figure, brilliant, eloquent, dominating; James K. Moorhead of Pennsylvania; and John Hogan of Missouri. Allison was also put on the Committee on the Audit of Expenditures of the Department of the Interior, an assignment that would give him the duty of checking the accounts of Secretary James Harlan. Allison's colleagues from Iowa also fared well: James F. Wilson was made chairman of the Committee on the Judiciary; John A. Kasson, chairman of the Committee on Coinage, Weights, and Measures; and Hiram Price, chairman of the Committee on the Pacific Railroad.[1]

America was now entering the postwar era of "moral collapse" in which the ethical standards of both business and government reached their lowest ebb. George Alfred Townsend, whose pen name was

76

"Gath," was an acute observer and reporter of the Washington scene of these years, and he wrote some biting comments on the "organic evils" of the congressional system of the time. In his judgment the "system" brought down the honest member, who gradually fell into corruption, and the honest client, who found himself paying for the passage of a bill because he was in a hurry. This seemed to be the only way to get action; everyone else was doing the same thing. Clerks and pages were often able to smooth the passage of a bill, and of course they were always receptive to tokens of appreciation. The real business of Congress was not that which appeared in the *Congressional Globe* and which was conducted according to the rules contained in the 500-page Speaker's Manual. "Very few members," wrote Gath, "have studied the manual: some have never looked into it." A "large proportion of those who know it best, have mastered it for the purpose of taking advantage of it," he continued. "The Ways and Means and the Appropriations Committee, and two or three other important committees are esquired by men who know the full value of a wink or a word, and of whom it will be impossible to expect anything better." [2]

Well illustrating Townsend's assertion that the real business of Congress did not appear in the pages of the *Congressional Globe* are certain letters showing the role of Allison as the agent of Platt Smith, a Dubuquer who was vice-president and attorney for the Dubuque & Sioux City Railroad in which Allison was a small stockholder. Smith's letters document perfectly the "system" whereby the railroads could use a member of Congress or of a state legislature to secure or forward the things wanted. The voracious demands of the expanding railroads and the low ethical standards of the time made this a heyday for the politician who was willing to go along, and Allison was willing.

A few of Smith's letters demonstrate the tie-up. In January, 1866, he sent Allison a bill for extending the time for construction of the Dubuque & Sioux City Railroad and asked that it be put through, adding that "your friend" Oakes Ames would give "all the assistance in his power." [3] In February, Smith wanted Allison to make a court motion for him to intervene in two cases before the Supreme Court, and he enclosed "fifty dollars so that you may not forget to make the motion." [4] In a letter in March to Oakes Ames, Smith complained that he had heard nothing from certain bills he had drawn up while in Washington and discussed other actions that Ames and Allison were taking on his behalf.[5] To Smith and his like, Congressmen were nothing more than legislative agents to be used as intermediaries between the railroads and the Eastern financial interests.

In spite of these many instructions from Smith, Allison does not seem to have been as active on the floor of the House in speaking on railroad bills as were some of the other Iowa members — Price, Kasson, and Wilson in particular. One proposal that Allison made, the origins of which are obscure, was an amendment to a House bill on bridges across the Mississippi River, which provided for the construction of a bridge between Dubuque and Dunleith.[6] Since it developed that Allison later became president of the company formed to build this bridge, it would be interesting to know whether such a company was in the formative stage when he made the legislative request. In other words, was he a legislative agent for his own company?

More important for Allison's future, however, and for his reputation as a legislator rather than as a "fixer" for the railroad interests, was the fact that in this term he began to emerge as the champion of the West and as an expert in the fields he would make his own — transportation, tariff, and revenue. His political and economic views appear in the records of his bills and in his remarks in this session of Congress.

One of Allison's most significant speeches as a Western man came on May 1, 1866, in support of the Niagara ship-canal as a boon to the West. New York interests had been collecting a tribute from the West by charging a tariff on goods going through the Erie Canal or over the railroads of that state, Allison claimed. The proposed Niagara canal would open up a new avenue, and by law the new avenue could be made duty-free. In fact, Allison's only objection to the bill was that it provided for construction by private interests; he thought the federal government should do the work. In his opinion, the Supreme Court decision in McCulloch *v.* Maryland indicated that the central government had the power to do this.[7] Such views, apparently, were not the heresy in that time that they would later become.

Allison's role as a Westerner affected his tariff views. On March 9, 1866, he made his longest speech to date, a rather sharp defense of the West against the East. Speaking as a moderate on the tariff question, Allison argued the subject of the regulation of trade with British North America with William ("Pig-Iron") Kelley of Pennsylvania. In the heat of the debate the Iowan showed a good command of statistics and was always ready with a retort to his opponent's argument, proving that he was not easily flustered. The farmers were as much entitled to consideration as the coal interests, Allison insisted. He reminded his listeners that in the previous session certain interests had defeated a needed Niagara ship-canal bill: "If we do not obtain such facilities the productive industries of New England and all the great central States must not expect us to join in giving them that protection which they enjoyed the last few years," he threatened. "Legislation on these questions must be mutual and reciprocal." [8]

Another statement of Allison's tariff views came in June, 1866. James F. Wilson was asking for a revision downward of the rates on railroad iron, and Allison supported him, firmly denying that the iron manufacturers deserved any protection added to the relief they had already received in the internal taxes bill.[9]

Taxation was also becoming an Allisonian specialty in these years. He gave indication of a new source of economic knowledge in his remarks on a motion to strike out an entire section of a tax bill which provided a "drawback" (refund) on a tax on cotton. In his arguments he cited evidence given by his friend Edward Atkinson of Boston, a distinguished manufacturer who claimed that American industry could compete with any other country's on equal terms.[10] Atkinson, with whom Allison kept up a friendly correspondence for years, played the role of tutor to the legislator: in this period Allison was a pronounced moderate on the tariff question and leaned heavily on Atkinson and David A. Wells, another tariff reformer, for advice and statistical evidence.[11]

On taxation, Allison joined hands with his colleague James F. Wilson in a contest with Justin S. Morrill in defense of the small manufacturers of the West, and perhaps of the East as well. Morrill wanted to tax equally the entire production of a company that exceeded $1,000; Wilson and Allison wanted to make a lower rate for production between $1,000 and $3,000, and they won their point.[12] In general, it could be said that in the consideration of the tax bill, Allison took a full part in the running debate and frequently supplied the exact information needed in short, terse speeches.

When the House and Senate disagreed on the tax bill, Allison was appointed as one of the three House members on the conference committee. Their report was adopted by a vote of 71 to 57. About the same time Allison proposed a reduction on the import tax on tea, admitting that the revenue would be cut in half from the nine million dollars of the previous year, but that the savings could go into reduced prices that would be mostly for the benefit of the poorer classes.[13]

A good example of Allison's attentiveness to financial savings is to be found in his opposition to a pork-barrel raid undertaken by the Representative from Oregon, James H. D. Henderson, who was seeking to secure a branch mint at Portland. Speaking for his Committee, Allison brought in carefully studied plans for the reorganization of the minting and assaying work of the government and followed the introduction of the bill with a fairly long speech on the history of the government's minting operations, the technical aspects of the process, and the cost. His clinching argument was that the British Empire with all its use of gold found that one mint was sufficient. This speech was characteristic of Allison's style and methods, and of his habits of thought.[14]

On money matters, Allison even dared to lock horns with the able but fearsome Thaddeus Stevens, the leader of the Vindictives and the bully of the House. The subject was the power of the Secretary of the Treasury to call in greenbacks. In a running exchange with Stevens and several others, Allison contended that the Secretary now had the very powers that some professed to fear. In this he was upheld by Roscoe Conkling, who, boss that he was, nevertheless had an ample fund of knowledge, a fact never doubted by his worst enemy. "I wish to say that, for one, I entirely concur in the statement which has been made by the gentleman from Iowa," said Conkling, "that the very power which the gentleman from Pennsylvania says would appal [*sic*] the country now exists." [15]

In contrast to factual speeches on tariff, taxes, and money, Allison gave an impassioned defense of Secretary Harlan on June 9, 1866. Walter A. Burleigh, the territorial delegate from Dakota, had attacked Harlan and D. N. Cooley, Commissioner of Indian Affairs, for an order that Harlan had secured from President Johnson for the removal of Indians from Minnesota and Nebraska. Allison was greatly indignant that anyone should insinuate any misdoings by these "honorable gentlemen" and demanded a full statement of the charges and a hearing. Burleigh made a lame reply, and the matter was dropped.[16]

All this activity would indicate that Allison does not quite fit into the "system" as described by Gath. Although he might be willing to push through certain bills for his friends, he also took a wider view of his duties, and he sponsored and voted for legislation for the benefit of his own region and for the nation as a whole. These activities, rather than certain minor special interest bills, made his reputation and insured his long career in Washington.

While Congress dealt with problems of tariff and taxation as a matter of course, the most important work of this Congress was the harrassing problem of the readmission of the seceded states to the Union. By 1866 the smoldering conflict between President Johnson and the Congress over this issue had burst into full flame. During the summer of 1865 Johnson had issued his Reconstruction Proclamation; immediately upon the convening of the Thirty-ninth Congress in December, the Radical Republicans had countered with the appointment of the famous "Joint Committee of Fifteen" to act as its agent in the battle with Johnson over control of Reconstruction. The executive-legislative struggle, begun under Lincoln, was nearing a climax.

Allison, on the best of terms with such members of the Joint Committee as Thaddeus Stevens, Elihu B. Washburne, Roscoe Conkling, and George S. Boutwell from the House, and with Grimes and William Pitt Fessenden from the Senate, gladly followed their lead in Reconstruction matters. In February of 1866 the President had won a victory over his enemies in Congress by courageously and successfully vetoing the Freedmen's Bureau Bill, but this was his last brief moment of triumph. A second bill was passed over his veto in July, Allison voting with the majority. Later, by his votes on the Civil Rights Bill and the Fourteenth Amendment, Allison continued to keep his Radicalism unsullied.[17] The lines were now sharply drawn between the Radicals and the Conservative "Johnsonites."

When the first session of the Thirty-ninth Congress recessed on July 28, 1866, Allison returned to Iowa to make a bid for a third nomination, thus defying the two-term tradition that was already slowly losing its force in Iowa. Finding his district organization badly split between Radicals and Conservatives, Allison made an uncompromising and successful appeal to the Radical element. The Charles City *Intelligencer* voiced the Radical position: Allison should be supported because of his sound votes on congressional Reconstruction and because putting in a new and untried candidate would give comfort to the Johnson men. The Chicago *Tribune*, a popular paper in the district, favored Allison's renomination as a "fearless and incorruptible Radical Republican and the most valuable member" of the Ways and Means Committee because of his opposition to the recent high tariff bill. The delegates in the Radical-controlled convention at West Union on August 22 followed this advice and nominated Allison by acclamation. The candidate accepted the nomination in a "short but eloquent" speech in which he emphasized the need for control of the government by none but loyal men and asked for the enfranchisement of the Negro and the disfranchisement of all who had taken part in the rebellion.[18] All this was good, orthodox Radicalism.

The nomination had not been easily procured, however. Shortly after the convention, in a spirit of "now it can be told," the Dubuque *Times* published a letter from one of Allison's colleagues in the House, J. W. Welker of Ohio, who had read of opposition to Allison and wanted to endorse him for re-election as an able man. The *Times* added the hope that the rift would soon be closed and the party united in Allison's support.[19] The cause of this rift was disclosed as a fight between Radicals and Conservatives over the postmastership in Dubuque. The incumbent in 1866 was Colonel E. C. David, a man of good war record but now the leading Johnson Republican in the area. David, who had been removed in favor of Captain V. J. Williams, presumably at Allison's request, had made a trip to Washington just before the West Union convention and had secured reappointment on a promise to support the administration.[20] To some the reappointment made it appear that Allison could not control the machinery of the party in his district, but his renomination disproved this.

In September, Colonel David emphasized his conversion to Conservatism by attending the convention of Johnsonites held at West Union. The meeting, held under the name of the "National Union Party," was described by the Democratic Dubuque *Herald* as a "Democratic Mass Convention." Colonel L. L. Ainsworth of West Union, a man of excellent war record, presided, and David was the chairman of the resolutions committee. The group chose Reuben Noble of McGregor, a man of heretofore impeccable Republican standing, as their nominee to oppose Allison. On September 13 the Democrats met at Independence and accepted the same nominee, thus enabling the Johnson men to draw votes from the Democrats as well as from their own wing of the Republican party.[21]

As the campaign moved on, Allison, needing a sure medium for the defense of his record, now under heavy attack from the *Herald*, bought an interest in the Dubuque *Times*, the party organ of his city; but he had to share ownership with his rivals in the party, D. N. Cooley, now a mild Johnsonite, and Julius K. Graves.[22] The *Herald's* charges against Allison were many. When he entered Congress he had but a "small competence," according to the *Herald*, but "now he pitches his yearly income well into the thousands." This was a charge that would be repeated against Allison for the rest of his public life. Allison's principal activity, continued the *Herald*, was the handling of patronage, a patently false statement in view of the work Allison had been doing in legislative matters during the last session of Congress.[23]

The Dubuque *Times* ignored most of the charges against Allison, but now and then consented to issue categorical denials. Its columns were devoted more to attacks on President Johnson and to glowing accounts of Allison's campaign speeches throughout the district. After some prodding, according to the *Times*, Noble had agreed to engage in a series of joint debates with Allison, a series in which Allison, as reported by his own newspaper, came off the winner each time.[24] In short, Allison was up to his ears in a political fight of the hardest sort.

Allison's was not a lone struggle, however, for all the districts in Iowa had shown intense factionalism before ever the fighting against the Democrats could begin. But in Allison's case the fight was between Conservative and Radical, whereas in most of the other districts it was a raw struggle for power between the Harlanites and "Dodge & Co.," neither camp being able to complain of the other's Radicalism.

Four of the six members of the Iowa congressional delegation were considered sufficiently Radical to be acceptable to Dodge & Co. — James F. Wilson, Hiram Price, Allison, and Asahel W. Hubbard. Only John A. Kasson, for all his amenability to Dodge, was considered insufficiently Radical, and yet no less an opponent than Dodge himself was required to deprive him of renomination.[25]

The other Congressman who was denied a renomination was Josiah B. Grinnell of the Fourth District. Whatever the reason or reasons, it was definitely not the refusal of Grinnell to fight back when caned by a Kentucky Congressman, General Lovell H. Rousseau, in Washington,[26] because the attack did not take place until several days after the district nominating convention had rejected Grinnell and nominated Judge William Loughridge of Oskaloosa. Loughridge's speech of acceptance emphasized his own intense Radicalism and his readiness to resign whenever anyone found fault with his policies,[27] a hint that perhaps Grinnell's Radicalism had not been strong enough to suit his constituents.

All six of the Iowa Radicals were returned victoriously. Allison lost Dubuque County as usual, although the city of Dubuque itself "went Republican at last" by the slim margin of 32 out of a total of 2,500 votes, a cause for banner headlines in the October 12 issue of the Dubuque *Times*. Even with the loss of his home county, Allison won the race against Reuben Noble by virtue of his ample margins in the other counties of his district. In the country at large the Radicals won a resounding victory over President Johnson. The nation could now look forward to a furious effort to defeat the entire program of that luckless individual.

In the short session closing out the Thirty-ninth Congress (December 3, 1866, to March 3, 1867), Allison made an important statement of his own personal beliefs. It is a good example of the Radical Republican views for which he was by that time well known.[28] The subject was the government of the "insurrectionary states." Thaddeus Stevens, probably the most implacable Radical in the House, was a firm believer in the policy of treating the defeated Southern states as "conquered provinces." Johnson, by contrast, had adopted the statesmanlike Lincolnian policy favoring a quick restoration of the Southern states to the Union.

Allison, in his speech on February 12, 1867, endorsed the Radical belief in the power of Congress to legislate for the seceded states. The President's plan, said Allison, had been defeated by the people at the polls. He disagreed with Nathaniel P. Banks of Massachusetts who said that for two and one-half years Congress could not "restore these States upon a loyal basis against the will of the President." This could be done, said Allison, by "treating as utterly void the governments organized by the President in those States." Congress had done this with respect to the "existing pretended government of Louisiana," he continued. "I so voted to-day and shall continue so to vote as often as opportunity is presented." New governments should now be organized "without distinction of race or color," said Allison, voicing another of the strong tenets of Radicalism.

I want no property qualification, no qualification of intelligence in the enjoyment of the elective franchise. Let intelligence follow, as it surely will, the enjoyment of this great privilege of voting for those who shall govern. . . . I have no fear but that now there can be found intelligence among the blacks to prudently and properly exercise the franchise.

I believe the hope of restoration of republican governments in those States rests in the masses of the people, the uneducated, the poor, and now powerless masses. Certainly not in the aristocratic few, who, though vanquished by our arms, are still wedded to the idea that the strong should govern the weak at their own pleasure and will without the consent of the governed. Therefore I believe to stop short of manhood suffrage in our legislation is to trifle with the great subject, and render us ridiculous in the eyes of all those who respect popular government based on the will and judgment of the people.[29]

This speech helped further to establish Allison's position as one of the Radical elite.

Allison took no other notable part in the debate on the bill, which became the famous Reconstruction Act of March, 1867, except that he joined his Iowa colleagues Price, Wilson, and Grinnell in voting for it. Hubbard and Kasson did not vote. On the successful motion to override the President's veto of the bill, all the Iowans voted yea except A. W. Hubbard, who again did not vote.[30]

A measure giving Allison another chance to show his Radical attitude was a proposal by George W. Julian of Indiana to extend the homesteading plan to certain Southern states. Kasson severely attacked Julian's plan and proposed instead to let "disloyal" men have access to the lands only if "loyal" men did not apply. Julian opposed the idea and was upheld, 97 to 30, Allison voting with the majority along with Hiram Price. The other four Iowans did not vote on this issue.[31]

On the tariff question, however, Allison deserted many of his Radical colleagues. A measure increasing tariff rates, sponsored by Justin S. Morrill, passed the House; in the Senate certain reductions were made at the suggestion of an independent tariff expert, David Ames Wells, then Special Commissioner of the Revenue. The Senate version was returned to the House and subjected to a lively debate, but was rejected through the technicality of failure to receive the two-thirds majority vote necessary for the suspension of the rules to bring it up for a formal vote. Allison was a leading critic of the bill even in its Wellsian version and voted against suspension of the rules on the ground that only a short time remained in the session and passage of the bill would give too much power to the inevitable joint conference committee; no harm would be done by letting it go over to the next session, reasoned Allison. A leading modern authority on tariff history has asserted that failure to pass the Wells amendments in this bill of 1867 was most unfortunate for the cause of future tariff reform. Thus

Allison, an anti-protectionist at this time, helped to defeat his own cause. In response to a reproof from Edward Atkinson, Allison made the reply that probably characterized his congressional voting policy for many years: "I always like to vote, if I can, so as to not be called upon to explain too much at home." [32]

In March, 1867, Allison entered the long session of the Fortieth Congress which had been arranged by the Radicals, instead of the normal December meeting, so as to keep guard over President Johnson. General Dodge, Kasson's successor in the House, wrote to Mrs. Dodge: "Mr. Allison, Mr. Wilson and myself have been looking for a home to live in next winter and we think we have found a place that will suit us at Wormleys, the finest place for eating in the city, where we can get our meals as we like and have a house to ourselves." [33] But when winter arrived something happened to these plans, and Allison did not join the others. It is most likely that he continued as a member of the Grimes household. [34]

These associations with Grimes, Dodge, and Wilson are of the utmost importance in an understanding of the development of Allison's career and of his position of influence. Dodge made it plain that Wilson was his first lieutenant and Allison his second, but it would not be long before Allison replaced Wilson in the triumvirate. And eventually, he would himself succeed to Dodge's position of "boss" of Iowa politics. In these years Dodge, as a friend of General John A. Rawlins, Grant's old chief of staff and closest friend, was close to the seat of forthcoming power. Grant wanted Dodge and Wilson to look after his interests in the convention of 1868. [35]

Allison steadily took a good part in the work of the Fortieth Congress. When in February of 1868 the Radicals in the House at last succeeded in voting impeachment of the President, Allison and the rest of the Iowa delegation favored the measure, and James F. Wilson was appointed one of the seven House managers of the impeachment trial before the Senate. The long trial was the sensation of the day. When rumors spread that a few Republicans, heretofore classified as Radicals, might vote against the impeachment, and when these rumors carried the name of James W. Grimes, the Iowans in Washington and at home were shocked, since the trial was frankly considered a political and not a judicial proceeding. On May 11 Grimes confirmed these rumors when he spoke in the Senate, announcing his belief that Johnson was not guilty of an "impeachable offense." Two days later Iowa's great Senator suffered a stroke of paralysis while in the Senate chamber. Since the vote on impeachment was very close, many Radicals must have breathed a sigh of relief. However, when the crucial vote came on May 16, an enfeebled Grimes appeared to cast his vote against impeachment.[36]

As a staunch Radical, Allison must have been pained by Grimes's vote; as a virtual member of the Grimes household, he must have found it embarrassing and difficult to know what to do or say. The only known evidence is a statement from Dodge that all the Iowa delegation except Wilson and himself were "down on" Grimes.[37] Most Iowa Republicans joined in the fierce Radical denunciation of their once idolized leader, and it would have been political suicide for Allison to attempt a defense of him at that time. It may be assumed that he discreetly said as little as possible either way and simply waited for the storm to blow over, a none too manly course of action in view of his obligations to the senior Senator.

After the failure of the Johnson impeachment, Congress continued in session until July 27. Meanwhile, even while the impeachment trial proceeded, the Republicans had met at Chicago and nominated the Radical's choice, U. S. Grant, for their presidential candidate. On July 4 the Democrats met at New York and named Horatio Seymour as their choice in a contest that was a foregone conclusion from the start. Of more interest to Allison even than the presidential contest, however, was his own campaign for a fourth term in the House. This time he had a close call, his difficulties coming from several sources.

By his own admission, Allison was under fire from early in 1868 until the election because of his known connections with the Dubuque & Sioux City Railroad, whose promotional program was much criticized.[38] Furthermore, he was troubled by an anti-urban complex in the hinterland counties which had a natural jealousy of Dubuque and Dubuque County. According to them, Dubuque County had almost all the offices, although it never gave the party a plurality. In addition, the charge was made against Allison that in 1866 he had promised that that would be the last time he would ask for renomination. Nothing has been found in the way of concrete evidence to uphold this charge, but it was made by one who was in good standing in the party, J. H. Powers of Chickasaw County.[39]

Allison faced opposition not only in the rural counties of his district, but at home as well. The rebellion in Dubuque County was led by the prominent and capable banker, Julius K. Graves, ably supported by Dr. Lewis A. Thomas. Up to this time, and for years after this rebellion was over, Graves was a most friendly and devoted follower and business associate of Allison's, and Dr. Thomas had been a loyal supporter in 1866. Just why they strayed off the reservation on this occasion has not been revealed. Perhaps it could be set down just to plain ambition. Two rival delegations were chosen in the county, and both made their way to West Union for the district convention. Among the twenty-one men in the Allison camp were Colonel David B. Henderson, Oliver P. Shiras, Henry L. Stout, S. M. Langworthy (a member of one of the oldest families in the city and holder of a fortune made in lead mining), George Crane (Allison's law partner and local business manager), and Captain V. J. Williams, Allison's choice for postmaster over David in 1866, and others. In the Graves camp there were General William Vandever and Shubael P. Adams, both old rivals whom Allison had out-distanced; their opposition was easily understandable. The others in the Graves group were prominent in local affairs only.[40]

The real contest was before the committee on credentials which heard arguments from both the Allison and Graves delegates and chose to seat the former. General Vandever then called off the fight in the interest of party harmony, and the convention proceeded to nominate Allison by a large margin over John E. Burke of Bremer County and others. Allison went on to win easily in October against the "whisky-ring and the devil," as he later expressed it.[41] His Democratic rival, Williams Mills, received only 14,120 votes as compared to 20,119 for Allison. Dr. L. A. Thomas received 149 votes; Graves, one solitary ballot.

Allison's victory was a part of the larger party triumph in which Grant defeated Seymour. Through his friend and supporter, General Dodge, Allison now had a contact with the new President which might prove to be helpful. Congressman Elihu B. Washburne, Grant's political mentor, was one of Allison's good friends and could be looked to for help if the occasion called for it.[42]

After three terms in Congress, Allison would still have to be classed as a "leg man" for others, but he was rapidly approaching the point where he would also have to be called a man of power in his own right. He was busy promoting and managing enterprises that were partly his own, as well as looking after the interests of others. Among his closest associates were Henry L. Stout, Platt Smith, F. W. H. Sheffield, R. A. Babbage, Rufus E. and Julius K. Graves, all bankers and railroad promoters of Dubuque; Samuel Hooper of Boston; Oakes Ames, a railroad Congressman; Morris K. Jesup, a heavy investor in the roads that ultimately were merged into the Illinois Central Railroad from Dubuque to Sioux City; and John I. Blair of the North Western.[43] Allison is said to have been offered the presidency of the Illinois Central at one time, and on another occasion he was recommended for the managership of the Jay Cooke interests in Washington.[44] In only one area was he at odds with the majority of his party: he was definitely a moderate in his tariff views. In these years began the friendship and intimate correspondence with such independent thinkers as David A. Wells, Edward Atkinson, Horace White, and Whitelaw Reid, economic and political liberals who attacked the doctrines and ethics of the Radicals. Somehow Allison was able to win and keep friends in both camps of Republicanism while maintaining his own Radicalism beyond doubt.

In the short session of the Fortieth Congress, 1868-1869, Allison and his colleagues, James F. Wilson and Judge Asahel W. Hubbard, came dangerously near real trouble in their mixture of business and politics. The charge was that the trio used their influence to secure a change in the route of the Sioux City & Pacific Railroad. The original chartering act had called for a continuation of the road into Nebraska in a westerly direction from Sioux City, until it would intersect the Pacific Railroad running west from Council Bluffs. By their activity, Allison and Wilson (Hubbard seems to have been inactive) secured permission to run the line south and southeasterly from Sioux City, on the Iowa side of the Missouri River, until it intersected the John I. Blair road at California Junction, just west of the town of Missouri Valley. Thus, the Sioux City road would act as a feeder to the Blair road instead of developing the country beyond Sioux City, as the original route would have done if used, and the road would not follow the most direct route to the point of intersection with the main line of the Pacific, as the original law specified.

At first glance this may seem to have been an act of service to Iowa as against Nebraska and therefore deserving of gratitude from Iowans. But the key question was, why did Allison and Wilson work to secure the change of route? Were they unselfishly serving Iowa or were

they serving someone else — for a price? Both men were stockholders
in the Blair road; had they been given the stock by John I. Blair in return for their services? Circumstantial evidence was certainly against
them, but they indignantly denied the charge, Allison going so far as to
name his assailant as Lewis A. Thomas of Dubuque, whom he con-
temptuously dismissed as the Independent Republican candidate
against him in 1868 who had received only 149 votes.[45] Blair was
quoted with great finality, as if he were an impartial witness, to the
effect that each man had regularly subscribed to stock purchases and
had paid the installments due. The famous contemporary journalist,
Gath, fulminated against Allison and Wilson, especially Wilson, whom
he called the "singed cat." [46]

But it was too late. Allison had already been safely re-elected to
Congress for his fourth term, and Wilson had voluntarily made way
for a new candidate in his district.

* VII *

A Time of Decision

By 1869 A NEW situation had arisen in Iowa politics. Senator Grimes had gone to Europe in search of health. His vote against the conviction of Andrew Johnson had destroyed his position of leadership in Iowa and had brought down upon his head attacks which reached their climax in the epithet of "Judas." The paralytic stroke that had sent him abroad for rest and convalescence made it almost certain that he would not be a candidate in January, 1870, for the next senatorial term beginning in 1871. If Grimes should send in his resignation before his term expired, this would mean that the lawmakers would again have the task of choosing both for the unexpired and for the regular term. Thus the short and long term contest of 1866 was about to be repeated. Most likely two men would be selected, one for each opening; the real contest would be for the regular or "long" term.

Iowa politicians did not wait for definite word on Grimes's intentions. That restless soul, Colonel Tichenor, was the first to raise the question of the succession. In his most forthright style he sent to his chief, General Dodge, a letter which was at once an invitation and a challenge.

Is Jim [James F.] Wilson going to make a fight for Senator I see your name mentioned in a number of papers. . . . Judge Wright [George Grover Wright of Des Moines] is a very anxious candidate and as our [county] nominating convention meets in a few days I want to know your wishes. We can control the legislative nominations in this county if necessary but I don't care to

91

make a fight against Wright unless you or Jim Wilson are interested. I can also do something in the matter of legislative nominations in Guthrie, Dallas, Greene, Adair & several other counties but have no relish for the work unless it be to serve you or Wilson.[1]

Thus prodded by Tichenor, Dodge wrote two letters to Wilson.[2] From the wording of Wilson's reply, it is obvious that the powerful Dodge had asked Wilson to run for the Senate and that Wilson had declined. "I have a taste now of the independence of private life and I don't think I will give it up soon," Wilson wrote. "I will not be a candidate for the Senate. Can you get Tichenor to stick a few pins for Allison I don't think we ought to send an inexperienced man to succeed Grimes." [3] Allison might well have thought this letter the most important ever written about himself.

In view of the tenor of the entire Dodge-Wilson-Allison-Tichenor correspondence, it is easy to supply the line of reasoning running through Wilson's mind. The term "inexperienced man" meant one who knew nothing about putting through Congress the plans and projects of Iowans and their friends; one who had no contacts with the Chief Executive and the Departments and no facility at making them; one who knew nothing about keeping a watchful eye on the Supreme Court.

Wilson was the perfect man for such work and was the natural choice for senatorial spokesman for Dodge & Co. He had had a distinguished career in the House since 1861, and he easily stood first in the Iowa delegation, head and shoulders above all except John A. Kasson. A brilliant lawyer, he had risen to the chairmanship of the Judiciary Committee and had helped to draft the Thirteenth Amendment. He had also helped to draw up the articles of impeachment of President Johnson and had served on the House Board of Managers during the trial. He had had much experience as a railroad promoter and investor and was one of the government directors of the Union Pacific Railroad; he was a bank president and a large buyer of securities; he was an effective writer and a forceful stump speaker. All in all, there was not an abler man in Iowa politics.[4] But he did not want to be a Senator in 1869.

Following the normal party practice and the constitutional rules of the time, Senators were nominated by party caucuses and elected by the General Assembly, each house voting separately. Both nomination and election usually took place early in the session of the Assembly; in the case of Iowa, this was in January. In a one-party state, such as Iowa happened to be by an overwhelming margin, nomination by the Republican party caucus was equivalent to election. Therefore, the real contest was within the party, and this usually brought out the worst aspects of factional fighting. In their zeal to win, men would stop at nothing to do or say, regardless of the fact that such words might later boomerang on the party if proved to be true or on the maker of the statements if proved to be untrue.

The management of a senatorial contest was something akin to the science of conducting a military campaign. There was a definite set of procedures that must be followed in proper and delicately timed sequence. First, each candidate must write letters feeling out the prominent local leaders of his party. In such letters the prospective candidate would not openly declare himself to be in the race but would ask for an expression of attitude toward himself if later he should decide to make the contest. One who received a satisfactory number of favorable replies or who was not otherwise discouraged would finally begin the active effort to have state legislators favorable to him elected in October. The candidate and his manager would have to write hundreds of personal letters in their efforts to get the right men chosen. Key leaders had to be cultivated, from the precinct caucuses to the county conventions that chose the party nominees for the legislative positions. After the October elections a furious fight would follow until the January session began, each candidate trying to win and hold the votes of as many legislators as possible. What went on during this period was usually known only to God and the men directly approached. Outright bribes were no doubt rare, but there were many forms of indirect assistance: business favors, loans on easy terms, promises of patronage. Every member needed something.

An unfavorable feature of this business was that a powerful candidate for the Senate could fill the legislature with a large body of unfit or disinterested members who had been chosen and assisted more for their loyalty to their leader than for their qualities as lawmakers for the state. On coming into the session, the senatorial election was the first item of business; that disposed of, the legislators must stay on for the remainder of their terms, performing duties for which they might have neither fitness nor inclination.

In April, 1869, the popular Iowa correspondent, "Linkensale," wrote that if the senatorial election were held then, the choice would be made from four possibilities: Allison, Judge E. H. Williams of Clayton County, George G. Wright, or James F. Wilson.[5] It seems to have been taken for granted, even this early, that Grimes would not run for another term, although his formal resignation did not come until August. Jacob Rich, who was closer to the scene and to the men than Linkensale, sized the situation up in a letter to Kirkwood, who was now "unavailable" as a candidate because of his residence in the southern part of the state, near Harlan's home.

> I suppose [Governor Samuel] Merrill will be renominated without opposition. The Senatorial fight will be the most exciting, and just how it will turn out I do not pretend to be able to fathom. I shall be where I shall not be able to take part in it. I think the North will be pretty well united for Allison, if he should be in the field. Are you not playing into the hands of Mr. Harlan and his friends and your enemies, in going for Wright? It looks a little that way to me at this time.[6]

Thus it seemed early in May to this acute observer. It is well to note that Kirkwood was not backing Allison. Rich, speaking for the Dodge-Kirkwood-Wilson-Allison wing of the party, clearly recognized and indicated that the Harlan faction was the real enemy. About the same time Tichenor pointed out to Dodge that John A. Kasson was another enemy who must be undermined.[7]

But the real worry for Tichenor was the fear that Dodge had not picked the right man in accepting Allison upon Wilson's recommendation. That he had done this is ascertainable from Tichenor's letter a fortnight after Wilson's boost of Allison as a man of experience to succeed Grimes. Tichenor began to bombard Dodge with a series of letters in this vein:

> Wilson says he will not be a candidate for Senator. He must change his mind or you must run. I feel sure either of you can be elected, but we had all fixed on Wilson. I don't think it is in "the papers" to elect Allison and the result I fear will be that Judge Wright or some other inexperienced and unfit man will be selected. We can come nearer electing Palmer [Frank W. Palmer], I think, than Allison although I can and will stick every pin I can for Allison if you say so.[8]

Tichenor's doubts and fears continued to mount rather than subside as the weeks went by. On July 14 he wrote Dodge a long letter, warning him of John A. Kasson's candidacy. It was a masterpiece of denunciation in which Kasson was virtually accused of being a Copperhead. Tichenor was all for fighting Kasson to the death even if in the process a Democrat slipped in as one of the Polk County representatives — this would be better than a victory for Kasson as United States Senator. Either through coincidence or through concerted planning, Frank W. Palmer, now Representative for the Fifth District in Congress, reported to Dodge on the very same day that Kasson was working hard, Judge Wright was overconfident, and Wilson should run and save them all from a Kasson victory.

Tichenor continued to blow hot and blow cold. In one and the same letter he expressed his desire to see Dodge succeed the late Secretary of War Rawlins in President Grant's Cabinet, and thus help Grant, and yet he added: "I am dissatisfied with the existing state of affairs concerning the matter of U. S. Senator I tell you Wright is not the man. Can't he be appointed to that U. S. Judgeship and you or Wilson or some good man take the Senatorship?" [9] This from the man who was supposed to be "sticking pins" for Allison, with the legislative elections just a few days away!

By contrast, Allison himself was confident, almost overconfident. During the hubbub over the War Department vacancy, he wrote to Dodge, offering to go to Washington in his behalf if Dodge desired it. At the same time Allison reported that his canvass was going well. Publicly, he managed to give an appearance of resignation to fate. A friendly newspaper wrote that Allison would like the senatorship but only if it came to him "naturally and spontaneously"; the office would have to "seek the man rather than the man the office." [10]

George Grover Wright, the leading contender, belonged to that class of pioneers who might well be called the "aristocrats of the frontier." He came from a prominent family in Indiana, where his brother had been a leading citizen, a former United States Senator, and a Minister to Prussia. After finishing his course of studies at Indiana University with high honors, and a brief period as a lawyer in that state, Wright came out to Iowa in 1840 and settled in the interior town of Keosauqua, then the center of land sales and a "lawyer's town." Here he made an enviable reputation at the bar, and by 1855 he had risen to be chief justice of the state supreme court. In the fourteen years since, he had established himself as a jurist and made his fame secure by the quality of his opinions.[11] Wright was well known as a Harlan man, and Harlan was on excellent terms with the Grant administration. So it is easy to see that General Dodge had challenged a formidable man when he insisted on putting Allison into the race against Wright. Further support came to the Judge when the rising power among the editors of the state, young, able James S. ("Ret") Clarkson, of the Des Moines *Iowa State Register*, threw his weight behind him, with Governor Samuel Merrill as a possible compromise candidate.

As the end of the year came on, Allison expressed conflicting sentiments to different people. Writing from Washington, where he was on duty in the House of Representatives, he told Edward Atkinson "I think it very doubtful whether I shall be able to make the Senatorship," but to Dodge he was confident of victory "if we work hard." His hopes rested on the theory that Merrill would detach enough votes from Wright to keep Wright from winning on the first ballot, and that would defeat Wright in the end. Allison also expressed great confidence in the power of Dodge and Wilson to control the matter.[12]

The year and the campaign closed with a long letter to Dodge, in which Allison reported to his field commander. The situation was paradoxical in that Allison, who as the candidate should have been commander-in-chief, was actually subordinate to Dodge. Allison listed ten points on which he accepted Dodge's view or on which he had executed Dodge's instructions.[13] It could hardly be said of Allison that he was letting the office seek the man.

There is no point in making a great mystery of the victory of an able and popular jurist, with excellent political connections, over a Congressman with only an average record and with the question mark of his railroad activities hanging over him. When the Republicans gathered on January 13 in the House of Representatives in the capitol building at Des Moines, Wright received 63 votes on the first ballot, Allison 39, and Merrill 24. Sixty-four votes were needed to secure the nomination. On the second try the votes were 66, 47, and 13 respectively, and Judge Wright was the victor.[14]

Almost an anticlimax was the vote for the short term, although it took three ballots to choose a candidate. The honor went to James B. Howell, editor of the Keokuk *Gate City*. Eleven men had been named for the post, with Howell and J. B. Grinnell leading. Grinnell had made a good showing, but he did not have the strength to overcome Howell.[15]

In retrospect, the learned and politically informed editor-correspondent of the Cedar Falls *Gazette* asserted that Allison had worked hard and that the Third District had proposed to win at all costs. Although he did not know whether this famous "Newell Letter" were true or not, wrote the Cedar Falls editor, he did know positively that Allison had used "every known means" to manipulate the Assembly. The fight had been tremendous, and there were "wild and uproarious performances when it was known that Judge Wright had won. . . . Allison is a badly used up man, and will never recover from the stunning blow." [16] In early January, State Senator Homer V. Newell of Clayton County had written a letter that was published in the Davenport *Gazette* and the Dubuque *Herald*, charging that Allison had been supported by a subsidized press, the whisky ring, the railroad lobbies, federal appointees, and others.[17]

Only the actions of the anti-Allison wing of the Dubuque Republicans require explanation. There is good reason to believe that Allison's own fellow-Dubuquers contributed largely to his defeat. This was the belief of Democratic editors in both Des Moines and Dubuque, and they could better afford to tell the truth than the Republican editors. The Dubuque delegation to Des Moines for the legislative fight was far from unanimous in its preferences. Describing Allison's contingent as the Radical element of the city's Republicans, the hostile *Herald* wrote: "It is the Allison crew on the wing. They are going down to lobby for Allison as Senator, and whew how the whiskey will fly!" Among those listed were General M. M. Trumbull, recently appointed as successor to Colonel David B. Henderson as Collector of Internal Revenue; Willis Drummond, an inspector in the Revenue office; V. J. Williams, the postmaster; Colonel Henderson, now assistant United States district attorney; O. P. Shiras, Henderson's senior partner; George Crane, Allison's law partner; F. W. H. Sheffield, president of the Merchants National Bank of which Allison was a director and in which Allison's nephew, James Emerson Allison, worked as a bookkeeper; and John T. Hancock, vice-president of the same bank and a prominent merchant. The list concludes with the vague expression, "and many others." Almost as an afterthought the article named three others as also going to Des Moines: D. N. Cooley, S. P. Adams, and L. A. Thomas. These three might well have been given more attention; perhaps it was only the art of the writer who was thus casually drawing attention to the principal actors in the drama, for these three men were the leaders of the anti-Allison faction in Dubuque. The names of E. C. David and Julius K. Graves, the latter temporarily estranged from the Allison wing of the party, were also added to the list.[18]

The Democratic Des Moines *Statesman* gave the full explanation of the defeat. According to its reporter, Allison, a very confident man, "moves among the Savery [Hotel] lobbyists with graceful mien, and accepts the situation as his." But "last night," Cooley "came as Banquo's ghost," accompanied by Graves.

> Everybody knows Graves. He trotted out Allison for Congress years ago, gave him money to buy the nomination, carried him on his shoulders into the representative's hall, made Allison's political history. Railroad complications [*sic.* combinations] made Allison rich and Graves tried to oust his protege and go to Washington in his stead. Alack! Allison counted noses among Graves' retainers and bought them up in a lump! So Graves is on the war path. So is Cooley.

The reference was to Graves's defeat by Allison in the congressional convention of 1868. There is no proof of the vote-buying charges, but otherwise the story runs close to the known facts about the convention. The Dubuque *Herald* editor added that Graves was now "avenged for West Union" (the site of his 1868 defeat), and the victory supper that Allison had ordered for three hundred was turned into a wake.[19]

Allison's *bête noire* in the case, however, was not Graves but Dr. Lewis A. Thomas. He had been the chief accuser of Allison and Wilson in 1868 for what he termed their services to John I. Blair. This man wielded a barbed pen which was always well informed. A long letter, anonymous but nonetheless preserved by Allison, written by someone well placed in or around the legislature, later informed Allison of the tremendous influence in the lobby enjoyed by Dr. Thomas and the great effect of his letters to the Dubuque *Times*, written under the pseudonym of "Jov." The anonymous writer attributed Allison's defeat to the effectiveness of Thomas' letters and his work around the legislature, saying that Allison had no idea how bitter the feeling had been in some quarters. Anonymous though the letter might be, it was clearly written by someone who had a vast knowledge of the inside manipulation of the legislature. The concluding point of the writer, and his asserted reason for writing the letter, was a warning that if Allison wanted to win in 1872, he must take steps to prevent this kind of opposition from originating again right in his home town.[20]

Dodge, Allison, and Wilson remained in Des Moines for a conference in regard to the forthcoming senatorial election in 1872 in which Harlan's seat would be at stake.[21] Their decision, if any were made, was not announced. It is safe to assume, however, that the defeat of Harlan was the chief topic, but later developments in the story prove that they made no irrevocable decisions at this conference.

In later years Dodge said that he had picked Allison and had run him in 1870 in a trial heat in order to advertise him and build up alliances for the 1872 race against Harlan. For example, Dodge recorded with great satisfaction that both Judge Caleb Baldwin and John T. Baldwin, Dodge's own business partner, were for Wright in 1870 but were surprised at Allison's good showing and promised to support him in 1872.[22] This is a facile explanation very likely derived from Dodge's habit of always seeing things more clearly in retrospect and more favorably to himself than at the time of the deed. In 1869-1870 Dodge & Co. were out to win and failed.

The important fact to remember is that Dodge and his business associates wanted to oust James Harlan from the Senate and from the No. 1 place in Iowa politics. The use of Allison was only incidental in this struggle for control of the party. Dodge's vast business interests and railroad engineering activities demanded too much time to allow him to replace Harlan in person, as he had replaced Kasson in 1866. James F. Wilson was well suited to his purposes but was not available. Samuel J. Kirkwood was a possibility, but he lacked pliability and geographical availability. Allison was both available and pliable; he had "experience"; he was eager and willing. The only practical course for Dodge was to take another chance on Allison and to hope that the work already done for him would be helpful.

In the meantime Allison went about his own business as usual, quite uncertain of his future. There were times when the prospects of a business career looked brighter than those for a continuation in politics. He was still a member of the House and had work to do for his constituents and his special friends. Dodge, who had many projects that had to be looked after, was using James F. Wilson as his personal agent in Washington. Wilson in turn looked to Allison for help and advice on the spot, inasmuch as Wilson had to divide his time between his banking and law business in Fairfield and his duties as a government director of the Union Pacific Railroad, which frequently took him on trips to the West or to Boston, New York, and Washington. Frank

W. Palmer, the member in Congress from Dodge's home district, was willing and eager to be helpful, but he did not have the flair for this work that Allison had.[23]

Dodge was primarily interested in three matters at this time: a bill to reorganize the company which then had a bridge under construction across the Missouri River between Council Bluffs and Omaha for the use of the Union Pacific Railroad; a land grant bill; and a reapportionment bill that would award three new Congressmen to Iowa. Of these, the bridge bill was seemingly the most important to him. At the same time, Dodge was having a fight with an element inside the Union Pacific crowd that was unfriendly to him; his friends Palmer, Allison, and Wilson were cooperating with Congressman Oakes Ames to improve that situation.[24] As if these manifold interests were not enough, a move was on foot in Iowa to set up a Capitol Commission to supervise the building of the proposed new capitol building. Tichenor wanted Dodge and Wilson to get places on this commission in order to use the leverage it would give them in state politics. In one letter to Dodge, Tichenor blithely reported, "we can hold about 20 votes for or against the bill as we please," and in another, "Let me tell you — we are forming a most powerful Allison-Dodge-Wilson organization. We can sweep the state clean." [25]

In the midst of all this, Allison had to think of his own immediate political future. He had four choices, one a fairly sure thing and three definitely involving a risk. He could run for re-election from the Third District and be pretty certain of victory, although he might court a fight with those who had so nearly embarrassed him in 1868. He might wait and see whether Iowa received the three proposed new Congressmen-at-large seats, and run for one of them. Thirdly, he might drop out of the House and take the big gamble on election as Senator over Harlan in 1872. And fourthly, he could follow a business career by making himself useful to General Dodge, to the Illinois Central people, and to his Dubuque friend, Henry L. Stout, and perhaps to a widening clientele as the years went by.

First, true to the office-hunter's technique, Allison sent out letters of inquiry to sound out the feeling about his seat in Congress, apparently writing as one who would not run again. Only two letters of response have been found; undoubtedly there were others. An editor in Waukon was rather noncommittal — "As to your successor — I had not contemplated any such event, and don't like to now. But if it be so, can't as yet say whom to choose." The editor-postmaster at Cresco was more explicit. "While you say you are not a candidate for re-election I infer that you would accept if nomination was tendered you." He expressed both the hope that Allison would run again and confidence that if he did he would win.[26] From these letters it is a fair inference that Allison was keeping a watchful eye on the succession to his place as a member from the Third District. After four successive terms one may be pardoned for a certain air of possessiveness. It was only natural that he should want to keep this place as an ace in the hole, pending the decisions about other possibilities.

The ever watchful Tichenor reported to Dodge on June 20 that he was planting articles in the papers suggesting Dodge and Wilson for Congressmen-at-large and either Allison or Hiram Price if a third place should become available.[27] A more positive suggestion came to Allison from Dodge's friend, Judge Caleb Baldwin of Council Bluffs.

It is now generally understood that Iowa will have three additional congressmen to elect in the state at large, and of course, that is bringing out a good many men that are anxious to go to Washington. . . . I also understand you will be a candidate. If so, I wish to assure you of my wishes for your success (and my support). I know that I can bring General Dodge's friends to your aid, and that you can also aid the General. Your respective locations and the positions you occupy, as former members, will by mutual work secure beyond a doubt your nomination and election. If you favor the Generals nomination, you need not hesitate one moment on account of any doubt as to his acceptance, as he will not decline, unless by being a candidate he should cross the path of such a strong personal friend as yourself.

I will be glad to hear from you, and while I done [sic] all that I could to secure Judge Wright's election last winter, allow me to assure you that it was not because I did not esteem you highly, but because of my friendship for the judge.[28]

As it happened, the "at-large" vacancies never occurred, for the additional seats were not added until April 17, 1872, and then on the basis of a redistricting of the state.[29] Meanwhile, in 1870 Allison's place as Third District Representative went to William G. Donnan of Independence, Buchanan County, but only after the convention had fought through 107 ballots.[30] Donnan was supported by Allison's friend and Grimes's protégé, Jacob Rich, who had once published a paper in Independence and was now editor of the Dubuque Times; it was probably Rich's influence that finally swung the victory to Donnan.

Thus, two of Allison's choices had been removed. There remained the possibility of succeeding to Harlan's Senate seat in 1872. Dodge's official biographer has cited the Council Bluffs "bridge imbroglio" of 1870-1871 in explanation of the Dodge-Harlan enmity that played so great a part in Allison's future. The biographer explains that Dodge urged and warned the Union Pacific people to remember that their eastern terminus was on the east or Council Bluffs side of the river, whereas the company was emphasizing its Omaha terminal. The Council Bluffs people, he avers, played into the hands of ex-Governor Alvin Saunders of Nebraska, blindly taking the Omaha side and denouncing Dodge in a mass meeting just three blocks from his own home. Afterwards they wired to Senator Harlan for help which he gave, and which provoked Dodge to favor Allison in the Senate contest, thus helping to give "Senator Allison to the nation." [31]

Unfortunately, all this is rather loosely dated in the biography. Some offsetting facts are these: Allison was chosen, as we have seen, as the Dodge candidate in lieu of Wilson early in 1869. This was well before any bridge controversy had arisen. Then came the defeat in 1870. While not a certain candidate for 1872, Allison was always the logical choice as the one to continue the race in an effort to get a "Dodge Senator" into the Senate. But more important is the fact that Harlan actually did not oppose Dodge in the quarrel as far as it can be traced in the printed debates in the *Congressional Globe*. The fight had been begun for Dodge by the Representative from his district, Frank W. Palmer, when he introduced a bill on February 14, 1870, to authorize a bridge over the Missouri between Omaha and Council Bluffs. A few days later Palmer explained that a previous bridge company had been authorized and work had been started, but that they had discovered that Union Pacific mortgages stood in the way. His bill was for a reorganized company that could resume work free of all financial and legal barriers. This was what Dodge and all Council Bluffs promoters wanted, but Omaha interests opposed. Senator Harlan aided the cause mightily by seeing the Palmer bill through the Senate over the opposition of Senators John M. Thayer of Nebraska and Samuel C. Pomeroy of Kansas. The bill received the presidential signature on February 24, 1871.[32] Harlan had made it plain that he was representing Iowa interests against all others in his support of the bill. He was not so politically blind as to work against his own state and against a political boss of Dodge's standing in that state. Thus it can be seen that there was no conflict between Harlan and Dodge over this particular bridge. Such an explanation, even if true, would not account of itself for the Dodge efforts to defeat Harlan.

The contest in 1872 was in the future, however. In 1870 Allison's career in the House was closing rather uneventfully. His reputation as a tariff moderate had been made. Although inclined toward compromise, as illustrated in the making of a book tariff rate that pleased the eminent Philadelphia publisher and historian, Henry C. Lea,[33] Allison was not always a compromiser. In making up the Tariff Act of 1870, he reminded the defenders of protection that many of the wartime tariffs were meant to be only temporary measures. "But I may be asked how this reduction shall be made. I think it should be made upon all leading articles, or nearly all. . . . I shall move that the pending bill be recommitted to the Committee on Ways and Means with instructions to report a reduction upon existing rates of duty equivalent to twenty per cent." His efforts against this bill later brought praise from a leading authority on tariff history.[34]

Perhaps the most striking thing about Allison in these years is the seeming contradiction in his friendships, both personal and political. Along with James F. Wilson and Dodge, he was up to his ears in railroad politics and railroad promotion, sometimes a shady business, nearly always a "high-pressure" type of promotion. His Dubuque friends relied on him implicitly as the man to take hold of a new railroad company, the Iowa Pacific, and get it under way.[35] Morris K. Jesup, the great New York financier, with heavy investments in Iowa railroads, wrote to him in a peremptory manner. In one cryptic letter he urged Allison to visit John Crerar, the Chicago capitalist, and John M. Douglas, president of the Illinois Central Railroad; in another he virtually ordered Allison to "take up the business without delay" of arranging for the "St. Paul Extension from Dubuque to Minnesota, a matter of such importance as to demand your personal immediate attention." Another road, from Cedar Rapids to Ottumwa, would not "require your personal care," he added.[36]

At the same time, Allison was on the most cordial terms with the liberals, Edward Atkinson and David A. Wells, and with such a Puritan in politics as Horace White, editor of the Chicago *Tribune*, a tariff reformer, monetary expert, and soon to be a leader of the Liberal Republicans.[37]

Was Allison running with both the hare and the hounds? Was he being all things to all men? Not at all. A considered answer is that he seemed to have a positive talent for securing and maintaining friendships with men of all types; Radicals and Conservatives, realists from the world of business and theoreticians from the world of ideas. Yet his versatility of talent and his social amiability presented him with a problem. The time for a great and final decision was at hand. His loss to Judge Wright had closed one door just when it seemed that elevation to the Senate would be easy; the delay in creating additional congressional districts for Iowa had precluded the hope for an immediate place as a Congressman-at-large; the decision to let the Third District seat go to someone else was now beyond recall. This left only two clear possibilities: the pursuit of a business career or the gamble of a political campaign against the redoubtable senior Senator from Iowa, James Harlan.

☆ VIII ☆

The Mantle of Grimes

PERHAPS THE DAY would come when Allison would wonder why he had ever had his doubts about making a second try for the Senate. However that may have been, his friends seem to have been more active and more concerned than he was. Just before the close of the year 1870 Allison heard from Jacob Rich, the guardian of his Dubuque and Iowa interests, that he had seen William Larrabee, a state senator from Clermont and a new star in the Iowa political firmament, who had indicated his support. Rich confidently assured Allison that he had widely planted two ideas: Allison's ability was equal to Harlan's; Allison was the man north Iowa could unite upon.[1]

Even the slightest and seemingly most remote matters had their points of relationship to the senatorial question. O. P. Shiras, of the law firm of Shiras, Henderson and Van Duzee, all strong Allisonians, was eager to have the state divided into two federal court districts, for not wholly unselfish reasons. He counted on Allison's support, but out of consideration for Allison's interests he warned him not to consent to an east-west division as desired by Pottawattamie County (Council Bluffs). "The charge would be made at once that the north part of the state had been sold out and a trade made on the senatorial question." [2] (It would be ten years before this court division could be settled.)

Another instance involved Dodge's man Friday, Tichenor, who was about to be ousted (through Senator-elect Wright's influence) as postmaster at Des Moines. It automatically followed that Dodge &

105

Co. must not only get Tichenor a new berth somewhere, where he could be helpful, but they must also have a hand in the new Des Moines appointment so as to reap the benefit from the disposal of the favor. The "programme" was to get Tichenor in as State Supervisor of Pensions, a post of increasing political influence due to the power of the G. A. R.,[3] and to throw the Des Moines plum to some one of political importance. Both aims were accomplished. Tichenor received the coveted supervisorship, and the postmastership, by suggestion of Dodge's friend, Frank Palmer, went to Ret Clarkson.[4]

James Sullivan ("Ret") Clarkson was now the rising star in Iowa journalism. Not yet thirty years old and of limited formal education, he had in four years risen to a place of prominence on the staff of the Des Moines *Iowa State Register*. His older brother, Richard, had come with him from a Grundy County farm to Des Moines in 1866 as a fellow-worker on the *Register*, and the two brothers and their father, Coker Fifield Clarkson, himself once a prominent Indiana newspaperman at Brookville, had bought the paper in 1870. James S. soon came to be known far and wide by his nickname, "Ret," a pen name originating in his custom of marking his copy with "Ret. Clarkson" (Return to Clarkson) so that all his editorials and articles, dashed off in a wretched handwriting, would be returned to him for proofreading before he would allow them to go to final press. But Ret and Dick and "Father" Clarkson, who later became famous for the agricultural columns he conducted in the *Register*, had something more to offer than catchy nicknames. They were men of positive views: staunch Methodists, once virtual Abolitionists who had operated a station on the Underground Railroad, they were now strong believers in Prohibition, Protection, and the Republican party as the divinely appointed agent of Progress. Their paper soon became the Bible of Radical Republicanism in Iowa and much of the Middle West. Ret dominated the editorial policy of the paper and therefore was the man who must be won by Dodge & Co.[5]

Another part of the program of Dodge & Co. was the selection of suitable candidates for the state legislature and the right man to be supported for Governor, one who, even if not pro-Allison, at least would not be pro-Harlan. As might be expected, it was the ubiquitous Tichenor, whom Dodge referred to as his "monitor," who made the first suggestion to Dodge along this line. "We must fix upon our men for Gov and Lieut Gov *at once*. Harlan is looking to these matters already. . . . Allen [B. F. Allen, Des Moines banker and state senator] will not be in the field indeed we cant spare him from the Senate. I think *you* are the man. Baldwin would be my next choice. . . . Who is your man for Lieut. Gov. That is important on account of Committeeships." [6] Dodge merely wrote a note on the back of Tichenor's letter and sent it on to Allison: "Cale Baldwin dont want to run. *I cant.* Suppose we put forth C. C. Carpenter of 6th Dist. We have no time to lose." Allison was not enthusiastic in his reply and neither was Tichenor when consulted, but Carpenter made a tactful reply when Dodge sounded him out on the senatorial question, and soon Tichenor fell into line. [7]

An important angle to the game of politics was the lining up of friendly newspapers. Since the Republicans had risen to power in Iowa they had managed to bring about an almost invariable association between editorships and postmasterships. Certainly it would be a rare Republican publisher-editor who at one time or another was not a postmaster. If such a man could also be put into the legislature, so much the better, especially at the time of a crucial senatorial election. If a friendly editor of an important paper were not available, then the paper must be bought, if possible, and put into loyal hands. Such a transaction as this can be traced out in detail in the purchase of the Glenwood *Opinion* by John Y. Stone, with assistance from Dodge and Allison. At least $1,000 in cash was put up by Allison as his part of the deal, perhaps more; whether it came out of his own pocket or from friendly sources in the East will never be known. Overnight a strong Harlan paper was converted into a strong Allison paper, and Stone's vote in the legislative election was assured. [8]

Allison was up against tremendous odds in his fight to unseat Senator Harlan. The veteran Senator from Mount Pleasant was not merely a power in the state because of an army of supporters built up by years of rich patronage disposals; he was a national figure and had a position of recognized leadership in the Senate. Only recently he had gone far to rescue the hapless Grant administration from embarrassment over its Santo Domingo policy. The President, blindly following the lead of his overly zealous but not overly scrupulous secretary, General Orville E. Babcock, had submitted to the Senate a treaty providing for the annexation of Santo Domingo, agreeing to guarantee that island in the meanwhile against foreign intervention. To this end Grant had dispatched a naval squadron to protect the pliant President Baez. But the military minded President soon found that he could not order or even maneuver Senators as he had armies. His policy aroused a hornet's nest of opposition led by Senators Charles Sumner and Carl Schurz. In a tremendous oratorical effort, Harlan answered their criticism with one of the most extravagant claims ever made for the power of the Chief Executive to determine day-to-day foreign policy, independent of Congress. Naturally this endeared him to the feckless President, and Harlan could expect the full support of the Grant administration in his fight to save his seat. Allison warned Dodge that Harlan had strengthened himself by his speech and that Grant had finally extricated himself from his difficulties by a skillfully written message to Congress. "You ought to write him a congratulatory letter," Allison suggested, probably relying on Dodge to use his military friendship with Grant to limit the President's favors to Harlan.[9] James F. Wilson, who was giving his wholehearted support to Allison's campaign, used strong language as he requested Dodge to call on Grant "and make him pull out of our senatorial fight. Make him give the Reps. of the several districts their rights in matters of appointments in their districts." [10]

In all the maneuvering for support or for actual votes, it is surprising to find a letter from Harlan to Dodge, asking or at least hinting for his help in the senatorial race. "I am frank to say I would feel disappointed should you feel compelled to throw your influence in the adverse scale. I would be gratified to hear from you." [11] This letter seems terribly naïve or else a deliberate effort to play on Dodge's sentiments of gratitude for favors of the past. It was public knowledge that Dodge had been Allison's principal backer in 1870; how could Harlan expect him to desert Allison in 1872? One can only speculate whether Dodge's answer was a frank statement of his pledge to Allison or a meaningless evasion.

The preliminary fight in Iowa was for members of the legislature. The individual voter must be convinced that if he wanted Allison (or Harlan), the "proper time to understand that is previous to the Representative and Senatorial contests," to quote advice given by Jacob Rich in an earlier contest.[12] In this kind of dogfight, Allison had a great advantage in the fact that George C. Tichenor was filling the double role of chairman of the Republican state central committee and director of the Allison campaign. Dodge's aide-de-camp was indefatigable in this kind of work; many others contributed their bits.

William Larrabee gave notable help; John H. Leavitt, the pioneer Waterloo banker, won a state senate seat in order to vote for Allison. Former Governor Kirkwood tried to do the same thing in Johnson County but lost to the Democratic incumbent, S. H. Fairall. In the October elections the Republicans walked off with their usual overwhelming victory. The 1872 legislature would have 120 Republicans in a total membership of 150. The successful candidate would have to win a majority of those 120 Republicans.

The interval between the October election and the meeting of the General Assembly in January might be called the "desperation period." Dodge & Co. were the aggressors in this particular war; they took the fight to Harlan with a ruthlessness that has seldom been equaled in any political contest. The Harlanites were put on the defensive and could only fight back by saying that their man was "not guilty" and neither was Allison a spotless lamb. The nearest thing to a special charge against Allison was the accusation that he and James F. Wilson had made a deal with John I. Blair to change the route of the Sioux City & Pacific Railroad. The Burlington *Hawk-Eye* rang the changes on this theme day after day; the Sioux City *Journal* under George D. Perkins, and Harlan's home newspaper, the Mount Pleasant *Journal* under Frank Hatton, seconded with enthusiasm. The assertion, made many years later, that involvement in railroad construction company scandals hurt Allison does not hold up. His defeat in 1870 was not due to this factor; the worst scandal, the Crédit Mobilier affair, did not break into the news until nine months after the election of 1872.[13]

The charges against Allison were puny in comparison with those hurled at Harlan. Harlan's long years in the Senate, plus his months in the Department most notorious for corruption, the Interior, left him in a vulnerable position. The charges involving his acts as a Cabinet officer did far more damage than those arising from the "Newman Letter." In the latter case John P. Newman, a prominent Methodist minister of Washington, D. C., was supposedly Harlan's tool in sending out a letter to Methodist ministers in Iowa, urging them to use their influence in behalf of Harlan, probably the best-known Methodist layman in the nation.[14] Harlan had been in office so long that his sense of propriety may have been blunted. Matt Parrott, one of the fairest editors in the state, thought that Harlan admitted complicity in the letter while trying to explain away its importance. It could easily be true that Harlan would not have thought in advance that this kind of "pressure" would be objected to; for years he had benefited from the friendly attitude of the members of the largest church group in the state, a group that was hardly distinguishable from the Republican party in its personnel and in Civil War and Reconstruction psychology.[15]

The influence of the Newman Letter was literally meteoric; it flashed across the political skies and soon disappeared. Not so with the charges of Harlan's misfeasance in office as Secretary of the Interior. For years the public prints had carried stories of Harlan's approval of a sale of Kansas lands belonging to the Cherokee Indians at an illegal price to the Connecticut Land Company. This contract was canceled by Harlan's successor, who then sold the lands to a railroad combination headed by the Detroit lawyer-capitalist, James F. Joy.[16] Under the treaty which regulated the Indians, their lands were not to be sold for less than a minimum of $1.25 an acre; also they were not to be sold without the approval of the Secretary of the Interior, in whose department all Indian affairs were located. Harlan, it was charged, had approved a price of $1.00 per acre. The Commissioner of Indian Affairs at the time was Allison's former partner, D. N. Cooley; J. B. Grinnell, who was said to have acted as the agent of the Connecticut Land Company in carrying out the transactions, was another Iowan brought into the story.

The general newspaper account was turned into an exposé by one of the foremost journalists of the day, General Henry V. Boynton, in a series of articles published in the Cincinnati *Gazette* in January, 1869; George Alfred Townsend added his strictures.[17] From time to time Harlan and his friends wrote letters of denial and explanation which appeared in friendly papers throughout Iowa, but no great concern was shown by him and his friends until the end of the race with Allison drew near. Then the Harlan forces frantically filled column after column with defensive letters and articles:[18] Harlan had used his discretion, so the accounts read, in accepting a bid of $1.00 per acre after finding that $1.25 was a price that no one would pay; the deal had only been approved by Harlan and was actually consummated by his successor, Orville Hickman Browning of Illinois, who first rejected the contract and later approved a substitute.

The question of guilt or innocence, however important for Harlan's place in history, is of no importance for the present study. The Allison forces were not interested in truth: they were interested in votes.

Very likely they were able to persuade themselves for the moment that their charges were true. Additional evidence for their case was furnished by material supplied by a colorful character, Hawkins Taylor, once a mayor of Keokuk and a member of the first territorial legislature of Iowa, now a government worker in Washington who made a business of running errands for his friends. He delved into the records at Washington and with the assistance of John Allison, the Register of the Treasury [19] (unrelated to William B. Allison), dug out a mass of items that seemed to support charges that had been bandied about for years. These were that Harlan had enriched himself by collusion with Perry Fuller and with Elijah Sells, Sr., and his son, Elijah, Jr., in fraudulent contracts for supplies for the Indians; that he had used horses and carriages, furniture and stationery belonging to the Department of the Interior, that he had put his son on the payroll even though the son was still in school. Taylor's letters were not published verbatim, but their contents were whispered about and shown to some of the members by W. G. Donnan of Independence, Allison's successor in the House.[20]

A serious blow to the Harlan cause was the open espousal of Allison by the Des Moines *Register*. All through the year this paper had been rather coy in its refusal to take a positive stand for any candidate, although it had seemed to lean toward the Harlan candidacy; certainly it had warmly defended Harlan against the charges in the Cherokee Land cases. It had also shown favor toward General Dodge. On December 13, 1871, came the first editorial positively favoring Allison; each day thereafter the paper became more violently anti-Harlan. The defense of Harlan's Cherokee policy was completely reversed, and the Hawkins Taylor material was used, although not credited to him. What happened to bring about this switch?

In later years it was revealed that Father Clarkson and his sons had split over this senatorial race, the former persevering in his favor of Harlan, a fellow-Methodist who in his eyes could do no wrong, and the sons veering toward Allison. Thereupon, the father had sold out to his sons and relegated himself to a politically innocuous position as "agricultural editor" of the paper, while Ret took over the editorial columns and Dick the business management.[21] Harlan later privately charged that Allison had furnished $5,000 to help Ret swing the deal; many years later a venerable figure in Iowa history, Ora Williams, was quoted to the effect that Ret had secured $30,000 through Jacob Rich in order to buy his father's interest, a story subject to serious doubt.[22] Although there is no proof that Allison owned stock in the *Register*, there is evidence that on one occasion he had the power to determine the paper's policy.[23]

As the race neared its end, the position of James F. Wilson became somewhat enigmatical. By September he was an acknowledged candidate and was receiving some support. Allison reported to Kirkwood in November: "I expected to meet you at Des Moines. . . . I met Wilson there and on the whole am satisfied with what he proposes, viz., to do nothing for himself, by himself or friends. But let the matter rest where it is in good faith." Allison added a powerful plea to Kirkwood to come to Des Moines and act as the "Gen'l in Chief of my forces. I will provide you with skillful subordinate officers who will under your guidance conduct the battle. I will see that your army is well equipped & supplied with all proper things to conduct a campaign." [24] But only a few days later Jacob Rich, Allison's *alter ego* in politics, wrote to Kirkwood:

I note what you say about the contest, and fully agree with you that we must not have a general fight in the Senatorial contest. It must be made straight between Allison and Harlan, and I have full faith that it will be. I believe that it is so coming [*sic*] as to make that imperative. I feel sure that Wilson is only a candidate to defeat Harlan, and will take his friends where they ought to be, to Allison. We have already had positive evidence in one case that he is already doing so.[25]

Kirkwood was now in a position to appear aloof. In one letter he adopted a casual attitude that must have been both baffling and irritating to Allison, but he ended by advising Allison to stay in the race against both Harlan and Wilson or else Harlan would win.[26]

The last few days of 1871 and the first few of 1872 were hectic beyond description. George Tichenor reported, "I fear my nervous system is prostrated. Dont be alarmed however. If I find that I cant keep up I will telegraph you and will go to bed and rest so as to be in fighting trim when the members come. Dont be alarmed if I cease writing you for a few days." Ret Clarkson, having started later, managed to hold up until the election was over but then wrote: "The over-work and excitement of the Senatorial fight have prostrated my nervous system so badly that I must take a rest in order to avert rheumatism." [27]

There were 120 votes to be worked for in the party caucus, where the real election would take place. The questionable methods used were later described by one of the participants, George D. Perkins, when, after three years of meditation, he remonstrated against the tendency to pursue Harlan "with the ghosts of a past that Iowa Republicans should be willing to put so far as may be out of sight — for the Allison-Harlan campaign was one to be ashamed of." As a Des Moines observer saw it, "the canvass here by the friends of the different candidates was active, earnest, and upon the part of some, we are sorry to say, vindictive and bitter." [28] Harlan's biographer was never more mistaken than when he wrote: "But it should be remembered that the candidates took no part in the war of personalities which followed, except to answer some of the most violent accusations, nor were they responsible for the bitterness of the campaign conducted by their admirers." [29] Each of the three candidates was on the ground directing his forces and furnishing material for his followers to use in conferences, letters, and newspapers. For several days the lobbies of the hotels were full of milling partisans, Allison's outnumbering those of Harlan and Wilson combined.[30] On the Sunday before the caucus on Wednesday, Governor-elect Carpenter and his wife attended the Fifth Street Methodist Church. "The House was full of politicians & preachers here from different parts of the State, in attendance at the Senatorial fight." [31]

The very last blow against Harlan seems to have been struck by Al Swalm, currently editor of the Jefferson *Bee*. A special pre-election issue of his paper appeared with all the charges repeated, summarized, and emphasized, and the colorful Swalm, whose partial Indian blood excused him for affecting an Indian-style hairdress, took copies to Des Moines and personally distributed them among the legislators.[32]

The Republican caucus met at seven-thirty on the evening of January 10, 1872, in the chamber of the House of Representatives in the State House. The excitement of the drama in the caucus room has been portrayed by journalist-politicians who were on the scene. One especially vivid account tells of the high-pressure lobbying that preceded the caucus, and the last-minute conferences between the principals and their lieutenants just before the members filed into the House chamber. On the first ballot, which was informal, the vote stood: Allison, 60; Harlan, 38; and Wilson, 22 — one short of victory for the candidate of Dodge & Co. The first formal ballot stood 59, 42, and 20, respectively, a total of 121 votes, indicating that one man had cast an extra ballot in order to invalidate this vote, whoever the winner — a clever but desperate tactic.

On the second formal ballot the Allison vote reached 60 with one more vote to be counted. Every eye was on the teller as he reached into the hat for that precious slip of paper. If it were marked "Harlan" or "Wilson" a third ballot would be necessary; if it were marked "Allison" the prospect was lifelong power for him and oblivion for Harlan. "Allison" it was, and suddenly all was pandemonium both inside and outside the hall. Finally order was restored enough to allow for some shifting of votes, and the count was announced as 63, 40, and 17. Harlan's manager, Dr. Charles Beardsley of Burlington, then offered the customary motion that the nomination be made unanimous.

Kirkwood was waiting for the members to emerge. "He is wild and goes rapidly from hand shaking to dancing, and finally I see him catching frantic young men and pressing them to his voluptuous vitals." Allison and his forces gathered at the Savery for a victory celebration that went on far into the night, while Harlan returned to his darkened room. "This ends my political life," he said to a friend, with more truth than he knew. Later he manfully controlled himself and called on Allison to deliver his congratulations in person.[33]

Governor Carpenter's laconic comment well expressed the mood of many: "Tonight the Senatorial caucus took place. Allison was nominated and the long agony was over."[34] But for some others the occasion could not be so briefly dismissed. For some who were able to take the long view, this was the climax of a fight that had been going on since the far-off days of 1865 when Harlan insisted on returning to the Senate, capriciously so his opponents thought, thus blocking the election of Kirkwood. Now the day of reckoning had arrived. Victory for Allison was not the one and only goal; revenge for Kirkwood and power for Dodge & Co. were the real ends in view. Control of the future of the Republican party in Iowa was the supreme prize at stake in this election.

After the first frenzy of jubilation had spent itself at Des Moines, the enthusiasm of Allison's supporters subsided into a proper modesty in victory. In Dubuque a reception was held at the Lorimier House with Christian Wullweber, leader of the German community and a strong Allison supporter, as the principal speaker. Allison responded with timely remarks followed by handshaking, feasting, and dancing.

No political party lines were drawn on this occasion.[35] The pro-Allison newspapers did not gloat over their victory, nor did Allison himself. The only comment of his own that has been found is in a note to his friend James A. Garfield. "I thank you sincerely for your congratulations. I had a severe contest and achieved a great victory. I hope in a humble way to be of some service to my country in the direction of lifting some burdens from the people, without laying on others more grievous. I shall hope to see you before the Ides of March." [36] To Dodge he wrote in a quite different vein, dutifully acknowledging his obligations and asking for an accounting so that he might at once place the money to Dodge's credit.[37]

President Grant's advisers were happy to acquire another friend in the Senate. General Horace Porter, Grant's personal secretary, commented pleasantly to Dodge about Allison: "He has always been one of our intimate friends here and we shall get along swimmingly with him. He is able and will make a valuable member of the Senate." [38] Knowing what we now know about the Grant administration, it is a doubtful compliment to Allison to be counted as one of Grant's "intimate friends" with whom the administration would "get along swimmingly." A "valuable member of the Senate" could mean more than one thing to a Grant operator.

Although Harlan was publicly gracious and courageous in the days following his defeat, privately he vented his disappointment with considerable vigor. He wrote Azro B. F. Hildreth of the Charles City *Intelligencer*:

I am grateful for your manifestation of friendship for me. The "Register" was indebted to B. F. Allen $25,000.00 on purchase price of the establishment. It was understood at Des Moines that Mr. Allison advanced $5,000.00 which had matured on the debt, at about the date of its first onslaught on me. Perhaps this was a loan to be repaid out of the profits of public printing. The management of the campaign, on their part, was, as I think, most disreputable. The fruit thus gathered ought to turn to ashes! But we must acquiesce and wait, and work, for a redemption, which will certainly come sooner or later.[39]

Harlan was perhaps nearer the truth than he realized, in view of Allison's influence over the policy of the Des Moines *Register*. A few days after Allison's election, Ret Clarkson's brother-partner Richard was elected to the profitable post of state printer. Members of Dodge & Co. regarded the fight as one for Ret's benefit as well as Allison's.[40]

The Burlington *Hawk-Eye* could not be as gracious in defeat as Harlan had been. It bitterly charged that "The man who has done most for the Republicans of Iowa must give place to one who has done nothing, and whose genius and purposes are not in accord with those of a very large majority of the people, even if his abilities and character were at all comparable with those of Mr. Harlan. . . . We do not propose, or desire to conceal our regret at what we deem a misfortune to the republicans of Iowa. We are not only dissatisfied but disgusted." A few days later this paper's correspondent at Des Moines, "X. Y. Z.," sent in his postmortem report. He attributed the defeat of Harlan to the railroads and to the use of money; not that votes were actually bought for cash but by "loans, promises of future assistance, or chances in profitable undertakings." The charges against Harlan were not the reason for his defeat but merely good excuses, he claimed. This writer praised the bearing and conduct of both Allison and Harlan, but observed that Wilson was a bad loser.[41]

George D. Perkins of the Sioux City *Journal* was equally bitter. He accused Allison flatly of having used cash and promises of office in order to win. He asserted that Allison could not win in a fair contest or in an election "left to the people." [42] The methods used would encourage "pothouse politicians" of the future. Perkins raised a more serious point by asking, "Shall the odium rest upon the party?" In an editorial on this subject he said it was up to the Dubuque *Times* and the Des Moines *Register* to carry on and either reform the party or else admit that all the charges of corruption made against the Harlan wing had been claptrap.[43] And John P. Irish, a fiery Democrat, tried to force the Republicans' hand by introducing a resolution into the General Assembly, calling for an investigation by the Senate of the United States of the charges against Harlan, with impeachment to follow if found true. The resolution was quickly tabled on motion of John A. Kasson, now a member of the Iowa House.[44] Only the future would tell whether the Allisonians, in a spirit of liberal reform, would purge the party of the corruption charged to the Harlanites.

In addition to the forty legislators who had shown their faith in Harlan by voting for him, there were others in Iowa who looked with distaste on the tactics used. Although not taking an active part in the contest, Governor Cyrus C. Carpenter, the choice of Dodge & Co., wrote in his diary: "I have no belief in the stories told about Mr. Harlan. If he was guilty of anything wrong it arose from his good heartedness and dislike to shake off shysters who hung around him." [45]

Nationally, Allison's moderate views on the tariff led some liberals to favor his election. James McDill wrote to his friend, Lyman Trumbull, a Senator from Illinois, that the Liberal Republicans of Iowa were "rejoicing just now over the defeat of Harlan and the election of Allison. If I have not misread your record you too will be pleased at the result. Allison is not a protectionist." [46] *The Nation* spoke out in all its righteous pleasure, now that Harlan had been defeated, rehearsing at length all the charges against him and asserting that "Civil-service reform, tariff reform, and all other reforms will gain by the election of Mr. Allison . . . in place of Mr. Harlan." [47]

Sixteen years later both Allison and Dodge reflected on the circumstances of this campaign and gave their remembered versions of how the election had been brought off. These are interesting examples of the softening effects of time and preoccupation with other business. Allison recalled meeting Grenville M. Dodge on the fateful trip to Washington in 1861, Dodge's successful army career, his entrance into politics, and his connection with the Union Pacific Railway. As for Dodge's part in the senatorial election of 1872, Allison could recall only the great energy with which Dodge had taken hold of the Des Moines electioneering. As to Dodge's motivation, "I think Dodge went for me quite largely because we were personal friends." [48] Dodge's account is valuable largely because of his attempted explanation of his pro-Allison, anti-Harlan position. He stressed Harlan's loss of contact with Iowa people and their needs, due to long absence from the state, whereas Allison was strong on this very point. Dodge made contradictory statements as to Harlan's policy toward Nebraska. All in all, his statement does not impress one as being forthright. [49]

One might ask what was the sequel of the election for James F. Wilson, whose original refusal to run in 1869 made him the sacrificial victim in this contest. Perhaps it was all a meaningless gesture, but the Chicago *Tribune*, edited by Horace White, bosom friend of both Dodge and Allison, now began a campaign to draw attention to Wilson as a potential presidential candidate. [50] Surely this could not have been anything more than a sop thrown to Wilson to assuage his feelings. A few days later Tichenor had reduced this campaign on Wilson's behalf to an effort for the second place on the ticket. H. M. Hoxie, now railroading for Dodge in Texas, assured Dodge that he would get the Texas state convention and the newspapers down there

started on the task of building up Wilson for Vice President.[51] This
was an even more fantastic idea. Politicians as a rule do not nominate
men from "safe" states for President and Vice President, and Iowa
was certainly "safe." Nor do they often nominate those who are from
adjacent states. Since Grant's renomination was inevitable, Wilson's
prospects for either post were illusory.

The Burlington *Hawk-Eye* noted the Wilson boom with scorn:

Western railroad interests, identified with the great lines from Chicago
through Iowa, to Omaha, and probably the Union Pacific interest, also, are
hard at work putting *one of their attorneys*, JAMES F. WILSON, of Iowa,
through his paces, so as to trot him out as a Presidential candidate. . . . *We*
of the West have understood for a long time past [the existence of railroad
influences in our national and local politics]. . . . We point out this new
development of railroad insolence, and we speak of it plainly, that it may
be known and thwarted by the people. This interest has made our judges,
has given us a Senator and now seeks to foist upon the people a President.[52]

So far as Allison is concerned, the records amply confirm the judgment of the historian who said: "To fortify their privileged position,
the railways . . . chose governors and sent their picked servants, like
W. B. Allison of Iowa, to the Senate." [53] Allison had been and was to
be a faithful servant of the railroads in Congress. Shortly after his
election he wrote to Dodge: "Your news about U. P. [Union Pacific]
surprises me. I suppose that accounts for the advance in the stock.
I will do everything I can in the matter. I think in view of that you
had better hurry along East as soon as you can so as to direct me." [54]

Less than a month after Allison had been elected to the Senate, death
at last released James W. Grimes from the sufferings which had racked
his body for so many years and for which the medicinal waters of
Europe had proved useless. Most Iowans had long ago forgiven him
for his vote on behalf of Andrew Johnson, and his funeral was an occasion for widespread public mourning. Allison was in the East on
business at the time and, strangely enough, did not return to attend
the last rites of his great friend, but he wrote to Mrs. Grimes, acknowledging his debt to her husband.[55]

Now, in 1872, it remained to be seen whether William Boyd
Allison had really won "the mantle of Grimes," and, if so, with what
grace he would wear it.

☆ IX ☆

Elections and Scandals

TROUBLES SOON invaded Allison's enjoyment of his new-found success. Perhaps none disturbed his peace of mind any more than the crusade of the disaffected members of the Republican party known as the "Liberals." Some of Allison's best friends were leaders of this movement, and it was no easy matter for him to steer a course between loyalty to the Radical Republicans and offense to his Liberal friends, especially when the Radicals carried their factionalism to such extremes. Well before his election, Allison had been taken to task by one of his Radical friends for consorting with Liberals and giving rise to the rumor that he was helping to plan the formation of a third party; the friend appeared to be greatly relieved when Allison sent assurances of his loyalty to Radicalism.[1]

The original Liberal Republicans were apparently truly scandalized by the methods and policies of the Radicals. Although only minor revelations of Radical misfeasance and malfeasance had yet been made, it is significant that even before the worst scandals had been exposed a large segment of the party had come to the point of secession.

The first positive move in this direction came in Missouri. Carl Schurz and B. Gratz Brown were the originators of the movement, but national leadership was soon taken over by Allison's good friends, Horace White, editor of the Chicago *Tribune*; Whitelaw Reid of the New York *Herald*; David A. Wells, the economist who earlier had been the victim of Grantism; Edward Atkinson, Boston banker and economic philosopher, who, like Wells, was one of Allison's intimate

119

correspondents; and Senator Lyman Trumbull of Illinois.[2] In Iowa the Liberals had a fair representation of respected names in Iowa history, but they were men who were only on the edge of political success: Josiah B. Grinnell; William Peters Hepburn; General Fitz Henry Warren; W. W. Merritt of Red Oak; Colonel J. H. Keatley of Council Bluffs. The Dubuque Liberals included Dr. E. A. Guilbert, distinguished Masonic leader; Joseph A. Rhomberg, distillery magnate; F. Hinds, banker; and Allison's old rivals, Shubael P. Adams and Julius K. Graves.[3]

The national convention of the new party had been called for Cincinnati, and some Liberals looked hopefully to Senator-elect Allison for support. Whitelaw Reid wrote to him with confidence in April: "The Cincinnati movement looks brighter than it did when you were here. Our people who are inside are all confident; the Administration, on the other hand, seems to be equally confident, and indeed pooh poohs the Cincinnati movement, though with a nervousness which indicates the reverse of satisfaction at the prospect. The only movement gaining strength is the Cincinnati movement. The Grant force has developed long ago." [4]

Reid's letter, with its mixture of enticement and warning, has the ring of a plea to join the movement. The remarkable thing about Allison's performance here is that he rejected the new party completely but at the same time retained the friendship and trust of his Liberal friends. Fortunately for him, the issue had not reached the crucial point at the time of his contest in January; now, as one safely elected, he could cling to the old rather than gamble on the new. The Liberals seemed to have been satisfied with his election; either they did not know their man or else they regarded him as the lesser of two evils. Harlan was definitely known to be a Grant man and a Radical wheel horse, as illustrated in the "great debate" of 1871 over Santo Domingo.[5] James McDill's letter to Lyman Trumbull is worth repeating: "We are rejoicing just now over the defeat of Harlan and the election of Allison. If I have not misread your record you too will be pleased at the result. Allison is not a protectionist." [6]

But protection was not the only issue. If the Liberals had only reflected a moment they would have known that the man who was the protégé of Grenville M. Dodge and the ally of James F. Wilson could not, if pressed, be other than an irrevocable Grant-Radical Republican. Fortunately, Allison could be himself and still satisfy both camps.

He was on record as "vindictive" toward the South, but nothing new was demanded on that subject. On civil service reform, he had said little but always acted with those who despised the subject and ridiculed it as "snivel service" reform. By his actions he approved the principle that the government should be the servant of business, especially of the railroads. These things pleased the Radicals. On the other hand, the Liberals liked his moderation on the tariff and currency questions.

A course of reading in the newspapers, speeches, and letters of the period is an excellent school for cynicism. The times cried out for Republicans to do something about the corruption that had been charged against Harlan — and all the other Harlans in the party. As George D. Perkins had said after the Allison victory, now it was up to the Des Moines *Register* and the Dubuque *Times* to reform the party or else admit that the cry of corruption known as "Harlanism" was all a game designed to bring victory to those who were themselves corrupt. The sequel demonstrates how well Perkins had divined the situation and how little disposed was the Dodge faction to purge the party of corrupt members, once victory was theirs. Dodge, Wilson, and Allison did not waver in their fealty to Grant and his regime, no matter what exposures were made. Meanwhile, their editorial spokesmen Ret Clarkson and Al Swalm ridiculed the Liberal movement incessantly.

Even Harlan now intensified his associations with the dominant wing of the party. Despite his rejection by Iowa Republicans, he served his party faithfully in the 1872 campaign. In June he acquired the vulgarly partisan Washington (D. C.) *Chronicle*. Henceforth his paper served as the apologist and defender of all things done by the Grant followers.[7] Moreover, Harlan served as chairman of the congressional campaign committee for the 1872 campaign. The man who was not worthy of re-election in Iowa after sixteen years as Senator and a year in the Cabinet was apparently quite acceptable as a manager for the election of others. On the morrow of his defeat, Harlan began to experience the bitter truth of his new political situation: he was acceptable enough as a party worker and civic and church leader but not as a Republican officeholder. Dodge & Co. demanded a more pliable agent in Washington than a man who, accustomed to the honors of leadership, expected allegiance from others.

In May the Liberal Republicans proceeded to turn their promising outlook into a gigantic joke at Cincinnati. They passed over many good men, Charles Francis Adams notably, and finally settled on that "extinct volcano," Horace Greeley, as their candidate for President. Several months later the *North American Review* summed up the situation:

The honor, to the utter surprise and merriment of the people, fell upon Horace Greeley. Precisely how this result was brought about is not known to this day, — whether it came from previous negotiations or understandings with Democratic leaders, of which there are some evidences extant, or was achieved through the skillful tactics of General Blair and Governor Brown of Missouri, in the convention itself, or is to be accepted as the last case of political spontaneous combustion, originating in the inflammable materials of a miscellaneous gathering.[8]

To make matters worse, the Liberals supplied Greeley with a low tariff platform, which he repudiated, and then asked the Democrats to accept him as their candidate as well. And the leaderless Democrats had to swallow him at the cost of becoming the laughing stock of the country. Small wonder that the Cincinnati movement, which Whitelaw Reid had thought so promising in April, became a lost cause by August.

Meanwhile, Allison and others continued to boost James F. Wilson for the second place on the ticket with Grant, instead of the top place as some had once foolishly suggested. This could hardly have been more than a gesture, however. "His locality if anything will prevent his nomination," Governor Carpenter recorded in his diary. Nevertheless, the correspondence about Wilson's chances was deadly serious in tone, even Wilson's own letters. If nothing else, Dodge's lieutenants were faithfully carrying out his orders to boom Wilson. Dodge himself reached out into all the states where he had a crony, a dependent, or a former staff man from the war days to call on. Allison reported to Dodge: "I believe we can nominate Wilson if we work heartily. How can we reach the Ohio delegates. . . . I know two or three of these delegates personally & will write to them." [9]

The Iowa Republican state convention had met in March, elected Dodge as one of the delegates-at-large to the national convention and passed resolutions endorsing Wilson for the vice-presidency. The Burlington *Hawk-Eye*, which seemed to have sworn eternal enmity to Wilson, cleverly wrote up this endorsement so as to give the impression to Grant that Wilson was a rival. Wilson, very much perturbed, begged Dodge to take the matter up with Grant and General Horace Porter and to assure them that he was strongly in favor of Grant's renomination.[10] In April, Dodge ordered Allison to intensify the drive for Wilson. Allison should go into Wisconsin and Minnesota, Wilson into Illinois, and Christian Slagle of Fairfield into Missouri. "Work alone will now pull Wilson through and we must give the next two or three months to it. Keep me posted on what you do." [11]

The Republican national convention met at Philadelphia on June 5 and made quick work of showing how practical politicians could run off the business of putting safe men on the ticket. Grant was renominated without difficulty. James F. Wilson's name was not even placed in nomination for the second place; for Grant's running mate the convention struck a blow at his nemesis, Senator Charles Sumner, by nominating Sumner's colleague from Massachusetts, Henry Wilson. Iowa, on the first and only ballot for Vice President, gave 19 votes to Henry Wilson and 3 to Schuyler Colfax. Evidently Dodge & Co. had found the Henry Wilson boom too strong for their man and had saved him embarrassment by not naming him at all. Governor Carpenter, who was in Philadelphia, had correctly predicted the result on the eve of the convention, "It now looks very much as though Henry Wilson would be nominated for the vice Presidency." [12] So much for this episode in the annals of Dodge & Co.

While the campaign was in the September doldrums, Charles A. Dana, dynamic editor of the New York *Sun*, exploded a bombshell. On September 4, 1872, he published the first accusation of the involvement of several Congressmen in the Crédit Mobilier Company. The burden of Dana's story was that Oakes Ames, a Representative from Massachusetts, and a vice-president and dominant force in the Crédit Mobilier, had put out shares "where they would do the most good." This contracting company for the construction of the Union Pacific Railroad was largely owned by the stockholders of that railroad. It had been working on the construction since 1864 and had completed the job by the junction of the Union Pacific rails with those of the Central Pacific Railway at Promontory Point, Utah, on Sunday, May 10, 1869. Among those accused of receiving stock under fraudulent terms was William Boyd Allison, Senator-elect from Iowa. Others were Senator Henry Wilson, the vice-presidential nominee; Representative James A. Garfield of Ohio; Speaker James G. Blaine; Senator James W. Patterson of New Hampshire; Vice President Schuyler

Colfax; James Brooks of New York; James F. Wilson; and Grenville
M. Dodge. In addition, as a corollary charge, Senator James Harlan
was accused of having received $10,000 from Dr. Thomas C. Durant
of the Union Pacific as a contribution to his 1866 campaign for the
Senate against Governor Kirkwood.

For some weeks the country refused to become excited over the
charges and the denials. *The Nation* said that the charges "amount
to little." [13] The matter then began to drift, and, but for the questionable zeal of one of those accused, the whole business might have passed
into obscurity. But James G. Blaine, eager to parade his innocence,
stepped down from the Speaker's chair with a great show of virtue,
turned the gavel over to S. S. ("Sunset") Cox, and moved the appointment of a special select committee to make an investigation of the
charges. This led to the naming of the Poland Committee in the
House, later supplemented by the Wilson Committee. On the first
committee, besides Luke P. Poland of Vermont,[14] there were Nathaniel
P. Banks of Massachusetts,[15] George W. McCrary of Iowa,[16] W. E.
Niblack of Indiana, and W. M. Merrick of Maryland. The latter two
were Democrats; their presence, plus the recognized integrity of
McCrary and Judge Poland, was later described as a "guarantee that
the inquiry would not result in a whitewashing report." [17] James
Ford Rhodes, the eminent historian who wrote those words, did not
take notice that four of those accused were from Iowa; that one of
those four was James F. Wilson, McCrary's immediate predecessor in
the House and a man to whom he owed a great deal; [18] and that
McCrary had senatorial ambitions of his own which he must not seem
to advance by too much zeal at the expense of his own party colleagues.
This is not to say that McCrary did not make a "fair" committee
member; but it does help to explain why he was not a bloodhound
in the long hours of cross-examination of the accused.[19]

The committee brought out the fact that the Crédit Mobilier was
a mere front for the Union Pacific Railway, and that there had been
a series of contracts let for the construction of the road and its ap-
purtenances, the first one going to Herbert M. Hoxie in 1864 for a
portion of the line.[20] What the committee did not bring out was the
relationship between Dodge (and therefore Allison and Wilson) and
Hoxie, or the fact that Hoxie could not finance such an operation. He
was set up as a "dummy" who would accommodatingly sublet the
contract to the very company that had given it to him. Furthermore,

the committee did not disclose that Dodge, as commander of the military Department of Missouri, had managed to combine a tour of duty as the leader of expeditionary forces against the Indians in 1865 with the congenial task of selecting a route for the Union Pacific.[21] The committee did not succeed in discovering these things, partly because Dodge avoided the service of a subpoena and dashed away from Texas, the current scene of his railway building, to a hideout in St. Louis. Even his henchmen, Wilson and Allison, criticized Dodge for this, but he brazenly defended his course on the grounds that he could not spare the time from his business. He told Allison that everyone connected with the Crédit Mobilier affair, except James F. Wilson, had "played the fool" by admission of guilt.[22] (Wilson had denied guilt and regretted only that he could not have bought more stock.)

In its cross-examination of Allison, the Committee leaned over backward to avoid the conclusion that he deserved some degree of censure for his relations with Oakes Ames. Much has been made of the point that Allison made a clean breast of his dealing with Ames; and that he expressed regret over the matter and insisted that he had withdrawn so soon as he discovered the nature of the deal. James Ford Rhodes and others have followed that interpretation; apparently it was also accepted by contemporaries, inasmuch as the subject was soon forgotten.

But Allison escaped more lightly that he deserved. A person hearing or reading his testimony, who did not know his background of years of experience in the sharp game of railroad promotion and his intimate dealings with Oakes Ames ever since he entered Congress in 1863, would suppose that Allison was an innocent making his first venture into the realm where finance and politics meet. His story was that he had bought ten shares each of Crédit Mobilier and Union Pacific stock, coming to $1,047; that they had almost been paid for before delivery by a stock dividend amounting to $776; this left a balance of $271 which presumably he had paid. "How this balance was paid, I do not now remember," said Allison. Later he received a dividend check for $600 which was deposited to his credit with the Sergeant-at-Arms of the House. This gave him an equity of $1,647 with an outlay of only $271, a neat profit of $1,376. Some time later Allison decided to return the stock and the dividend voluntarily; he did so after deducting the $271. According to Oakes Ames's testimony, the stock certificates were returned from Dubuque in an envelope without the sender's name or any covering letter; he could only assume that they were from Allison because there were no other stockholders of record in Dubuque.

The natural question is, of course, why did Allison return the stock? Did he hear the rumors that were in the air, the vague criticism that was springing up? Not by his own account. He said that it was because he was being criticized during the campaign of 1868 for his part in the shifting of the route of the Sioux City branch of the Pacific railroad; he wanted to prevent further criticism that might come from a revelation of his connection with the Crédit Mobilier. Oakes Ames insisted that Allison's alarm had been due to his fear that a lawsuit by Henry L. McComb of the Crédit Mobilier might have embarrassing results, and therefore he would not want the stocks to be found in his name. Ames further testified that he had "bought" back the stocks from Allison for a consideration, the amount being five cents, as a cover for the transaction, and that the stocks were to be returned to Allison if the outcome of the suit were favorable. Under questioning, Allison denied that the whole matter was a "ruse" to allow him to keep the stock under some conditions or not to keep it under others. The Committee made no effort to choose between the conflicting stories.[23] About all one can say is that Allison was not censured, and that Oakes Ames and James Brooks, of New York, were strongly censured by the House.

Most of those who were accused managed to come out unharmed and suffered no political damage. Allison was the beneficiary of very lucky timing throughout the whole episode. He had been elected to the Senate on January 10, 1872; the story of the scandal did not break until September 4. He gave his testimony before the Poland Committee in January, 1873; the report was submitted in February. On March 4 Allison was sworn in as a Senator, and the matter was never officially referred to again.[24] There was much criticism in the pro-Harlan papers of Allison's acts and of his air of innocence, but all to no avail.[25]

When he entered the Senate, Allison had reached the prime of life. Of average height — five feet, eight inches — he carried his two hundred pounds well. His head was set well upon broad and sturdy shoulders; his dark eyes had a piercing intensity, and his mouth was firm. His brownish hair was profuse but well ordered, and his beard and mustache were neatly trimmed, almost pointed. In a group picture of the Senate not a man cut a finer figure than Allison. He was always elegantly tailored; from New York and Washington haberdashers came the best of everything. He enjoyed cigars and was considered a prodigious smoker; otherwise, he was notably temperate in food and drink. In manner the soul of courtesy to colleagues and constituents and business associates, this is clearly an Allison capable of holding his own in senatorial combat.

Allison's senatorial career began quietly and without fanfare. He took the oath of office on March 4, 1873,[26] in a special session of the Senate called by President Grant, whose second inauguration he witnessed on the same day. The session was uneventful for Allison except for the negative fact that his credentials were not challenged in any way, the Crédit Mobilier scandal notwithstanding. Among his colleagues in the Senate were such notable men as Justin S. Morrill of Vermont, an old friend of the House days; Roscoe Conkling of New York, whose "turkey gobbler strut" was one of the jokes of the day, an able but vain and pompous man who might have caused observers to wonder "whether this was an actor burlesquing a senator or a senator burlesquing an actor";[27] Simon Cameron of Pennsylvania, who had left Lincoln's Cabinet under a cloud; John Sherman of Ohio; General Richard J. Oglesby of Illinois; Oliver P. Morton, the strongly Radical war Governor of Indiana; the carpetbaggers Stephen W. Dorsey of Arkansas and General Dodge's old staffer George E. Spencer of Alabama; General John B. Gordon of Georgia, a Confederate hero; the ultra-Radical John J. Ingalls of Kansas; A. A. Sargent of California; and John P. Jones of Nevada, of silver bonanza fame. The competition offered by this group was not threatening to a man of Allison's talents and industry; only Morrill and Sherman combined ability, character, and prestige in the highest degree. Happily, these were the ones to whom Allison was most closely attached, and with them his friendship proved to be most enduring.[28]

Allison's committee assignments offered uneven attractions.[29] A place even though near the bottom of the list on the Committee on Appropriations was much to his liking and was a suitable recognition of his years of experience on the House Committee on Ways and Means. In addition, Allison was put on the committees on Indian Affairs, for what good reason it would be hard to discover, and the Congressional Library. Years later his colleague Blaine recalled Allison's "enviable reputation" for "industry, good judgment, strong common sense, and fidelity to every trust, both personal and public."

Allison, wrote Blaine, "devoted himself to financial questions and soon acquired in the Senate the position of influence which he had long had in the House." [30]

The special session lasted only twenty-two days. The following months are unaccounted for in the record but easily lend themselves to the imagination. In June a brief item appeared inconspicuously in the Burlington *Hawk-Eye*:

Honorable Wm. B. Allison of Dubuque, and Miss Mary Neally [Nealley] of this city, were married at 5 o'clock yesterday afternoon. The wedding, which was strictly a private one, took place at the residence of Mrs. Grimes, the bride being a niece of that lady, long an intimate of the family and practically an adopted daughter of the Senator and Mrs. Grimes. Mr. and Mrs. Allison left on the eastbound train last evening, intending to go directly to New York, and to sail on the 18th inst. for Europe, to be absent four months. Many friends will wish them a pleasant tour and a safe return.[31]

The ceremony was performed by the distinguished Congregational minister and author, Dr. William Salter, a long-time friend of the Grimes family, who had officiated at a similar service in 1846 for James Wilson Grimes, a pioneering young lawyer from New Hampshire, and a little school teacher from Bangor, Maine, named Elizabeth Nealley.[32] At the time of his marriage, Allison was forty-four years of age, his bride twenty-four. The young lady was mature in mind and manner, even when Allison first met her. She had enjoyed advantages far above the ordinary — wealth, social prestige, and associations at home and abroad with the great and the near great because of her doting uncle's position. She was perfectly equipped by nature and training to carry out all the duties and to realize upon all the opportunities of a Senator's wife. This opinion was expressed by many; for example, Mrs. James A. Garfield "considered Mrs. Senator Allison one of the most cultured and loveliest women of Washington." [33]

After a pleasant tour of Europe, the Allisons returned in October to Dubuque, where the Senator was caught up in the backwash of the Panic of '73 that had broken in September. Among the countless institutions that had gone down in the crash was the Merchants National Bank of Dubuque. Probably no single event of his private business career ever disturbed Allison so much as this or placed more burdens upon him. As a director, he had both moral and financial responsibilities and so did his friends. President F. W. H. Sheffield and Mrs. Sheffield were intimate companions; R. A. Babbage, the highly trusted cashier, was a close business associate. Babbage escaped to Europe after hiding for a month; the Sheffields eventually moved to Utica, New York.[34] The solid financial pillar left to sustain the defunct bank was Henry L. Stout, the lumber magnate. The role of Allison was to furnish advice at Stout's request and to act as senior counselor. Their correspondence shows that Stout had great faith in Allison's advice and in his ability to get things done.[35]

The first Monday in December, 1873, found Allison answering the roll call on the opening day of the first regular session of the Forty-third Congress. His committee assignments were unchanged, but he moved up one notch on the Indian Affairs roster, due to the departure of Senator Alexander Caldwell of Kansas. A few days later he was appointed to the Committee on Pensions to take the place of Senator Orris S. Ferry of Connecticut, excused.[36]

At the moment there seemed to be a lull in politics as well as in business. One item in which Allison was particularly interested was a bill to divide Iowa into two federal judicial districts instead of one. Years of backstage maneuvering were necessary before this bill could be passed. The principal proponent of the measure was Oliver P. Shiras of Dubuque, senior member of the firm of Shiras, Henderson and Van Duzee. He prodded Allison and Henderson mercilessly and gave no one a moment's rest until the matter had been finally consummated. Colonel Henderson had to make it his chief interest for years. Part of the difficulty was in agreeing on the geographical division of the proposed two districts; a north-south line was illogical because of transportation difficulties, and an east-west line was hard to agree upon because of the rivalries of so many cities. General Dodge pushed his favorite, Judge Caleb Baldwin, for the judgeship and insisted that Shiras should be withdrawn. For once it seemed that Dodge and Allison were about to have a serious difference of opinion.[37] This bill finally passed in 1882, and Shiras received the appointment.

Little action of great moment came from the Forty-third Congress, yet the session gave Allison several chances to keep his name before the public. A committee had been appointed to investigate charges made against Alexander R. Shepherd, Governor of the District of Columbia — "Boss" Shepherd of questionable reputation. Opinion is still divided on this figure: was he a crook or a benefactor? There is no doubt that he took Washington out of the mud; did he do so at an unfair profit? Did he use the method known as "the purchase of influence," or was he falsely accused? Allison was chairman of the select committee that investigated Shepherd; others on the committee were Senators Allen G. Thurman of Ohio and William M. Stewart of Nevada, plus five members from the House.[38]

The committee heard many witnesses. The testimony ran to some 2,500 pages; the report and its exhibits, to about 700 pages.[39] The comment of *The Nation* was typical of the critical journals. In its opinion, the report sent in by Allison and his colleagues was an improvement over the whitewashing verdict of a committee that had carried out a similar investigation in 1872. A later judgment of the report described it as being "as friendly in its tone as the circumstances would permit, [but] it clearly declared that Shepherd had assumed complete control of the government [of the District] and had exercised it in an entirely arbitrary manner." [40] The general assumption from that day to this has been that Shepherd was guilty of both malfeasance and misfeasance.[41] However that may be, he wrote to Allison on friendly terms, offering helpful and concrete suggestions for the improvement of the government of the District.[42]

The Allison Committee, in its report, made some constructive recommendations. From the language of the debate it is certain that Allison and his colleagues did not know that they were building so well. The committee proposed creation of a commission to govern the District pending the development of a more suitable method, not realizing, of course, that the commission itself would endure. Congress jumped for the idea, however, and the system has not been changed to this day.[43] Thus was the basic plan of municipal government known universally as the "commission plan" born, a plan that has been adopted by many cities since Galveston chose it in 1901.[44]

Far more important in the history of the times, although apparently not disturbing to Allison, was the wave of protest politics that swept over the nation, particularly the Midwest, in the trough of the Panic of 1873. The term "agrarian radicalism" has been used so long that it is now too late to suggest a new name for the politics of the period. Actually the movement was not confined to the agrarian elements of the population, and its radicalism, in the popular present-day sense of that word, was very mild.

Organizationally, the protest was channeled through the Order of the Patrons of Husbandry, better known as the Grange, hence the terms "Granger Movement" and "Granger Laws," not altogether

John M. McDonald, Dubuque

MARY NEALLEY ALLISON

Historical Society, Iowa City

WILLIAM BOYD ALLISON

JAMES HARLAN

JAMES W. GRIMES

JAMES F. WILSON

GRENVILLE M. DODGE

satisfactory labels. The protest did not originate with the Grange, and often the higher spokesmen of the organization repudiated the proposals and methods of some of the protestors. But the protest took the form of a drive for economic relief for farmers; many farmers were members of the Grange; many local Granges passed resolutions on the subject; hence popular logic easily associated the two.

Politically, the protest found two outlets. The constitution of the Grange forbade participation in politics, but this did not stop all political action. Many participants followed the counsel of those who advocated staying with the Republican party as the only wise course. This solution to the conflict of loyalties between present needs and past sentiments could be successfully resolved for agricultural relief only by converting the Republican party into a farmers' party, a thing impossible to do. The other outlet was a curious thing called the Anti-Monopoly party, an invention of the times which absorbed the Democrats, the Liberal Republicans, and the reforming element. This definitely was not a Grange party, although it enrolled some Grangers. It was more Democratic in leadership and composition than anything else. In the Iowa election of 1873 the Anti-Monopolists won fifty out of the one hundred seats in the House and ten out of the twenty-three seats in the Senate at stake that year.

The protest movement focused itself on the current demand for more equitable railroad freight rates, by law if necessary. This raised the constitutional question of the state's power to regulate the railroads. The state legislature, elected in 1873, proceeded to pass the Railroad Act of 1874, providing maximum freight tariffs for each of four classes of railroads, and left the question of constitutionality up to the courts. The overwhelming vote for the bill was 93 to 4 in the House and 39 to 9 in the Senate. The Iowa law was approved by a United States Circuit Court decision handed down in May, 1875, by Judge John F. Dillon, whose ruling was upheld by the United States Supreme Court in Chief Justice Morrison R. Waite's famous opinion in the case of Chicago, Burlington and Quincy Railroad Company *v*. Iowa.

Allison seemingly was little concerned with these events. The best explanation for this indifference lies in his political and social calendar and in his personality. His senatorial career began in March, 1873; from June to October he was in Europe on his honeymoon. Thus his participation in the legislative election campaign of 1873 was negligible. After Congress convened in December, he was chiefly interested in the political and social life of Washington and with issues of national rather than local implication. He would not have to concern himself specifically with re-election until the campaign of 1877. In the meantime, he could leave his local interests to trusted lieutenants such as Jacob Rich and Colonel Henderson and work quietly in the interests of moderation. Allison was never one to go out on a crusade. It would be unfair, however, to assume that he was totally oblivious to Iowa's internal affairs and uninformed and without convictions on the questions of railroad regulation. The subsequent story will show his participation in Iowa politics and also his attitude toward the railroad question.[45]

The panic-ridden politics of the time brought Allison chances for service and publicity without participation in the questions raised by the Grangers. The congressional elections of 1874 proved a stunning rebuke to the Republican party nationally. In Iowa the Republicans did not fare so badly, losing only one House seat out of nine, and that to an able opponent, Colonel L. L. Ainsworth of West Union, who ran as an Anti-Monopoly candidate with Democratic support. Even so, this was the first time since 1854 that an "enemy" had been elected to the House from Iowa. The only consolation for regulars was that they had been able to defeat General James B. Weaver's bid for the Sixth District congressional nomination, even if only by one vote. Weaver, a man of independent views, was out of favor with the Radical leadership.[46] Nationally, the party losses were a turning point in the history of Reconstruction politics.

The net result of this defeat was to force the Republicans to do something about the depression. Because of the deflation that had set in even before the end of the war, the topic of greatest urgency had become the monetary problem. A demand arose for an increase in the quantity of greenbacks in circulation. "Greenbacks" were simply fiat money, printed paper notes worth whatever the holder thought of the government's credit. Since the close of the war the demand for greenbacks had fluctuated, but Congress had never even closely approached the mark advocated by the extremists. In 1868 the Democrats had made a bow to the inflationists by writing into their platform George H. Pendleton's "Ohio Idea" for the redemption of government bonds, whenever possible, in greenbacks.

The failure of Congress in 1873 to continue silver dollars on the list of mintable coins was soon followed by the discovery of new lodes of the white metal in the West. By 1875 a cry of the "Crime of '73" was added to the demand for more greenbacks. Not many people understood the intricacies of the economics involved. They simply knew that times were hard and that there was a shortage of money. They knew that silver was plentiful, and they could not understand its sudden undesirability as money when only recently it had brought a premium; they could not understand that the greenbacks which had been suitable for bank capital in Salmon Chase's national banks were now unsound money. Clearly, something had to be done to appease the discontented. Allison's mail from his Iowa constituents was full of suggestions, advice, and urgent pleas for action. Not all of it was on the side of inflation, however. Two of his banker-politician friends wrote letters that surely would have matched any that could have been written by Eastern bankers in favor of caution, moderation, and soundness.[47]

In December, Congress met for the short session, the last chance it would have to deal with the currency situation before turning the problem over to the newly elected majority of Democrats and Anti-Monopolists. It is in this light that the work and the achievement of Allison and his colleagues should be considered. The Republican high command set up a committee of eleven to work out new financial legislation, with John Sherman of Ohio as chairman. The rest of the committee consisted of Morton, Logan, Edmunds, Ferry, Frelinghuysen, Howe, Boutwell, Conkling, Sargent, and Allison. After disputes that threatened more than once to break up their work, they finally reached agreement on a bill known to history as the Resumption Act of 1875. Allison had come a long way since the currency debates earlier in the year, when Sherman had been forced to make some pointed remarks to him. At that time Allison had not believed that the issue of more paper money would take the country further away from the resumption of specie payments. Sherman had retaliated sharply, although acknowledging Allison's "intelligence and ability."[48] Now Allison was "accepted" on the committee as an acknowledged leader.

The Resumption Bill, a caucus job through and through, passed both houses of Congress with a minimum of debate and was signed by the President only after he had attached a message pointing out its defects. It perfectly illustrates the spirit and method of compromise with which Congress has to do most of its work. The principal provisions were that the amount of greenbacks in circulation was to be reduced gradually to $300,000,000, with an expansion of national bank notes as an off-setting factor, and the redemption of greenbacks in specie beginning in 1879.[49] No one could be quite certain what changes would be made in the intervening four years or what would be the effects of the act if it were left intact. Greenbackers everywhere deplored the reduction in volume and later secured an act "freezing" the amount at whatever the volume outstanding might be when resumption became effective.[50]

A few months later a new scandal barely missed Allison's political household. On May 10 federal agents swooped down on the revenue office in St. Louis and arrested General John McDonald, chief collector of the St. Louis district, and his secretary-assistant and handy man, Colonel John A. Joyce, on charges of defrauding the government by permitting distilleries to market some of their products without buying the required revenue stamps. For years there had been suspicion and some public discussion about a "Whiskey Ring," but always some one in Washington had tipped off the operators of the game, and they had been able to put their houses in order before the arrival of the inspectors. President Grant's latest appointee, Secretary of the Treasury Benjamin Helm Bristow, had outwitted the suspected men and had successfully put his inspectors in St. Louis before the operators could doctor up their accounts. McDonald and Joyce were tried and found guilty.

Fortunately for Allison, few people knew that Colonel Joyce was his protégé. The Colonel was somewhat of a wandering minstrel whose career was well described by the title of his autobiography, *A Checkered Life.* According to his own story, Joyce was born in Ireland, and he seems to have inherited the gift of song and words traditionally associated with the sons of that isle. After being brought to America, he had lived in various states, principally Kentucky, and had served in the Union Army until discharged because of wounds in 1864. Somewhat by chance he came to Allamakee County in Iowa to visit with an uncle and remained to eke out a living as a teacher and tax collector's assistant. In Waukon in 1865 he happened to be in Congressman Allison's audience, and an acquaintance began which led to an invitation to call on Allison in Dubuque. In due time the invitation was followed up, and Allison made good by assisting Joyce to find a clerkship in a good office in Dubuque, at the same time allowing him use of the offices of Allison, Crane and Rood for reading law. After a few months of this, Joyce went to Washington, where Allison found him a minor clerkship in the office of the Collector of Internal Revenue after getting him past a Civil Service Examination Board. Promotions followed, and after a few years Joyce went into the field and served in a number of places before catching on at St. Louis, where he acted as secretary and manager for McDonald, a man of ability but little formal education. In addition, Joyce's facility with words helped him to write editorials and speeches which were fed out to papers and politicians who needed them.[51]

Both men later wrote autobiographies in which they presented their versions of what had happened and their apologies for their actions. McDonald's book, called *Secrets of the Great Whiskey Ring*,[52] is much more convincing than Joyce's. McDonald admits the crime and makes a good case that he and Joyce were shielding President Grant's secretary, Orville E. Babcock, and behind him, Grant himself. McDonald describes vividly the visit of Grant and Babcock to St. Louis in September, 1875, on their way to an army reunion in Des Moines and the promises made by Babcock to secure pardons from Grant for the two men before they had served long in prison. But Babcock was unable to deliver on these promises because of various embarrassments that kept arising for the Grant administration, and McDonald's conclusion was that he and Joyce found themselves unwilling martyrs for the good of the Republican party and the Grant regime. McDonald was finally released after threatening to expose those whom he considered to be the real offenders.

Letters of a personal nature from the other culprit, Colonel Joyce, and Mrs. Joyce to Allison indicate their closeness to him and their dependence upon his help. They also reveal that Allison had once borrowed money from Joyce on a note.[53] The kindest thing that can be said of Allison is that he was a poor judge of character on this occasion; the worst, that he should have wondered how a poorly paid government clerk would be able to accumulate money to lend to a Senator of the United States. Nevertheless, when Joyce was pardoned by President Hayes on December 19, 1877, it was done on the personal intervention of none other than Senator Allison.[54] It is impossible to avoid the feeling that Allison had narrowly missed serious involvement in the operations of the shady crowd headed up by Grant's secretary, General Babcock.[55] Nor can one forget the comment of

General Horace Porter, another of Grant's secretaries, when informed of Allison's election to the Senate: "He has always been one of our intimate friends here and we shall get along swimmingly with him." [56]

Allison had other problems than the Whiskey Ring in early 1875, however. He and his lieutenants were thinking of the state convention in Iowa and the nomination of a candidate for Governor. C. C. Carpenter was completing his second term; it was time for a new man. Kirkwood had been mentioned by many as the best candidate, but the ex-Governor preferred a term in the United States Senate to another two years as Iowa's Governor. A United States Senator would be elected in January, 1876, and almost a year before that date Senator Wright had let it be known that he did not intend to seek another term. "I am tired," he wrote to Kirkwood in February. "Want to get home. Sick of this life. Dont you want my place? Come & take it. As I now feel, & believe I shall, you or any other man can have it two years from now, for all that I care." [57]

A few days before receiving this letter, Kirkwood had rejected a flattering diplomatic offer. With the assistance of "Tama Jim" Wilson of the Fourth District (not to be confused with James F. "Jefferson Jim" Wilson), Allison had secured an appointment as Minister to Turkey for Kirkwood.[58] Allison's actions in this matter raise the question of his real attitude toward Kirkwood. Was he genuinely interested in an honor for his friend, or did he want to remove him from the political scene? Whom did Allison want for Governor and whom did he want as his partner in the Senate? Answers to those questions would have to be given before the year was out. The effort to "ship" Kirkwood to Turkey definitely conflicts with Allison's later use of that gentleman; either he had not thought the matter through or else there were later developments that could not be foreseen at this time. The problem was partly resolved for Allison by Kirkwood's rejection of the Turkish post.

Jacob Rich, now generally recognized as Allison's manager and mentor, wrote Kirkwood a strong letter in April, 1875, urging him to run for the governorship because he was the one man who could assure the party success in carrying the legislative ticket, so necessary in winning the Senate seat. Rich told Kirkwood that election to the governorship would not remove him from the list of possible senatorial candidates. On the contrary, it would enhance his chances. Allison's wise mentor then said that George W. McCrary, the brilliant Representative from the First District, would be the second best man for the party to put up for Governor, but that he could not be spared from Congress.[59] A few days later M. C. Woodruff, the able editor of the Dubuque *Times*, wrote to Kirkwood, giving him the same arguments in even more forceful style. Rich repeated his plea some ten days later. Thus it is evident that a group of politicians no less important than Allison's own circle had decided that Kirkwood should be their candidate for Governor. Assuming success in this, if later he wanted to try for the senatorial honor in the election to be held in the very month of his inauguration, that would be quite all right. "One thing at a time" seemed to be their motto: control must be maintained at any cost.

But Kirkwood would have nothing to do with this game; he refused to make any kind of announcement for the office. There were several other names up for consideration, among them John Russell, W. B. Fairfield, James Harlan, and General James B. Weaver. The convention was clearly headed for the nomination of the gallant Weaver, who was considered by many of the rank-and-file Republicans to be a party man in good standing and deserving of recognition for his long service to the party and the nation. But to the Allisonians, Weaver was *persona non grata* because he was a strong Harlan man; to political leaders of the "safe" type, he was undependable: he was too emotional in his championship of prohibition and too outspoken in his friendship for the masses. Weaver had been defeated in his bid for a nomination to Congress; now he must be defeated at any price in his bid for the governorship.

When the convention met at Des Moines, the strategy was to delay the nomination until Kirkwood's consent could be gained for the use of his name.[60] Telegrams to Iowa City did not produce the desired result; in desperation, the Kirkwood men resorted to a "strong arm" scheme. At a critical moment in the proceedings, just when it appeared that the nomination of General Weaver was inevitable, the voice of the gigantic Dr. S. M. Ballard of Audubon County roared out the name of the old war Governor, Samuel J. Kirkwood. A delegate from Allison's county then came to the front of the platform and asked the crucial question, "By what authority do you give his name?" Dr. Ballard answered, "The authority of the people of the State of Iowa."

The convention was thrown into an uproar, and the result was adjournment to the next day to give time for communication with Kirkwood. In this emergency an engine and coach were secured from the Rock Island Railroad, and Jacob Rich and Joseph Morgan, the latter now beginning his long service as Allison's secretary, made the trip to Iowa City to work their personal persuasions on the reluctant nominee.[61] Finally securing his grudging and half-hearted assent, they telegraphed the good news to Des Moines. The next day the convention met, proceeded to scuttle the Weaver candidacy, and formally selected Kirkwood.

Thus the day was saved for the Old Guard. R. S. Finkbine, a former Iowa Citian living in Des Moines and superintending the construction of the new capitol building, wrote Kirkwood the next day to explain how it happened. Very astutely he played on Kirkwood's prejudices by first asserting that D. N. Cooley had led a movement of some preachers and temperance men to put Weaver to the front. Something had to be done to head this off, and so Kirkwood's friends held a conference. Other candidates were nominated by counties; hence the decision was made to have Dr. Ballard nominate Kirkwood in the name of the whole state. Finkbine then explained the many telegrams that were sent to Kirkwood and ended forcefully: "Had that answer not come you would have had a delegation of at least 100 there this morning. . . . Now do not buck the inevitable. Get some one else to take care of your little bank. Canvass the State." [62]

The simple truth is that the Allison people were using the governorship, which of course Kirkwood would win over any Democratic opponent, and its influence over the legislative elections as a means of holding off the Harlan people in the senatorial election of January, 1876. There is ample proof in the correspondence within the Allison-Kirkwood circle that the motivation for Kirkwood's forced nomination was the fear of Harlan's return to power.[63] The most convincing evidence comes from Kirkwood himself. Worried over the possibility that the governorship might be used to knock him out of the coveted senatorship, he wrote to James S. Clarkson after his election in October:

I notice in your paper articles from some two or three other papers in the State, opposing my election to the U. S. Senate for the reason that I have been elected to the office of governor. . . . Now you know (perhaps better than I do) how I came to be nominated for Governor — you know as well as I do that I did not seek that nomination, on the contrary that I did all I could to avoid it and only accepted it when it was in a manner forced upon me. You know also that the controlling reason for nominating me was the fear that if someone else were nominated such nomination might result in the loss of the General Assembly and the consequent loss of the Senatorship. Well the nomination was made and accepted — I made as good a canvass as I could and we have the General Assembly by an overwhelming majority and the Senatorship is secure to our party. Under these circumstances is it fair that my name must be ruled out as a candidate for the Senatorship because I did the very thing that many of our most clear headed men deemed absolutely essential to prevent the loss of the office to our party? [64]

There was only one possible answer to a letter such as this. The way must be prepared for a Kirkwood victory in the coming senatorial election, whatever the opposition. In addition to the ever present threat of James Harlan, eager for a return to power, there was a mild boom for the modest and self-sacrificing George W. McCrary of Keokuk and a very menacing challenge from his fellow-townsman, General William Worth Belknap, Grant's Secretary of War. McCrary wanted the honor but recognized the futility of a contest between two residents of the same city.[65] It would be hard to imagine two men of greater contrast. McCrary was quiet, dignified, reserved, intellectual, judicial; Belknap was ebullient, scintillating, mawkishly sentimental, in short, the complete extrovert. At the time Belknap was riding a wave of popularity, and Iowa rather narrowly missed finding herself saddled with a Senator-elect who would shortly afterward be plunged into disgrace over the sale of army post traderships. But this was apparently undreamed of in 1875.[66] Belknap was supported in his try for the Senate by such powers as Ret Clarkson of the *Register*, Al Swalm of the Fort Dodge *Messenger*, J. Fred Meyers of the Denison *Review*, and by the Ottumwa *Courier*. So shrewd a judge of men as Colonel D. B. Henderson ranked Belknap second only to McCrary and ahead of Kirkwood; Swalm thought that Allison preferred Belknap to Kirkwood as a young man who would be more serviceable to him than the old war Governor.[67]

If Allison did not favor Belknap, he certainly did not oppose him. While the informal canvass was going on, the two men were brought into close cooperation; Belknap wanted Allison, a member of the Senate Committee on Indian Affairs, to be one of a group he was organizing to go on a junket to Yellowstone Park that summer. Allison regretfully rejected this invitation but accepted appointment as chairman of a presidential commission that went out in September to negotiate with the Sioux Indians over the rights of white settlers to go into the Black Hills and engage in gold mining. Allison might have used this mission to the Sioux to make a name for himself by working out some kind of constructive treaty that could have been a step toward the solution of the higher problem of relations between the races, but perhaps this was expecting too much from Allison or anyone else at that time. Few were interested in anything but driving a hard bargain at the Indians' expense.

The commission actually underwent some danger as well as hardship. On one occasion the young braves of the tribe surrounded the President's agents in menacing fashion and were restrained only by the older men of the tribe and by a show of strength by the soldiers guarding the commissioners. One smiles a bit at this picture of Allison, the most peaceful of men, who had escaped military service during the Civil War, now faced with the possibility of dying for a mob of gold-seekers straining against the restrictions of the treaty rights of the Indians, with the mob all too readily backed up by military men itching for a fight. The Indians were not to be persuaded to sell out for the trivial sum that Allison was authorized to offer, and the mission ended in failure. The white men pressed on into the restricted territory, however; Indian resistance gave the soldiers an excuse to use force; the episode came to an end — a very bitter end — with the massacre of Custer's forces at the Little Big Horn in 1876.[68]

A small by-product of the expedition was the securing of a clerkship to the commission for Al Swalm. Allison had interceded with Belknap in behalf of Swalm after the post had first been offered to and refused by the eminent economist, David A. Wells. Perhaps this accounts in part for the enthusiasm shown by Swalm for Belknap's candidacy for the Senate. Belknap carried on a lively correspondence with Allison all during the summer and fall regarding their western trip and the Senate race, seemingly quite confident of Allison's favor. It is unlikely that Clarkson or Swalm would have supported Belknap so strongly if Allison had objected. Allison apparently was playing it safe with two pro-Allison candidates, Kirkwood and Belknap, either of whom would most likely defeat Harlan.

The conventional account of the senatorial election of 1876, in a sentimental history of Iowa politics, is that the victory of Kirkwood over Harlan (such history seems to be unaware of the great threat posed by Belknap) was made possible by the dramatic withdrawal of

Harlan due to the emergency of his son's illness and a trip to his bed-side in the West. This explanation will not hold up, however. Harlan had first tried a form of political blackmail on Allison, writing him in November: "I am curious to know whether your friends under-stand that one feature of the warfare likely to be made against me . . . would weigh as heavily against you. . . such as the 'Credit Mobilier' nonsense." Allison did not fall into this trap; his answer was non-committal.[69] Shortly after this, Harlan was called West by the illness of his son in Wyoming, but he returned to Iowa before Christmas day.[70]

The senatorial fight came to its climax in the Republican caucus on January 12, 1876. In the afternoon Harlan received word that his son had taken a turn for the worse; he sent a letter to the caucus, with-drawing his name, and the next day left for the West again. Kirkwood was chosen on the first formal ballot. If enough Republicans had been inclined to vote for Harlan to elect him, this second departure to his son's bedside would not have deterred them; rather it should have in-creased their affection for him. Had Harlan been sure of victory, he would not have withdrawn. In other words, his son's illness was used as an alibi for defeat. It is quite understandable that, after the distinguished career he had earlier enjoyed, Harlan would find it gall-ing to be defeated again and would want a story to hand out for public consumption.

Rich wrote a full report of the battle, ending with the observation that Allison's situation now was better than he had any right to ex-pect: his friend and benefactor, Kirkwood, had been elected; Harlan, Belknap, and Hiram Price of Davenport had all been squelched. "There is no one to contest with you in 1878 but George McCrary, and if you can't keep him out of the field, with the certainty of succession four years from the time of your reelection, you are not the man I take you for." [71] So many wrote to Allison about the effect of this race on the prospective one of 1878, when Allison's own seat would be at stake, that it is impossible not to believe that this was a strong factor in Allison's thinking. James F. Wilson revealed this line of thought when he asserted his lack of fear of Harlan two years hence, saying in his best Lincolnesque manner, "We will take care of that pig when it gets fat." [72]

Belknap's friends were bitterly disappointed and charged his de-feat to ungrateful people who had forgotten their debts to him for political appointments. But a few weeks later these same friends could breathe a sigh of relief that Belknap had not been elected. On February 3, 1876, the Fort Dodge *Messenger* reported that stories were being circulated about Secretary Belknap by a certain man named Armes, a relative of Senator-elect Kirkwood. The man had been discharged from the army, so the story ran, for an outrage against some ladies and was now against Belknap because he refused to reinstate him. A few days later the paper reported that serious charges were being brought against the Secretary but that it would refuse to believe them until they were fully confirmed.

The full story broke on March 2, 1876. Disclosures were made by the Committee on Expenditures of the War Department showing that army post traderships had been sold to those who would "kick back" into the Secretary's private purse. Belknap's recently deceased wife and her sister, whom the Secretary had married, were both accused as accomplices to whom some of the money had been paid. Rumors spread that Belknap had committed suicide after the disclosures, but these were unfounded.[73] The House of Representatives rushed through articles of impeachment but not until President Grant had with unseemly haste accepted the accused man's resignation. Not one member of the Iowa delegation made any kind of public statement on the subject of their fellow-Iowan's actions.

The House persisted in its efforts to secure a conviction on its impeachment charges but failed because a sufficient number of Senators, including Allison and Wright of Iowa, refused to vote for a verdict of guilty, claiming that Belknap's resignation had removed him from their jurisdiction. Most of those who so voted admitted that they thought him guilty.[74] Belknap dropped out of sight for a short time and then re-entered the practice of law in Washington and Philadelphia.[75] Eventually the scandal was forgotten, the ex-Secretary came to be respected and admired both in the East and in Iowa, and when he died in 1890 he was buried in Arlington Cemetery.[76]

✯ X ✯

Allison and Silver

WHILE THE BELKNAP scandal was still before the country, the political calendar brought on the quadrennial drama of a presidential
election. Little did anyone suspect that the election of 1876 was to
prove one of the most exciting in American history. But first there
came the madness known as political conventions. General Grant was
finishing his second term of office, and the field was wide open as the
Republican party began its search for a successor. The leading aspirant
was James G. Blaine of Maine, Allison's congressional colleague since
1863; other contenders were Roscoe Conkling of New York, Oliver
P. Morton of Indiana, Benjamin H. Bristow of Kentucky, and
Rutherford B. Hayes of Ohio. As his most recent biographer points
out, Hayes was a conspicuous candidate throughout the campaign,
rather than a last-minute entrant.[1]

All of Allison's closest friends were enthusiastic Blaine men, but
Allison's own sentiments were well concealed. Just as the race was
getting under way, Blaine was implicated in a shady piece of railroad
finance that would have completely destroyed a man of lesser abilities.
He had acquired some worthless bonds of an Arkansas railroad; these
later turned up in the possession of the Union Pacific Railroad that
had reputedly bought them for $64,000. Blaine bullied an investigating
committee and the House with questionable justification for his actions
and with half-explanations of some of his own letters held by a
James Mulligan.

Such was Blaine's popularity with orthodox Republicans like

143

Kirkwood that they remained skeptical of the charges against him. They certainly preferred him to Bristow of Kentucky, who, although a strong Union man during the war, had stayed aloof from the Vindictives, or Hayes, who seemed little known outside of Ohio even though he would answer the need for a "clean handed man." Kirkwood pondered the rivalry of Blaine and Hayes. "I am still for Blaine," he wrote to Allison. "Of course if there is reasonable ground to fear that this nomination would bring defeat we should take someone else. But I do not like the idea of taking Hays [*sic*]. This thing of taking a man who has not a *national* reputation always has to me a flavor of humiliation. Besides it destroys measurably the laudable ambition of public men to earn a national reputation." [2]

As the time for the Republican national convention approached, every eye was turned toward Cincinnati, and every expert had his own guess as to the winner. Most of them were sure that it would be Blaine. "He has completely vanquished the enemy, the country is disgusted with these investigations," wrote J. K. Graves of Dubuque, who predicted a sure victory for Blaine and hinted that Blaine should then call Allison to his Cabinet.

Ret Clarkson wired Allison on May 29 that the Iowa delegation to the national convention would be "solid for Blaine" but asked if the delegates should be instructed. Allison replied: "Cannot advise from this distance as to what would be wise." A few days later Ret was not so sure; Blaine, his favorite, was ruining his chances by his testimony before the House committee, and this left the Iowa delegation free to move to someone else. Clarkson expressed confidence that he could swing many votes at will and asked Allison to name his choice. [3]

Although Allison almost certainly supported Blaine, neither he nor his Iowa friends appeared ready with a positive alternative policy, should Blaine be rejected. [4] And rejected he was, although only after six ballots and then for expediency's sake; on the seventh ballot the relatively obscure Hayes emerged as the winner. Iowans supported Blaine consistently, but changed to Hayes when the band wagon rolled.

Allison sent a perfunctory message of congratulations to Hayes, but Kirkwood was unable to cover up his real feelings of disappointment. "When I can do so without swearing I may write you again" was one of his milder comments on the action of the convention. [5] James F. Wilson was equally disappointed but more rational in his remarks. First asserting that the ticket was not what Iowans wanted, but that it would win, Wilson went on to say: "Blaine was beaten by bad management in the Penna. delegation, aided largely by the fact that Edward McPherson could not control the convention. A president who could have held the convention in hand would have brought on a ballot on Thursday and Blaine would have been nominated." [6] Blaine's chances were at their peak just after Robert G. Ingersoll made his great speech on Thursday, calling Blaine the "Plumed Knight." [7]

The Democrats at St. Louis a week later had no such difficulties in choosing their nominee. The brilliant New York lawyer and reformer, the recent conqueror of Tammany Hall, Governor Samuel J. Tilden, was chosen for the head of the ticket. Thomas A. Hendricks of Indiana, a "soft-money" man, was put in for the second place, acting as an offset to Tilden's known financial conservatism. The Independent, or "Greenback," party nominated Peter Cooper of New York and Samuel J. Cary of Ohio as their standard-bearers.

The closing act of the drama was more exciting than the first. When the first election count was made, Tilden had 184 electoral votes undisputed with only 185 needed for victory, and Oregon, South Carolina, Florida, and Louisiana were still uncounted. Hayes went to bed resigned to defeat and by his own statement relieved at the prospect. Not so those two hardy battlers for Radical Reconstruction, Zachariah Chandler of Michigan and William E. Chandler of New Hampshire, unrelated by blood but kindred spirits in politics. Old Zach hurriedly sent off telegrams to the local Republican leaders in the four states, telling them to hold fast, claim everything, and concede nothing. If every vote from these states could be secured for Hayes, he would be elected. Oregon was later conceded to Hayes, but visiting statesmen were soon on their way to the three Southern states to assist the returning boards in making out their reports. The vital question of the day was the method of deciding the award of the contested votes. Congress was badly divided on the question, and practically every local politician in the country had his own notion of the solution and his own idea of the best way to enforce the decision.

Major A. R. Anderson of Sidney, a lightweight but extremely voluble politician of southwest Iowa, expressed to Allison the typical Radical Republican viewpoint: "What we want now is no yielding. A firm hand and we are all right. . . . We have played the coward for four years and have well nigh frittered away our birthright. . . . Civil Service and all kindred part-your-hair-in-the-middle Geo.

William Curtis frauds must be put aside till the Rebellion is over and all such meddlers with frauds must incontinently be kicked out of the party." [8] The chairman of Iowa's Republican state central committee, H. C. Leighton of Oskaloosa, took the same position in answer to Allison's query. "You ask as to the temper of the Iowa people on general questions. I think they are unanimous in our party, in sticking up and standing firm for everything our own. If the Senate believes Hayes elected, and so declares him, Iowa will back it up with 100,000 men if necessary." [9]

The great controversy over the election commanded wide attention during the early months of 1877. Allison's mail was full of suggestions from friends and interested parties who offered plans for settling the dispute. Governor Kirkwood, soon to be sworn in as Iowa's junior Senator, wrote a five-page letter which was a good essay on the subject, although he did not have a plan for which any favor could be found. More important than his proposal was the expression of Kirkwood's attitude: "I would regard the accession of Mr. Tilden to the Presidency as a great public misfortune but not so great as another civil war or a dual presidency." [10]

On January 18, 1877, a joint congressional committee introduced a proposal, soon to be known as the "Compromise Bill," providing for an Electoral Commission of fifteen members, five each from the Senate, the House, and the Supreme Court. [11] Credit for being the chief architect of this plan has been accorded to Senator George F. Edmunds of Vermont, but to Representative George W. McCrary of Iowa should go credit for originating the idea that a joint conference committee should prepare a measure "best calculated to accomplish the desired end" of getting the votes counted. [12] There were to be three Republican and two Democratic Senators, three Democratic and two Republican Representatives, and four Supreme Court Justices named by circuits. The four justices were then to name a fifth, to make the fifteenth man on the Commission. The bill passed the Senate, 47 to 17; the House, 191 to 86. [13] The remarkable thing about the bill was that fewer Republicans voted for it than Democrats.

James F. Wilson, close to the grass roots opinion in Iowa, sent this advice to Allison: "If the Senate comes to a vote today I believe your safest course is to vote *No*. . . . If it passes and Tilden is elected, it will ruin any man in the Western states that voted for it." A more powerful protest came from the eccentric but able Al Swalm of the

Historical Society, Iowa City

Samuel J. Kirkwood

Nat'l Cyclopaedia of Amer. Biog.

Jacob Rich

Historical Society, Iowa City

David B. Henderson

Historical Society, Iowa City

James S. Clarkson

SENATORS JONATHAN P. DOLLIVER AND WILLIAM B. ALLISON

Fort Dodge *Messenger*. "Three hundred Republicans of Fort Dodge ask that you oppose the Compromise measure. Count us in or out but no compromise with threatening bull dozers." There were those, however, who took the other side. The Burlington Chamber of Commerce sent Allison a copy of their resolutions favoring the plan; Kirkwood wrote that Republican politicians were afraid of the bill but the non-politicians were for it.[14]

In spite of the warnings, some more violently phrased than others, Allison summoned up his courage and voted for the Compromise Bill, as did George Wright, whose senatorial career was closing; in the House, the nine Iowans divided six to three on the bill. In later years Allison testified that he was fully aware of the risk that he was taking.[15] He anxiously watched the fight before the Electoral Commission as the votes were counted.

The work that went on secretly to bring about a Hayes victory and the acceptance of that victory by the South was not known to many people in 1876-1877.[16] Certain Northern Republicans saw a chance to deal with certain Southern businessmen of former Whig associations who were ready to bargain Southern support of Hayes in return for Republican votes for federal assistance to internal improvements in the South, especially harbor clearance and grants to railroads. Deep in the plot was General Grenville M. Dodge of Iowa, who stood to gain by a grant to one of his interests, the Texas & Pacific Railroad. While these leaders worked quietly, excitement ran high, and there was much talk of "war" on both sides. It is hard to believe that Dodge's good friend Allison did not know what was going on.

Early in February, Allison and his friends, apparently assuming that a victory for Hayes was a sure thing, began to work for an Iowa man in the Cabinet. Their special candidate for this honor was, quite naturally, George W. McCrary of Keokuk, not only because of his brilliance and his service to Hayes as part-author of the Electoral Commission Bill (assuming a victory for Hayes), but also with some thought of removing him from the senatorial scene in 1878. As the Commission's hearings drew to a close, and all the contests were being decided in Hayes's favor, the pressure on him to name his Cabinet increased. Wilson and others urged McCrary for Attorney General in view of his pre-eminence as a lawyer.[17] McCrary received his reward, but it was for the War Department rather than the Attorney General's office.

At long last the Electoral Commission finished its work. By a strict party vote of eight to seven, the Commission gave every contested vote to Hayes. At four o'clock on the morning of March 2, 1877, Allison, acting as teller for the Senate, announced the electoral vote as 185 for Hayes, 184 for Tilden.[18] Thanks to the work of General Dodge and his companions, and to others who helped to arrange compromises at the very last, the way had been prepared for Southern acceptance of Hayes, and the inauguration went off without a hitch. Certain people had taken a long chance by their determined interference with the democratic processes in this affair; fortunately, the country had enough reserves of political resilience to survive the experience.

Hayes proceeded to give the country an excellent example of enlightened statesmanship by policies and actions designed to heal the breach between the North and the South. He has been called a mediocre President, but something should be said for the moral courage he displayed in insisting upon the return of the South to the Union. However much this may have been a part of a plan incorporated in the bargain between Northern Republicans such as Dodge and Southern Conservatives of the old Whig strain, this plot was not known publicly then. Hayes had to bear the burden of a raging criticism within his own party. Apparently Dodge did not tell his Iowa friends that Hayes was in office because of the machinations of a handful of Republicans, for no one attacked Hayes more violently than James F. Wilson and Ret Clarkson. Both spoke for a large wing of the party that seemed to forget that Hayes was their own alternative to Tilden.

The bitterness of their unreasonable feelings can be gathered from some of their statements. After Hayes had helped to bring about the ouster of S. B. Packard as Governor of Louisiana and Daniel Chamberlain in South Carolina, Wilson wrote to Allison: "Be careful not to give a shade of belief that you approve of Hayes' Louisiana blunder — if not crime. . . . Even Jacob Rich is under suspicion as being too much so." [19] Wilson's aversion to any but the Old Guard Republicans is colorfully set forth in his letter to Allison concerning the confirmation of John Marshall Harlan of Kentucky for the Supreme Court. "I hope you will not vote to confirm Harlan for the Supreme Court. He is unfit for the place. He is not a first class lawyer and is a mere politician. For God's sake give us no more of that kind of cattle on the Supreme bench. If he is confirmed we will all live to regret it. Tell Kirkwood so." [20]

Other things occupied Allison's mind during 1877, especially his role as friend, adviser, and sometimes agent for Charles E. Perkins of the Burlington Railroad. "Railroad politics" put Allison in a delicate position just at this time. Perkins wanted him to support a Pro Rata bill, so called, which would compel the Union Pacific to share its business with the Burlington from Kearney, Nebraska, eastward. The presidents of other roads, particularly the North Western and the Rock Island, also good friends of Allison, objected violently to the plan and urged him to work against it, as did others who lived along these lines. A reading of these letters brings out the difficulties of a politician when caught between two forces, both friendly to him but rivals to each other. The preponderance of numbers and therefore potential votes seems to have been against Perkins, but Allison serenely stayed on his side. [21]

Perkins also put Allison on the spot by asking him to exert control over the policies and actions of the editor of the Dubuque *Times*, Mark C. Woodruff, a leading opponent of the railroads' drive to secure repeal of the Iowa Railroad Act of 1874. To do justice to Perkins, it must be said that he was not seeking repeal of the Act but modification only. In this he probably resembled Allison more and his brother railroad presidents less. Both men seemed to realize the inevitability of some degree of regulation of the carriers. Even so, Perkins wanted the newspapers to be friendly, and he repeatedly complained of Woodruff's editorials. In addition, Perkins wanted Allison to have Woodruff use his power in Republican circles by getting a plank in the 1877 platform in favor of modification. [22] In the light of Woodruff's position in opposition to repeal or even modification — a reflection of the desires of the merchants of Dubuque — such a request by Perkins was ridiculous. No such plank appeared in the Republican platform. Any effort to change Woodruff's attitude might have harmed Allison's chances in the forthcoming senatorial election.

Allison's seat in the Senate would be on the block in January, 1878; he must see to it that a safe majority of Allison men were elected to the General Assembly in 1877. The number of major interests that he had to carry along at this time is impressive. He was in the midst of debate in the Senate on the silver bill which would become the famous Bland-Allison Act. In addition, there was the Iowa election; the fight over Hayes's Southern policy; railroad matters, especially the movement for repeal of Iowa's Railroad Act of 1874; the struggle to divide Iowa into two federal court districts; Mrs. Allison's failing health; and many other matters, large and small. Any one of these would have been enough to occupy all his time.

Fortunately, Allison had able lieutenants who helped him in the work of electing the right men to the Iowa legislature and in delivering their votes according to plan. His trusted Dubuque manager, Jacob Rich, checked his speeches and arranged meetings; Colonel D. B. Henderson sent many letters of advice, some of them critical of Allison's neglect of important party leaders throughout the state; General Dodge saw to his own district; Edgar Pickett, a young lawyer of Waterloo, began his political career at this time by working to carry Black Hawk County; John A. Hoffman and H. C. Leighton of Oskaloosa helped to suppress a movement to throw Marsena E. Cutts of that city into the race, a project that Cutts himself disowned. A. H. Neidig of the Marshalltown *Republican* was a valiant worker. Matt F. Parrott of the *Iowa State Reporter* of Waterloo wrote that he wanted to work for Allison for Senator without having to drag the senatorial issue into the fight for state printer, a hope that was not realized. Judge Nathaniel M. Hubbard of Cedar Rapids, chief counsel for the North Western Railroad in Iowa, worked steadily for Allison and secured the cooperation of other railroad officials.[23] Charles E. Perkins of the Burlington added his influence.

Above all, Allison enjoyed the powerful support of Ret Clarkson, who was still fiercely Radical on the Southern issue and who rang all the changes in his condemnation of the Hayes policy. Actually, the *Register* had little time and space for the silver fight then going on; a casual reader would not have known that anything was before the people except the Hayes "Policy," the word currently used in sneering fashion by Radicals when referring to Hayes's program of restoration of the South to the Union. One issue of the paper carried a long editorial letter from Washington, reassuring the people of Iowa that their delegation in Congress was safely "anti-Policy." The next week the people were told that Allison was the man to vote for because he was the leading spokesman for Western Republicanism and the first to have spoken out against Hayes's "Policy." [24]

When the appointed night for the Republican senatorial caucus came around, there was the usual excitement, but it was a waste of emotion. State Senator William Larrabee of Clermont nominated Allison; Representative John Y. Stone of Glenwood made the seconding speech. A motion was then presented by Representative William Allen of Henry County, heretofore a strong Harlan man and leader of a "stop-Allison" group, asking for the unanimous nomination of Allison; a seconding speech to that motion was made by Senator Alfred Hebard of Montgomery County. The motion carried, and Allison's name was put before the two houses with as much unanimity as anyone could ever claim.[25] In the formal election, Allison received 104 out of 142 possible votes, the Democrats giving the compliment of their minority vote to Daniel F. Miller.[26] C. C. Carpenter had written Allison that it would not be necessary for him to be there in person, a prediction amply upheld by the event.

Among the many letters and messages of congratulations that Allison received, surely none could have been more deeply appreciated than one from his boyhood friend, now a successful businessman:

I avail myself of the present opportunity of congratulating you upon being your own successor to the United States Senate. Ever since your election to the House of Congress, and also the Senate, I have always watched your course with interest, and now it gives me great pleasure to see you so highly endorsed by your constituents, and I feel sure they will have no cause to regret the confidence they have reposed in you. Wishing you success in the future and hoping you may live to reach the highest position in the gift of the people of this nation, I remain your old friend and school mate, Clem Studebaker.[27]

During the 1877 campaign the great currency question came up in Congress. Allison had observed a rising clamor over the so-called "Crime of '73" for some time. In 1873 Congress had innocently dropped the silver dollar from the coinage lists, recognizing the fact that silver, then scarce, was seldom offered for coinage owing to its higher value in the open market than at the Treasury. But in the mid-1870's new mines in the Mountain West began pouring out fresh silver in vast quantities. Meanwhile, the Panic of 1873 and the agricultural crisis brought demands for an expanding money supply. The frustration of the Greenbackers in 1875 by the Resumption Act had only served to add vigor to the movement. Inflationists now developed an affection for silver and urged that Congress provide for its coinage in unlimited quantity.

The greatest enthusiasm and the most urgent demand for silver were naturally found in the West. Wherever debtors outnumbered creditors, wherever mortgagors were having difficulty in making their payments, and wherever silver was produced as a commodity, there you would find believers in the possibility of the use of silver as a monetary medium regardless of its price on the market in comparison with gold. Western politicians were made or broken by their response to this sentiment. The most complete embodiment of a favorable response was Richard Parks ("Silver Dick") Bland, a Democratic Congressman from Missouri. Bland combined real ability with an evangelical and self-denying temperament. He fought for free silver because he honestly believed in it, not because it was politically expedient. Term after term he had introduced bills on this subject and had frightened the moneyed men of both the West and the East. In October, 1877, he introduced a far-reaching bill calling for the free coinage of silver at a ratio of sixteen to one. This bill passed the House on November 5 by a vote of 163 to 34, with 93 not voting. Every one of Iowa's nine Representatives voted for the bill.[28]

On November 21, 1877, Allison reported the Bland Bill out of the Senate Committee on Finance with amendments that not only changed the intent of the bill, but its name as well — henceforth it would be known as the Bland-Allison Act. The principal alteration placed a brake on the unlimited coinage for which Bland's bill had provided. The Senate committee now proposed coinage of silver dollars, with the Secretary of the Treasury authorized to buy not less than $2,000,000 and not more than $4,000,000 per month.[29] (The word "worth" was not inserted until later.) Another provision was for an international conference on the subject of bimetallism.

The exact date of the submission of these amending clauses is of vital importance. It has been suggested that Allison was moved to the use of his influence on this occasion by his friend, John Sherman, now Secretary of the Treasury and presumably the spokesman of the conservative financial interests of the East.[30]

Now it is true that Sherman wrote to Allison on December 10, 1877, saying:

Permit me to make an earnest appeal to you to so amend the silver bill that it will not arrest the refunding of our debt or prevent the sale of our four per cent. bonds. I know that upon you must mainly rest the responsibility of this measure, and I believe that you would not do anything that you did

2.3

not think would advance the public service, whatever pressure might be brought to bear upon you.

Sherman then went on to explain the problem of the existence of a surplus then facing the Treasury Department. This surplus not only invited raids on the Treasury for high pensions and needlessly high appropriations; it excited the taxpayers, who felt that they were over-taxed and that such overtaxation was a deflationary force at a time when some inflation was needed. More technically, the surplus was harmful, because it could not be effectively used for the retirement of the nation's debt, which was largely held in the form of long-term non-callable bonds.

It was this latter problem that particularly worried Sherman. He feared that a decision for the free coinage of silver would create such a shock to the national credit that United States bonds held abroad would come back to this country, and "our people will then have a chance to buy the existing bonds and we cannot sell the four per cent. bonds. This will be a grievous loss and damage to the administration and to our party, for which we must not be held responsible." [31]

But Allison had reported his limiting amendments from the Finance Committee on November 21, well before this letter was written by Sherman. Unless the letter was merely a confirmation of previous conversations, it seems fair to give Allison credit for making up his own mind. In Poore's memoir no reference is made to the influence of Secretary Sherman; Allison is presented as the odd man on an other-wise evenly divided committee, and it seems that by common con-sent the committee turned to him for leadership. [32] He had known Sherman since 1855 or perhaps a little earlier, and of course would know his views even had they never been expressed in a letter. On December 13 Allison gave strong prosilver arguments for the amended bill on the grounds that the country could stand a limited amount of silver per year, an amount that he predicted would not exceed $30,000,000, and that with such a limitation both silver and gold would circulate side by side without discrimination. He also put great store by the necessity of securing an international agreement for the use of silver, hence his insistence on the amendment for an international conference. [33]

No cause in which Allison had enlisted up to this time drew from him such complete devotion and such spirited and unwavering defense. The full record of this fight in the Senate for a fair recognition of

silver belies the picture of him as a weak, spineless, noncommittal compromiser. Beginning with his speech on December 13, which drew
many contemporary compliments, Allison bore the brunt of the fighting against such able opponents as George F. Edmunds of Vermont,
James G. Blaine of Maine, Thomas A. Bayard of Delaware, A. A.
Sargent of California, and finally President Hayes himself. He had
to carry the handicap of working for amendments to a bill that had
been introduced by a Democrat and the added handicap of the Stanley
Matthews Resolution, which declared that payment of government
bonds in silver would not be an act of bad faith or an invasion of the
bondholders' rights.[34] Allison had to vote for this resolution, although
he would have greatly preferred to postpone consideration of it until
the main fight for silver was over.

After a long Christmas recess, the debate on silver raged on through
late January and into February, 1878. Conservative journals such as
Harper's Weekly and *The Nation* criticized Allison or anyone who
offered the least concession to the silver interests. In Iowa, the Davenport *Gazette*, almost alone in opposing silver, attacked him for his
admission that "the chief cause for the depreciation in value of silver
has been the action of other nations in adopting the single standard"
and for his assertion that the adoption of the silver dollar as a standard
depended on international agreement. The *Gazette* thought this a
damaging admission to make.[35]

In mid-February the course of the Bland-Allison Bill was nearing
its end. The climax of the debate, with the Senators at their best in a
battle of wits and knowledge, came in the all-night session which began on Friday afternoon, February 15, and did not close until five
o'clock on the morning of the 16th.[36] In such a marathon session
every one had his chance to say his piece. Several speakers seemed eager
to ascribe to Allison the authorship of the two million-four million
limiting clause, but he was always prompt to attribute it to the entire
Committee on Finance. He made one prepared speech, summing up
the case for the bill, and in the course of the running debate he held
his own against such doughty opponents as Edmunds and Justin S.
Morrill. He was the soul of courtesy, but he could not be sidetracked
or tricked in any manner.

Near the close of the debate Allison rose:

Mr. President, it seems now, at twenty minutes of five o'clock in the morning, by the action of the Senator from New York (Kernan) we have had

thrust upon this bill not only the question of the remonetization of silver, but the whole question of the resumption of specie payments and the volume of the paper circulating medium. If that question is to be opened up again and added to this bill, I think the motion of my friend from Vermont (Mr. Morrill) would be quite opportune, namely, that this bill should take effect on the 1st of July, 1878, because we shall not probably finish it until about that time. Therefore I beg the friends of this bill not to lumber it up with questions of paper money. Let us settle the silver question now and the question of paper issues afterward.

The vote was at last called for, and the amended bill passed by a vote of 48 to 21, with 7 absent. In an editorial on February 22, Ret Clarkson announced triumphantly that the Senate had passed the bill and reminded his readers that the Iowa Republican convention of June, 1877, had been the first to endorse the remonetization of silver. He pointed out that the Iowa delegation in the House had supported the proposition unanimously and that Allison had led the fight in the Senate. Pointing out that 999 out of every 1,000 Iowans wanted the silver bill as passed, Clarkson derided the Davenport *Gazette* for its opposition.[37] On the Monday after the Saturday passage of the bill, according to the *Register*, Sherman and Allison had had a talk, and Sherman had promised to enforce the act to the letter, agreeing that it would help him to prepare for resumption in 1879. C. C. Carpenter wrote from Fort Dodge and congratulated Allison on his speech and on his leading position in the contest and expressed his pleasure with the law: "I wish now the men of money and enterprise could be assured that the financial question will be let alone as I believe it would help more than anything else to restore confidence and business activity."[38]

Meanwhile, the amended bill had passed the House by a whopping vote of 196 to 71.[39] The Iowa delegation did not take part in the debate, but they voted unanimously for the bill. The separate amendments all carried easily, but none by as large a vote as the one for a limited ($2,000,000 to $4,000,000 worth monthly) coinage. On this the vote was 203 to 71. Representative James Abram Garfield expressed perfectly the mood of the country when he wrote in his diary on February 17, 1878: "If there were any temper in Congress or the country which would tolerate or listen to discussion, I should be glad to debate this case fully — but it is an epoch of madness."

Nothing daunted, President Hayes sent the bill back with a short but forceful veto message. Without debate the Senate passed it over the veto by a vote of 46 to 19, with 11 members absent. Allison and Kirkwood naturally voted with the majority.[40] In the House the Speaker's announcement that the bill had carried over the President's veto by a vote of 196 to 73, with 23 not voting, was greeted with great applause.[41] Again, the entire Iowa delegation voted for the bill. Garfield noted in his diary that "The President was not only unable to influence a single vote but lost some in each House. He has pursued a suicidal policy towards Congress — and is almost without a friend." Again the Des Moines *Register*, which is to say, Ret Clarkson, exulted, and the editors of *Harper's Weekly* lamented.[42] The latter stood by their contention that the bill was largely a Democratic achievement by pointing out that of the 73 votes in the House to sustain the veto, only 20 were Democratic; of the 19 on Hayes's side in the Senate, only 9 were from that party. Furthermore, of the ten Republicans who wanted to sustain the veto, all but three were from New England. Clearly Allison was not acting with the "regulars" on this occasion.

Allison received some criticism. Charles E. Perkins, sharply disagreeing on this question in spite of his friendship for Allison, ended up a rambling letter with the warning, "There is a future in store for you Silver men!" A more positive denunciation came from another friend from the world of railroad finance, Morris K. Jesup. The fight that Allison had made for his ideas about silver, in the face of the opposition of some of his best personal friends, helps further to disprove the belief that he was a man of no opinions of his own, even if it be granted that he had popular support in Iowa for his stand.[43]

Nothing has been found to show that there was the slightest contact or collaboration between Bland and Allison on the act that bears their names. One was a Democrat, the other a Republican; the only thing they had in common was their residence in Western states that wanted free silver. Bland introduced his bill and put it through the House; Allison had a key part in getting it amended in the Senate, although he made no extensive claims for honor here, merely saying that he was the odd man on the Finance Committee and had the power to throw the vote of the committee either for an unfavorable report or for passage with amendments. He chose the latter course.

Thus Allison helped to write another chapter in the long history of American experimentation with silver as a money. "His" act was destined to survive for twelve years. It is easy to pass judgment on his policy, if one remembers one thing above all else: Allison was a politician, not an economist. He was on the side of the debtors of the West and South, with his own state party organization safely on record in favor of silver before he acted. He was enough of a neutral to help the extremists in each group to find a point of agreement. In effect, Allison was saying, "a little inflation will not hurt us; this country is big enough to stand a little bad economics in return for political peace in the West." He had predicted that the amount of silver dollars going into circulation would be about $30,000,000 per year; at the end of twelve years the total figure was $378,000,000, a remarkably close estimate.

If the techniques of quality control could be applied to legislation, Allison's bill would rate well. It gave the Westerners enough to appease them temporarily and a hope that silver would soon return to a favorable price. By its limiting clauses, the bill relieved the Easterners of the fear of something much worse — the bugbear of unlimited coinage of silver. It satisfied John Sherman, Secretary of the Treasury, because it destroyed the threat to his plans for carrying out resumption of specie payments in 1879 and his plans for the sale of new bonds. If the act "both disappointed its friends and failed to effect the dismal results foretold by its enemies," which is the judgment passed on it by a leading economic historian,[44] it rather well met the utilitarian test of providing the greatest satisfaction possible to the greatest possible number of people.

☆ XI ☆

A Garfield Republican

ALLISON SETTLED down to his usual routine of personal and public business after the excitement of winning a second term election and the passage of the Bland-Allison Act. As a Senator he had definitely "arrived." Safely elected for a second term, a member of important committees, possessed of a charming wife, and occupying a home in which Mrs. Grimes shared the expenses and contributed her prestige and intellectual prowess, life was now about as full and rich as Allison could ask for.

Countless invitations to dinners, teas, and receptions, and frequent requests to stop in and see the President, a Cabinet member, or a fellow-Senator show that Allison was in his element. There is no indication that he ever let any of this "go to his head"; he was approachable, he was attentive to his constituents when they came to Washington, and he ran countless errands for Civil War soldiers or their relatives wanting pensions, inventors wanting patents, homesteaders wanting titles to land, and so on almost *ad infinitum*. But the real pleasure came from both social and political recognition. William Boyd Allison had come a long way since those days in the small farmhouse near Ashland, Ohio, or even those days when he came to Dubuque as an almost penniless young lawyer and camped on his brother's hospitality until he could get started on his own. Possibly the rewards of social recognition resulting from Allison's services to Big Business were more highly prized by him than any others he may have received.

Washington was no longer the overgrown and muddy town that

Allison first saw in 1861 when he attended Lincoln's inauguration or in 1863 when he came for his first term in Congress. The city had been rescued from the mud by "Boss" Shepherd; the housing situation had caught up with the influx of population; and a number of people of wealth, including some Senators, had established residences there. Washington at last was beginning to have some of the advantages of a large city and a world capital as well as the convenience, the charm, and the intimacy of a small Southern town.

Senators kept open house one afternoon a week to receive their constituents and others who came to Washington for business or social reasons. Such visitors, usually under the escort of a Congressman's wife, called on the President and other high officials.[1] Allison would have only limited obligations and demands made upon him compared to certain Cabinet members and the older and wealthier Senators, but he and his wife and Mrs. Grimes combined their resources sufficiently to make a place for themselves in a small circle of official society and to extend their hospitality to their closest out-of-town friends.

In addition to his social life and his senatorial duties, Allison had personal business enterprises to keep him occupied during 1878. He enjoyed an annual retainer from the Illinois Central Railroad; when it began or for what purposes it was paid it is impossible to say.[2] He was deeply involved in a scheme whereby his Dubuque friends, H. L. Stout, General C. H. Booth, and the Graves brothers, and his New York boss, M. K. Jesup, were trying to sell a "paper" railroad — called the Iowa Pacific — to some Boston capitalists. It is impossible to piece together the whole story, but the fragmentary correspondence available is quite intriguing. Allison's potential reward seems to have been some farm land near Belmond, presumably to be carved out of the lands the road would receive.

In this scheme, Allison is revealed as the leg-man running between interested parties. R. E. Graves wrote in March, 1878, that "in Boston this week they will decide to buy the I. P. [Iowa Pacific] or drop it entirely." Stout planned to build the line, then lease it. "Stout, Booth and I want you to be a Director and help us in our negotiations for the purchase of rails, etc." [3] After some months of fruitless negotiations, Stout became anxious. R. E. Graves wrote Allison that Stout had instructed him to "write the Senator that his big farm out West has vanished and that I say he hasn't done anything yet, and he is going to be paid accordingly to the work he does. . . . He smiled as he said it but the foregoing is a scene from real life. Give us a ray of sunshine if you *can*." [4] The next day Graves wrote Allison again: "I enclose copy of letter from M. K. Jesup. . . . You know all the particulars of the situation and our anxiety to have the business concluded as agreed. Also the bearing on other Cos . . . your fertile brain is equal to the emergency. We depend on you, and if any modification becomes necessary you will see it, and put it in train. We are anxious not to *appear* anxious." But Stout was more imperious. After expressing annoyance and fear over the delay, he wrote Allison: "Now I think you should look up that old cotton umbrella [and] go to New York and stay there until you get this matter settled. . . . I am still [a] doubting Thomas and need to be comforted in some way. This unfortunate delay is killing our project by inches." The matter seems to have come to a close with a letter from Stout: "The unaccountable delays of the New York parties in carrying out the contract for constructing the D. & D. Road [Dubuque & Dakota, successor to the Iowa Pacific] renders it impossible for us to place anything to your credit here, but if they ever do . . . you will be remembered accordingly." [5] From the demands made by these friends on his time, one would never know that Allison's real business was that of a Senator representing Iowa in the Congress of the United States.

There always seemed to be things to do for Allison's railroad associates. His correspondence with Charles E. Perkins, the managing genius of the Burlington, reveals the opposition of the roads to the early efforts to secure government regulation of railroads. To be sure, opponents of Iowa's Railroad Act of 1874 had secured repeal of that legislation; it had been replaced by an act of 1878 that created a commission pretty much controlled by the railroads. But the magnates were not even satisfied with this, and they kept up a running fire on the idea of regulation. Their protest was well expressed by Perkins in 1879:

A word about Iowa politics. A prominent politician remarked lately that an anti-railroad cloud was gathering in the political atmosphere, and that the marked difference between the present impending storm and the storm of 1872 [*sic.* 1874] was that it came from the country, from among the farmers, while this year it seems to take its rise "in the cities." Now this gentleman came a good deal nearer the truth than perhaps he thought. The truth is that a few Republican politicians, who live in cities, are making the serious political mistake of trying to raise an anti-Railroad wind.[6]

A long series of letters followed in April, May, and June, 1879, in which Perkins continued to complain of the antirailroad spirit of the Republicans and to urge Allison to use his influence to get it stopped. The fact that the groundswell of antirailroad sentiment was not political but economic, and that it was a part of the whole protest sentiment of these years, seems to have escaped the business mind of Charles E. Perkins. Neither Allison nor any other politician could have stopped it, and certainly Allison was too astute a politician to have tried.

In addition to railroad affairs, personal business took up much of Allison's time in these years. One small but significant matter was the creation in 1879 of a corporation made up of some of his friends who bought a section of land in Butler County and marked it out as a townsite. They named the town after Allison on the condition that he buy a one-sixth share in the corporation and also use his influence with the Post Office Department in arranging the use of his name for the new town. He met these conditions, and thus originated the pleasant little county-seat town whose name honors the public servant with the longest tenure in Iowa's history.[7]

Legislative affairs were not neglected by Allison, however. Because of his part in the writing of the Resumption Act and his joint authorship of the Bland-Allison Act, he had a great interest in the monetary situation. As the time drew near for the resumption of specie payments, he was on the alert for all signs of success or failure. The act had provided that "on and after January 1, 1879, the Secretary of the Treasury shall redeem, in coin, the United States legal-tender notes then outstanding on their presentation for redemption." An article in the Chicago *Tribune* advocating the free coinage of silver drew Allison's ire and served as a text for a letter of advice to his friend, John Sherman, Secretary of the Treasury.

As to how you will manage Silver, if redemption grows apace, I would throw out [pay out] the Silver. If people only present G. B.'s [greenbacks] for legitimate purposes & not to exhaust you or make a corner on you, I would pay out gold. You have more of it than Silver. But without promises, pledges or complications I would reserve the right to pay out either. If the New York banks want to discredit silver they will do so only to their injury, as it is certain in my judt [judgment] if what is called the Single Standard people press their views as they now seem to be doing, they will have a Single Standard but not the one they want. We are too near success in 1880 to divide our people on the mere question of a metallic Standard. The

Tribune article was written by [Joseph] Medill and he thinks that is the sentiment of the West and I fear he is too near right for a good state of public health & morals.[8]

Here again, as in dealing with the Bland-Allison Act, Allison is more the politician than the economist. A sound monetary system is not his primary interest: the people, the voters, must not be divided "on the mere question of a metallic Standard." What counts is to win in 1880.[9] It would have been easier for Allison to go along with the West without reservations; this he would not do.

Sherman passed Allison's letter on to President Hayes, who wrote a note of approval. Allison replied with a restrained note of thanks and expressed the belief "that our party will be strong in 1880 & with its strength the country will be safe." This was the best he could manage in view of the unhappiness with the Hayes administration which he had already expressed to one of former President Grant's advisers.[10] It turned out that Allison's concern over Resumption was needless: the process went forward without a hitch.

The year 1880 is notable in Allison's career for the interest he and his close friends took in the presidential election of that year. It had long been known that Hayes would not seek a second term. Even those best qualified to predict the Republican presidential nominee were in a quandary, but the names of James G. Blaine and Ulysses S. Grant were most frequently heard. James F. Wilson was strongly for Blaine. "I want a candidate of deep, earnest convictions (i. e., a Radical), whether it be Blaine or Grant. . . . If the convention should say Blaine, I should give him my cordial support *as I did in 1876.* I want our party held together in harmony, and I dont want any more dark horse performances." General Dodge was for Grant, if he would run again: "He is the strongest man in the party, no matter what they think." His second choice was Blaine. Ret Clarkson, as usual, was a Blaine enthusiast, but he also worshipped General Grant.[11] The candidacy of Grant, who had just returned from his European tour, was the result of the zeal of certain bosses in the party, notably the malodorous Thomas C. Platt of New York.

The Iowa members of the convention were led by four delegates-at-large of strong character, personal ability, and unusual political acumen: James S. Clarkson, Samuel M. Clark, David B. Henderson, and George D. Perkins. Under Clarkson's leadership Iowa voted for Blaine on thirty-five successive ballots, as the deadlock between the man from Maine and Grant continued to tie up the convention. Totally ignoring the scandals of Grant's previous terms in office, his supporters now urged his name upon the convention and corraled 306 votes for him, making up a group that fought unflinchingly to the bitter end of the voting and then went on to order medals for themselves as mementos of their work. Not a delegate from Iowa was in this list.

The delegates at last selected a dark horse, in spite of the wishes of James F. Wilson. After Blaine and Grant, the third man in the balloting had been John Sherman, whose floor manager was James A. Garfield, a Senator-elect from Ohio whom Allison as an old friend had welcomed into "the companionship of the Saints on the right wing of the Capitol." After many wearisome ballots a few delegates threw their votes to Garfield, and his strength quickly developed. When the stampede came on the thirty-sixth ballot, Iowa climbed on the band wagon in approved style, and Garfield was nominated.[12] For Vice President the convention threw a sop to the Eastern machine by nominating Chester A. Arthur of New York.

The Democrats tried a scheme to overcome their Copperhead reputation by nominating a Civil War hero of unassailable reputation, General Winfield Scott Hancock; for his running mate they chose William H. English of Indiana. To complete the picture, the Greenbackers nominated Iowa's own General James B. Weaver as their candidate.

From the viewpoint of Allison and Iowa, the Republican choice was most fortunate. Garfield and Allison had been friends and colleagues and coadjutors through good times and bad, through palmy days and the dark ones, when both were grilled for their parts in the Crédit Mobilier scandals. With Garfield as President, Allison would have a close friend in the White House, one who knew him well and who would accept him as an adviser. Allison's telegram of congratulations was soon followed by an intimate letter full of advice:

Hancocks nomination is strong & weak. His patriotism & his soldierly qualities cannot be assailed. His utter want of experience in civil affairs, at a most critical time for the wisest & most enlightened statesmanship make him weak with the voters. . . . I feel uneasy about the chmanship [of the national committee] you must have somebody that can raise money & the Cong Committee & Nat'l must work in complete harmony. John M. Forbes or Don Cameron can raise all the money needed. The Comitee [sic] should feel that it is Garfield & Arthur that we are fighting for, not the battles of the past or the one to come four years hence. That will take care of itself if the campaign is not frittered away. If I can be of any service in any way command me.[13]

Allison took a full share of the work of campaigning. Apparently he was in close consultation with Garfield and in a position to give advice. On September 27 ex-Senator Simon Cameron, Levi P. Morton of New York, Allison, and others stopped over at Mentor, Garfield's home, to discuss the campaign. "Had a full conversation on the political situation in Indiana. Allison and Morton spent the night with us . . . the campaign was quite fully discussed," Garfield reported.[14]

Allison later wrote to Garfield from Indianapolis about his travels and findings in the pivotal states of Indiana, Ohio, and New York. Everywhere he found the party leaders hopeful but alert against "Democratic fraud." His usual pessimism was overcome: "I think I am naturally conservative and not disposed to take rose colored views of things. But I predict a victory here, unless some reverse shall come unexpectedly at the last moment." He made the same report to his friend Whitelaw Reid, publisher of the New York *Tribune*, and praised the work done in that state.[15]

The "last moment" moves were made by his own party, however, carrying Indiana and other necessary states into the victory column. The secretary of the Republican national committee, Stephen W. Dorsey, an Arkansas carpetbagger of questionable reputation, saved the day for his party by sending out agents who could outbid the Democrats. For this feat of wholesale vote-buying he was roundly denounced by press and pulpit, but many leaders of his party feted him with a great dinner at Delmonico's.

Allison and Garfield circumspectly avoided attendance at the dinner and maintained complete silence. Yet the correspondence as quoted by Garfield's biographer and a letter from Allison to Garfield, hitherto unnoticed, show that both men were well aware of Dorsey's methods. Garfield had interceded with Levi P. Morton, the New York banker, to get funds for Dorsey's use. On November 3, the day after the election, Allison wrote to Garfield: "After leaving you I made the journey as contemplated. . . . While in Harrisburg I telegraphed Dorsey & he answered that all required would go to Ind. starting from New York on Thursday night. With this information I thought it not wise for me to go to New York & I returned home."[16] It must be said, with benefit of hindsight, that both Allison and Garfield knew more than they wanted to tell.

On election day Allison sent a telegram to Garfield: "Iowa sends you cordial greetings with sixty thousand majority and full Republican delegation in the new house." [17] This message was based on a rapid and tentative calculation of the vote and was actually under the mark. The final count showed that Garfield's plurality over Hancock was 78,000, but the 32,000 Iowa votes for James B. Weaver cut Garfield's over-all majority to 46,000.

Hardly had the votes been counted when men began the second battle, the battle over the make-up of Garfield's Cabinet. As Garfield's ablest biographer puts it: "The presidential term of James A. Garfield practically began the day after his election." [18] The President-elect ensconced himself in his farm home near Mentor, Ohio, a few miles from Painesville, and from this refuge conducted a heavy correspondence, meeting and sometimes entertaining the visitors who came to seek favors or to give advice as to the membership of his official family. In this way Garfield could carry on business, keep a balanced view of national problems, and at the same time stay in close touch with his family and home.

Two impressions about Allison have been given in the literature on this subject, both false. One, found especially in writings on James G. Blaine and in his own letters, conveys the impression that Blaine, who had been chosen for Secretary of State, virtually forced Allison on Garfield as first choice for Secretary of the Treasury, even implying that Allison was little known to Garfield and that it was necessary for Blaine to describe Allison's virtues before the President-elect could be brought to accept the Senator from Iowa. The second impression, that Allison accepted a place in the Cabinet and then inconsiderately "broke down" on Garfield's hands on the very morning of the inaugural, needs more extensive examination.[19]

Nothing could be further from the truth than the idea of Allison's dependence on Blaine. Garfield and Allison were much more nearly two of a kind than Garfield and the brilliant but domineering Blaine. Their acquaintance had begun at least as far back as that December day in 1863 when the two men began their service in the Thirty-eighth Congress. They had served together on the Committee on Ways and Means, and they had been through the fire of the Crédit Mobilier investigation together. In fact, it is hard to imagine any two men in congressional life whose careers had run more nearly parallel. The letters cited above in regard to the presidential campaign illustrate their friendship and their brotherly feeling, and, specifically, that Allison had acted as confidential agent for Garfield. On one occasion he had even acted as ambassador to old Simon Cameron and his son Don, in Pennsylvania, to iron out any prospective difficulties there with regard to Cabinet claims.

One of the first to begin action designed to put Allison into Garfield's Cabinet was that man of action, James S. Clarkson, who wrote to Kirkwood just a month after the election: "You and I agree perfectly as to Iowa & the Cabinet. We want a man there, & that man should be either Allison or Wilson. I believe Garfield will prefer Allison. If he does he ought to take it, and then the Lord have mercy on us in Iowa next year with two Senators to elect. I should feel like taking my long contemplated trip to Europe." [20] Clarkson, not unwittingly, had put his finger on the real problem. Kirkwood's seat would be up for election in January, 1882. If Allison should resign from the Senate in order to accept a Cabinet post, the same legislature would have to elect someone to fill out the remaining two years of his term, as well as choose a man for Kirkwood's seat, presumably but not necessarily by the re-election of Kirkwood himself. The agonies of decision suffered by a number of men in the next three months would never have been experienced if the senatorial fates of three men — Allison, Kirkwood, and Wilson — had not been involved. Since only two could go to the Senate, the little drama became a game of "odd man out." Which two would be given the security of six years (or more) in the Senate, and which would be given a Cabinet membership with all its honor but also its hazards?

Allison made the first move among the Iowans by writing to Garfield on December 10; the letter has not been found, but in reply Garfield said rather cautiously: "I am anxious to oblige the friends to whom you refer but I do not think the position could go in that direction. A good place can be found however which I hope will be satisfactory. Dont fail to call & see me on your way to or from Iowa." [21] The "friends" Allison had referred to were undoubtedly Wilson and Kirkwood. Before Garfield's letter had been received, Allison headed a list of petitioners recommending James F. Wilson for a place in the Cabinet. Senator Kirkwood joined Allison on the petition, along with five members of Iowa's delegation in the House.[22]

The first important letter in the series from Blaine to Garfield, which gained for Blaine the ultimate reputation of being Garfield's Cabinet-maker, is of double interest because it is largely a special plea for Allison. Asserting it to be self-evident that the Secretary of the Treasury must come from the West, Blaine ruled out Senator William Windom of Minnesota as "profoundly and absolutely ignorant of finance except as appropriation bills teach," and James F. Wilson as one who had been too long out of public life. He then came to the name of Allison. After managing to throw himself a bouquet by citing John Sherman's opinion "that he thought Allison better posted in financial legislation than any man in Congress, except Garfield and Blaine," he described Allison as "true, kind, reasonable, fair, honest, and good. He is methodical, industrious, and intelligent. . . . In the whole United States I do not believe you could do so well." Blaine closed rhapsodically by picturing a triumvirate of Garfield, himself, and Allison — a "picture without precedent — poetic as well as political." [23]

Day after day this business of Cabinet-making went on. For some it was hardly more than an intellectual exercise. For others it was a matter of political success or failure, perhaps political life or death. For Garfield, as for any President-elect, it was a gigantic problem of satisfying sectional, state, and sometimes personal claims, and at the same time finding personalities who would make up an agreeable official circle. Callers came by the dozens, and an immense correspondence had to be handled.

Allison's stock went up and down, as did that of many others. Major William McKinley, an Ohio Congressman, boomed Allison, but Kirkwood came along and offset this by realistically expressing his fears that Eastern interests would not accept Allison because of his record on silver.[24] John Sherman, who knew the strength and weaknesses of all the prospective appointees as well as anybody, recommended William Windom as his first choice and Allison as his second, but he also warmed to Garfield's suggestion of John Jay Knox of New York.[25]

On January 16, 1881, Allison, in response to an insistent telegram, came to the country home that had become the political capital of the country, and Garfield, apparently full of doubts, put the burden of decision on him by telling him that there were objections to him for the Treasury and asking him for his own opinion of them. The objections were that Allison was unsound on four points: the silver question, currency, the tariff, and deference to the "machine." Allison said he was ready to stop the coinage of silver, was not bound on the tariff, and thought the last point not well taken. He would be satisfied, Allison added, if Iowa had either Wilson or Kirkwood in the Cabinet.[26] Garfield was far from a decision on that mid-January day, and on February 3 he was still debating among six men for the Treasury, including Allison and Wilson.[27]

Factional struggles within the Republican party made Garfield's decisions even more difficult. The "Stalwarts" led by Roscoe Conkling were opposed by the "Half-Breeds" led by James G. Blaine, and Garfield must try to appease both men. Blaine and Whitelaw Reid, publisher of the New York *Tribune*, were beside themselves in their fears that a deal would be made between Garfield and Conkling, and Blaine was getting desperate in his determination to keep out Conkling and Windom at any price.[28] Of the former, Blaine said: "His appointment would act like strychnine upon your administration — first, bring contortions and then be followed by death." As to Windom, Blaine thought that he was not only incompetent but "has the Presidential bee in his bonnet *terribly*. My bee is dead or has ceased to sting, but Windom's is just fully hatched and is very active, buzzing all the time." [29] On February 3 Garfield drew up another tentative list for his Cabinet, with no less than six possibilities for the Treasury: Charles J. Folger, Edwards Pierrepont, Knox, Wilson, Allison, and Windom.

Meanwhile, Allison was having troubles in other ways. Mrs. Allison was in very poor health. For some time the beautiful and charming young wife had suffered from nervous and mental strain over which she could establish no control. In one letter she quotes her doctor at the sanatarium as saying that her trouble was "hysteria." In a great many rambling letters to her husband, most of them addressed to him as "Dear Boy," although he was twenty years her senior, she reveals quite clearly even to one not learned in the science of psychiatry the extent of her derangement.[30] One of the consulting physicians was the eminent Philadelphia specialist, Dr. S. Weir Mitchell.[31] Mrs. Allison avoided the strain of life in Washington by spending the winter of 1880-1881 at Atlantic City.[32] Her trouble was later speculatively traced to an illness called "Roman fever" that she had contracted while in Europe with her foster father, Senator Grimes, on his search for health in 1869.

Then there were troubles connected with the shifts in political positions in Iowa, if Allison were to go into the Cabinet. These were complicated by the fact that his lieutenants, who owned and ran the Dubuque *Times*, were about to sell that enterprise to his former partner D. N. Cooley. This paper was the natural medium for Allison's political releases. He had once held a small block of its stock and could virtually dictate its policies; now it appeared likely to get away from him. Indeed, there were probably times when Allison must have thought that the gods had conspired against him. Seemingly at the top of his career, acting as adviser to a President-elect, and with his name on everyone's tongue as a possible Cabinet member, he was nevertheless unable to control the comparatively petty affairs of his own little feudal principality.

The first to break the news to him of the possible sale of the Dubuque paper was the most trusted of all his vassals, Colonel David B. Henderson, who was well aware of the need for a dependable and efficient staff for the Dubuque headquarters of Allison's machine. Henderson worked hard in an effort to keep the paper in the hands of its able editor, Mark Woodruff. George Crane, Allison's former law partner, was now the postmaster at Dubuque. Henderson reminded Allison that he had once said that if he should go into the Cabinet he must have Crane with him as adviser. If Allison would let him know his plans for accepting the Cabinet place, suggested Henderson, then he could notify Woodruff that he would succeed Crane as postmaster and thus be able to keep the *Times* as well. Unfortunately Allison did not like this audacious display of initiative on Henderson's part and showed his pettiness by rebuking the faithful manager, and Henderson had to swallow this rebuff and make an humble apology.[33] The sale of the paper went through in spite of all the efforts to save it.

Meanwhile, Allison and his lieutenants untangled the knotty problem of Iowa's claims upon the Garfield Cabinet. Allison approached both Wilson and Kirkwood. Wilson, he learned, was more confident of his ability to win Kirkwood's seat than Allison's, and Kirkwood seemed happy enough to have Wilson replace him. Allison and "the boys" thereupon gathered in Chicago to endorse a scheme that would leave Allison in the Senate, place Kirkwood in the Cabinet, and elevate

Wilson to the vacant Senate seat. Allison undertook to gain Garfield's assent. He wrote unfavorably about other proposed Cabinet members; Kirkwood, he assured Garfield, "likes you so well that he like Barkis would be willin' if the fates & your judgment point that way. . . . So now you see how to make of Iowa a happy family." [34] Allison's personal supporters were delighted with the decision, for they recognized the insecurities of a Cabinet appointment. They rejoiced that Kirkwood would sacrifice himself for the good of Iowa Republicanism. Jacob Rich prepared Kirkwood: "I have hinted to some of them the possibility that you may be selected, and every one approves the plan under the idea that Wilson will succeed [to your place in the Senate], and *we shall have all three of you in influential places.*" [35]

Thus again the main point in the game is clearly set forth by one of the principal players. The irony in this plan is that Kirkwood had been prevailed upon to agree to his own sacrifice. Looked at under these circumstances it is not possible to agree with the pronouncement that the ultimate selection of Kirkwood for the Cabinet was an "insignificant non-political appointment." [36] In later years Kirkwood could look back on 1875, when he had been pressured into the race for Governor, and 1881, when he had been "kicked upstairs" to the Cabinet, and think of himself as a badly used man.

Garfield did not readily accept the plan of Iowa's strategists, however. Indeed, he startled Allison with a quite contrary proposal: "I have gone over the ground thoroughly, and have reached a point where I must have your help — I want you to take the Interior Department — and I earnestly hope you will do so — Please let me know soon after I reach Washington." [37] Allison's answer was prompt and decisive: "I regret to say that my obligations to others are such that I cannot honorably accept the place." [38]

So now Allison could boast that he belonged to that relatively small group that had been offered places in the official family of a President of the United States, his invitation being for a place then considered more important than it is today. [39] One by one he had checked off as his the items on the list of political honors available to citizens of the United States: delegacy to both state and national party conventions, membership in both houses of Congress, and now Cabinet membership if he so desired.

On March 1, 1881, Garfield arrived in Washington, still undecided about several places on the Cabinet. He was at once besieged by callers with advice, suggestions, and demands. Allison wrote him a note that day which shows him in the role he graced so well:

Don Cameron says to me he called before six & Swaim [G. G. Swaim, Garfield's secretary] told him to come at half-past six and you would see him. He called at 6:35 & you sent word that you were engaged, & then again after seven you sent him the same word. He feels sore. I told him you could not have seen his message. You should send for him so I think. *He feels very sore.*[40]

This is Allison, ever the peacemaker, trying to prevent Garfield from angering Conkling's Stalwarts, of whom Cameron was one. Allison's role was useful to Garfield, who noted at the end of that day: "The rush and swirl of callers was too much to be remembered without discomfort. Interviews with Blaine and several leading men — Slate generally approved — but Allison is pressed in place of Windom — Morton [Levi P. Morton of New York] pleased with his new place but his New York friends not." [41]

Thus, on Tuesday, March 1, Allison was "pressed in place of Windom." On Wednesday, March 2, late in the day, Garfield wrote in his diary:

Only four hours of sleep, last night. Morton broke down on my hands under the pressure of his N. Y. friends who called him out of bed at four this morning to prevent him taking the Navy Dept — I told him he must ask to be released if he wanted to go — which he did by letter in the afternoon. The N. Y. delegation are in a great row because I do not give the Treasury to that State. . . . It seems important to get a volunteer soldier into the cast if possible and I am discussing Judge Gresham of Indiana — and that would require a change in the Treasury — Allison instead of Windom. On some accounts this change will be more agreeable — I had James of N. Y. telegraphed for. I want to measure him for P. M. G.[42]

But there is a contradiction that must be reckoned with. An Allison letter to Garfield, dated "Mch. 2, 1881" and obviously written in the morning of that day, reveals an offer, hitherto unnoticed in any discussion of this subject, of the Treasury to Allison on March 1, possibly after he had refused the Interior Department. The fact of a conference between Garfield and Allison on that date is on record.[43] Allison wrote:

A full night's reflection, I regret to say, has led me to see it to be my duty to withdraw the hasty promise I made yesterday regarding the Treasury, and I must be considered as out of the way wholly and irrevocably. I feel this to be my duty to myself & those about me. I hope the way will be clear for my colleague or Mr. Wilson. I write this hopeful for your success in your great office — & in every other way.

I would say this & more in person but am so unwell this morning that I fear I cannot be out today.[44]

Meanwhile, Garfield finally dodged the New York roadblock by selecting T. L. James of that state as Postmaster General.[45] This provoked an amusing though trying scene when Conkling, Platt, and Arthur called on Garfield, and Conkling dressed down the President-elect in his best oratorical style,[46] a proceeding which Garfield lightly dismissed in his diary for March 3, concluding with the statement usually thought of whenever mention is made of Garfield's proffer of the Treasury to Allison: "In the evening I offered the Treasury to Allison and he accepted." [47]

There is evidence in the Garfield Papers that Garfield had not given up on Allison, in spite of his first refusal of the Treasury on March 2. It is in the form of a note from Allison on that date, saying "I will come to see you at 3 p. m. or about that time." The note is endorsed "March 2/81. In ans to note requesting him to come." [48] The vital point is that Garfield has now, apparently for the second time, offered the Treasury post to Allison and has received his acceptance. Whether we are entitled, in view of the above, to say "again has offered" is of interest only in that it might reveal Garfield's resoluteness or his belief that Allison could be broken down. In passing one wonders a little about the unfortunate fate of Windom and also about Allison's carefully nurtured plans for Kirkwood's elevation and the easy succession of Wilson to the Senate.

But the story has a quick turn. Early on the morning of March 4, only a few hours before the inaugural ceremonies, Allison again "resigned." On the slender evidence given in Garfield's diary, the story has been built up in such a way that Allison gets none of the benefit of the preceding exchanges. Here are Garfield's words: "Friday, March 4, 1881. . . . At 8:30 a. m. Allison broke down on my hands and absolutely declined the Treasury, partly for family reasons, but mainly from unwillingness to face the opposition of certain forces. Though this disconcerts me, the break had better come now than later."

There is another story of the incident of Allison's last-minute rejection of the offer. It was written many years later by James Rockwell Sheffield who, in the seventies and eighties, was Allison's protégé, and who received from Allison part of the tutelage which enabled him to become a distinguished lawyer and Republican leader in New York City and to serve with distinction as Minister to Mexico. As a boy Jimmie Sheffield spent many holidays with Allison in Washington, and he happened to be there on this occasion. Allison sent him to Garfield at 6:30 on the morning of the inauguration with a message. Jimmie gained admission to the Garfield suite, delivered his message, and was so cordially invited to remain for breakfast with the family that he did so. On returning to Allison's home, Jimmie found him closeted in serious conference with Blaine.[49]

The inaugural went off as planned, few in the audience knowing of the little drama that had taken place earlier in the day. The dark and gloomy skies and icy streets of early morning were conquered by a persistent sun,[50] and the pageant of the inaugural ran its course. Any plans that Garfield might have had for announcing the Cabinet were completely upset. Whitelaw Reid wrote: "We are in a turmoil over Allison's action in refusing the Treasury. The Blaine people have now been urging Gresham . . . but not with much success." [51] Very late that night President Garfield made the diary entry regarding Allison's "breakdown" and then added: "Met Windom by appointment [at eleven] and, after a full hour's talk with him, offered him the Treasury. Retired at twelve-thirty, very weary."

The entry for the next day shows the resolution of the difficulty. Noting that Windom had accepted at 10 o'clock that morning, Garfield says he then sent him and Blaine to make inquiries about Gresham, Hunt, and Kirkwood for the Interior post. On their return they agreed with Garfield that Kirkwood was the "safest suggestion." At 2:30 that afternoon Kirkwood was appointed, and the full list sent to the Senate. Thus the scheme of Allison & Co. was carried out.

Whether or not Allison had a final hand in this choice of Kirkwood, or whether he even attended the inaugural ceremonies, cannot be said. When the Senate roll was called that day, Allison was reported confined to his room by an indisposition.[52] All that we know is contained in a polite and expressive note from Allison to Garfield:

I have not words to express to you my gratitude for your kindness to me throughout this whole affair of the Cabinet. I assure you that Iowa is satisfied & grateful and you may rely upon her & her representatives alwas [sic] to be yours for the work you have in hand. Your Cabinet is a good one, a strong one, and your inaugural splendid in thought — tone & spirit. No one could have done better.[53]

The new Cabinet was only fairly well received. One can merely speculate as to the reception that might have been given to Allison's name, had he been in Windom's place. Their views had not been far apart, so anything said of Windom might generally be said of Allison. While *The Nation* was especially critical of Windom's record, *Harper's Weekly* was more kindly disposed and more optimistic about his possibilities, relying upon Garfield's "financial rectitude" and Sherman's recommendation of Windom's ability.[54] Well might the editors have taken comfort in these assurances regarding Windom. If Allison had been the choice for the Treasury post, it is doubtful if either editor could have changed a single statement in his appraisal.

Allison and his friends had wanted "all three" — Allison, Kirkwood, and Wilson — to be in prominent places. This may be accepted, along with Mrs. Allison's precarious health, as the obvious reason for Allison's final refusal of the Treasury. But one other reason should not be overlooked. Allison undoubtedly knew that the next man in line for the Treasury was Windom; he also knew very well that if Windom accepted, his claim on the chairmanship of the Committee on Appropriations would be vacated. Nothing would please Allison more than succession to that spot. He was well trained for it by virtue of his experience on the House Committee on Ways and Means and more recently as ranking member on Windom's committee. Allison succeeded to this very spot in the Forty-seventh Congress and remained there (except for the first two years of Grover Cleveland's second term, when the Democrats controlled both houses of Congress) until his death in 1908, surely one of the longest of such tenures in the history of Congress.[55]

These reasons combine to deliver a blow to the thesis that Allison refused the Cabinet offer because of reluctance or fear to oppose the powerful Roscoe Conkling. This point has been argued on the basis of Garfield's statement that Allison "declined . . . mainly from unwillingness to face certain forces." The proponents of this theory base their beliefs on Allison's seeming support of Conkling in the affair of the Robertson appointment which embroiled the Garfield administration early in its career.[56]

Late in March, 1881, President Garfield flew in the face of many of his closest and most powerful Republican advisers and gave the choice political plum — Collector of the Port of New York — to the anti-Conkling Independent Republican, W. H. Robertson. The incumbent, General E. A. Merritt, was transferred to a foreign post. Merritt was not a Conkling man, having been appointed by Hayes in place of the Conkling vassal, Chester A. Arthur, when Arthur's operations in favor of the "machine" and his opposition to reform in his office had been exposed some years earlier. But in 1881 Conkling preferred to stay by Merritt rather than fly to the ills of a known opponent such as Robertson.[57] Eventually the fight took on the character of a duel between Conkling, who was head of the powerful Republican organization based on control of the New York patronage, and Garfield, who sought to reform the civil service and to save his own prestige by showing that Conkling could not run the national government as he did the state of New York.

In such a fight it is easy enough to applaud the victory of the reformer and to impugn the motives of all who resisted reform by supporting Conkling. It may seem that all merit in the dispute was on Garfield's side, but many of his best friends told him he had made a mistake,[58] and Senators Allison, Logan, and Frye urged him to withdraw Robertson's name before the issue was fully drawn.[59] Garfield had gone along with Conkling to the extent of giving his men nine posts, and now the President's friends might well wonder why he had chosen to fight the brilliant but domineering New York boss on this unnecessary appointment — unnecessary at this time, since Merritt's term had not yet expired.

Under these circumstances the fight became, at least to some, a simple contest between the executive and legislative branches, with some Senators — among them Allison, Edmunds, Dawes, Frye, and T. C. Platt — standing on the rule of "senatorial courtesy," [60] at least until their colleague had had a chance to present his case. It certainly was not fear that prompted them to act; with the possible exception of Platt, these men were not afraid of Roscoe Conkling. Allison, for one, was fully aware of Conkling's pompousness; Sherman had only recently described Conkling for Garfield's benefit in language that probably many Senators would have endorsed, admitting his great ability but stressing his petulance, his personal pettiness, and his political power based only on control of the patronage.[61]

It is unnecessary, therefore, to read fear of Conkling into Allison's intercession with Garfield when he presented Conkling's complaint that he had not been consulted about the appointment of Robertson. To this Garfield replied, "I stand joyfully on that issue. Let him who will fight me!" [62] Allison's role was that of mediator and peacemaker when he wrote to Garfield: "I had a long confidential talk with R. C. yesterday on New York politics. This was not of my seeking but I am at liberty to unfold it to you if agreeable to you. So if you care to occupy a *half hour* in that way & will name the time I will be at your service." [63]

In short, Allison's case has been considered in too narrow a context. Not only has the rule of senatorial courtesy been overlooked by most writers, but also the fact that each Senator might have had his own private reasons for appearing to support Conkling. For example, Senator Edmunds opposed Garfield and therefore seemingly supported Conkling, largely because he believed the nomination of Robertson had been dictated by his hated enemy, Blaine.[64] Furthermore, those who seek to condemn Allison do not seem to be aware that he had run many errands for Garfield between November and March and had investigated many people for him. Proof that a majority of the Senators finally swung over to the side of Garfield, and gave up their insistence on senatorial courtesy, came when Conkling and Platt resigned at the prospect of an adverse vote on the Robertson appointment. Robertson was confirmed by a vote in executive session without the formality of a roll call.[65]

Allison's position was now secure. He entered the Forty-seventh Congress as a friend of the President, as chairman of the powerful Appropriations Committee, and with political affairs at home fairly quiet. This peace would not continue for long.

Iowa Politics, 1881-1882

•

For Allison the remainder of the year 1881 was mostly taken up with the twists and turns of Iowa politics, senatorial and gubernatorial. As soon as Kirkwood's appointment to the Cabinet had been confirmed, James F. Wilson came out with an announcement of his candidacy for the Senate. If there were any doubt that Allison had manipulated events so as to give Wilson a clear field, Wilson's letters to Allison and Kirkwood would remove it. To Allison he wrote: "I recd your dispatch announcing Kirkwood's appointment. . . . I suppose Henderson is in Washington, at least so the papers say, and of course you have had him to understand the situation. Please see that all your friends in the North are posted. Give me any suggestions you deem proper. . . . I am greatly obliged to you for your entire line of action in the matter."

Wilson's letter to Kirkwood, written the same day, is either utterly selfish or else a cold discussion of a plot in which Kirkwood was as deeply involved as anyone else. Without even the grace to offer congratulations to the old War Governor on his selection for the Cabinet, Wilson began fishing for Kirkwood's assistance: "So things have turned out! And now I have a job on my hands. I have written to a number of persons today. . . . It is important now to fix your friends as soon as possible, and I wish you would give this matter a little attention." [1]

James F. Wilson proved to be a most indefatigable campaigner for the senatorship. His principal opponent in the early stages was Governor John H. Gear of Burlington, although John A. Kasson developed some support, and James Harlan's name was frequently mentioned. Wilson's main concern was with the attitude of the railroads: to whom would they throw their great influence? The general assumption was that they favored Gear. As early as March, Jacob Rich reported to Kirkwood on this subject:

Ret spoke to Hughitt and Potter of the N. W. and CB & Q, respectively, and I have written Ackerman and Duncombe of Ill. Cent. and Merrill of St. Paul R. R., as well as Withrow [of the Rock Island]. The two first repudiate all affiliation with Gear as I wrote you. I have not heard from Merrill yet. Hughitt and Potter told Ret they wanted to keep aloof from the fight. The only danger is Perkins. We must have Allison see him sometime in New York. He can do more with him than any one else. The CB & Q mixes more in politics than any other Co. and has the most power. We must spike them.[2]

On his own part, Wilson first took notice of the question of railroad support in a letter to Allison on March 11: "I am writing all around the board. I am going to keep this thing going. I have got to make the fight without the R. R. peoples help. I think they are all Gearish. He is trying to revive the Granger issue on me but if he does, and the R. R. people let him go you will see fur fly before that card takes a trick." Apparently Wilson was harking back to the days of 1876-1878 when an effort was being made to repeal the Iowa Railroad Act of 1874. At that time Wilson helped the railroads, but so did Gear when, as Governor, he signed the repeal act of 1878. Wilson did not mean to let Gear appear to be "the people's friend" when actually he had been for the railroads.[3]

A few days later Wilson wrote to Allison again, reporting that he had a meeting with such party leaders as J. H. Easton and Captain Theodore Burdick, the Decorah bankers, and Henry L. Stout and J. K. Graves, the financial leaders of Dubuque. All gave him good reports. In this letter Wilson indicates that Kirkwood had been well aware of the "deal" to put Wilson in the Senate. The revealing sentences are: "I find many are anxious to know how you and Kirkwood stand. If it can be understood that both you and he favor me it will help mightily. This is our fight — your future and mine."[4]

On March 23 Wilson, in his most forceful style, wrote Allison that Gear had cleverly taken Henderson out of the fight by having offered to appoint him to the Senate, in case Allison had accepted the Treasury post, thereby neutralizing Henderson toward Gear's candidacy if not actually winning him over to his camp. Now Henderson would not be able to help Wilson in the northern part of the state as he had hoped. Wilson also repeated the allusion to Gear's tactics of raising questions about Wilson's relations with the railroads, although Gear himself was vulnerable on that point.[5]

Wilson's next report to Allison consisted of a complaint against James G. Blaine's rumored interference in Iowa politics, with the object of defeating Wilson. "Now I dont want this thing to drift, and I want you to ascertain definitely about this. If he is to meddle in Iowa politics let us know about it, but I want no stroking of the beard and stabbing under the fifth rib at the same time by Mr. Blaine."[6] Allison promptly replied that Blaine would not interfere in Iowa politics. Evidently without noticing the contradiction, Wilson then asked Allison to get Blaine to write to Ret Clarkson, Blaine's great friend in Iowa, and tell him that he was for Wilson. Instead of writing Blaine, Allison wrote directly to Ret, stating his preference for Wilson and asking Ret for his support. Four days later Ret reported that although his brother Richard was for Gear, he himself favored Wilson but had no objections to Gear; therefore, neither he nor the *Register* would get in too deeply.[7] Wilson next urged Allison to work with Kirkwood and Robert T. Lincoln, now Secretary of War, to get a foreign appointment for Harlan and thus remove one of his rivals from the race.[8]

Late in May, James F. Wilson antagonized Charles E. Perkins. Both Gear and Wilson spoke before the Northwestern River Improvement Convention in Davenport on May 25 and 26.[9] Gear's address lauded a system of water transportation, reviewed the efforts at state control of railroad freight rates, and concluded by tossing the whole problem into the lap of Congress. Wilson advocated the improvement of water transportation in order to compete with the railroads. He attacked the railroads for stock watering and pooling and insisted on the public character of transportation. The *Register* praised both speeches and printed them in full, Wilson's under the heading, "A Masterly Exposition of the Whole Question." Clarkson prefaced the Wilson speech with a paragraph complimenting Wilson on his "intelligent and statesmanlike" effort. What Wilson said would win applause and votes from the people, but it brought a furious letter from Charles E. Perkins, who exhibited the railroad man's confusion of his own wishes with the good of the public. Even the imperturbable Allison must have reeled a bit when he read the letter from Perkins, the man with whom he was supposed to be able to "do more than anyone else."

I am greatly astonished to read in the Register of yesterday a strong endorsement of Wilson's Davenport speech which is so distinctly opposed not only to good sense, but also to the interests which I have & represent in Iowa.

I feel that the time has come when I must ask you to carry out fully the agreement which we made in 1877 in consideration of the purchase by me of an interest in the Register and the payment of $15,000. In that agreement you undertake that the Register shall not occupy ground antagonistic to my interests. Mr. Wilson has experienced a change of heart which will surprise and disappoint all right minded men. He has enunciated doctrines which no one knows better than he does are utterly false. He has taken a position opposed not only to his own previous record and to my interests, but equally opposed to the interests of all property rights. Take what he says about the surplus earnings of Railroads and apply it to your newspaper or his own bank! How can you endorse such absurd communistic theories which are far worse than absurd coming from Wilson.

He has at the crisis shown himself not only the cold and selfish man you always said he was, but an arrant demagogue and a shorter sighted one than I had supposed possible. . . . Whoever may be the next Senator I cannot believe the people of Iowa want a man who has proved untrue to his friends and to himself.[10]

There is no evidence that Allison was in any way affected by this ultimatum from Perkins. He went right on with his support of Wilson, again proving that he was no rubber-stamp for a powerful railroad president, even when that president was his good friend and staunch ally.

Whether Allison passed on Perkins' demands to Clarkson is not known, but the *Register's* attitude during the rest of the campaign was one of wary neutrality until the assassination of Garfield gave it a way out. Following Garfield's death in September, 1881, all Cabinet members went through the traditional practice of handing in their resignations, Kirkwood along with the others. While the new President, Chester A. Arthur, did not immediately accept their tenders, it soon became well understood that there would be a general shuffle of the Cabinet. Kirkwood's retirement did not come until the following April, but his resignation permitted the introduction of his name into the list of available prospects for the senatorial seat, actually the one from which he had resigned to enter the Cabinet as a convenience to the plans of Allison and Wilson. Gradually, the *Register* made its way over to the support of Kirkwood, and thus came about the strange spectacle of Allison and Ret Clarkson in separate political camps. The fact that Kirkwood was not working for a return to the Senate, and that he was writing his friends that he positively would not allow his name to be used against Wilson, did not deter the *Register*.[11]

Meanwhile, Allison & Co. had let the gubernatorial politics of 1881 get out of hand. Their choice was State Senator William Larrabee of Clermont. Larrabee was a Connecticut Yankee who had come out to the West and settled in northeastern Iowa, where he had gradually accumulated a fortune as farmer, miller, timber man, and railroad promoter. His greatest asset at the moment was the friendship and support of Colonel David B. Henderson; his greatest handicap was that he had gone into the race too late. The advantage had been seized by State Auditor Buren R. Sherman of Vinton, who had come up through the political ranks and had worked with the Allison machine in 1877 when he ran for auditor. Now he was the first to announce for the governorship and the first to campaign for delegates to the party convention. Larrabee entered the race in a cautious way, and only gradually did his candidacy pick up momentum.[12] Harlan, "available" for either Governor or Senator, was another contender.

The attitude of the Allison men is shown by two letters; first, one from Jacob Rich to Kirkwood in March:

> Our friend Larrabee is quite anxious, naturally, to have an early solution of the question as to whether Sherman is to have a place in the Territories, or somewhere else, that will take him out of the Gubernatorial fight, and asks me to drop you a line on the subject.
>
> I hope sincerely that it may be done, for it will give Larrabee a fine start of all other racers that may be entered, Harlan not excepted. I have no particular fear of Sherman, but he has some strength that Larrabee ought to have.[13]

The other letter, written in May, is from Colonel Henderson to his good friend, I. M. Fisher, superintendent of H. L. Stout's vast stock farm in Butler County, out of which the townsite of Allison had been formed:

> My old & intimate friend, Senator Larrabee of Fayette Co. is a candidate for Governor. He is one of the soundest of Republicans & one of the truest of men. I know him & will stand by what I say. All our interests as business men & as Republicans will be safe in his hands. . . . But Sherman who "is all things to all men" to get support, has worked up considerable support. . . .

If you can aid in this matter you will support a true man and place me under personal obligations, as my friendship for Larrabee dates back to early days when we worked side-by-side on neighboring farms in Fayette Co.[14]

All these efforts to capture the nomination for Larrabee were in vain, however. The party convention met in Des Moines on June 29 and gave the prize to Sherman.[15]

While the campaign was at its height Allison had new cause to be thankful for his decision not to go into Garfield's Cabinet. Shortly after the tragedy of the assassination, Allison's own home was struck by near-disaster. In September his wife, still suffering from mental disorders, made an unsuccessful attempt to take her own life. The matter was not greatly publicized at the time, but it was freely mentioned later. The nervous strain and the expense of the nursing care now required must have been great for Allison. At the time there was no proved method for the treatment of such cases; the only solution seemed to be rest and care.[16]

Politics went on in spite of personal tragedy. The fate of Wilson's candidacy depended, of course, on the outcome of the October elections. Under these trying circumstances, Allison had to do what he could to influence the vote. The preponderance of Republican strength in Iowa made the result certain; the only question was one of factional distribution. Buren R. Sherman easily won the race for Governor, and a safe Republican majority was carried for the General Assembly. In January, 1882, this Assembly met at Des Moines, and the Republican caucus proceeded to nominate James F. Wilson by acclamation, in spite of the favoritism of the *Register* and the Sioux City *Journal* for Kirkwood right down to the eve of the meeting. Kirkwood did the handsome thing for Wilson by having his name withdrawn from consideration; Governor Gear and the backers of John A. Kasson followed suit. Wilson's brief report to Allison made light of the *Register's* opposition and expressed "everlasting gratitude" to Kirkwood, "for he has acted magnificently."[17] Of course Wilson went on to win in the formal election held by the General Assembly, and James W. McDill of Union County was elected to fill out the remainder of Kirkwood's term. One is a little puzzled by the display of unanimity for Wilson. Surely there were unknown and unseen forces at work; if so, they were well covered up. It does not seem unreasonable to suppose that Allison had made known his desire for Wilson as his colleague and that his wishes were carried out. Little did the public dream of all the correspondence that had gone on behind the scenes; of such a letter for example, as Charles E. Perkins had written to Allison, demanding the repudiation of James F. Wilson's speech, or the letters relating to the original Allison-Wilson plan to have Kirkwood eased out of the Senate and into Garfield's Cabinet.[18] Allison had now repaid in full his debt for Wilson's favor of 1869.

The large and small affairs that filled the year 1882 have little to do with the Allison story except that they illustrate the kind of matters that occupy the life of the boss of a state political machine (who was all the more a boss because he never put on the appearance of one) and a leader in the Senate, where he was a conscientious and indefatigable committee member. Above all things else Allison performed faithfully and promptly the hack work that makes up the life of the dutiful and efficient legislator. Most people think of it as deadening and boring, a necessary evil to be endured if one is to have the other more attractive features of the role. Not so, Allison. He had always been a good committee man and a leader in the congressional debates which eliminate the flaws in the routine legislation that keeps the wheels of government rolling. Now that he was chairman of the Appropriations Committee, he seemed to find new interest and new strength for this kind of work. It became his life; it supported him when all other things seemed to have gone against him.

In spite of the terrible heat of a Washington summer in those days of Nature's air-conditioning, the Forty-seventh Congress stayed in session until August 8. Allison's hard work attracted attention. Henry Villard, the railroad magnate, wrote a friendly warning: "I am sorry to infer from the scarcity of your visits to New York that you are worked too hard in Washington. Don't overdo it." [19] On one occasion Allison wrote to his wife that he had entertained two of his colleagues at dinner, after which they had returned to the Capitol and worked until after midnight on sundry bills; there was no telling when they could get away from Washington, he added.[20]

One particular matter caused Allison a vast amount of trouble and threatened to weaken his political empire just at the moment when he could least afford it. For years the O. P. Shiras scheme for the division of Iowa into two federal court districts had been grinding its way through the legislative mill and now was nearing fruition. The earlier opposition of Council Bluffs forces to the plan had been allayed; now it was Burlington that objected to the latest plan because

that city wanted a court session, and this was not in the provisions of
the bill. Allison's friend Charles E. Perkins proved to be a powerful
spokesman for the Burlingtonians, ably aided and abetted by Frank
Hatton, the editor of the *Hawk-Eye* and a one-time ardent supporter
of James Harlan. Sam Clark, editor of the Keokuk *Gate City*, predicted the loss of his county to the Democrats if Keokuk were passed
over.[21] Allison was so certain that some sort of bill could be passed
that he promised the district attorneyship to a brilliant young Des
Moines lawyer, John S. Runnells, the state chairman of the party.[22]
Colonel D. B. Henderson gave up all other interests for a time in
order to direct the fight. Finally, a bill was passed that offended the
least number of people.[23] Burlington was the loser, and Perkins philosophically bowed to the result. A few weeks later Shiras was nominated
and confirmed for the district judgeship that he had all along planned
for himself.[24] Frank Hatton, the other complainant in the court
matter, was finally appeased by an appointment as First Assistant
Postmaster General in the Arthur administration. His case had been
complicated by the fact that he owed a sum of money to Senator
Wilson's First National Bank of Fairfield — a debt about which he
appeared singularly indifferent — and about which Wilson harassed
Allison with correspondence on the topic as if it were Allison's probable loss instead of his own.[25] From the vantage point of his new
position, Hatton went into publishing and, as the owner of the Washington *Post*, became a wealthy man. It is to be presumed that the
debt to Wilson's bank was retired and that everybody emerged happily
from the once embarrassing affair of the court division.

   In 1882 the outstanding question before the people of Iowa was
prohibition. The state legislature had proposed an amendment which
would make possible the adoption of such a law. This was truly a
"hot potato" for the politicians of the day. The Democrats as a
party solidly lined up against the idea, since the large German and
Irish populations in the river counties were the center of most of their
strength. A good many Republicans were also against prohibition,
most of them from the same cities where the Democrats were strong.
For example, Samuel J. Kirkwood from Iowa City, J. K. Graves from
Dubuque, and John H. Gear of Burlington opposed prohibition.
Allison was no more inclined than many another leader to make his
position known until the drift of opinion could be safely determined.
Illustrative of the challenge put up to Allison is a letter from the

editor of the Democratic newspaper in Dubuque: "Your neighbors here, and undoubtedly the people throughout the state as well, would like to know whether you are in favor of or opposed to the proposed prohibition amendment."[26] The editor offered to publish Allison's reply or keep it confidential as he preferred. Allison managed to keep out of a public decision on the matter by making a noncommittal statement. The prohibitory amendment was approved in a special election in June by a vote of 155,436 in favor to 125,677 opposed.[27]

Before that time, however, Allison's good friend and political lieutenant, David B. Henderson, had announced himself as a candidate for the Republican nomination for Representative in Congress from the Third District. In May, Henderson was selected to serve as the secretary of the Congressional Election Committee of the Republican party, an honor that Allison probably managed to send his way. Henderson won his party's nomination in June and stepped into the unusual role of manager of his own campaign while assisting in the election of his future colleagues from almost every state in the Union. These activities entailed a heavy correspondence with Allison and frequent appeals for advice or for the use of influence in the confirmation of appointments which Henderson wanted to bring about for political purposes.[28]

As the November elections approached, Henderson registered his own concern and that of many others.[29] His fears were well founded. The Iowa Republicans gained 15,721 votes over their 1881 totals, but the Democrats gained 28,931 and the Greenbackers, 2,705. The distribution was such that the Republicans elected only eight of the state's eleven members of the House — including Henderson. The Democrats took two of the remaining seats, and the Greenbackers one, that much abused but really admirable humanitarian, Luman H. ("Calamity") Weller, being their candidate.[30] The Republicans lost one of their eight seats almost at once by the death of Marsena E. Cutts in August of 1883, before the Forty-eighth Congress met. Cutts was succeeded by a Democrat, John C. Cook of Newton. To add to the Republican woes, "Tama Jim" Wilson's election was successfully contested by a Democrat, Benjamin T. Frederick, but Wilson managed to serve during the whole of the Forty-eighth Congress before the decision was made.

In Republican circles this election was interpreted much as was that of 1874: the people had merely suffered a temporary aberration.

Pathetically unable to fathom the revolt of the people against the hard times, even so liberal a Republican as Secretary of the Interior Henry Moore Teller, whom his biographer calls "Defender of the West," could see nothing more than a passing perversity. "I think the people occasionally get wild," he wrote to Kirkwood, "and this time they were wild sure. Burrows [of Michigan] was beaten by a 'fiat money man' of no character whatever; nearly as bad as 'Calamity Weller.' Kansas, Michigan, Massachusetts and Colorado, all with Democratic Governors — it beats the d—l." [31] Kirkwood's comment to Allison was: "How do our Republican friends feel since the deluge in Nov.? I think I was lucky in getting away from Washington when I did." [32]

Well might Kirkwood congratulate himself on escaping from Washington and from the political scene forever, although the mood did not last. Allison, by contrast, had long since put aside any doubts about his political life. In one of his rare moods of frank expression, he confided his inner feeling to Mrs. Allison. Late in 1882, in describing a gathering of prominent people of Iowa, he referred to Kirkwood, who "did not seem to be in a very amiable mood politically. I think he likes well to be in public place. I am afraid I will feel the same way when the fates decree that I shall retire, although I often feel that I have had more than my share of the blessings & burdens." [33] He little knew how prophetically he wrote.

☆ XIII ☆

A Man of Influence

VERY LIKELY ALLISON looked back later on 1883 as the worst year of his life. The politics of the time were nightmarish. His party was not at all chastened by the defeats in the congressional elections of 1882. "Prohibition" was the great divider of the times, and nothing else seemed to be of any importance in the thinking of many Republican leaders in Iowa. Their fanatical zeal approached that of the prewar Abolitionists. The Republican party was not officially a prohibition party, but popular opinion regularly tended to pair the two. At the same time, it was generally known that most Democrats were strongly against any effort to control the liquor traffic. Allison, a man of reason, was pained to see his good party friends throw caution to the winds and dash headlong into a local fight that threatened to do the party great harm in national politics.

The year opened with keenest anticipation of a forthcoming verdict from the Iowa supreme court in the case contesting the validity of the prohibition amendment that had been approved at the polls in a special election the preceding June. In October the amendment had been declared invalid by a Scott County district court decision given by Judge Walter I. Hayes, who happened to be a Democrat. In December opposing batteries of the outstanding attorneys of the state argued the case before the state supreme court. Counsel for the state, pleading for the validity of the amendment, was headed by Attorney General Smith McPherson of Red Oak, assisted by William E. Miller of Iowa City, J. A. Harvey of Fremont County, Senator-elect James F.

187

Wilson, and C. C. Nourse of Des Moines, veteran politician and Republican leader, the most rabid of all the prohibitionists. Finally, there was John F. Duncombe of Fort Dodge, the near-Copperhead of Civil War days, attorney for the Illinois Central Railroad in Iowa, and undoubtedly one of the best lawyers in the state. Although not a prohibitionist by conviction and not a Republican, as were all the other attorneys for the state, Duncombe had been brought into this fight by James S. Clarkson in frank recognition of the value of his ability. George G. Wright, Allison's nemesis in 1870, and John C. Bills of Davenport represented the forces opposing the amendment.

On January 18, 1883, the court's answer was given. In an opinion by Justice William H. Seevers the amendment was declared invalid. Justice Joseph M. Beck dissented at length. Not satisfied with this decision, by which the proposal had been thrown out on a technicality, the prohibition forces petitioned in March for a rehearing. This time the court's decision was handed down in an opinion by Chief Justice James G. Day: the petition was denied. Again Justice Beck dissented.[1] A great wave of indignation swept down over Justice Day, a Republican. The prohibitionists inconsiderately denounced him for not rendering a decision favorable to their cause, seemingly expecting him to construe the law in their favor regardless of his judgment. In the meanwhile, Governor Buren R. Sherman, a prohibitionist, refused the demands of his colleagues to call a special session of the legislature to re-enact the amendment and to pass a total prohibitory statute.[2]

All this happened at a time when the party was on the defensive following the defeats of 1882. The temper of the times on corruption, prohibition, and great corporations was well illustrated by a letter to Allison from Major Albert R. Anderson of Sidney, heretofore a violent Radical Republican but now veering toward another kind of radicalism.

I could understand the widespread distemper that prevailed in last fall's election and could well feel the effects of the scratching itch that the many wrongful acts of the party had produced. . . . The truth is that many people have for many years been voting the Republican ticket under protest. I have been in that class largely myself. The past good record of the one party and the past bad one of the other has done the work. But this will do it no longer. Our party must convince the masses that it is not in the hands of the corporations of the country. To this end two prime things would be to declare against all [railroad] pools and in favor of the abridgement of the jurisdiction of the U. S. Courts. Allison, you are perhaps not aware of how much demoralization grows out of this last matter. You do not hear it. There is no one to tell it. The people do not itemize and formulate but they bear these grievances as long as they can then smash things. They are now in the smashing mood. The temperance question may absorb all things else. There is no telling where it may land us . . . there must be a bold prompt step forward in some such direction as I have indicated or there is nothing but trouble ahead.[8]

Kirkwood, a strong antiprohibitionist, wrote to Allison, suggesting some kind of action at the party's state convention and asking his views and advice on the prohibition issue. In his reply, Allison expressed himself with a mixture of evasion and positive advice. He left no doubt of his own adherence to the Kirkwood view that it would be a mistake for the party to try to carry a prohibition amendment and also to advocate legislative prohibition in the party platform; he feared the radical prohibitionists would dominate the state convention; and he expressed a strong hope that Kirkwood and others "taking more conservative ground" would go to the convention and help to make the platform.[4]

If Kirkwood attended the state convention, he had no success in stemming the prohibition tide. From the keynote speech on, it was a triumph for the amendment forces. Lieutenant Governor O. H. Manning of Carroll County coined the sentence which became famous as the slogan for their movement: "A school house on every hill and no saloon in the valley." Colonel Henderson, notoriously loyal to his Scotch ancestors, accepted the chairmanship of the convention with these words: "The wife and child of the drunkard are raising their hands to you for aid. . . . Every Republican accepts the idea that we will help them." [5] Riding roughshod over all opposition, the "drys" nominated Joseph R. Reed of Council Bluffs for the place on the supreme court held by Justice Day, defeating Day, Senator McDill, and others for the place.

Kirkwood now went so far as to advocate scratching the ticket so as to elect antiprohibitionists. It thus became obvious that the prohibition fight was jeopardizing the Republican chances for success in 1883 and 1884. No one recognized this more clearly than Allison. In a long letter to Kirkwood in July of 1883 he remonstrated with the old war horse who was in the strange role of trouble-maker within his own party, although Allison was careful not to make the advice too personal. Admitting that there was much dissatisfaction in the state, Allison argued against local ticket-scratching by appealing to loyalty to the national party. The next year would bring a presidential election; a victory "by a scratch" in Iowa in 1883 would give hope to the Democrats for victory in 1884, so he said. Furthermore, the Senate was now in a tie; the Republican party needed victories in both Iowa and Ohio in order to preserve its national position.[6] Thus Allison used one of the most effective but questionable devices of political leadership: loyal party members must give up a chance to deal with a local issue in order to win on the higher level of national politics.

Kirkwood was pelted from both sides. The eminent C. C. Nourse sent two letters in defense of the moves that the majority had made; others wrote letters of approval of Kirkwood's position. Carl W. Snyder, an editor and party leader of Cedar Falls, wrote that "we have some here who are intemperately insane on the prohibition question," but that most people would remember the great record that Kirkwood had made and would think of him now accordingly, although not all would follow his extreme advice and scratch the ticket and vote for the Democrat, Walter I. Hayes, in place of Reed. The best letter in the series is one from Justice Day in which he expressed a fear of the reflex action of this affair on the supreme court, the defeated jurist giving an excellent statement of the evil of punishing a court for an unpopular opinion.[7] The feeling of crisis was just as real as if the issue had been war or peace; it illustrates the trials of a democracy when honest men must make up their minds between party and principle.

A few weeks went by, and Allison joined all the faithful for a party celebration at Clarinda. The Republicans were torn as never before, with the prohibition issue and the tariff issue driving good men from the party fold, with Kirkwood counseling a scratched ticket, and Horace Boies of Waterloo announcing his intention to support the Democrats.[8] The regulars met at Clarinda, William P. Hepburn's home town, to provide a sounding board for speeches by Allison, James F. Wilson, and Governor Buren R. Sherman. All the newspapers edited by the orthodox gave the speeches in full, some printing special supplements for distribution, and readers were reminded that the Democrats were the party of treason and that only the Republicans were fit to govern the country.

Allison had left Dubuque for Clarinda and the party gathering on Thursday, August 9, 1883, planning to spend the following week speaking throughout the state. Mrs. Allison, who remained in Dubuque, had been ill but was improving when Allison left. On Sunday, August 12, she told her nurses that she was going to make a short call on Mrs. D. B. Henderson and was allowed to leave the house unattended. Carrying two "gossamers" filled with sewing, she made her way to a slough of the Mississippi River, weighted down the gossamers with stones, waded into the water, and sank below the surface.[9] Upon hearing the terrible news, Allison's railroad friends provided a special train for a fast trip all the way across the state, but the grief-stricken husband could only join the throngs of mourners.[10]

Friends were exceedingly kind and considerate in this hour of grief and distress. Ex-Governor Kirkwood sent condolences and an offer to fill Allison's speaking engagements; an intermediary reported, "I delivered your kind message to Senator Allison, whom I found very much depressed over his terrible affliction. He would be glad indeed to have you make a few speeches in this section." [11] Mrs. Grimes packaged up Allison's letters which Mrs. Allison had preserved and sent a picture of Mrs. Allison dated "Heidelberg, 1873," taken during the couple's honeymoon tour of Europe. Mrs. Grimes pronounced it "very beautiful," a judgment in which one can readily join. For the next year or so, many letters from old friends made some allusion to Mrs. Allison's charm and beauty and expressed sympathy for the bereaved husband. Ret Clarkson later wrote Cyrenus Cole of Mrs. Allison: "She was a beautiful, splendid woman, one of the loveliest I have ever known, refined, high spirited, and gentle and lovable in every way." [12]

Allison's Washington neighbor and colleague, Senator Justin S. Morrill, wrote from Vermont, expressing deepest sympathy. "Permit me to hope that you and Mrs. Grimes will return to your Washington home and keep its memories bright. Mrs. Allison loved and was justly proud of you. I cannot think she would want you to shirk any duty that may concern your continuance in public service." [13] Morrill must have known how his friend would react to this tragedy, for Allison wrote him, "I am broken up. I realize how vain a thing is ambition. I shall try to do my duty, but this is a warning[?] to me, to be prepared to join my wife in a better world as I am sure she is where pain does not come." He had no plans for the future, he added, "as Mrs. Grimes is in deep grief." [14]

Mrs. Allison's inheritance from Senator Grimes had been well managed, and she was able to leave a considerable estate to her husband and to members of her own family. To Allison she gave $30,000 outright and a fifth of all remaining after certain specific provisions had been carried out. In later days it was asserted that his share of the estate came to about $50,000. A most harmonious relationship existed between Allison and the other heirs. He continued to share the home with Mrs. Grimes and carried on a lively and stimulating correspondence with her during his absences. As co-executor with Edward B. Nealley of Bangor, Maine, he was deferred to in every matter that came up; not a step was ever taken without his advice.[15]

Although bowed down by grief, Allison had no choice but to work at his business of politics. The prohibition question had so badly divided the party that the possibility of defeat in October was openly discussed. With such a leader as Kirkwood advocating a scratched ticket, and with General Weaver's Greenback party pulling other votes away, it actually seemed possible that the Democrats might elect enough legislators to enable them to choose the Senator in January, 1884, when Allison would be up for re-election. "Success in that direction would be a national calamity, and tend to throw the balance of legislation forever into their hands. Let every Republican be forewarned and cast his ballot accordingly," wrote the Dubuque *Times*.[16] Allison decided not to have Kirkwood speak in Dubuque, for fear that a strong antiprohibition speech to please the people there would antagonize the "dry" forces in southwestern Iowa. He also dissuaded J. K. Graves from publishing an article favoring local option.[17]

All through the summer Allison was concerned over the forthcoming senatorial election. It is hard to believe that he could have been seriously and sincerely worried about the outcome, but he wrote to Kirkwood as early as May: "Some say I must be a candidate for re-election & that I will have no trouble if the legislature is Republican but I know this cannot be so unless I shall have the cordial support of all or most of the leading Republicans in the State. If I have such support I am willing to take the chances. Without it I do not wish to be set up merely for the pleasure to other people of knocking me down."[18] Kirkwood was ready with advice which Allison accepted readily; his answer was more confident. "Carpenter expressed himself warmly for me," Allison wrote a month later, "& is ready to aid me in any way possible. I think Kasson will not appear on the stage as a candidate. He told me [he] had received many letters asking him to run but that he had answered them all saying I ought to be returned."[19]

As part of the campaign against Allison, General James B. Weaver resurrected some of the "dead cats" of the years 1869-1872. To do this, he had only to quote the earlier charges made by the Harlan faction of the Republicans. Allison's lieutenants fought back valiantly, and Ret Clarkson used the columns of the Des Moines *Register* for fierce denunciations of General Weaver. First charging that the General and the Greenbackers had made a trade with the Democrats to help the latter by attacking Allison and Wilson, Clarkson then repeatedly called Weaver a liar. He took up the charges and disposed of them one by one. That Allison had voted for the subsidy of railroad lands and bonds for the Sioux City branch of the Union Pacific Railroad could not have been true, because this was done in 1862, a year before Allison took his seat in Congress. That Allison was connected with the company that was prosecuting suits against the settlers in southwestern Iowa was not so, because Allison was not connected with the Cedar Rapids & Missouri Railroad Company, the plaintiff in these suits. That Allison and James F. Wilson, as Congressmen, voted in 1864 to double the volume of government bonds loaned to railroads in 1862 was called a barefaced lie, because it was the railroad lands that were doubled, not the bonds. That Allison and Wilson had helped to get the route of the Sioux City & Pacific Railroad changed was denied by passing the responsibility to John I. Blair and Secretary Harlan, who should have rejected it if it were not proper. The route was defended as one dictated by engineering requirements. That Allison and Wilson had made millions out of these actions was denied; the company itself had not made millions, and Allison's and Wilson's shares were small.[20] Of all these charges, those concerning the change of route of the Sioux City road were the most valid. Certainly the answers differed from those given in 1868, when Allison was on the defensive in his campaign for re-election, or in 1873 when testifying before the Crédit Mobilier inquiry.

At last the campaign ended, but not until Senator Benjamin Harrison of Indiana and others had been imported to help the cause. Hard work plus the traditional beliefs of the party carried the day; Governor Buren R. Sherman was re-elected by a vote of 164,182 to 139,093 for his Democratic opponent, L. G. Kinne of Toledo, while Weaver, the Greenbacker, received only 23,089 votes. Dubuque County returned a Democratic majority of 3,597, by far the largest of any county. The Republicans carried the legislature, but only the holdover vote in the Senate gave them a confortable margin. The new General Assembly would have 39 Republicans in the Senate and 11 Democrats; in the House there would be 52 Republicans against 42 Democrats and 6 Greenbackers.[21]

A loyal supporter of Allison, who was also his cousin, reported that "Republican speakers whom I have heard during the canvass have all defended you against the slanders of Mr. Weaver; H. J. Budd, of Knoxville, spoke of you as the grandest and noblest man that had ever represented Iowa." [22] Even so, Allison continued to worry about the outcome, perhaps fearing that some members of his badly divided party might vote against him. Writing to Kirkwood a few weeks before the election, he said: "Do you hear of any opposition to my return, or do you believe that any such opposition will develop among Republicans. If so, I would like to have your aid at Des Moines." [23]

While waiting for the General Assembly to meet, a second visitation of sorrow came to Allison. His father's health had been failing for some time: the end came on January 5, 1884. The old gentleman had made his home with his youngest son, James H. Allison, called by his middle name "Harrison," who had a comfortable farm home near Peosta, about ten miles from Dubuque. The Senator had come from Washington in order to be with his father during his last illness.[24]

A few days later Allison made his triumphal trip to Des Moines to direct his own re-election as Senator. On January 15 the Republican caucus proved his worries groundless by unanimously renominating him for the position. One of the nominating speeches was by ex-Governor, now Representative, C. C. Carpenter of Webster County; John A. Kasson, a former rival, openly supported Allison for re-election, probably in the hope of winning the Senator's favor in a ministerial appointment Kasson wanted. A committee made up of Senator William Larrabee and Representative Benjamin F. Clayton notified Allison of his success, and he responded with a "short graceful speech" in which he promised to do his best. On January 22 the houses voted separately, after the House had suppressed a small revolution led by Representative Joel Stewart aimed at investigating the charges made against Allison during the campaign. On the 23rd the houses compared their journals and found that Allison had received 90 votes; B. J. Hall of Burlington, 48; D. M. Clark, 10; and L. J. Kinne, 1.[25]

Jacob Rich's report to Allison was not the customary outpouring of six or eight pages but a short letter reporting a glorious victory and blaming Weaver for the abortive investigation. Perhaps the thrill of an Allison election was dwindling, now that it was becoming so commonplace. At Ret Clarkson's invitation, Rich wrote the editorial for the *Register* the day after the victory. In searching for material for his paean of praise for Allison, Rich could not seem to rise above the thought that Allison had been offered a Cabinet place in 1881 and, had he accepted, could have served a useful purpose by acting as mediator between the President and the dissident Senators.[26]

Allison and the Republicans had won in Iowa, but the fate of the party nationally hung in the balance in 1884. The state convention in May, 1884, would be of more than customary importance, since it would have a chance to express a preference for President and would elect the delegates to the national convention. Jacob Rich, as usual, gave Allison the inside report. He wrote that the convention had been held down with difficulty to the expression of a preference for Blaine without instructing the delegation in his favor; actually many were heard to say that they would like to go for William B. Allison.[27] So far as is known, this is the first time that Allison's name had been seriously discussed for the presidential office.

Iowa sent twenty-six delegates, headed by Clarkson, to the Republican national convention at Chicago in June. The contest was between James G. Blaine and President Arthur, with George F. Edmunds running a poor third. Four ballots were necessary for the nomination, with Iowa casting her twenty-six votes for Blaine for three ballots. On the fourth, when Blaine was nominated, two Iowans, W. G. Donnan and Dennis Morrison, broke from the others and voted for Arthur. A hue and cry went up, as if they had betrayed their country in time of war. Morrison was an inconspicuous man, but Donnan had been fairly prominent, a former member of Congress as Allison's successor in 1871, and a former state chairman of the party. The enthusiatic Blaine men hounded him out of the ranks, never again to be heard from politically.[28]

In spite of the Iowa delegation's loyalty to Blaine, there was some sentiment at the convention for Allison. John S. Runnells, a loyal Allison man and one of the delegates, wrote to Allison that many had been waiting for the right moment to leave Blaine and come out for him; among them, he said, was Nelson W. Aldrich of Rhode Island.[29]

The Democratic party nominated Grover Cleveland as their standard-bearer. The story of the campaign, probably the most unsavory in American history, is a familiar one: the accusations of moral lapses on the part of both candidates; the emotionalized attacks on both men; the tactless remarks of Dr. Samuel D. Burchard about the Democrats as the party of "Rum, Romanism, and Rebellion"; the closeness of the vote in New York; and Cleveland's victory by a margin of 1,149 in that key state.

Perhaps it was time for a change. The Republicans had had their way pretty much since 1860; a new day was at hand. Allison's close friend, the liberal Edward Atkinson of Boston, viewed the changing situation in this light:

You are right in assuming that I was greatly opposed to the Democratic Party, so long as it sustained slavery, but a transmutation is in progress. The Republican Party has become corrupt and has become the chief support of an exorbitant tariff and of an intolerant system of protection, while the new South, permeated by new industries and new interests, is becoming truly Democratic, and therefore entitled to full consideration. . . . Philosophically speaking, I am a radical Democrat, and therefore welcome the reconstruction of the Democratic Party on right principles.[30]

The year after Cleveland's election proved to be comparatively uneventful in the Allison calendar. He was now secure in his Senate position and had only to wield the power that was his. The Senate of 1885 has been pictured as follows: "Half of the seventy-six Senators were wealthy and respresented large vested interests, among them such men as Dolph, Jones, Brown, Allison, Cameron, Aldrich, Sewell, Spooner, and Sawyer." [31] The name of William M. Evarts might well have been included in this list, which was made up by his biographer, but Allison's name should not have been included. He was, to be sure, a friendly worker for large "vested interests," but he was by no stretch of the imagination a wealthy man. He was not in a class, financially, with the Senators listed here. Allison could not possibly have kept up an estate such as Senator Evarts maintained at "Runnymede" in Vermont; only by careful management was he able to maintain his home at Dubuque and to keep up his half of the Washington home that he shared with Mrs. Grimes.

Modest as were his resources, when compared with some other Senators, Allison launched a new venture in February, 1884, when the Iowa Trust & Savings Bank of Dubuque began its operations. G. L. Torbert was the president, Frank D. Stout, the vice-president, Allison's nephew James E. Allison was the cashier, and the Senator was elected as a director. It was a small institution, with only $50,000 in capital stock, but with the Stout family supporting it, the bank was sure to grow. Above all else, from Allison's point of view, it gave a secure berth for his nephew and provided an effective agency for the handling of his own financial affairs.

In the management of his personal business, Allison does not measure up to what one expects from a man who was an authority on national finance and the chairman of the Senate Committee on Appropriations, the "housekeeper" of the nation in those times when Uncle Sam did not operate on a budget. Many of Allison's letters about his personal affairs give the impression of a little man, somewhat spoiled by the adulation showered on him in Washington by self-seeking people who needed his favor for their projects. He could be penny-pinching and grasping on occasion; he often overdrew his account at the bank; and he was a hard man to deal with because of his procrastination and his tendency to use figurative and indefinite language.

Examples of these traits are numerous. One remembers the tedious correspondence with his man Friday in Dubuque, George Crane, representing Allison in a deal to sell the Dubuque *Times*; at last, provoked beyond endurance, Crane asserted flatly that Allison ought to come home and attend to his own business, where so much money was involved. Then there was the case of William L. Bradley, a banker, who handled the sale of some lots for Allison. The amount of money at stake was not large; Allison was vague and indefinite but said enough that Bradley felt authorized to go ahead with the sale; when Allison tried to block the completion of the deal, Bradley was much chagrined and deeply hurt. At last, he deferred in a cringing manner, as he had to do on another occasion when Allison complained about the collection charges on a draft paid through Bradley's bank. After several letters of patient explanation, Bradley gave up in disgust and refunded the amount. One cannot escape the conclusion that Allison was acting the bully toward these lesser men; toward Bradley he was especially unreasonable and overbearing.[32]

Meanwhile, in the Senate, Allison helped to shape up a bill to regulate interstate commerce. The demand for some degree or form of congressional action had been growing, and the air was full of speculation on the subject. Nearly everybody in public life had some plan or portion of a plan to propose. In this somewhat bewildering situation, after Senator Shelby M. Cullom of Illinois had reported his bill from the Committee on Interstate Commerce, and the debate had proceeded a short time, Allison came to Cullom and said: "Cullom, we know nothing about this question; we are groping in the dark; and I believe that there ought to be a select committee of the Senate appointed to investigate the question, to go out among the people, take testimony, and find out what they know about it, — what the experts know, what the railroad officials know, what public opinion generally is, and report their conclusion to the Senate at the beginning of the next session. I am willing to help you secure the passage of a resolution with that end in view." This was done, and the resolution was adopted on March 17, 1885. These ideas were the same as those expressed by Charles E. Perkins in a letter to Allison of December 15, 1882,[33] and which Allison had then ignored, probably because he felt that the time was not right.

During the summer of 1885 Allison put the problems of interstate commerce and currency behind him and enjoyed a carefree trip to Europe. He loved travel; it was his only effective means of escape from his slavish devotion to committee work. As companions he took along his able young secretary, Joseph Morgan of Dubuque, who for some fifteen years was to be his eyes, ears, and hands, and Jimmie Sheffield, now a student at Yale University.

While Allison enjoyed the sights of Europe, his lieutenants in Iowa carried on his political work for him. Allison men saw to it that State Senator William Larrabee of Clermont was properly announced for Governor early in the campaign, now that Governor Buren R. Sherman, the victor of 1881, had finished his inevitable second term. They carried Larrabee to an easy victory in the nominating convention and in the fall election. After service in the state senate since 1868, Larrabee had come to be known as a man of strong views but eminently "safe" judgment. He was probably the largest landholder in the state, and additional banking, brick and tile, and grain-milling interests made him one of the state's wealthiest men. From his first session in the legislature, he had consistently supported the idea of regulation of the railroads by the state, yet he was not thought of as a radical on the subject. He had voted against the Railroad Act of 1874 because he thought it inadequate; perhaps some people mistakenly interpreted this vote as one of opposition to regulation.[34] He and Colonel Henderson were friends of long standing, and Larrabee's nomination and election might be regarded as a personal triumph for the old soldier who had become the guiding genius of the Allison machine.

Allison and his railroad friends found nothing alarming in the 1886 inaugural address of Governor Larrabee.[35] Further railroad regulation was generally regarded as a sure thing — better to have it in the hands of friends than enemies. The drive for federal legislation drew more attention just then than the possibilty of more state action. On May 12, 1886, the Senate passed Senator Cullom's interstate commerce bill, providing a modicum of regulation and differing somewhat from a bill piloted through the House by John H. Reagan of Texas. A joint conference committee was set up to work out the differences, and this committee spent the remainder of the year over into 1887 in study and in search of a workable compromise.[36]

Meanwhile, Allison had probably given more thought to the money question than to the Cullom bill. His reputation as a bimetallist brought him many letters pro and con, plus one speaking invitation from an unusual source. Jimmie Sheffield was importuned by the Yale chapter of the Phi Beta Kappa Society to secure Allison as a speaker in a series of public lectures sponsored by the society. "They wish a lecture on the silver question by some one who takes a different ground from Prof. William Graham Sumner who lectures in the recitation room daily." [37] Correspondence with regard to the proposed lecture went on from February to November. As late as November 12, Allison wrote that he would come, the date to be agreed upon later. No record has been found to show that he ever gave the lecture, however.

In spite of national issues, Allison was more interested in the 1886 congressional race in Iowa. This campaign aroused feelings that disprove the easy assumption that these were "the good old days" when ideologies did not matter. Much of the discontent that had been smoldering in the Republican party for years now exploded. Perhaps it was not surprising that General James B. Weaver was re-elected to Congress; the surprise was that those stalwarts of the party, Samuel J. Kirkwood and William Peters Hepburn, were defeated.

The Republicans could blame themselves for their defeat. In this year of all years, they needed to maintain an unbroken front. In the Second District the Democratic opposition was led by the very able Judge Walter I. Hayes of Clinton, a strong candidate in his own right. In spite of this, the Republicans allowed themselves to be split in the district over a choice of candidate. The old Civil War Governor, who had been a United States Senator and a Cabinet member, accepted the congressional nomination from the Republicans, but one faction of the party, reflecting the widespread industrial conflict of 1886, notably in the eastern River Cities, broke away and supported T. J. O'Meara, the candidate of the Knights of Labor. Hayes, of course, was elected. The loss was a galling one for Kirkwood, who had probably forgotten his ticket-scratching ideas of 1883. He had the comforting alibi, however, that the Iowa City-Clinton district that he was trying to redeem had always been a stronghold of the enemy and for the past two terms had elected a Democrat.[38] He could also say that he had received little help from friends outside the district. David B. Henderson reported that he was too hard-pressed in his own district, where there were 3,000 members of the Knights of Labor, to be able to help.[39] He offered to try to send Allison, after the latter's return from Maine, where he was campaigning for Eugene Hale, a senatorial colleague and close friend, but Allison never appeared in behalf of Kirkwood.

Hepburn, who represented the Eighth District, was the victim of the agrarian discontent that was so strong in the southwestern corner of the state. He claimed to be the true friend of the farmer and the "little man" but had the handicap of being known as a "railroad lawyer." The more discontented members of the party brought out the fiery Major Albert R. Anderson of Sidney as an independent candidate, and he was endorsed by the Democratic-Greenback fusion. For some reason Allison would not come into Hepburn's district and speak for him; Senator James F. Wilson also turned tail and ran, actually canceling five dates that had been made for him.[40] Only "Tama Jim" Wilson stood by Hepburn in what proved to be a losing fight. Allison's desertion seems hard to explain in view of the valiant blows that Hepburn had struck for him in 1883 when Weaver was reviving the charges of Allison's complicity in the Crédit Mobilier affair.

Many years later David Brant, editor of the Iowa City *Republican*, published a series of political memoirs in which he gave the following explanation of Allison's reaction to Anderson's candidacy:

Clarkson urged Allison to get an appointment for . . . Anderson, who was a decided populist and greenbacker in the bargain, in order to get him out of the way and where he could not make trouble. Senator Allison declined. He said that Anderson represented a condition, that if he was removed, somebody would take his place. The senator said that what was good in the Anderson proposals should be adopted and what was bad should be met in debate and in the press, so that the people could be educated in what was for the best. He said that while Anderson might win that year, he could not make his success permanent unless founded upon the right.[41]

If this story is true, it shows that Allison had the political wisdom and foresight not to associate himself with a certain defeat of his candidate. As it turned out, Anderson's success was not permanent. He served only one term in Congress and was replaced by a Republican, James P. Flick, for two terms, after which Hepburn returned to his seat in the House, where he remained until 1909.[42] In this same campaign Allison also ran out on a current promise to help Senator Benjamin Harrison in the Indiana campaign, on the plea that he must help out in three Iowa districts, where the fight was close and where he was "under great obligation to the people in many ways." [43]

But in spite of the loss of Kirkwood and Hepburn, Allison's party did pretty well. The First and Fifth Districts were recovered from the Democrats, and Anderson, Hepburn's conqueror, was nominally a Republican. Party regulars took no comfort in Anderson's victory, however.

Once the election was over, Congressmen could again turn their attention to the needs of the time. The dying days of the lame-duck session of the Forty-ninth Congress in 1887 were memorable for one thing above all else — the passage of the Interstate Commerce Act. The joint conference committee that had been holding sessions since June, 1886, had been unable to resolve a conflict over an antipooling clause. The House spokesman on this question was John H. Reagan, a Texan who had been a Confederate brigadier and a member of Jefferson Davis' Cabinet. He was adamant in his insistence on such a clause; Allison's close friend, Senator Orville H. Platt of Connecticut, was equally insistent that pooling should be permitted. After long delay, Senator Cullom, the nominal sponsor of the bill, which was actually the brain child of many people, asked advice from Allison and other Senators. They urged him to yield to Reagan on this point. This he did, although uncertain as to the wisdom of his course, and the bill was finally put through on the theory that some bill was better than none at all.[44] Allison, of course, was among those voting for the bill.

The year did not close without its share of troubles, giving Allison a chance to demonstrate his political power and also his ability to put his political house in order after a minor revolution had threatened it. It was a year for the election of a Governor and a legislature in Iowa; both elections would affect directly the results of the senatorial election in 1888 when James F. Wilson's seat would be on the block. For the governorship there was no good reason not to support William Larrabee for re-election. The full revelation of Larrabee as a reformer had not been made during his first term, and it was only natural that Allison should support his bid for a second inning in office; the selection of a legislature that would re-elect Wilson was a matter of more concern at the moment.

A difference of opinion within the Allison camp, however, came to light at the annual state convention held in August. Ret Clarkson, presumably Allison's principal reliance in editorial circles, strongly opposed Wilson's re-election and suggested that Larrabee should be elevated to the Senate in Wilson's place. Charles E. Perkins, on the contrary, had seen enough of Larrabee's theories to make him distrustful of another term for the man from Clermont, and he was equally distrustful of Wilson. This was indeed a strange and confusing development. Only the need for harmony in the party, and a growing enthusiasm for the idea of "Allison for President," prevented an open break.[45]

During the campaign Wilson diverted attention from himself by reviving the bloody-shirt tactics of Reconstruction days. By denouncing President Cleveland's pension bill vetoes, alleged abuse of the pardoning power, and subservience to the Solid South, Wilson made a strong appeal to the lingering elements of Radical Republicanism. The results of the canvass were not startling, however. Larrabee was re-elected, but his margin of votes was smaller, percentage-wise, than in 1885.[46] This letdown in Larrabee's popular support, and the *Register's* dislike of Wilson, encouraged Charles E. Perkins to support ex-Congressman Hepburn for the Senate. Thus a three-cornered fight developed in which Iowa was furnished with the strange spectacle of Allison, Clarkson, and Perkins, ordinarily a close corporation in politics, working against each other. Allison was not a "Railroad Senator" on this occasion.

It was a campaign of much name calling. Perkins could not forgive either Larrabee or Wilson for what he considered a betrayal of their former views toward the railroads. He wrote to Clarkson: "Larrabee & his friends naturally lay his small majority to the Railroads which is all nonsense — The real reason is that his course like that of Wilson has not been honest & the people feel it. Both Wilson and Larrabee have gone back on themselves." [47] The Wilsonites ridiculed Hepburn for his loss to Major Albert R. Anderson in 1886, in spite of a normal majority of 3,000 in the district; the Hepburnites sought to injure Wilson by linking him with Crédit Mobilier memories, forgetting that in Allison's previous campaign Hepburn had accepted a commission from the state central committee to absolve both Allison and Wilson of this very charge. Wilson was joshed for dragging out his old shiny black suit, much too short, and his slouch hat, his "campaign uniform . . . which always comes out when the Senator is running for office." [48]

Amidst charges of trickery and refusal to postpone the caucus so as to give the Hepburn men a fair chance to build up their candidate, the caucus was held on January 10, 1888, and Wilson was nominated. The triangular fight thus ended abruptly, and all Republicans rallied to support Wilson. The more remarkable thing is that Clarkson and Perkins returned to the Allison fold without a whimper or a sign of punishment, as did Hepburn also. A casual observer would never have known that a revolution had just been squelched.

The victory for Wilson clinched Allison's place as the dominant political leader in Iowa. Although preferring to work through others most of the time, he nonetheless directly controlled the selection of all men for the key positions and was consulted on many lesser ones. The object lesson of his victory over the leading editor and the biggest railroad man in the state would not be lost on the rank and file of the party. As for national affairs, after fourteen years in the Senate, Allison was a recognized leader of that body, where, besides being chairman of the Appropriations Committee, he was a member of the Finance Committee along with Morrill and Sherman. [49] It is not surprising then to find his name on practically everyone's list of presidential possibilities in the forthcoming contest of 1888.

☆ XIV ☆

The Great Prize Eludes Allison

IOWANS IN 1888 believed that Allison was cheated out of the Republican presidential nomination in that year by Chauncey Depew, a Senator from New York and the guiding genius of the New York Central Railroad. He unfairly blackballed Allison, they thought, because of his residence in Iowa, a state that had just passed legislation providing stringent regulation of railroad freight rates. As in many other good stories, there is a large element of truth in this one, but it is not the whole truth by any means. The opposition of Chauncey Depew was not the only obstacle Allison had to overcome. The New Yorker's objections to the Iowan certainly deprived Allison of a quick nomination early in the convention, but on the last day of balloting he still seemed to have a fighting chance. Then this fighting chance evaporated. What happened? The answer can hardly be given in anything less than a full account of the events of 1888.

The American national nominating convention [1] is sometimes an inspiring example of a party's delegates conscientiously and freely selecting a candidate for the highest office in the land. Unfortunately, this it not always the case; often a convention is a form of madness in which irresponsible delegates collectively perform deeds which no one of them would ever perform individually. Boss-ridden, they vote blindly under orders and deliver their votes in execution of a deal that has been made in the traditional "smoke-filled room." This is especially true in the convention where circumstances have combined to create a wide-open race.

204

One of those who fought in the Republican national convention held at Chicago in 1888 [2] was William B. Allison. According to the custom of that time, he had not made a formal announcement, but his cause had been taken up by his friends. A year before the Chicago meeting, people were aware that he was an avowed candidate. The first letter in which Allison's interest in the nomination was dicussed in businesslike terms was one from James S. Clarkson. Dated April 1, 1887, the letter is couched in vague language and would be meaningless unless interpreted as part of a series. James G. Blaine was scheduled to make a trip west, and Clarkson planned to persuade him to visit the Clarkson home in Des Moines, where they could meet and "talk over the situation. I think it is better that I should see him and gain some information as to the future before he goes abroad. . . . I shall have this interview hoping we may learn something definite, and which may be something of advantage to us all." [3] But Ret's hopes for a Blaine tour of Iowa were disappointed, and he had to be content with correspondence and second-hand reports.

Other bits of evidence can be pieced together to show the build-up of Allison's presidential effort. In April, 1887, he had commissioned that master of congressional biographies, Ben: Perley Poore, to do a campaign biography of him for *The Magazine of Western History*. Poore wrote: "I . . . thank you sincerely for the generous enclosure. I am not certain that you have not overpaid me for my services, but I don't consider them ended, and hope you will find me a lot more material, to be worked in where it belongs." [4]

There were many little ways in which the presidential topic could be kept before the public and a forum provided for the expression of Allison's views. During commencement week of 1887 Allison spoke before the six literary societies at Cornell College in Iowa and was rewarded with a gold-headed cane. The presiding officer felicitously remarked that they hoped the cane would in the near future help him up the steps of the White House. Allison, taken by surprise, replied haltingly: "I assure — I assure you, that like David Davis said in his letter — that would be something neither to be sought nor declined." [5] In June, 1887, the State University of Iowa sought out Iowa's leading political figures, Governor Larrabee and Senator Allison, to grace the occasion of the inauguration of a new president, Dr. Charles Ashmead Schaeffer.[6] In introducing Allison to the throng that packed the Iowa City Opera House, retiring President Josiah L. Pickard alluded to the possibility that the Senator might be "called to the Presidency of the United States." Allison replied, after the applause that greeted this statement, that "Dr. Pickard's most intimate friends knew that he would occasionally joke." [7]

Only the enthusiasm for "Allison for President" prevented a bad rift in the party's annual state convention in August, 1887, torn as it was by the bitter senatorial fight between Wilson, Hepburn, and Larrabee. On Allison's own advice, and Colonel Henderson's as well, the convention contented itself with going on record as being in favor of the party's interest alone; if this called for Allison for President, good; if not, Iowa Republicans would support the party's choice. [8]

Following the convention, Allison made an appearance at a reunion of the surviving members of Crocker's Brigade, practically the same thing as a Republican rally. The other speakers were Samuel J. Kirkwood, now nearing the end of his life, John H. Gear, and General William W. Belknap, who seems to have suffered no loss of prestige because of his impeachment and near conviction in 1876. [9] Allison's invitation to appear was a personal one from Colonel Addison Sanders, whom he had assisted in the hectic days of 1861 when recruitment was so great a problem. Sanders tried hard to create the impression that Allison was a bona fide veteran, entitled to all the honors of the occasion, [10] since status as a veteran was a political asset beyond price at that time.

The question that Clarkson had raised and that he hoped to have directly answered, concerning Blaine's availability, was the first question in the minds of everybody. Admittedly, Blaine was the most popular man in the party and a certain winner of the nomination if he would only give the word that he would accept. He had been narrowly defeated in 1884 in spite of the embarrassing disclosures of his business dealings. However vain, pompous, and erratically brilliant he may appear today, in 1888 Blaine was a god in the Republican Pantheon. It is hard to believe that Allison shared this idolatry of Blaine — he had been too close to the man since 1863 — but with Ret Clarkson leading the chorus he could not help but know of its existence.

Clarkson was unable to get a definite answer before Blaine departed for Europe. Evidently Blaine himself had not made up his mind. As late as October 11, 1887, he wrote from Paris, not very prophetically: ". . . although I think it probable that I could be nominated there will

be a contest, serious with Sherman and incidental and irritating with
Allison, Lincoln, possibly Harrison and some other favorite sons."
But in January, 1888, he wrote to a friend from Florence: "I am going
to withdraw my name from the list of candidates for the Republican
nomination. . . . Sherman is a determined candidate from Ohio,
Harrison will be equally so from Indiana, and Hawley will have the
delegation from Connecticut. Indiana and Connecticut are pivotal
states, and the candidate should not be one that they are unwilling to
. . . support." [11] He also sent a letter to the chairman of the Republican national committee, withdrawing his name.

Blaine, a hypochondriac, was depressed at the time of the second
letter by a cold caught on the train going to Italy.[12] But in 1888
voters were not concerned over his health or psychological reasons for
his attitude. Their only questions were: was he sincere in writing that
he would not compete again for the nomination; and, if so, to whom
would the Blaine blessing and the Blaine support go? [13] These questions were not to be definitely answered for many months to come.

Allison was only one of many seekers after the nomination. A
clever quip in the Chicago *Inter-Ocean* neatly illustrates the confusion. Asking "Who will it be?" the answer was arranged as follows:[14]

Gresham
AllisOn
Depew

CullOm
BlaiNe
ALger
JerrY Rusk

ForaKer
LincolN
HarrisOn
HaWley
Sherman

More seriously, it has been convincingly demonstrated that the contest of 1888 was the first Republican convention since 1860 that would
be truly free-for-all in nature.[15] In 1864 Lincoln's renomination was
never in doubt; in 1868 and 1872 Grant was the only logical choice;
in 1876 and 1880, James G. Blaine had been the man to beat; at
last, in 1884, he had won the coveted nomination only to lose the
election. Now, in 1888, there were at least four men to whom the

convention might give the nomination, assuming the unavailability of Blaine — Judge Walter Q. Gresham and General Benjamin Harrison of Indiana, John Sherman of Ohio, and William B. Allison of Iowa. There were others, but they can be dismissed as able men whose following was local or regional at best or dependent upon the exigencies of a deadlocked convention to bring them to the fore.

John Sherman of Mansfield, Ohio, was undoubtedly the front-running candidate. Since 1855 Sherman had been in the public eye as a member of Congress, first in the House (1855-1861) and then the Senate (1861-1877). In 1877 he became Secretary of the Treasury under President Hayes, and at the end of Hayes's term he returned to the Senate, where he stood next to Justin S. Morrill on the Finance Committee. As already indicated, his paths and Allison's had frequently run closely parallel. They were now friendly rivals, although there is no doubt that Sherman considered himself more deserving of the prize than Allison or anyone else in the race. A keen student of the period regards Sherman, Allison, and Shelby M. Cullom as "fence-sitters" — a peculiar product of the period of 1865-1900 when many politicians tried to maintain a balance between the older conservatism and the rising progressivism.[16] Sherman was definitely at the peak of his career at the age of sixty-five, six years older than Allison; this would probably be his last chance at the nomination.

General Benjamin Harrison of Indiana was the dark horse of the convention. In view of his limited experience it is difficult to account for his strength, and it is small wonder that many people discounted his chances well in advance. He had been moderately successful as a corporation lawyer and had had one colorless term in the Senate but had been denied a second by the Indiana legislature. His lineage and his title of "Brigadier General" were probably less valuable assets than his residence in the doubtful state of Indiana; the Hoosier preference for him over his rival, Walter Q. Gresham; and the astuteness of Louis T. Michener and W. W. Dudley, his campaign managers.[17]

Judge Walter Quintin Gresham had a name and a record that appealed to men of liberal spirit and to men favorable to one who ruggedly opposed his views to those of the "machine" — a man who truly would rather be right than President. He had risen to the rank of major general during the war and had been a federal district judge since 1869.[18] His cause had suffered at the hands of the Indiana Republican state convention, which favored Harrison; but this blow was partly offset by his strength in Illinois, where he was favored by Joseph Medill's *Tribune* and the Chicago *Inter-Ocean*. He also had general support among the rank and file of the Western states. James S. Clarkson reported that it was difficult to keep the state convention in Colorado from giving Gresham its endorsement; that he found Nebraska strongly inclined to Gresham; and that all Gresham people were strongly anti-Blaine.[19]

Against these formidable rivals, Allison had such assets as "safeness"; reliability as a party wheel horse; a general reputation as a Senator well versed in the intricacies of finance and the tariff; and the assumption that he could be trusted by both the East and the West. Close observers might have noted that he was from a state temporarily "doubtful" due to the growth of agrarian unrest. Possible liabilities were the activities in railroad promotion that had led to his link with the Crédit Mobilier affair; the fear that he might be subject to the pressures of agrarian radicalism; and the fact that he had not been a soldier. His moderate views on the tariff were an asset or a liability, according to one's views. In short, it must be remembered that this is the story of 1888, when memories of the war, of railroad politics, of the tariff debates of 1870, of the fight for silver in 1877-1878, and of Iowa's pre-eminence in railroad regulation were still green; Allison would profit or suffer according to the views of politicians on these subjects.

Perhaps as judicious a summary as could be found in the current literature of 1888 was the appraisal of Allison given in *Harper's Weekly* of March 17, 1888. This dignified and sometimes pontifical journal, edited by the reformer George William Curtis, began a series of articles on Republican presidential possibilities with this issue, leading off with Allison. The cover drawing was an excellent likeness that caught something of Allison's rugged physical strength at the peak of his career. The essay praised his freedom from the passions of the moment, his industry, and his knowledge of all legislative matters, especially fiscal problems. "Men like him are oftener found in the British Parliament. . . . He is as familiar with his work as a British undersecretary would be." Such things as financial deficiency and urgency bills would be unknown, said the article, if the Appropriations Committee had heeded Allison's pleas for systematic appropriations. The concluding statement was surely a pleasing compliment: "His fortune is ample, his tastes are refined, and those who know him best like him most."

If a fifth name were to be added to this quartet, it would surely be that of Chauncey Depew of New York. Such was the opinion of former President Rutherford B. Hayes, who wrote in his diary on June 22, 1888: "I am interested in the success of Sherman at Chicago. A noble President he would make. It is probable he would prove also available as a candidate because he is the fittest. The other names are good men. Harrison, Depew, Allison especially." [20] In a wide-open convention each favorite son has a certain importance as a trader, and of these Depew was by far the most important. As one of Allison's friends expressed it: "It looks to me now very probable that Mr. Depew will be the *expediency* man of our party because of alleged ability to carry New York but I should fear the effect of his being identified with the R. R. interests more especially with the Western voters." [21] But any man able to command New York's seventy-two votes plus others scattered here and there was not to be ignored. And this Depew could do, as he proved on the first ballot.

One of the most cheering letters received by Allison came from that highly intellectual man of honor who was the editor of the Keokuk *Gate City*, Sam M. Clark. Now president of the Iowa Press Association, which was virtually a club of Republican editors, Clark was in a position to wield great influence in the state. He assured Allison as early as January, 1888, that the time had passed when Iowa's delegation should go to the convention bound and consigned to Blaine. He then proceeded to dispose of the argument that Iowa was a "safe" state and that therefore no Iowan was available. Taking his theme from a statement by Governor Dennison of Ohio that Iowa was a "nursery" state like Virginia and Ohio, he argued that Iowa had great influence with the younger states to the West because so many Iowa men had gone to them. An Iowan who could carry their votes would be a distinct asset to the party. Therefore Iowa's delegation should go to the convention for Allison, as the Illinois delegation had gone in 1860 for Lincoln, with every intention of fighting for victory. [22]

This letter, so full of cheer and determination, was soon offset by disturbing news from Des Moines. Here Governor Larrabee's biennial message of January 10 and his inaugural address two days later had just sounded a declaration of war against the railroads. [23] Larrabee's specific legislative proposals called for the fixing of maximum freight and passenger rates and for control of such rates by the Board of Railroad Commissioners. The tenor of his remarks in his inaugural, in which he reviewed the history of railroad legislation in Iowa and the railroad efforts to block enforcement, was strongly provocative to nearly everyone who had a direct interest in railroads. There has been much speculation as to why this man of property, a faithful party regular since his first election to the Iowa senate in 1867, and the choice of the Allisonians for Governor in 1881 and again in 1885 and 1887, had gone "off the reservation." The simple fact is that Allison's candidacy happened to coincide with a growing demand for railroad regulation, as was clearly set forth in both the Republican and Democratic platforms in Iowa in 1887.[24] The question was bigger than either Larrabee or Allison. The people — the masses of the voters — were not thinking of Allison's presidential possibilities when they voiced their complaints of many years' standing and demanded more effective regulation of the railroads. Nor is it fair to make Larrabee the villain of the piece. A modern observer is more likely to be impressed with the reasonableness of Larrabee's statements than with their extremeness.[25] Contemporary reaction was immediate. The Des Moines *Register* commented caustically: "The whole color and tone of the message . . . are intense and exceedingly radical, and show more than public feeling and suggest a sense of personal animosity, based on fancied personal grievances." [26]

Ret's private remarks in a letter to Allison were even more vehement:

Governor Larrabee's biennial message was bad enough, but his inaugural . . . is absolutely unaccountable. Weaver and his demogoguism [*sic*] has never equalled this. It is bound to hurt the party very much. . . . He cares nothing for the party, and says . . . he will never be a candidate again, and seemingly does not care what may happen to others or the party. His conduct as compared with his long record as Senator, is unfathomable. I very much regret it, and sincere long friendship for him makes it as much to be regretted as anything else. . . . This will alienate many friends.[27]

Charles E. Perkins seconded this with an even stronger denunciation of Larrabee:

The situation in Iowa looks to me pretty threatening, and something ought to be done to hold Larrabee and his followers — Cant you come out here and make the Jackasses see the harm they will do if they carry out Larrabee's insane notions — Rates are so low now that Railroad property is in serious danger and the State will be greatly damaged.[28]

Perkins was not on sound ground here, because the roads had been forced to admit that their profits had been greater under the rates used since regulation began. His basic position was that government regulation simply would not work.

A month later (February 17) Perkins renewed his condemnation of the legislature and Governor Larrabee for interference with the railroads. He regretted that a Senate committee had reported favorably on two bills, one for an elective Railroad Commission of five and one requiring the Commissioners to fix freight rates. Of more direct concern to Allison were these two sentences: "Blaine's letter about the Presidency has it seems to me largely helped your chances if Iowa does not frighten the East by some extreme Granger legislation. I believe nothing but political consideration will hold them out there now and you and Henderson and others in Washington from Iowa are the only ones who can have any influence." He closed with the supposition that Jacob Rich was on the ground as a railroad lobbyist in Des Moines and the belief that the party might be spared "from blindly following so blinded a leader as Larrabee." [29]

Such fulminations from Perkins were of no avail. It seems never to have occurred to him that he could be wrong and Larrabee right in this matter. The philosophy that the railroads could be regulated in the public interest had apparently made no impression on him. At any rate, Larrabee and the legislature went right on with their reforming efforts, and if Allison and Henderson exerted any influence from Washington it is not on record, other than a claim that Allison's friends helped to "check" the tendency toward "wild legislation." [30] Allison could no more have controlled the Iowa legislature against the expressed wishes of the people of Iowa in 1888 than could Canute have restrained the waves. As admitted by Dr. Charles Beardsley of Burlington, Republican state chairman, there was a strong antirailroad feeling in both houses of the General Assembly. [31]

The Iowa state Republican convention, meeting in Des Moines on March 21, drew a larger attendance than usual, in spite of a blizzard in the extreme northern counties that made travel difficult. Hundreds of the men with whom Allison had been associated over the years since he came to the state in 1857, joined by others whose associations had been briefer and less intimate, met in Des Moines and paid him the supreme tribute of endorsement for the presidential nomination by the national convention scheduled to meet in Chicago in June.

Under the magic of the oratory of young Jonathan Prentiss Dolliver, the West Virginia circuit rider's son who was now a rising lawyer in Fort Dodge and whose oratorical gifts had been discovered by C. C. Carpenter and James S. Clarkson,[32] the delegates were brought to a frenzy of enthusiasm. If Allison had been present he would surely have found it difficult to suppress his emotions.

A month earlier Jonathan Dolliver had written three long pages to Allison, pledging his support and devotion, a pledge which he was to honor to the end of Allison's life. At the convention he let himself go in an orgy of flag-waving, appeals to the memory of Lincoln, denunciation of the Democracy, and glorification of Republicanism, all delivered in a style combining the zeal of an old-fashioned Methodist "spouter" with the polish of a trained rhetorician. The man was a genius at this business, and his role as keynoter for practically every state convention from 1884 until 1910 is proof of his ability to carry a political audience with him.[33]

A lively contest ensued for places on the delegation, in spite of the spirit of enthusiasm and unanimity that had been created. The chief troublemakers were Governor Larrabee and Colonel Hepburn, those very men who a few months earlier had challenged Allison's wishes in the senatorial matter and now were fighting for prominent places in the delegation of Allison boosters to be sent to the Chicago convention. Larrabee was beaten for delegate-at-large by Colonel D. B. Henderson, but Hepburn won a place on the delegation from the Eighth District. The other delegates-at-large besides Henderson were Dolliver, Clarkson, and George D. Perkins, the editor of the Sioux City *Journal*, who had been so staunch for Harlan in 1872. The only district delegate of note besides Hepburn was James F. Wilson. Rich reported to Allison that the delegation was "not all that he had desired — quite a few mediocre men got in." [34]

Allison could count himself fortunate in the managers who served him in his campaign for the nomination. It is doubtful if official appointments were ever made — rather, James S. Clarkson was by common consent of all concerned the active, full-time manager, with Colonel Henderson a close second in authority, and Jacob Rich the third man in the triumvirate. All three men worked in complete harmony and mutual trust. Nor should General Grenville M. Dodge's help be forgotten. Since 1872 Dodge had been content to let Allison run his own team, but his advice was always welcome because of his role as Allison's sponsor in 1870 and 1872 and also because of his financial support. These men were not neophytes. Clarkson was Iowa's member on the Republican national committee and had friends throughout the country with whom he carried on an immense correspondence on behalf of Allison. He also made numerous trips through the West and South in the interests of his candidate.

Shortly after the Iowa state convention Clarkson, who was in Washington at the time, came down with a sudden illness in which he narrowly missed "snapping a blood vessel of the brain" and was ordered by his doctor to lay off work for a year, an order that he refused to carry out. He reported to Dolliver: "The outlook for Allison, from this standpoint, is more than good. It is generally conceded that the nominee will be Blaine or Allison." [35]

In many ways there were points of contact between the Harrison and the Allison campaigns. There were straws in the wind indicating that the Harrison strength might have gone to Allison in case of its own lack of success; but there was little to indicate that the Sherman forces felt that way about Allison. What can be stated more positively is that the Blaine men preferred Harrison as a vicarious choice. The spokesman for this point of view was Senator Stephen B. Elkins of West Virginia, and there is proof that Clarkson knew of such an understanding well before the convention opened. [36] To say this is not, however, to argue that Clarkson was insincere in his promotion of the Allison candidacy. In a race such as the one in 1888, anything might happen. The wise thing to do was to work for one's own candidate as long as there seemed to be any chance of victory; if that appeared impossible of attainment, one switched to the man who constituted the second choice.

Questions about the sincerity of Blaine's self-denying letters and the identity of his heir would not cease. The Chicago *Inter-Ocean*, for example, ran a lengthy feature article in February, made up of these questions and its own answers and also those of many others, including Allison himself, Clarkson, Jacob Rich, and Governor Larrabee. [37] The paper thought that both Allison and Sherman were in a position to profit from Blaine's decision, each man having a number of virtues that appealed to the voters, but it leaned strongly toward Allison as the candidate to be preferred for two reasons: Iowa was a more doubtful state than Ohio; and Allison was more of a revisionist on the tariff question than Sherman, therefore more appealing to the farmers of his state. The unexpressed inference was that Allison would make more of an appeal throughout the whole agricultural West.

The paper quoted Allison and Clarkson as believing firmly in Blaine's sincerity. Clarkson said that Blaine was "all *for the party* in 1888" and that Iowa, which had supported him in three successive national conventions "believes in him now more than ever, now that he is out of the field." Clarkson apparently was so much interested in defending the sincerity of his hero that he omitted an opinion as to the probable heir of Blaine's strength. Of course he would have named Allison, if pressed on this point. Larrabee, Rich, and other Iowans spoke strongly in favor of Allison. Congressman Nelson Dingley of far-off Maine said that Blaine had not committed himself to any second choice, "but he had said that Allison was the most available," but did not say when or where Blaine had made such a statement.

Every such comment favorable and encouraging to Allison could be matched by one received by Harrison or Sherman. Certainly Harrison was not without strong support. A letter from Blaine to Elkins, probably received in January, 1888, named Harrison as the most eligible candidate.[38] Such news was undoubtedly passed along to the right parties. A letter which listed a number of Harrison's advantages came from James M. Tyner of Brookville, Indiana, a strong leader and spokesman for a large segment of the party. "I can think of no one so likely to inherit Blaine's strength as you and Allison, and your chances are the better in two respects — your public record is not so long as his, nor are there chapters in it that might be revived (such as supposed warm friendship for Pacific Railroad capitalists, etc.), and you were a soldier. Other things being equal the soldier record is an important element." [39]

Another example of good news passed on to Harrison was a letter from Elkins to Louis T. Michener, Harrison's astute manager. Elkins believed that Harrison's residence in Indiana, a doubtful state, gave him a real advantage over Allison, Sherman, Cullom of Illinois, and General Alger of Michigan, all of whom came from certain states. This was a rather arbitrary opinion of these states in view of the temper of the times, but it was the traditional view of Iowa's politics in the light of her record since 1854. Elkins admitted that the trend toward Blaine was increasing, but that if he were not nominated, "Harrison is bound to be and it is the wisest and safest thing to do." [40]

Harrison received even more encouragement from Elkins in a letter written from New York on May 2: "Things look fairly well in the East. I have seen and talked with a great many leading Republicans on the situation. . . . Clarkson of Iowa (Allison's friend) has been here for a week. He goes home a wiser man as to the situation. I told him I thought Harrison and Allison ought to make an alliance — he agreed with me." [41] This letter has cryptic overtones, but when coupled with another of later date, all doubts are removed. Years later Clarkson wrote to Michener, reviewing the events of 1888. "Yes," he wrote, "I remember the conference you and I had in New York in 1888, a few weeks before the Repn Natl Convention of that year, and when we practically reached an understanding that my second choice would be Harrison and that your second choice would be Allison, although we made no positive agreement; but I always felt that after that if we could not nominate Allison we would be for Harrison." [42]

Corroboration of the potential tie-in between the Harrison and Allison forces is given in a letter to Russell Harrison, the candidate's son, from R. C. Kerens, an influential national committeeman from Missouri:

Depew is constant and persistent for Blaine to be nominated. . . . While I was in New York we had a big conference with some of the old time workers and I can say to you confidentially that we decided so far as we were concerned that there were but two men to be considered, that is Harrison & Allison. Clarkson was present . . . and of course was urging Allison. This was leaving Blaine out entirely. Still I feel that when the Convention assembles the delegation from New York will likely demand the Blaine nomination. Elkins and I shall work together in the matter and *you know what our desires are.*[43]

Clarkson revealed his deference to Elkins in a letter to Henderson from New York, virtually summoning Henderson there at Elkins' request, a summons that the doughty colonel rejected by finding an excuse in the pressure of business in Washington.[44] It is not quite fair to Clarkson to impute that he was disloyal to Allison when he "conferred" with the enemy Elkins. Clarkson had never made a secret of his loyalty to Blaine and of his love for Indiana, his native state. But nothing has been found to throw any doubt on Clarkson's zeal as long as Allison had a fighting chance to attain the nomination.[45]

The city of Chicago had made elaborate provisions for the convention. Sensing the widespread complaints about the inadequate facilities and the poor acoustics of its old Exposition Hall, Chicago had arranged for the convention to use its still incomplete Civic Auditorium, which had the advantages of better visibility, much better acoustical qualities, and — something so new that it aroused the awe-struck admiration of at least one journalist — artificial lighting of the building by several thousand electric lights. "No daylight enters the hall" was his proud discovery (deponent sayeth nothing as to how the building was ventilated). The structure was oblong in form, with the stage in the center, and seats for the delegates and their alternates on the main floor. There were three great galleries and spacious boxes for the observers.

The Allison headquarters, along with those of all the principal candidates, were located in the Grand Pacific Hotel, another building that excited the admiration of the Iowa correspondent. Sleeping quarters were available for 1,500 people; 3,000 could be fed in one day; its halls and parlors could hold 8,000. The Sherman and Gresham headquarters were on the first floor; those of Allison, Harrison, Depew, and others were on the corridor of the second floor, Allison's being the spacious corner room that had been used by Blaine in 1884. In charge of hospitality in the Allison rooms was Sidney A. Foster, a prominent insurance company official of Des Moines. The candidates, as was traditional, did not attend the convention but kept in touch with developments by telegraph.

Estimates of the number of Iowans in Chicago, brought there mainly by the desire to boost Allison's cause, ran up to 3,000. They even included many Democrats from Dubuque who were enthusiastically wearing Allison buttons and talking up his merits. On the night of June 19 an Allison parade of 1,200 men, attired in the Allison uniform of blue Middlesex flannel suits and high brown hats, formed at the Grand Pacific and toured the district that contained the other leading hotels such as the Palmer House and the Tremont. Four hundred members of the Allison Club of Dubuque, 200 from the Corn Palace Club of Sioux City, and 200 from the Des Moines Club made up the principal contingents, with brass bands from Dubuque, Sioux City, and Decorah marking the cadence.

The pre-convention arrangements at the Auditorium were in the hands of a subcommittee headed by James S. Clarkson, a fact that rather automatically assured that good care would be taken of the Iowa crowd. Clarkson delegated the Iowa assignment to a Grinnell manufacturer and capitalist, George M. Christian, who procured a life-sized crayon drawing of the Senator for display in the Iowa sector and had medallions struck which set forth a front view of Allison's face. Certainly nothing had been left undone in the effort to make Chicago aware of Iowa's pride in her favorite son.[46]

Numbered among the unofficial visitors and observers were several people with a special interest in Allison's success. Former Governor Kirkwood and his wife were there, thanks to the intercession of an Iowa City friend who called Allison's attention to the old man's desire to witness the proceedings and his claims on Allison's gratitude; [47] the Senator's nephew, William Boyd Allison, Jr., son of his brother Harrison, a student at Grinnell College; [48] three granddaughters of Joseph Medill, daughters of Robert W. Patterson, who regretted very much that the Chicago *Tribune* was supporting Judge Gresham instead of Allison; [49] Miss Nina L. Gillett, member of a socially prominent family in Illinois; [50] Mrs. James S. Clarkson and Mrs. David B. Henderson, sincere admirers of Allison and keen observers of their husbands' strategic moves on the convention floor; and Mrs. Annette Hicks-Lord, a feather-brained but vastly wealthy widow whose efforts at engaging in politics were tolerated by Allison and Clarkson, it is feared, only because of the financial contributions she could make to the Allison campaign fund.[51]

Iowa journalists did their part in trying to keep up the hopes of Iowans that Allison had a good chance for the nomination. Ret Clarkson served as chief correspondent of the Des Moines *Register* as well as Allison's manager; Jacob Rich was the source of news for the Dubuque *Times*; the Council Bluffs *Nonpareil*, generally amenable to General Dodge, supplied southwestern Iowa with a favorable version; and the Fairfield *Ledger*, a James F. Wilson organ, was the best Allison booster in the southeast, along with the Keokuk *Gate City* under the erudite Sam M. Clark.

The *Register* kept up a running fire of comment stressing Allison's hold on the second choice position in many delegations and their readiness to vote for him as soon as they had paid their compliments to their favorite sons. The *Nonpareil* echoed this sentiment and prophesied that the real contest would be between Allison and Governor Russell A. Alger of Michigan. A few days later the *Nonpareil* joined those who held Iowa to be a "safe" state, noting Allison's handicap in coming from a state that could be counted on for a Republican majority of 30,000. Many papers carried a brief Allison biography which was prepared by a New York *Herald* writer on the basis of quick interviews secured in Dubuque. Even Allison's brother Masons tried to help by electing him to honorary membership in the Grand Lodge of Iowa.[52]

A short time before the convention met, railroad men held their annual meeting at Chicago. There they received word of the schedule of rates drawn up by the Iowa Railroad Commissioners. The Iowa legislature, in spite of the editorials by Ret Clarkson and the lobbying of Jacob Rich, had passed a bill providing for a stronger Railroad Commission with power to set maximum freight rates, to forbid rebates, pooling agreements, and other special arrangements for certain shippers, and to require the posting of rates. An additional bill had changed the Board of Railroad Commissioners from appointive to elective, and from railroad-supported to state-supported.[53] The rail leaders meeting in Chicago were given information on the schedule of rates before it was made public. Clarkson saw a good deal of them and knew and reported to Allison their true thoughts. "I never saw so angry a lot of men," was his pronouncement on their reaction to the new schedule. All of them, including Clarkson, who should have known better, tended to blame Larrabee. Strangely enough, some of them, most notably John I. Blair of the North Western, also blamed Allison and threatened to take revenge on him, calling him a Granger and promising to throw all their power against him in the convention. These men could not understand that Allison and Rich and other former lieutenants of General Grenville M. Dodge could no longer dictate the actions of the Iowa legislature in the face of a rising tide of popular opinion. Clarkson, aided by Thomas Withrow, Marvin Hughitt, and other Westerners, tried to counteract the Easterners' tendency to blame Allison, warning them, without much success, that it would be "madness & suicide" to fight "the very people" who stood for fair play for the roads.[54]

At the same time, unknown to Allison, Charles E. Perkins wrote to his father-in-law, John Murray Forbes, the great Boston capitalist and dominant stockholder in the Burlington road, asking him if he would support Allison if nominated, calling Allison the "safest" man on the list of prospects, but suggesting that if Forbes's answer were in the negative, he should announce that it was because he could not support any man from a state that was "confiscating property" as the Iowa Railroad Commissioners were doing.[55] Thus relentlessly did Perkins insist on the pursuit of Larrabee and all others who were carrying out the wishes of the majority of the people of Iowa.

The convention opened on Wednesday, June 20, with John M. Thurston, a Union Pacific attorney, as temporary chairman and keynote speaker; and with California's Morris M. Estee, leader of a diehard Blaine element, as the permanent chairman. The nominating speeches ran true to form. Sherman was put forward by General D. H. Hastings of Pennsylvania and seconded by one of the greatest of the wavers of the bloody shirt, Joseph B. Foraker of Ohio. Harrison's name was put up by Albert G. Porter; Gresham's by Leonard Swett; and so on around the circle. For reasons not altogether clear, Colonel William P. Hepburn made the principal nominating speech for Allison. Hepburn was an able man and a better than average speaker, but still one wonders at his selection, especially with the magnetic Dolliver available. Possibly Hepburn's wider national acquaintance may have been the explanation. Only recently Hepburn had opposed Allison's man, Wilson, for the Senate, and many bitter things had been said; now his words of praise sounded hypocritical to those who knew of that campaign. Allison had been warned specifically against his treachery,[56] but still he invited him to do the honors. Perhaps it was a gesture of peace.

The Chicago *Inter-Ocean* gave elaborate critiques of each orator's nominating speech but had little that was good to say about Hepburn's efforts. He spoke too long; "an eloquent speech became tedious from iteration and prolixity." His gestures were awkward, and he had to look at his manuscript too closely. The seconding speech was made by a total stranger to national politics, Benjamin M. Bosworth, an obscure Rhode Islander, "young, handsome, well dressed, slow and deliberate of speech. . . . He had the commencement-day oratory." [57] Was his selection a bid to the powerful Rhode Island leader, Nelson W. Aldrich, a rising force in the Senate? Certainly it is inconceivable that Bosworth would have acted contrary to the wishes of Aldrich, whose biographer asserts that his support for Allison was purely complimentary in the early stages of the convention while waiting for the swing to Harrison to develop.[58]

At last, at 11:30 on Friday morning, the balloting began, with the general understanding that several tests of strength would be required before a definite trend could be established. The first ballot produced this result:

John Sherman	229
Walter Q. Gresham	107
Chauncey Depew	99
Benjamin Harrison	85
Russell A. Alger	84
William B. Allison	72
James G. Blaine	35

A few scattered votes for minor figures completed the total of 830 votes cast. The minimum necessary to win the nomination would be 416. Allison's 72 votes included the solid Iowa block of 26, plus 8 from Rhode Island and 7 from Texas; the remaining 31 came in driblets of one to three from sixteen widely scattered sources. Louisiana, Missouri, Nebraska, Nevada, and Virginia gave him three each; Maine, Maryland, Massachusetts, Utah, and Wyoming, two each; Dakota, Idaho, Montana, and Washington territories, Colorado, and Tennessee, one each.[59] Thus nineteen states or territories contributed to his total, but there were no great possibilities of increase here; only Massachusetts had a sizable block of votes. John Sherman had almost a monopoly of the hand-picked delegations from the South. Either Allison's managers had fumbled or else the drawing power simply was not there. Harrison's vote, while only thirteen more than Allison's on this first ballot, was much better distributed.

The second and third ballots saw some shifting, and Allison's vote grew slightly to 88, Sherman's rose to 244, and Harrison's to 94. After the first three ballots on Friday, the convention recessed until evening. No ballots were taken at the night session; the main feature was the withdrawal of Chauncey Depew. Admitting his inability to command the Western votes needed for victory because of his position as president of the New York Central Railroad, he withdrew in the party interest.[60]

It was during the Friday recess that the conference took place at which victory was placed in Allison's hands, only to be snatched away by the vengeful Depew. There are several versions of the story: the most familiar is the one made public in 1899 by the venerable Senator George Frisbie Hoar of Massachusetts and published in Scribner's Magazine and later repeated in his Autobiography of Seventy Years.[61] Senator Hoar tells the story of a meeting of delegates from Massachusetts, New York, Wisconsin, Illinois, Iowa, California, and Missouri, at which they agreed to vote for Allison, the New York delegates qualifying their promise by saying that it was subject to the approval of their leader, Chauncey Depew. When informed of this conference and asked for his approval, Depew haughtily refused to go along with the plan. Having been forced to withdraw his own name by reason of objections from the Western states, where railroads were under attack, Depew refused to "submit to such an unreasonable and social-istic sentiment" and permit that region to name the party's candidate. Thus the plan to switch to Allison on the fourth ballot fell through. "I think no other person ever came so near the Presidency of the United States, and missed it," commented Hoar.

The same story in essence appeared in the friendly-to-Allison Chicago *Tribune* of Saturday morning, June 23, thus indicating that the conference and its results were in no way secret. A condensed ac-count appeared in Clarkson's *Register* on Sunday, June 24. The *Tribune* article was outspoken in its designation of Depew as the villain in the story. The paper further attributed Depew's action to his pique over the deflation of his own boom and asserted that Iowa delegates had let it be known that the nomination of Depew would make Iowa a doubtful state.[62]

Direct testimony on the incident from Depew himself was not given until thirty-four years later. In his memoirs, published in 1922, he had not mentioned the decisive conference.[63] Cyrenus Cole, the well-known Iowa editor-politician-historian, wrote to Depew saying that he had heard that the real reason for his veto of Allison was the offensive nature of some remarks by Colonel Henderson, who, as Cole tried to put it delicately, "liked to take a drink of Scotch." He asked for Depew's own version of New York's switch to Harrison.

Depew answered cordially and at some length, emphasizing several points. He acknowledged that it was the Iowa delegation's hostility, to which other Western states contributed, that had led to his with-drawal from the race. His own delegation responded by giving the disposition of their full vote to the four delegates-at-large: Depew, Thomas C. Platt, Warner Miller, and Frank Hiscock. John Sherman was absolutely unacceptable to Platt but just as strongly preferred by Warner Miller. Platt's second choice was Allison. In this impasse, Frank Hiscock, the fourth man, deferred to Depew to make known his choice. Depew said that he then explained that "Allison's friends" had been "most unfair and bitter" in attacking him, that New York as a "capitalistic state" could not be carried even by Senator Allison because of Iowa's antirailroad legislation. Depew's own candidate was General Harrison because of his war record, his family name, and his lack of corporate associations. He closed with a brief but misleading paragraph indicating that his designation of Harrison led to an immediate action in which Pennsylvania and other great states followed New York into the Harrison column and victory.[64]

The question as to whether his feelings had been antagonized by the exaggerated remarks of a drunken Iowa delegate was neatly sidestepped by Depew. That rumor was a persistent one, however, and is met more than once in the history of this incident. If true, however, it would have been only a tiny factor in a great struggle which had gone far beyond personalities. Even so, it is one of the ironies of this chapter in Allison's life that his cause was being hurt to some extent by the necessary political course of one friend, Larrabee, whose place as Governor had been made possible by the support of the Allison faction, and by a trivial story involving another friend, Colonel Henderson, whose devotion to Allison was unsurpassed.

On the night of Friday, June 22 — "Black Friday" Allison might have called it later had he been inclined to moroseness — the Allison cause might be described as "damaged but not ruined." His managers could fall back on the copybook maxim, "while there is life there is hope," but one can easily believe that they were a glum lot. A telegram from Clarkson to Allison in Washington shows that he was fully aware of developments. "New York has just decided to go to Harrison. We are going to fight for immediate adjournment." [65]

On Saturday the convention held a brief session, took the fourth and fifth ballots with little change in the totals, and then adjourned until Monday morning. One Iowa correspondent reported that this move would be in Allison's favor if taken,[66] but another was nearer the truth when he wrote:

The members of the Allison brigade are returning to their homes . . . and some . . . say that it is conceded by all of them that there is no show for Allison. They took away the magnificent large crayon portrait of the Senator last night. Much interest is manifested here [Cedar Rapids] over the probable outcome. Fully four-fifths of the Republicans of this city and vicinity are for Gresham, and the old soldiers, of whom there are fifteen hundred in this county, are anxious that a soldier shall be nominated.[67]

The Des Moines *Register* had a number of convention stories in its Sunday issue, but the principal one declared that the "experts" had counted out Sherman, Gresham, Alger, and Harrison, that there was much speculation on Allison for Monday. The Depew boycott of Allison might well boomerang on the New Yorker, according to the *Register*, because many "resented" this effort to punish the Granger states, although some were of the opinion that Depew's action had effectively disposed of the nomination. The Council Bluffs *Nonpareil* of Sunday reported that Gresham had lost out and the fight now seemed to be between Allison and Harrison. Senator Cameron of Pennsylvania had persuaded Senator Matthew S. Quay to support Allison, but New York was leaning toward Harrison. McKinley was now the dark horse.[68]

While Allison and Sherman were sweating it out in Washington, Harrison was undoubtedly having his own anxious moments in Indianapolis. There were the embarrassing importunities of Thomas Collier Platt for the Treasury Department, the slightly depressing effect of a declining vote from 217 on the fourth ballot to 213 on the fifth, and the sure knowledge that if ever selected he would be beholden to Elkins and the Blaine crowd, whose strength was greater than the 32 to 46 votes they had so far cast. On Saturday came an offer from a prominent New York newspaper publisher and politician, Elliott F. Shepard, to unite with Alger and Sherman in support of Depew. Depew could surely then be elected, he thought, and Harrison, Alger, and Sherman could "have the government" to themselves.[69]

The Shepard telegram was probably ignored or passed on to Harrison's managers for acknowledgement. One very important negotiation had to be handled by Harrison personally, however. This was carried on in a meeting at Indianapolis. The story is a roundabout one. On Saturday night Senator Aldrich, Nicholas Murray Butler of Columbia University, and other pro-Harrison men met to try to win over certain uncommitted delegates. The Harrison strength was already shored up by a block of one hundred Negro delegates' votes that had been bought at fifty dollars per head, by way of General Alger who first owned them. Other wavering delegates were almost ready to come to Harrison, but they wanted positive answers to certain questions, answers which only Harrison himself could give. Consequently an envoy was sent off to Indianapolis for a personal interview. Not until morning church services had been properly attended would Harrison permit his Calvinist meditations to be disturbed by the vulgarities of politics. The questions and answers are not on record, but it took no seventh son of a prophet to sense a change for the better for Harrison when the convention resumed its sessions on Monday morning.[70]

Another trip, not so well publicized in later days, undoubtedly had some effect on the result. The envoy in this case was self-appointed — Wharton Barker of Philadelphia, publisher and essayist on public questions, particularly finance, and a strong Harrison backer since 1883. Having been convinced by Senator Elkins that the nomination of Blaine on the following Monday was inevitable unless both Harrison and Sherman remained in the field to hold their respective votes, Barker first wired Sherman an entreaty to stay by his guns until he could talk to him, then made the trip from Chicago to Washington to add his personal persuasions. "I think you will consider my work at Washington so necessary that you will approve my going from Chicago," was his boastful report to Harrison.[71] According to one student of these proceedings, Barker persuaded Sherman, and later Allison, to agree that any candidate showing a decided gain on the first ballot on Monday would get full help from the one who showed a loss.[72] This same student points out that Colonel Henderson was afraid to tell Clarkson of this arrangement, knowing that Clarkson would be opposed to it.[73] One cannot condemn too harshly this act of deception which kept Clarkson in the dark.

The Monday session was dramatically opened by the reading of a cablegram from Blaine, asking his friends to respect his wishes and "refrain from voting" for him.[74] Andrew Carnegie, in Europe with Blaine, wired a confirmation: "Too late. Blaine immovable. Take Harrison and Phelps." [75] Blaine's act of self-denial, however motivated, was his last effective move in presidential politics.

When the convention proceeded to the first ballot of the day, the sixth of the convention, Allison's vote came to 73; on the next, it rose slightly to 76. Conversely, Harrison's had grown to 231 and 278, respectively, and Sherman's had dropped from 244 to 231. Allison and Sherman — the two friends at the end of the telegraph wire in Washington — now fought a little battle of their own.

Sherman, obviously, could not win. He could throw his votes to Allison or to Harrison, as the Wharton Barker plan would have required, or he could stand fast and let matters seek their own course.

The "stand-fast" policy was his choice, even if it meant Harrison's victory, and it cannot be interpreted other than an indication that Sherman preferred Harrison to Allison.[76]

But this coin had two sides. Allison too had some choices. His seventy-odd votes were not enough by themselves to give the victory to either Sherman or Harrison, but they might start a break for their recipient. Thus it was that Allison in defeat really won the privilege of naming the next President. The decision was not made by Allison himself, but by his managers, Clarkson and Henderson. The latter acted as the messenger and spokesman; a superficial observer might have thought him to be the leader.[77]

Beyond doubt, however, the active lead had been taken by Ret Clarkson. Ret's loyalties ran in this order: James G. Blaine, William B. Allison, and Benjamin Harrison — Blaine, Iowa, Indiana. Blaine had taken himself out of the contest; Allison had had his "run" and had lost; now the contest was between Harrison and Sherman. Confronted with these choices, there was no contest in Clarkson's mind.

It still remains to be seen how Ret engineered the shift to Harrison and put him across. The best possible description would be one by Ret himself, a newspaperman of the old school and a fascinating letter-writer. Fortunately, such a personal document is available. Here, in a long, reminiscent letter written in 1915 to Louis T. Michener, is Clarkson's own move-by-move account of his shift to Harrison and the strategy employed by him to give Harrison the victory. Recalling their New York meeting in the spring, a meeting that saved the final day for Harrison, Clarkson wrote:

. . . I always felt that after [that meeting] if we could not nominate Allison I would be with you for Harrison. . . . For, with my liking for you and other Hoosiers, and my father's desire to have me support Harrison . . . [I] kept the way open for that. . . . On Monday, Senator Hoar, of Massachusetts came to me and said "I think it is time some one gave way for the good of the party." I said I thought so too, and that I had a letter in my pocket from Allison authorizing me to withdraw his name whenever I thought it should be done, but that I would not do that unless we could get a majority of delegates pledged to some one before we made the new move. He asked me who I thought was the best man to unite upon, and I told him Harrison, and went on to tell why I thought so, and told him how much I believed you and Dudley and other Hoosiers had told me of Harrison that I believed, and then referred to my father's friendship for the Harrisons, and spoke of how my father had gone on horseback from Brookville over the Alleghenies to Harrisburg, Pa. in 1839 to help nominate the elder Harrison for 1840, and he exclaimed, "Why my father was a member of that Convention too, and if the Harrisons were good enough for the elder Clarksons and Hoars they were certainly good enough for the later ones." So we finally agreed — although the Senator at first was pretty strongly inclined to Sherman, as they were kinsmen in some degree, and Sherman was very strong in New England, but we finally agreed we would go together. Then I said "if you will canvass the Eastern delegations I will canvass the Western ones, and if we get a majority of votes pledged I will withdraw Allison's name at the close of the next ballot, and announce that Iowa was going to support Harrison." We made the canvass and after that and after consulting you and Dudley and finding how many votes you had pledged, found we had a majority for Harrison, and then proceeded to carry out our programme. My effective plea with the other delegates was that if we could get a majority of the delegates to go with us, Iowa would withdraw Allison and cast its vote for Harrison. As I was going back to my seat with the Iowa delegation Senator Quay, who had seen us at work among the delegations over-took me and asked, "What are you and old man Hoar up to?" I told him, and he said it was impossible, and that we hadn't had time to get such an agreement with so many men. I told him that we had, and added, "We have 18 votes pledged from your own State, headed by Oliver, and you had better get on the wagon." But he wouldn't and stuck to Sherman.[78]

All this evidence would certainly seem to clear the air of any suspicion of treason on Clarkson's part. It lay in his power to make the decision as to Allison's ability to go forward or backward after the seventh ballot. It was a fearful responsibility, but it is obvious that Henderson, Dolliver, and the others accepted his decision as correct. There was no revolution within the Iowa delegation. Allison had given Clarkson authority to withdraw his name whenever he saw fit. Nothing has been discovered to indicate that Allison had a preference as between Harrison and Sherman or that he tried in any way to steer Clarkson's choice. Clarkson chose Harrison instead of Sherman or Gresham. At least he had the later consolation of knowing that he had picked a man who could win, a man who would divide the party less than Sherman.

Letters poured in from Allison's friends and supporters expressing their grief over his defeat; practically all those written by "insiders" at the convention blamed his rejection on Chauncey Depew. Not a one has been found who blamed or censored Clarkson and Henderson for their decision to give up the fight after the seventh ballot.

Charles E. Perkins wasted no time on sympathy but took one last fling at Larrabee and the reformers. It is hard to realize that this letter is a criticism of the Republican party as the party of reform:

I was in Chicago all last week. Henderson & Clarkson made no mistakes. They managed things as well as possible. But when New York & Penna got together on Harrison that seemed to settle it unless Blaine could be agreed upon by all concerned which I feared might be the result.

Now I think our danger is that the spirit embodied in Larrabee & Al Anderson, which had more to do with your defeat than anything else, will break up the party.

We can not go on confiscating railroads & telling people what they shall eat & drink — and the successful party of the future has got to go back to first principles & stop interfering with individual liberty either by giving or taking away without proper consideration. It's as bad or worse to pension everybody as to confiscate railroads — I go to Des Moines in the morning to see if anything can be saved from the threatened wreck of the Commissioners.[79]

Another approach to the problem in hand is to study the content of the post-convention statements on the Harrison side. One very pointed message was telegraphed to Harrison by Elliott F. Shepard, who knew the story from the inside. "You are greatly indebted to Chauncey M. Depew who opposed Allison's nomination in the New York delegation proposed you in his stead as against Platts effort to carry Allison and got you first 55 votes & then seventy two when the latter fact became known this morning before the convention assembled it could be felt in the air   Hurrah for Tippecanoe & victory too." [80]

Senator T. C. Platt later claimed much of the credit for Harrison's victory. In his *Autobiography*, well described by one able authority as an "erratic work," Platt sings the praises of his own deeds for the Republican party, citing James S. Clarkson as an authority who had vouched for the importance of Platt's services. As to the convention of 1888, Platt quotes Clarkson: "In 1888, it was the New York delegation that, choosing in the final decision between Allison and Harrison, nominated Harrison; and it was Platt that took the New York delegation to this choice." [81] Of course this is claiming much too much in view of the well-attested facts about Depew's role; in part Platt is "compensating" for his own disappointment in failing to receive the Department of the Treasury that had been promised to him, as he always claimed, by John C. New of Indiana on behalf of Harrison, in return for Platt's delivery of the New York votes.

James G. Blaine cabled his congratulations from Scotland, and Harrison answered in this revealing fashion:

Your cablegram was so prompt, so generous, and so stirring that I could not refrain from giving it to the press. . . .

From your most intimate and trusted friends I had the assurance that in a possible contingency you and they might regard my nomination with favor. It was only such assurances that made my Indiana friends hopeful of success, and only the help of your friends made success possible.[82]

And what of Allison's reactions? First he wrote a handsome letter of congratulations to his successful rival. "I heartily approve of your nomination and sincerely congratulate you. I believe we can succeed. But it will require great vigilance & activity on our part. We have a wily foe with a leader strong in will & firm in purpose & not over scrupulous as to methods. After adjt I am ready to enlist under your banner & fight until victory comes to us." [83] Harrison replied in a holograph letter: "I need not tell you that the early and hearty offer of your congratulations, and the hearty and timely aid the [Iowa] delegation gave me are very highly appreciated by me." [84]

Thus closes the story of Allison's hard try for the Republican presidential nomination in 1888. Never a whimper came from him nor a sigh as to what might have been. He was a good enough card-player to know that games are not won by retrospective playbacks of the hands. As a realist he would know that he had not held the right cards to be a winner in the tournament of 1888. There was no vindictiveness toward his managers or his rivals. He might have written a bitter note to John Sherman — but he wrote no such note. He might have questioned the skill of Clarkson and Henderson and their lesser allies — but he did not. A reporter for the Chicago *Inter-Ocean* found him soon after the bad news had been received and gave a picture of Allison in defeat:

Mr. Allison was seen in his Committee-room immersed in appropriations. He simply said "Bully," that all was well. In answer to questions at to whether he had ordered the withdrawal of his name he said that his friends had full authority to act and had no doubt done so without instructions from him. And he reminded the *Inter-Ocean* correspondent that four years or more ago he had told him he would rather be Senator from Iowa during good behavior (which he hoped would be for life) than hold any other position.[85]

And a Senator for life he would be!

* XV *

A Party Wheel Horse

THE ALLISON STORY does not end with his defeat at Chicago. However disappointed he might have been over his own failure, and however little enthusiasm he might have for Harrison as a standard-bearer, Allison played an important part in the fight for a party victory in 1888. It had been hard for Harrison's friends to secure his nomination; it now became even more difficult to secure his election. He was not a glamorous man who could charm or persuade a great popular following. He was merely the candidate on whom a majority could agree after the withdrawal of Blaine; the one candidate, apparently, who was acceptable to the delegations from New York, Indiana, Connecticut, and New Jersey — states that had been lost in 1884 and whose recovery was deemed essential for a Republican victory in 1888.

Allison was certainly one of the first to see that Harrison was running under the twofold handicap of President Cleveland's hold upon the independent vote and the weakness of the high tariff plank in the Republican platform. To almost everyone except certain Republicans it seemed completely obvious that there was an inconsistency in asking for a high tariff at a time when there was a surplus in the Treasury. Yet this was what the Republican platform called for. Democrats in the House, where they had a majority, at once saw their golden opportunity to make capital out of this situation, especially since Cleveland had devoted his annual message in December, 1887, to this subject. In reality, Cleveland had used the message as a medium for

230

the education of the people on this topic. Why pile up money in the Treasury by collecting tariff revenues? The surplus could not be used to any advantage. If used to buy bonds, the government would have to pay a heavy premium, and speculation would be encouraged; if used in lieu of excise taxes on whisky, beer, and tobacco, the moral sense of some people would be offended; if deposited in banks, it would seem that the government and business were in partnership.

Under the leadership of Roger Q. Mills of Texas, chairman of the House Committee on Ways and Means, and long an advocate of lower taxes, economy in government, and a tariff for revenue only, the House passed a bill in July, 1888, bearing his name. The measure forthrightly called for a reduction of duties on manufactured articles and a free list for lumber, wool, salt, and certain other raw materials.[1] Although the purposes of such a bill were to lower taxes on imports and bring about a reduction of the Treasury surplus, the bill also had definite political overtones.

Allison was not slow to perceive the Democratic strategy and to suggest counteracting tactics for Republican use. In reply to an inquiry from Harrison about the prospects for adjournment, Allison had predicted that the Mills Bill would be passed late in July and then the Republicans must pass some kind of countermeasure. If the House should adjourn without passing a bill, the Senate could afford to do likewise, but a Democratic House bill must be matched by a Republican Senate bill that would reduce taxes. "To do this will require about three weeks after we get the bill." [2]

George William Curtis pointed out the same truth in almost every issue of Harper's Weekly [3] during July and August, namely, that the Republican party stood to lose much of the independent vote and the pro-reform Republican vote unless something were done to rectify the situation created by the Republican tariff plank and by the failure of House Republicans to develop a substitute for the Mills Bill. Almost every day brought announcements from prominent Republicans who said they were going to vote for Cleveland. As one man put it, so many others doubtless thought: he was not leaving his party; his party had left him by putting up an immoral candidate in 1884 and an unsupportable tariff plank in 1888.

The Mills Bill, finished on July 21, was passed on to the Senate. With Allison the practical politician urging his party colleagues on, it was but natural that they should put upon him, a moderate in all things, the main burden of framing an alternative or substitute. What was really needed was not a tariff bill to substitute for the Mills proposals; what was desired was a campaign document to replace the tariff plank of the platform.[4] The Republicans did not expect to pass the bill; they merely wanted to use debate on it for campaign purposes. And in providing the bill, Allison made his great contribution to Harrison's victory.

Allison was just the man for this kind of job, and he worked at it manfully from August to October. After weeks of hard committee work, the Senate bill was introduced on October 3 in the form of an amendment to the Mills Bill, Allison reporting the new version from the Committee on Finance.[5] Printed in fine type, it filled over eighteen pages in the *Congressional Record*. Appearing in the daily press on September 25, it met with instant favor, judging from Allison's correspondence.

An analysis of the bill, which showed how much Allison and his colleagues had accomplished, was given in *Harper's Weekly*, a journal that could be depended upon to be critical of anything that smacked of protection. Editor Curtis found that the bill proposed a reduction of 50 per cent in the protective tax on sugar, abolition of the internal tax on tobacco, an increase of the free list by a remission of about $6,500,000 in various taxes, and the freeing of alcohol used in the arts — a cut of about $74,000,000 in all. "The real question of the campaign is not free-trade, but reduction of the surplus by tariff revision," wrote Curtis. He thought that Allison must have "chafed under the necessity of calling a moderate diminution of the duties free-trade," as most Republicans had referred to the Democratic program under the Mills Bill; "his wise counsels have prevailed" and the only question is whether his or the Mills method was the better way of reducing the surplus.[6]

Gardner Cowles, prominent Algona banker, wrote for a copy of the bill and the majority and minority reports, adding a postscript: "Iowa is all right. The more the matter is discussed, the stronger the Republican position becomes with the people. As to the question whether the surplus income shall be reduced by cutting off internal taxes or abandoning the protective system, Republicans as a unit are for the former."[7] Another influential Iowan wrote his praises of the bill and expressed the hope that it would pass just as it came from the Committee. "If we had *free* lumber provided for in your Substitute we would be a little stronger in Iowa, but we can get along and the party is strengthened in other States by the protection you afford lumber interests," he added, thus illustrating the truth of the assertion that the tariff was often a "local" question.[8]

Both Allison and Nelson W. Aldrich took prominent parts in the running debate that went on in the Senate for days, Allison making his principal speech on October 8.[9] He received requests from James G. Blaine, just then on a stumping tour of Indiana, and from Nicholas Murray Butler and others for copies of his remarks; James S. Clarkson sent congratulations.[10] Even Harrison, famous for the "ice-water in his veins," sent almost unreserved compliments to Allison and Aldrich: as to Allison's speech, "the exposition you gave . . . is eminently satisfactory"; as for the report of the Committee, "I have been told by those who have read it that it is the best tariff document that has ever been issued." [11]

The Senate adjourned on October 20 without a vote on the measure but with thousands of words in the *Record*; the entire period from late July to October had been virtually a Republican committee meeting at public expense. Perhaps a faint smile came to Allison's lips as President-pro-tem John J. Ingalls of Kansas thanked all the members for their faithful service in what had been the longest continuous session in the history of the Senate.[12] Surely no one deserved such thanks more than Allison and the members of the Finance Committee, more especially his own subcommittee members, Nelson W. Aldrich of Rhode Island and Frank Hiscock of New York.[13] Allison and his colleagues in the debate had carried the responsibility of party success or failure. "If the Senate does not spoil the situation by a blunder in dealing with the Mills bill I believe we will win," Clarkson had written to Harrison in July.[14] The Senate had not blundered.

Although Harrison had asked Allison to come to Indiana after the adjournment, he did not stop on his way West, and when the time came to fulfill his promised speaking engagements in Indiana, he sent his regrets. One cannot escape the conclusion that Allison simply reneged on his promise to come into Indiana to speak. His plea was that he was needed in the campaign at home — a plea of doubtful validity since he had received assurances from Gardner Cowles and Maurice D. O'Connell that Iowa was perfectly safe. Harrison graciously excused him, and Allison proceeded to meet the engagements made for him by Dr. Charles Beardsley of Burlington, the Iowa state chairman, who assessed Allison $300 as his share of the expenses of the campaign.

The ticket of Harrison and Morton pulled through by methods that should have mortified those devout souls. Harrison ran behind the rest of the ticket in his own precinct and did not carry his own county; [15] Indiana was saved only by the device invented, ordered, and described by Colonel William W. Dudley, treasurer of the Republican national comittee, as "blocks of fives." This consisted of putting four "floaters" or uncertain voters under the care of one safe and financially fortified party member whose orders were to deliver the four votes under his supervision without fail. Although Harrison won in the electoral college, 233 to 168, the voters preferred Cleveland, 5,540,050 to 5,444,337.

The results in Iowa were heartening to the G. O. P. One jubilant Republican expressed the sentiment in this outburst: "Hurrah for Harrison and Morton. It is too glorious. Weaver and Anderson and Cleveland all gone. There is yet a God in Israel." [16] Ten out of the eleven Iowa members elected to the House were Republicans, among them Jonathan P. Dolliver of Fort Dodge for his first term. The lone Democrat was Judge Walter I. Hayes of Clinton.

Immediately after Harrison's nomination, an undercurrent of questioning had begun as to the men who would direct his campaign strategy; as soon as he had been elected, the rumor mills began to grind out the names of probable and possible Cabinet members. Such speculation frequently referred to both Allison and Clarkson.

Clarkson had been a busy man following the convention, where his role had been so decisive. But the hard-working and ever-thoughtful political manager had left the convention in no mood of elation in spite of his role of king-maker. His first act had been to write his tender of congratulations to Harrison, and with it he offered the information that he had remained in Chicago a few days to try to mollify the powerful Joseph Medill's disappointment over the defeat of Gresham. Shortly after that, Clarkson confided in Allison his own disappointment over Harrison's failure to offer him any position of definite responsibility in the campaign.[17]

An even keener disappointment was yet to come to the Des Moines editor. In July the national committee had met for purposes of organization. Senator Matthew S. Quay of Pennsylvania had been made national chairman a short while before the convention, but because of his vulnerability to charges of "bossism" a majority of the committee wanted to replace him with Clarkson. Quay was admittedly a master politician but a late-comer to the Harrison cause, having first supported Allison and then Sherman; he could now help greatly in swinging the big Pennsylvania vote. Clarkson, on the other hand, was not so well known and not yet tested as a manager on a national scale. Although the Harrison forces were singularly obligated to Clarkson, realism triumphed over sentiment, and the Harrison influence was thrown to Quay. Clarkson was asked to take the vice-chairmanship, which meant that he would receive far more work than honor and fame. It was only after much persuasion and much consultation with his own conscientious sense of obligation as Iowa's member of the national committee that Ret finally consented to serve under Quay.[18]

Clarkson established his headquarters in New York City, and gradually his fighting spirit rallied under the heat of the battle and the responsibility and privilege of the full direction of the campaign which Quay placed in his hands. In addition to the public headquarters of the committee, he maintained a "hide-out" at the apartment of the wealthy and eccentric Mrs. Hicks-Lord for secret conferences and for periods of uninterrupted recuperation from his strenuous labors, which went on day and night at great risk to his health.[19]

After the election of Harrison, Allison and his friends worked for a place for Clarkson, not Allison, in Harrison's official family. In one friendly letter Harrison, apparently in response to a statement by Allison, reassured him: "I have been perhaps more in correspondence with Mr. Clarkson than any other member of the National Committee and I am assured of his personal friendliness and of his great efficiency as a member of the Committee." [20] A much stronger assurance came from Jonathan P. Dolliver, the new Congressman-elect from Fort Dodge and a grateful protégé of both men. He informed Allison that he had written a strong letter to Harrison for Clarkson.

As for Allison's chances for a Cabinet post, his friends advised against it. J. Fred Meyers, a keen observer of the Iowa political scene, wrote Allison and urged him not to accept such a post. First, Allison could not afford to become Harrison's clerk; second, too many political implications would arise in Iowa; and third, Larrabee and Hepburn would aspire to Allison's place, and the "organization" would be broken up. Allison's best course would be to wait until 1892, when Harrison might not be renominated.[21] Still another good friend,

Maurice D. O'Connell, urged Allison to stay out of the Cabinet and told him not to let any fears about his re-election in 1890 cause him to take the Cabinet place as a substitute. "Don't allow yourself to be influenced by any doubt as to your strength at home. You can be your own successor." [22] A letter from Dolliver, dated December 28, indicates that Allison had notified his friends that he had already declined a Cabinet offer. This would suggest that Harrison had made an offer or at least a "feeler" earlier than is commonly supposed. Dolliver expressed his pleasure over Allison's rejection of a place in the Cabinet for himself; the only step up for Allison was to the presidency, and the Cabinet was not a steppingstone to that. [23]

As George William Curtis saw it, the selection of the Cabinet had resolved itself into a "contest." Blaine was taken for granted as the new Secretary of State and was credited with the statement that he would accept the place if offered, a situation that appealed to Curtis as being preposterous and, if carried through, equivalent to a clear surrender by Harrison. Even the Union League Club of New York City passed a resolution aimed against Blaine, as well as against John Wanamaker of Philadelphia and Thomas C. Platt, the notorious New York boss. [24] In spite of these objections, Blaine became Harrison's Secretary of State.

It seems safe to assume that Allison had sure knowledge all the way through late December and all of January that the Treasury post was his if he would only accept it. But what effect would acceptance or rejection have on the chances of Clarkson? That gentleman was suffering, very justifiably so, from a bad case of injured pride. On January 25, 1889, he wrote to Allison that he had had a conversation with a man from Philadelphia, a prospective member of the Cabinet (undoubtedly John Wanamaker), who had assured him that Iowa would not necessarily be limited to one place in Harrison's Cabinet. Another man close to Harrison was even more certain that Clarkson still had a chance. Therefore, Allison had been all wrong in telling Clarkson that he had no chance in the race. Ret said that he felt it was his duty to inform Allison of this, "yet I do not want to affect or influence your decision in the matter." His principal grievance was that after all his labors he had not been called into a conference. [25]

The country was tormented by rumors. Even so experienced a politician as Joseph H. Manley of Augusta, Maine, one of Blaine's most trusted lieutenants, allowed himself to be taken in on one occasion by a baseless report. On January 29 he wrote to Michener: "Saturday the W. U. T. Co. placed a bulletin on its board in this city saying 'President Harrison has tendered to Mr. Blaine Secretary of State and Mr. Blaine has accepted. Allison Treasury and Wanamaker P. M. G.' The news instantly spread over the city. Every one accepted it as an authoritative announcement and were wild with joy. . . . Supposing it to be authentic I telegraphed Genl. Harrison. It now turns out to be a newspaper story." [26]

At that, the bulletin was not far wide of the mark. Late in January, Allison had finally made the journey to headquarters at Indianapolis; the trip occurred at approximately the time referred to in Manley's letter. He was closeted with the President-elect for a large share of the time during the twenty-seven-hour visit, even moving his baggage from the New Denison Hotel to the Harrison home. Reporters could get nothing from him except the trite remark that he had had a pleasant visit and that something had happened to cause him to return to Washington instead of going on to Dubuque as planned.[27] Everyone believed that he had been offered a Cabinet post, and of course everyone expected him to accept. The well-informed George William Curtis wrote that the reports from Indianapolis were to the effect that Blaine and Allison had been "called" to the State and Treasury departments. Fully assuming that both men would accept, Curtis expressed approval of Allison's appointment, although his "present views on the tariff are not those which he formerly expressed, but he had doubtless felt constrained by the exigencies of political life to keep step with his party." Curtis felt that the appointment would be generally regarded with favor.[28]

But Curtis' dictum, dated February 1, was obsolete before it reached his readers on February 9. On February 1, 1889, Harrison had written to Blaine:

I thought I had nearly everything [settled] in my own mind that required attention before I reached Washington. If the newspaper reports today as to Mr. Allison's position is [sic] correct, it may unsettle some of my own plans. I said to a friend today that if all of the seven Cabinet officers could have been found in Alaska it would have promoted harmony in the party in the states. Maine, I believe, is the only state that has no interests to offer.[29]

Thus, strange as it may seem, Harrison learned through the papers of Allison's possible declination before he received the formal letter

of regret. Allison must surely have been pleased with the President-
elect's reply:

You know that your letter was very disappointing to me, but after our
very full conversation I do not think of any further consideration that I
can urge.

It seemed to me that I could not take the responsibility for not offering
you the Treasury, and urging it upon you by those public and party considerations which so closely and so strongly pointed to you as the right
choice. Added to this, there were general considerations that would have
made your acceptance of the place very agreeable to me. I shall probably take
no further step in this matter until next week and if anything should occur
in the meantime I will be glad to hear from you.[30]

Allison's sorry handling of Garfield's invitation to join his Cabinet
in 1881, and this rejection of Harrison's offer in 1889, make one think
that he is seeing the same show twice. And for the second time, the
Treasury went instead to William Windom.[31] But this time there
was an unfortunate element in the story that was not present in 1881.
At that time Allison had managed his end of the negotiations in such
a way as to assist his friend, Samuel J. Kirkwood, to step into the
Cabinet, and another friend, James F. Wilson, into the Senate. This
time his ineptness had disastrous results for his friend, James S.
Clarkson, who was eager for a Cabinet position, but who had sub-
ordinated his claims while waiting to see what Allison would do. By
the time Allison had made up his mind to say "no," it was too late
for Clarkson to push his own case. The full effect of this *contretemps*
on the personal relations of the two men did not show up for some
time, but Clarkson and his friends were keenly aware of the results
of Allison's hesitancy on Clarkson's chances for the Cabinet, even
while the "contest" was in full swing.

Clarkson was for the time being in Chicago, investigating the po-
sibilities of purchasing a newspaper there, and at the same time hopefully watching the situation. On January 30 he received a telegram
saying: "I just saw Senator Wilson he says he thinks Allison will not go
in the cabinet"; shortly afterward Clarkson received a letter from
General Dodge, in response to his complaint at Allison's delay:

You know how our friend is; his timidity would make him seem to be doing
what you say. . . . I am satisfied from a letter I got today from Washington
that [Allison] will not accept. I saw Vice-President Morton last night, and
he was very positive in his declaration that it would be the mistake of his
life if he did. If he should, there is going to be a general scramble; and in
my opinion the succession will go to Central Iowa or Western Iowa. . . . I

want to say to you that I think your course in this matter is so high and so straight, that no matter what anybody says, they cannot criticise it.[32]

But by February 2 it was known that Allison would not accept. One of Allison's fellow-townsmen, J. K. Graves, tried to console Clarkson with a copy of a letter that he had sent to Harrison, boosting Clarkson for a Cabinet post, and with the well-intended but probably galling words: "I believe if the Senator had been decided and positive at his two interviews with Harrison you would now be one of the coming members of the cabinet." [33]

As matters turned out, Clarkson's natural place, the Postmaster Generalship, was given to John Wanamaker, the merchant prince of Philadelphia, and Ret was persuaded to take over as First Assistant. To at least one keen observer this seemed a promising solution. Charles E. Perkins wrote to Clarkson:

For the sake of the party in and out of Iowa I am glad you have been induced to become the 1st Asst. P. M. General — but of course its hard work, and I don't suppose you want it. You ought to have been P. M. General and I suppose it will end in your being there — I trust it does not mean that you are going to give up the general direction of the Register. If you and Allison work together I don't see why you can't have things pretty much your own way in Iowa and let Larrabee permanently retire. If I can do anything to be of service let me know.[34]

Why did Allison reject the Cabinet honor? There were all the usual reasons: the comparative security of his Senate seat as against the uncertainty of the length of tenure in the Cabinet; the greater expense involved in Cabinet social obligations; the vast amount of petty desk work. But the real reason was the possibility that his successor might be the hated William Larrabee, the man whose ideas on railroad regulation were now anathema to Allison's best friends and supporters, General Dodge and Charles E. Perkins. These men would never have forgiven Allison had he made Larrabee's succession possible.[35] The only good prospect for holding the seat against Larrabee was for Allison to run again; even that would be no guarantee of success against the great crusader for railroad regulation. But this was all crystal clear from the first; it should not have been necessary to play along for weeks before making a negative decision. It was unfair to President-elect Harrison and to Clarkson or any other Iowan whose political future was hanging in the balance.

With the new administration in office, the Republicans turned their attention to local politics, and the elections of 1889 revealed how hard-pressed they were. Even a party of such overwhelming basic strength in Iowa found that it could not afford the indulgence of losing some voters because of a continuing fight for prohibition, some others because of Larrabee's antirailroad fight, and still others because of the general feeling that the party belonged to big business rather than to the small farmer.

Dozens of letters from Gilbert B. Pray of Fort Dodge, Charles Pickett of Waterloo, and the "old reliable," Jacob Rich, testify to the strenuousness of the campaign and the difficulty in getting pledges from the candidates for the General Assembly.[36] Allison himself was well aware of his situation. In a report to President Harrison he said: "I have had rather a pleasant summer but have been obliged to keep my mind on the matter of my re-election, and am not yet 'out of the woods' as it were but think I see the opening beyond. . . . I think we will do well this year, as our people are feeling well. We have an unprecedented crop of everything that grows in a temperate climate." [37]

The election results of 1889 and the even more significant upcoming Republican defeat of 1890 proved that the Republican party of Abraham Lincoln and, more important, the party of Thaddeus Stevens, James F. Wilson, James S. Clarkson, and William Boyd Allison, the Radical Republicans, could no longer win by a wave of the bloody shirt. For the first time since the term of Governor Stephen Hempstead (1850-1854), the Democrats put their man in the Iowa Governor's seat: Horace Boies of Waterloo.[38] They secured 45 out of the 100 seats in the lower house and 20 out of the 28 senatorial togas that were up for election. This gave them 65 votes out of a total of 150 in the combined houses — not enough to defeat the Republican senatorial nominee, however.

But the Democratic strength made it absolutely necessary for the Republicans to bury their factional differences. There could be no permanent doubt that Allison would be the party's nominee. The only question was whether essential Republican votes would be cast independently for Larrabee, flouting the caucus decision. Thus the success of Allison finally depended on Larrabee and his followers. When confronted with this situation, Larrabee adopted a policy of nonaggression, and Allison squeezed by with a vote of 79 to 63 for S. T. Bestow, his Democratic opponent. Larrabee "die-hards" cast eight votes for their hero.[39]

According to David Brant, in attendance in Des Moines as a reporter for Fred Faulkes of the Cedar Rapids *Gazette,* a few malcontents in the Republican party had done their best to defeat Allison by putting up Larrabee, but the Governor had refused to be their "catspaw," as he expressed it, and the rebellion had collapsed. During the campaign Allison had at last answered the stories circulated by Weaver and others as to his great wealth: in an interview with Brant he gave an accounting of his finances, and Brant persuaded him to agree to publication of the facts. Thus the story that Allison was one of the "Senate millionaires" was at last scotched. When the people of Iowa learned that "for several years [Allison] had borne with personal attacks without giving them the dignity of a denial," Brant wrote, "they loved the man more than ever. In fact it was in his later years that the people had real affection for their great senator." [40]

The year 1890 opened auspiciously for Allison. This was the fourth time in a row that he had been given endorsement by his party. The election by the legislature did not occur until March because of a fight over the speakership, a fact that in no way threatened Allison's certainty of victory.[41] It was a good thing that Allison was not tied down to a hard campaign for re-election: his full time and all his talents for the arrangement of compromises were needed in Washington. The Fifty-first Congress, famous as the first "billion-dollar Congress" in American history, convened on December 3, 1889. Three great issues concurrently occupied the attention of the solons: amendment of the Bland-Allison Act; revision of the tariff; and an elections bill. The issues were quite diverse but were made to relate to each other by the clever maneuvers of the members of the Silver Republican bloc mostly from the newly admitted states of the West, who permitted one of the three measures to get by only at the price of a favorable compromise on one of the others and a crippling action that killed the third. Specifically, they permitted a tariff act to be passed as the "regular" Republicans wanted it only at the price of a silver purchase act that the regulars did not want and the ultimate defeat of an elections bill that they very much wanted.[42]

Neither President Harrison nor Secretary Windom could be classified as an expert on the currency question. In a report made on December 2, 1889, Windom advocated the purchase of all silver bullion as offered, this to be stored and only enough of it coined to redeem the treasury notes that were used to pay for it originally. Harrison cut the ground from under this suggestion by admitting in his first annual message, delivered the next day, that he had given the plan but little study.[43] Congress droned away on the subject for many months before approaching the serious stages of debate and final decision. The state of mind of Congress can be judged by a letter from Allison to his old friend and mentor, Samuel J. Kirkwood, in June of 1890. "I think your view about silver the correct one. There will be no compulsory coinage, but a purchase of bullion and the Treasury notes therefore made a legal tender to the extent of about four million and a half of money. You are right about things being muddled here. What the outcome will be with the tariff and other questions, I do not know." [44]

This prophecy was based upon three test votes that had been taken: one in the House, where a silver purchase bill had been passed on June 7 by a vote of 135 to 119, with Iowa's ten Republican Representatives voting for it; one in the Senate, where a free coinage amendment by Senator Preston B. Plumb of Kansas had been adopted (Allison, of course, voting no) by a vote of 44 to 25 but promptly killed in the House.[45] Eventually a conference committee was appointed and its report adopted in the form known to history as the Sherman Silver Purchase Act.[46] This provided for the monthly purchase of four and one-half million ounces of silver, to be paid for by treasury notes redeemable in gold or silver at the discretion of the Secretary of the Treasury. There were to be no silver dollars coined, as the Bland-Allison Act had provided, but the metal was to be stored and certificates issued against it.

As a convinced bimetallist, Allison could not object to this slight increase in the use of silver. Joined by many whose names show Allison to have been in good company, whatever might have been said about "dishonest money," he supported the Sherman measure. Representative Henry Cabot Lodge explained his vote to his friends: "You may say that it is economically unsound to make the government a buyer of vast quantities of silver bullion. But it is better for the government to issue notes on silver bullion bought on a gold basis than it is to issue even two million depreciated dollars monthly." [47]

As for the tariff, the measure sponsored by William McKinley received the President's signature on June 12, 1890, not to become effective until October 1.[48] This tariff act is probably the best known, at least by name, of all tariff legislation. Its general reputation is that of a "high" or protective act that boomeranged on its creators by bringing about their resounding defeat in the congressional elections that soon followed. This generalization needs a guarded interpretation. Actually, the defeat would have to be assigned to the probable oncoming effects of the act, not its actual results. The American economy is not supersensitive enough to register the effects of a tariff act within one month of its effective date — but the American political party balance can be upset in five months of hard campaigning against a vulnerable opponent. The Republicans had left themselves open to an attack based on fear, and the Democrats cleverly seized the opportunity. The inevitable increase in prices of goods was harped upon; John Wanamaker the merchant ran far ahead of Wanamaker the Cabinet member by advertising from his Philadelphia store: "Buy now — don't wait for higher prices." Then, too, the Democratic and Populist gains of 1890 continued the state legislative gains they had made in 1889.

Allison is personally credited with responsibility for one famous provision of the act: the protection of an infant tin-plate industry. Probably no portion of the act was more severely criticized at the time or more effectively utilized by the Democrats in their campaign. Peddlers were sent up and down the country offering tin cups at twenty-five cents and tin pails at one dollar.

Yet Allison's own generation soon came to think of the tin-plate provision as a good thing and praised him for it,[49] although no monuments have been built to his memory in Wales, whose rolling mills were put out of business. It is clear that Allison and his colleagues knowingly undertook to create an American production of this commodity by putting in a barrier against the importation of tin plate, with the provision that American production must reach certain proportions within two years or the protection would cease.[50] American producers were equal to their opportunity. Capital, labor, and "know how" migrated from South Wales to America, and by 1914 the United States was the leading producer and consumer of tin plate in the world.

Allison was unable to see the virtues of reciprocity as set forth by James G. Blaine and written into the McKinley Act. It was Blaine who reputedly "smashed his hat in anger in the Finance Committee room because such men as Morrill, Aldrich, Sherman, and Allison could not appreciate the glories of reciprocity."[51] All in all, it seems that the Allison of 1890 is quite a different Allison from the tariff moderate of 1870.[52]

In 1890 Republican strength in Iowa reached the lowest point in the party's history between 1854 and 1932. Six out of eleven seats in the national House of Representatives were lost. Jonathan P. Dolliver must have blushed over the good-natured boast that he had made earlier that "Hell would go Methodist before Iowa would go Democratic." The Democrats nearly won three additional seats, failing by only narrow margins in the Third, Eighth, and Eleventh Districts. An analysis of the voting in all eleven districts shows that the total Democratic vote was 194,832, the Republican, 185,783, a margin of 9,049, to which should be added a protest vote of several thousand cast for the minor parties.[53]

Yet Iowa was probably not as "radical" as many of her neighbors. First, one should point out that many of Iowa's so-called "radicals" were not really very radical. A roll call of the Democratic and Populist leaders, closely associated in the public mind, reveals such names as Governor Boies, millionaire farm owner and lawyer; John F. Duncombe, chief counsel for the Illinois Central Railroad and one of the leading attorneys of the state; Martin H. Moore, a well-to-do lumber man of Dubuque but a strong advocate of a larger per capita circulation; Luman H. ("Calamity") Weller, dealer in lands and publisher of a small protest journal in Nashua; E. H. Gillette of Des Moines; and General James B. Weaver. These people were often prone to defeat their own cause by refusal to work together in a close party manner following the discipline of a recognized leader. For example, a prominent labor leader in Dubuque wrote to Weller expressing general approval of the success of the "opposition" candidates but rejoicing that "still we have saved Henderson by a closely contested fight. I worked for the Col. but not for the party. I am not among those that weep. The Col. is my friend. He is sound and educated." [54] One can easily detect the fallacy in the gentleman's reasoning in not equating Colonel Henderson with the Republican party which he completely personified but can also admire the Colonel's ability to draw men to him by sheer magnetism.

Early in 1891 Allison had another chance, or was at least favorably mentioned in some circles, for the Treasury post. Secretary William Windom died on January 29, 1891, and there was the usual speculation as to his successor. Allison's brother-in-law, Bowd Nealley of

Bangor, Maine, expressed the sentiments held by Allison's best friends: "Of course your friends need not fear that you would exchange the comfortable position of senator for six years for the Treasury for two. I am almost rejoiced that Iowa has got a Democratic governor so that they will not persecute you to take this place." [55]

Undoubtedly the most important event of early 1891 was the defeat of the Federal Elections Bill, better known as the "Force Bill," because of its provision for boards of overseers under judicial supervision which would certify federal elections in the South. The President was empowered to use the army and navy if necessary in the enforcement of the law. The bill was part of Harrison's effort to build a Republican party in the South by safeguarding the Negro vote rather than by trying to build a white man's party there.[56] The emotional aspects of politics could never be better illustrated than in this effort to force the election bill on the South. James S. Clarkson resurrected the bloody shirt that had never been very deeply buried, and his brother Richard editorially pictured a national calamity if the bill were not passed. Ret equated Republicanism with the "duty" to protect the Republicans of the South "at the polls and in their homes." "There is no other real question in present politics but this. . . . Civil service [reform] is the toy of a child, the trifling thing of hobby riders, thrust in to keep the Republican party away from its duty under conscience of settling this great overshadowing question." [57]

As the issue neared a final vote, Ret Clarkson, now living in Philadelphia, wired frantically to his brother Richard:

Can't you telegraph Allison saying that all earnest Republicans in Iowa are anxious to know whether it is he or Ingalls who is against the election bill and Republican party. His pair with Ingalls makes Ingalls treachery count two votes against the bill. It is important Allison should break the pair and vote for the bill to save it.

Allison's answer was clear and decisive and laid the Clarksons' fears to rest. He was paired with Ingalls only on questions on which they were in disagreement. "I have power to transfer my pair to any absent Republican who agrees with me," he assured them.[58]

Allison's part in the debates was a minor one and makes evident the deterioration of his once flaming Radicalism of the 1860's. The most that can be said for him is that he voted for the bill; he did not work for it in spite of pleas from the Clarksons, General Dodge, and Dr.

Charles Beardsley, the Republican state chairman of Iowa. The bill was defeated according to plan by Northern and Southern Democrats. For several weeks, through December and January, with only a brief Christmas recess, the Senate was treated to a clever exhibition of Democratic delaying tactics managed by Senator Arthur Pue Gorman of Maryland — tactics that amounted to a filibuster, although the word was never used. Just when it appeared that the short session would end without any action whatsoever, Senator Wolcott of Colorado, a Silver Republican, moved the consideration of another bill. Aldrich admitted his defeat, and the Elections Bill was never heard from again.[59]

The greater significance of the defeat of the Elections Bill is not often pointed out, but it has been thoroughly analyzed and described as a turning point in post-Civil War Republican party history.[60] It was the last link in a chain of events made up of Cleveland's election in 1884, the admission of the "Omnibus States" (four Western states admitted by a "lame duck" Democratic Congress in 1889), and the Republican defeat in 1890. Never again would this party make a major effort, in the post-Civil War sense, to inject the warmed-over issue of Negro suffrage into national politics. There would be no more Radical Republicanism, although there might still be a few Radical Republicans. Of those who had entered Congress during the war, yea, even of those who before the war had helped to bring Radical Republicanism into being, Allison was now nearly alone. The "last of the Radical Republicans" we might call him, along with Justin S. Morrill of Vermont and John Sherman of Ohio, who were the only other members who could look back over a congressional career that actually began during the war. Shelby M. Cullom of Illinois came nearest to these in vintage: he had entered the House in December, 1865, as a member of the Thirty-ninth Congress. To be sure, there were younger Radicals, such as Joseph B. Foraker of Ohio and Clarkson of Iowa who were just as "Radical" as their elders, but their status in the party was not the same; they, too, now went on to other interests.

The new leadership in Congress, especially in the Senate which was now to enjoy a distinct pre-eminence in government, belonged to men for whom the Civil War and its offspring, the Negro question, as issues had little interest. More and more would the power of decision pass into the hands of men who spoke for big business.[61] Nelson W.

Aldrich, the traction and textile magnate, to whom Rhode Island was as truly a pocket borough as any ever owned by the Duke of Norfolk; [62] John Coit Spooner, the constitutional law authority from Wisconsin; Eugene Hale of Maine; General Joseph R. Hawley of Connecticut; Orville H. Platt of Connecticut; and James McMillan, multimillionaire shipping magnate and investment holder of Michigan [63] — such were the men who now dominated the Senate. McMillan was host to an exclusive group known as the "School of Philosophy Club," whose members settled many an issue over dinner and the card table.

Allison, a poor man compared to most of these leaders, was a charter member of McMillan's little club, very much one of the "boys," and apparently a regular in their friendly little poker games. Other Senators and Cabinet members felt themselves fortunate when they were occasionally invited as extras to share the conviviality of the group. Although the picture of the Senate as a millionaires' club has been overdrawn, it is easy to see where the idea came from. No one has yet demonstrated that a poor man's patriotism is any more sincere than a rich man's love for his country, or that a poor man is any more blessed with a spirit of industry than a rich man when it comes to willingness to hack away at a committee assignment. Allison might well have testified on this score: he knew equally well both the rich and the poor. On this, as on so many things, he was safely "in the middle" but definitely leaning toward the right.

☆ XVI ☆

Allison Finds His Level

THE GREAT LEGISLATIVE battles of 1890-1891 were followed by years of seesaw politics in which each party was harassed almost as much by internal factionalism as by the opposition. Academic arguments over the tariff and free silver took on realistic tones as economic hard times came to a climax in the Panic of 1893 and its resulting depression. Probably never did party workers appeal to the American people with more intensity and earnestness, as many factions tried to convince the voters that truth was on their side.

In all of this, Iowa was a battleground, and Allison was directly involved. The odd-year politics of 1891 brought up the prospect of the re-election of Governor Horace Boies of Waterloo, a bitter pill for Republicans to swallow. As an Iowa Democrat, Boies opposed prohibition and the protective tariff and mildly favored free coinage of silver. As for the Republicans, a majority favored prohibition, protective tariffs, and bimetallism; a small minority, led by Albert B. Cummins,[1] strongly opposed prohibition, spoke moderately on the silver question, and challenged the need for high tariffs. Allison's strategy, that of a wary politician rather than a dynamic leader, called for alignment with the majority Republicans but enough friendliness toward the minority to keep them loyal to him personally and to avoid a clean break within the party.

As a party standard-bearer to throw into the battle against Boies in 1891, the Republicans had chosen Hiram C. Wheeler of Odebolt. Not many had sought the almost certain martyrdom of the role.

248

Everywhere there was a tendency to rely on the party's record. Perhaps the attitude of a party wheel horse, Major John F. Lacey of Oskaloosa, was typical. Availing himself of his wife's illness as an excuse to avoid a hard campaign, he cultivated a false optimism. Admitting that the party was split over prohibition, he went on to say: "I think we will make a better showing in Mahaska county than we did in 1889 or 1890. Our town and county are very prosperous and ours is the party of prosperity and the good business outlook will surely help us." [2]

Allison rallied to the cause by speaking extensively throughout the state, as did Colonel Henderson and others of the delegation at Washington, but all to no avail. Boies was again elected. Many were the post-mortem efforts at explanation. One member attributed the defeat to the revival of Know-Nothingism in the party. In his opinion, foreign elements in the party were being persecuted, and such people were going over to the other side. [3] A more expert observer, Colonel Henderson, writing in privacy to Richard P. Clarkson of the *Register*, thought that the railroad influence had not been properly directed into the usual Republican channels: "I am not prepared to say that the railroad organization, through their management, fought Wheeler, but I am clear on one point that Boies is a very satisfactory Governor to the railroad interests, while Wheeler was an untried force." [4]

Internal difficulties among the Republicans continued to beset the party nationally in 1892. There was little enthusiasm anywhere for the renomination of Harrison, and, indeed, he himself was indifferent to the idea in the early part of the year. His cold and austere manner, his indifference to political machines as built and used by such men as T. C. Platt and Matthew Quay, his capacity for inspiring grudges in such men as Platt, Quay, and Ret Clarkson made him a most unlikely possibility for renomination. Clarkson and W. W. Dudley, two great pillars of support in 1888, were now among his enemies. This raised the question of an alternative and inevitably revived the hopes of those who wanted James G. Blaine as their candidate. Of these, no one was more enthusiastic than James S. Clarkson. Early in the year he wrote to Blaine of the successful results coming from the reciprocity features of the tariff of 1890, for which Blaine had been responsible, and then gave a long list of reasons why Blaine could win in 1892. [5] In March a capable observer in Iowa, B. F. Gue, wrote to Ret's brother and agreed with him on Blaine's chances. "You are sound on Blaine. He can carry Iowa by our old time Republican majorities and *be elected without doubt.* With Harrison both are doubtful. Blaine is infinitely stronger than ever before. He can save the Republican party from defeat. With any other candidate there is doubt." [6] The evidence could be multiplied. The *Register* came out with a strong editorial for Blaine on February 28. Asserting Blaine to be the strong man of the administration, who had made it popular throughout the world by his policies as Secretary of State, the *Register* urged the party to choose its strongest man regardless of sentiment, and that man was Blaine.

But there were those who shied away from Blaine, even though they did not like Harrison. This division of sentiment brought other names into the field, including the familiar ones of Russell A. Alger and William McKinley from the 1888 list, and, among several new prospects, James S. Clarkson, who deserved consideration in his own right after years of service to others. Carl Snyder, a former Iowan now a journalist in New York, wrote that Ret was considered by political leaders in that city to be a serious contender for the nomination at the coming convention at Minneapolis. [7]

About this time and under these circumstances, an event happened which nearly destroyed the Allison-Clarkson friendship and political alliance, and which put a black mark on the Senator's personal record that is hard to forget. In an interview given to "Gath" Townsend about February 22, 1892, Allison discussed a number of subjects, including the chances of Governor Boies for the Democratic nomination for President, but his principal remarks were about Clarkson's effort to secure a Cabinet appointment under Benjamin Harrison. In a wholly gratuitous manner, Allison belittled Clarkson's chances of ever having been called to Harrison's Cabinet, boasted of his own chances by contrast, and inferred that Clarkson had expected Allison to use his influence in securing a place for him. [8]

The contents and the tone of the interview must have been shocking to Allison's friends as well as to Ret, his wife, and their friends. Everything about the incident was so unlike Allison that it is an almost unbelievable story. Clarkson's letter to Allison, on the other hand, demanding a retraction of the statements and presenting his own version of the Cabinet negotiations, is a masterpiece of its kind. Many a lesser man would have resorted to abusive name-calling, and to unsupported assertions of innocence. Not so James S. Clarkson. The fact that the letter was dictated from Clarkson's bed of pain in Asheville, North Carolina, where he was undergoing treatment for a severe case of rheumatism, only adds to one's amazement at the man's self-control. Undoubtedly driven on by white-hot anger, the aggrieved man remained calm and cold on the surface, the better to express his indignation and his conviction that Allison had been guilty of base ingratitude. In some three thousand words he reviewed the history of their long association, summarized the involved story of the negotiations whereby he had been deprived of the fullest possible consideration for a Cabinet position because of the wavering uncertainties of Allison's own course, and finally discussed the appointment of John Wanamaker in such detail as to throw some light on that point.

Surely Allison had never been called on to read such sentences as these about himself:

. . . this testimony you are made to give to history is about as complete a perversion of facts as could well be made. . . . I never believed that you would urge me seriously and sincerely for a Cabinet place. For I knew that you did not want a division of power in Iowa. . . . I may say it to you now that I did think then and believe now that you did more at Indianapolis . . . to try and weaken General Harrison's faith in me than to strengthen it. As I did not care for a place, and as I was philosopher enough to know that a man who like yourself devotes his whole life to a career in politics develops that remarkable instinct of self preservation which in common people is called selfishness, I did not resent it then and bear no resentment now. . . .

So far as I can remember, I have never asked a personal favor of you. After twenty-five years of intimate association, it is late perhaps to make such a request. But I do now ask, and feel that I have good and honorable reasons for insisting upon it, that you shall publicly correct these false statements to which the currency of your powerful name has been given in a wide circuit of the American press.[9]

It is a fair assumption that Allison's belittling remarks about Clarkson were made in an effort to squelch or at least minimize the attention being given to Clarkson for the presidential nomination. At the time it was generally believed that Harrison would not run for a second term, and Clarkson was being mentioned freely as one deserving the honor. It may be assumed that in Allison's eyes this was little short of preposterous. Allison had known Clarkson for years as a faithful manager, and now the two were being mentioned in the same breath as equals!

This analysis is not wholly conjectural. On March 6, a few days after the interview, the Des Moines *Register* carried a story from Washington quoting both Allison and Jonathan P. Dolliver on Clarkson's chances. Allison was curt, almost disdainful: "I have not, up to date, received any intimation from Mr. Clarkson that he will be or has any desire to be a candidate for the presidency." Dolliver, who had a greater capacity for warm friendship, was more generous. He said that Clarkson had never given him any authority to use his name, indeed he had reproved him for using it in that connection. Even so, said Dolliver, "I am impressed with the belief that he is the best available presidential timber, and I believe that he could be nominated and elected."

The next day, March 7, Mrs. Clarkson wrote a stinging letter to Allison:

> Brother Richard telegraphs that you perfer waiting — until you hear by letter from my husband — before correcting the impressions given to the public in your interview with Mr. Townsend. I do not think that you can be too prompt in rectifying that damaging and most unkind criticism upon one who has served you so patiently and well.
>
> I write you because Mr. Clarkson is very ill, and will not for some time be able, to either write or read letters.
>
> I believe that your interview has had much to do with his sickness, as I have never known him so distressed and hurt before, and your judgment and kind heart will tell you that the sooner you set it right, the sooner it will be over. . . .
>
> I trust you are well and I know you will sleep better nights if you get that interview off your mind — and I may add so will the undersigned.[10]

On March 12 Mrs. Clarkson must have received word of some sort from Allison as to a forthcoming correction. She telegraphed him as follows: "Thank you I am glad. Mr. Clarkson is improving slowly but surely. Still bedfast." [11] On the 13th the *Register* published a long article in which Allison made restitution of Ret's good name as well as he could without abjectly confessing his mistake. Clarkson was generous enough to forgive Allison. Aside from the telegram from Mrs. Clarkson, the proof rests upon the course of their later relations. But surely there could never again be the same warm friendship, the same unhesitating support that Clarkson had always given since those hectic days of the senatorial election of January, 1872.

In spite of his illness, Clarkson corresponded voluminously and discussed presidential politics with many who came to his recuperative

retreat at Hot Springs, Arkansas. At the Republican national convention in Minneapolis in June, he opposed the Harrison forces.[12]
His tactic was to try to win the Iowa delegation away from Harrison
and commit it to Allison; in short to do anything in order to start a
movement against the President, whose early reluctance to seek renomination had been overcome. Clarkson's efforts failed, however,
because Allison and James F. Wilson were going along as "regulars"
in support of Harrison. This clash put further strain on the Allison-
Clarkson friendship, whatever appearances the two men managed to
display in public. On June 5 Clarkson sent Allison four telegrams,
three of them long and urgent appeals for help; the fourth simply
read: "I am waiting at the wire to talk with you." [13] Apparently
Allison ignored the entire effort to switch from Harrison.

After Clarkson's stratagem had failed, Dolliver tried to swing the
nomination to McKinley. From Washington he wired Clarkson that a
canvass of Republicans in Congress showed that the younger element
wanted McKinley, and that he had asked Foraker of Ohio to forget
the past and help put McKinley over. Foraker yielded to this appeal
and to Mark Hanna's pleas for McKinley, but all in vain.[14] The convention went ahead with the renomination of Harrison, a result
cleverly manipulated by Harrison's astute manager, Louis T. Michener,
but the delegates made a real mistake when they rejected the incumbent, Levi P. Morton, for Vice President in favor of another New
Yorker, Whitelaw Reid. The excuse was that Morton had not declared
himself. Allison wrote to the Vice President: "There continues to be
deep regret respecting the action at Minneapolis towards you, no
hostility that I know of to Mr. Reid, but a feeling that your interests
were not thoroughly cared for." [15] Clarkson was much more outspoken in his letter to Morton and blamed the defeat on two unnamed
members of the New York delegation who were trying to win the
friendship of Reid's newspaper, the *Tribune*.[16]

Factionalism was as prevalent among the Democrats as among the
Republicans. In the end the antisilver group led by Grover Cleveland
triumphed and nominated him rather than Iowa's Horace Boies or
any other candidate nearer the protest groups of the Midwest or the
South. These dissatisfied agrarian elements met at Omaha and, under
the name of People's, or Populist, party, made James B. Weaver of
Iowa their nominee, after Judge Walter Q. Gresham had rejected the
honor.[17]

In spite of his antipathy toward Harrison at Minneapolis, Ret was persuaded to accept the second place in command and actually to take charge of all the details of the campaign, much as he had had in 1888. As the heat of the battle increased, he threw himself into the work without reservation. He told Morton: "Our work is heavy & the result by no means assured. Still I think that our chances, plus the work we shall do between now and November, will pull us through if no accident shall intervene." [18] Allison did what he could for the cause. He toured Iowa and delivered a speech which was a cleverly planned defense of the McKinley Tariff Act, basing his remarks largely on the Aldrich report on "Retail Prices and Wages." [19] In addition, he cited comment by his friend, Edward Atkinson, who was "more of a Democrat than a Republican," that prices were low, wages high, and the workman never better off. Allison was at his oratorical best when he stood before the people and spoke as their agent or trustee, gladly giving an accounting to his employers.

His efforts were not in vain as far as Iowa was concerned, even though the nation as a whole turned to Cleveland. In Iowa only one Democrat, Walter I. Hayes of Clinton in the Second District, was elected to Congress, instead of the six of 1890. Allison was of direct help to William Peters Hepburn [20] and perhaps to others. The Republicans were also aided by the fact that the Populists were badly divided amongst themselves; some concentrated their attention on free silver while others fought "corporate aggression." Populists and Democrats should have maintained perfect unity in their separate parties and worked together in support of a common ticket if they hoped to enjoy any success whatever. This they did not do in 1892 in Iowa or elsewhere. [21]

Allison spent the remainder of the year pleasantly as a member of the American delegation to the International Monetary Conference at Brussels, which began its sessions in November. As one whose insistence had ever been on international bimetallism, going back to his amendments to the Bland Bill of 1877, Allison had more than a casual interest in the success of the conference. He found himself helpless, however, as did all the others present, in the face of a world economic situation that simply could not be manipulated by conference edicts. "It was an empty farce, as its predecessors had been, devised as they too, for the most part, had been to make the West think the Republican Party was 'doing something for silver,'" was

the harsh judgment of a leading historian of the period.[22] It proved
to be an interesting social experience for Allison but hardly anything
more.[23]

Heretofore, when Congress had attempted to guarantee a place for
silver by providing for purchases of stated amounts, Allison had
played a prominent role; by contrast, it would seem that he took little
part in the great debates of early 1893 on the subject. He did not
seem to be very excited about the matter, in spite of the fact that the
business situation had been deteriorating steadily in 1892. Early in
1893 he wrote his close friend and confidant, Richard P. Clarkson:
"I note what you say about repealing laws. I am in thorough sympathy with you in your view upon the subject. There is not such hot
haste as is suggested in many Republican quarters nor is there the
slightest chance that the Sherman law will be repealed during this
session." [24] He was speaking, of course, of the short session that
would end on March 4, 1893. To some extent the statement forecasts
the Republican strategy to lay the crisis on the Democratic doorstep
with the advent of Cleveland's second administration.

This crisis had been building up for a long time — since 1890 at
the very least. In part the trouble was due to the inexorable workings
of the business cycle, which the statesmen of that day did little to
control or modify. For example, the banking system was open to
the criticism that it shut down on credit at the very time that credit
was most needed; a crying need of the times was for a more elastic
currency system rather than inflation through the injection of more
cheap silver into the monetary stream. The slightest difficulties in
European financial circles reacted on the American economy by
forcing the return of securities from abroad as Europeans scrambled
to build up their gold reserves by resale, thus automatically draining
American sources and causing the markets to collapse.

The impending disaster had somehow been staved off during 1890-
1892, but it was imminent throughout the winter of 1892-1893.
The rumor that the gold standard would have to be abandoned would
not down and, in fact, was nourished by each new report of purchases
of silver made under the Sherman Act of 1890. The failure of the
Reading Railroad in February, 1893, was an indication that the end
had been reached; the failure of the National Cordage Company in
May actually precipitated the panic. The Erie, Northern Pacific,
Union Pacific, and Santa Fe roads soon joined the Reading in the list

of bankrupts; banks, especially in the West and South, failed or suspended in great numbers; unemployment figures mounted to four million or more.[25]

Allison was understandably in a difficult position. There were many pressures bearing down upon him. Iowa was not unaffected by its proximity to the Western states that made a fetish out of support for silver. The Democrats, most of whom were for free silver, were an ever present threat to Republican supremacy. The strongest Democratic leader in Iowa, Governor Horace Boies, was aligned with the silver forces, although not vociferously so, and he was a likely candidate for a third term as Governor. Republicans, under Allison's leadership, must not allow him to make too much capital out of his friendliness for the agrarian-labor interests that wanted free silver coinage. With Philip E. Studebaker writing him, on the one hand, a strong letter critical of his monetary views and advocating free silver with a legal tender of $10,000, and Charles E. Perkins, on the other hand, advocating bimetallism, not to mention the pleas of the masses for relief for their distresses, Allison indeed might have wondered which way to turn.[26]

Even James S. Clarkson, full of strange sentiments for an old-line Republican, came up with a speech in which he went far beyond the usual pleas for bimetallism and urged extensive and sincere consideration of the needs of the small farmer. Accusing his own party of a lack of interest in the welfare of the masses, he advocated specific remedies such as small banks "near enough to the people of the small communities to give them confidence in them. . . . If the Farmers' Alliance shall help to bring this about, it will not have existed in vain. A million of honest men do not rise up in revolt unless they have some actual grievance. The republican party may well adopt the policy of remedy rather than repression towards all discontented elements among the people." True enough, this speech was a valedictory from a disillusioned Clarkson laying down the presidency of the National Republican League, but it was not a speech to be ignored, especially when there were those who were urging Clarkson to come back to Iowa and make the race for the Senate.[27]

Even foreign affairs had to be reckoned with. Taking a very long view, Allison's colleague, Senator Anthony Higgins of Delaware, called his attention to a threat to Republican prospects in the German situation of June, 1893. The government of Chancellor Caprivi was in jeopardy over an army bill. "Should it come about that Germany abandons the gold standard and adopts bi-metallism, England will likely follow, and whether England should or not, France and the continent I think will, and the question would be settled for us, Cleveland would get the glory, we would be thrown back on the tariff for an issue, we would probably come into a long course of Democratic control, or maybe something else would happen." [28]

President Cleveland, applying his conservative financial views to depression problems, called an extra session of the Fifty-third Congress to meet on August 7, 1893, to consider repeal of the Sherman Silver Purchase Act, an action much needed because of the flow of United States gold to Europe. The episode makes up a chapter in a long, long American story that began with Shays' Rebellion. Party lines meant little or nothing in this fight between spokesmen for the creditors and the debtors. The President's forces beat down an attempted filibuster, all offers of compromise, and an effort to apply cloture. The editor of *Harper's Weekly* called such men as Bland of Missouri, Teller and Wolcott of Colorado, John P. Jones and William M. Stewart of Nevada "enemies of the public welfare." [29] These gentlemen in turn could only tug at the heartstrings of the public by picturing the pathetic poverty of a silverless West and give off rumblings that clearly foretold the class war of 1896.[30] On October 30 the Senate finally gave the *coup de grace* to the Sherman Act by a vote of 43 to 32. Allison was paired with Mitchell of Oregon; the former would have voted "yea" if present, the latter, "nay." [31] Such action and such circumstances lend point to the oft-quoted statement attributed to Allison, which a mutual friend passed on to Cleveland, that "it was God's mercy that you were elected President in 1892 instead of Harrison or any Republican because no Republican President could have procured the repeal of the Sherman Silver Purchase Act, however strongly he might have tried. . . . No other Democrat than yourself *would* have done it." [32] This was hindsight on Allison's part; he certainly did not oppose Harrison in 1892.

Allison and other Republicans kept up an interest in bimetallism, even though the Sherman Act had been repealed. It is hard to see anything in this except the preservation of a talking point for use in the West. In May, 1894, Allison joined Aldrich, Hoar, O. H. Platt, and others in sending a cablegram to the London Conference on International Bimetallism, to which the United States had sent Brooks

Adams and Senator Edward O. Wolcott of Colorado as delegates. "We believe that the free coinage of both gold and silver by international agreement at a fixed ratio would secure to mankind the blessing of a sufficient volume of metallic money, and, what is hardly less important, secure to the world trade immunity from violent exchange fluctuations." [33]

From this distance of time it is hard to see how bimetallism, as a practical prospect rather than as a theory, could have attracted so many and such outstanding devotees, but it did so in great numbers and from both parties. Cleveland's Secretary of the Navy, the great New York traction and utilities magnate, William C. Whitney, was converted and tried to convert Cleveland, but without success. "If Whitney ever approached fanaticism on any subject, it was over bimetallism," is his biographer's comment.[34] Henry Cabot Lodge, a new Senator now, was another who would not let the subject drop. He was severely criticized by a Republican editor, who deplored not only Lodge's "idiotic" scheme to force Great Britain into bimetallism by means of a tariff war, but also deplored the number of Republican conventions in Eastern states which were currently passing resolutions favorable to silver, after the issue had presumably been killed.[35]

The great battle of 1894 was not over silver, however, but over the tariff. All through 1892 and 1893 the Democrats had been making studies which looked toward revision of the McKinley Act. A leader in this work was a brilliant scholar and statesman from West Virginia, Representative William Lyne Wilson.[36] A bill could have been ready for presentation at a special session of Congress, but President Cleveland could not be persuaded to call one for this purpose. Therefore, the Wilson Bill had to wait until the regular session opened in December. It was briefly debated and then passed by the House on February 1, 1894, by a vote of 204 to 140. Of Iowa's delegation of eleven members, only the lone Democrat, Walter I. Hayes, voted "yea." [37]

The bill now went to the Senate, where it was taken over by the badly divided Democrats. Some, such as Roger Q. Mills of Texas and George G. Vest of Missouri, were outright free traders on principle; some, such as David B. Hill and Edward Murphy, Jr., of New York, and Calvin S. Brice of Ohio, were inclined toward protection, especially on certain products in which they were personally interested. Murphy, for example, was from Troy, New York, and was always cartooned with collars and cuffs, his "pets," sticking out of his pockets. Others, such as Arthur Pue Gorman of Maryland, were inclined to compromise. As the months dragged by, Gorman emerged as the one whose amendments were cutting the heart out of the Wilson Bill, so much so that it came to be known as the Wilson-Gorman Bill, although Wilson and Gorman were poles apart in their views.[38]

Allison's role was that of a watchdog. "I wish you & I could be empowered to make a tariff," David A. Wells wrote to Allison, with nostalgic sentiment. "I think we could as of old, agree, & make a better job than has been done of late."[39] Allison drew on his long experience as he hacked away at the thousands of details contained in the bill. He made only one major speech and saw to it that it was well distributed in Iowa.[40] In this speech he began with the premise (which would have pleased many of his Democratic opponents) that "in time of peace we should in the main, carry on the Government by means of duties upon imports." This had been true from the beginnings of the government up to now, he said, and on this all citizens were agreed. If this premise were accepted as true, then the only important question was: "How the duties upon imports are to be levied." Allison then proceeded to show the superiority of Republican proposals over those made by the Democrats. He was frequently interrupted, often by leading questions seemingly designed to help him bring out the strongest points for his cause.

The vote was at last taken on July 3, 1894, and the bill passed, 39 to 34, and was immediately referred to a conference committee. Allison strongly protested against such referral before the House had had a chance to vote on the Senate amendments.[41] One of the most contentious points in the bill had been the one providing for an income tax. Charles E. Perkins bombarded Allison with objections and arguments,[42] but without avail. The tax was included in the bill, and there is no indication that Allison used Perkins' material by way of argument against the provision. After the adoption of the conference committee's report, President Cleveland resignedly allowed the bill to become law without his signature.

In the meantime, Allison had had his hands full in rescuing Iowa from the Democrats. The 1893 Republican standard-bearer against Governor Boies was Frank D. Jackson of Greene County. Unfortunately Jackson's involvement in a heavy debt and in a near pension scandal in August threatened to ruin him and leave the party without a candidate. Only some firm action by Gilbert B. Pray, the state chairman, and a New York draft which Allison procured from some source, enabled the party leaders to cover up the mess and permit the campaign to go on.[43] Probably very few Iowans knew how closely the party came to disaster. All they knew was that the Republican split over prohibition was sufficiently healed to permit Jackson to beat down Horace Boies's attempt to gain a third term.[44]

The next thing on the Iowa schedule was the election of a Senator to succeed James F. Wilson, who was seriously ill and would not be in the race. There were a number of aspirants for the vacancy, notably John H. Gear of Burlington and Albert B. Cummins of Des Moines. Gear was the choice of his fellow-townsman and son-in-law, Joseph W. Blythe, counsel for the Burlington Railroad and a rising boss of Iowa Republicanism.[45] Cummins was a brilliant lawyer whose promise of a great career was being fulfilled. He had courage and ability, as shown by his stand against prohibition and his victory over the Barbed Wire Trust when he brought suit on behalf of the Iowa Grange. He was obviously shooting over his head at this time, although he received strong backing from Des Moines interests spoken for by Richard P. Clarkson and the *Register.*[46] George D. Perkins of Sioux City was another possible nominee. Whether Allison remained neutral toward all the contenders, as Perkins hopefully supposed, would be hard to prove. Most of his closest friends were pro-Gear. He was warned against making a combination with Gear, because that would give both Senators to the strongly Democratic River Counties, a deal that was manifestly unfair to the counties that delivered the big votes for the Republicans.[47] But such men as Blythe and Charles E. Perkins, and the power of the railroads, were not to be denied. They took the long chance that the election of their man in 1894 would not operate against the election of Allison in 1896, and they put in Gear as his colleague.

In the remaining months of 1894 Allison not only campaigned effectively in Iowa but in South Dakota, Nebraska, and Minnesota as well. Illinois Republican managers also pleaded for his assistance. He was now beginning to receive letters from all over the country, encouraging him to consider a campaign for the presidential nomination in 1896. Perhaps the one that gave him the most pleasure was from James S. Clarkson, who told of his travels and work in twelve states, all with a long view of 1896. George M. Reynolds, cashier of the Des

Moines National Bank, wrote of the recent convention of the American Bankers Association at Baltimore, where he found bankers from all sections strong for Allison as the party nominee in 1896.[48]

It is of paramount interest that the first known letter urging Allison to look ahead to the presidential contest of 1896 was written by Albert B. Cummins in the early spring of 1894. Cummins, however ambitious and independent-minded he might be, was wise enough at this stage to keep a foot firmly planted in the Allison camp. In this letter he wrote of his belief that Allison was superior to McKinley for 1896 because of his greater ability to speak authoritatively on the currency question. Cummins asked for permission to present Allison's case at a coming meeting of the National Republican League in Denver. Allison replied that he did not want the nomination, but if the party insisted on choosing him, he would accept as a matter of duty.[49]

The great theme of the Allison story of 1895, then, was the increasing attention being paid to him as a presidential possibility. Stronger men than Allison might have been pardoned if their heads had been turned by the flattering attention given to him by President-makers far and wide, especially by able businessmen of the East. For that matter, Iowans could be proud that not only Allison but James S. Clarkson and Colonel David B. Henderson were mentioned as possibilities for the nomination.[50] Allison's name was bracketed with men of the highest standing. John Hay wrote to Henry Adams, then sojourning in Europe: "If you don't hurry back, there won't be a silver man in America except you and Peffer [the Populist Senator from Kansas], and even Peffer said in an interview the other day that the jig was up. I think Reid and McKinley and Allison and Harrison and Morton are good gold-bugs now." [51]

During these months of possibly premature agitation of the presidential question, Allison lost two old friends. In September, 1894, Samuel Jordan Kirkwood died at his home in Iowa City, at the age of eighty-one. In the following spring, just a month after he had completed his second term in the Senate, James F. Wilson died at Fairfield. The passing of two colleagues who had been with him from the start of his career must have saddened Allison at a time when the future looked so bright.

Allison took part in the Iowa campaign of 1895 with special attention to the legislative elections, in view of the forthcoming senatorial election of January, 1896, when his own seat would be at stake.

He permitted himself a rare burst of confidence in a letter to another old rival, John A. Kasson, now safely left far behind in the great game of politics: "I made a full campaign this fall, and our victory exceeded my expectations. I expect to be returned to the Senate this winter. We have ninety majority on first ballot 36 in the Senate and 54 in the House." [52]

It almost goes without saying that Allison was re-elected. Even he had come to look upon such an event as inevitable. This time, however, re-election carried with it a special significance. As a part of the developing campaign for the presidency, the event had to be given a dramatic setting so that publicity values would accrue. This was done in a very effective way. The Republicans in the General Assembly of Iowa made a public ceremony out of their caucus and gave Allison a unanimous nomination. A number of high ranking dignitaries of the party were present: former Governor and Mrs. William Larrabee, Governor and Mrs. Frank D. Jackson, Governor-elect Francis M. Drake, Lieutenant Governor-elect and Mrs. Matt Parrott, and other state officers. James S. Clarkson and Gilbert B. Pray, now ranging far and wide to build up an interest in Allison, came in from their travels and joined the effort to impress the nation with the devotion of Iowa to Allison's cause. After the rising vote of all those present, a committee waited on Allison and ushered him in, to the accompaniment of an ovation. [53]

Clarkson, a well informed and influential political manager, was counted as a great asset by those who were watching Allison's second trial for the prize. His first concern was to secure some one to write an adequate campaign biography that would make Allison seem as attractive and colorful as his rivals, McKinley or Thomas B. Reed. For this work Clarkson called on the star reporter of the Des Moines *Register*, Cyrenus Cole, a product of the Dutch settlement of Pella. Many letters were required before Clarkson succeeded in conveying his ideas to Cole. [54] It would have taken less time and effort if he had done the job himself, and he could have done it better. Cole had put in long years under Clarkson's editorial supervision; now Clarkson coaxed and wheedled and drove his former employee on until the job was done. The finished essay was ready early in 1896 and appeared in various papers throughout the country in February; in the *Register*, for example, on February 12.

Allison's candidacy was formally launched at the Iowa Republican state convention on March 11, where he was given an enthusiastic endorsement after the convention had listened to an impassioned address by Congressman Jonathan P. Dolliver.[55] Clarkson's strategy was to pledge delegates far and wide to give Allison their second votes after they had given their favorite sons the first ballot as a matter of courtesy. He sent out a story from St. Louis, the site of the national convention, where he had gone to make arrangements, that Allison was sure to win because McKinley did not have enough second-choice votes pledged to him.[56] An incentive to hard work was the belief that nomination was equivalent to victory, because the opposition was split into Silver Democrats, Gold Democrats, and Populists.[57]

Walter Wellman, the outstanding Washington correspondent of the time, had warm praise for Allison's virtues as a candidate. Conceding Thomas B. Reed to be the brainiest of all the known candidates, Wellman asserted that Allison was the Washington favorite for President. His skill and his diplomacy as chairman of the Appropriations Committee had won friends in all walks of life. Democratic Senators "without exception" liked him, and as for Republican Senators, they were almost unanimously in favor of Allison for President. Reed and McKinley had a few friends, but the remainder were all for the Iowa Senator. "A large number of states are preparing to cast their votes for McKinley at St. Louis which would go for the Iowa man if the senators from those commonwealths could have their way. The senators feel that if Allison were in the White House they would be able to get along without friction or trouble. He would understand them, and they him." [58]

But as convention time approached, Allison himself seemed to realize that the fight had been in vain. Writing in confidence and perfect candor to a close friend and warm supporter, General James H. Wilson of Wilmington, Delaware, Allison admitted as much as early as May 4.[59] He and the other condidates could see that none of them had a manager with the skill and resources of McKinley's guiding genius, Marcus Alonzo Hanna. Other managers might have as much personal devotion to their chiefs, but none had the singleness of purpose, the ruthless, cold-blooded efficiency, and the amplitude of financial resources of this successful businessman from Cleveland, Ohio. For years Hanna had studied the game of politics and observed other masters of its rules and methods. Now it was his turn to enter the field as a full-fledged participant.[60]

The futility of the work of Allison and Clarkson must have been sensed by others. Well before the convention the editor of the Waterloo *Courier* urged Iowans to remain loyal to Allison to the end; Lincoln was quoted to the effect that every political race had its high and low points; Allison's race was now at a low point, but courage could yet win the day.[61] Clarkson had earlier appealed to his old friend, Louis T. Michener, to remember Iowa's assistance to Benjamin Harrison in 1888. John H. Gear importuned Harrison directly for aid, but Harrison replied that he was helpless to do anything, because any interference by him in Indiana politics would have the effect of bringing himself into the field. He went on to say:

I have said to a good many personal friends that I believe Mr. Allison's nomination and election would give us a safe and conservative administration that would not be followed by an ebb tide. . . . The favorite son business has been sadly overworked. The bringing into the field of some persons whose candidacy was not regarded as sincere and the apparent attempt to take large blocks of delegates to the convention for the purpose of transferring to somebody else very naturally excited popular resentment and the benefit has accrued to Mr. McKinley. I think Mr. Allison's managers have been too cautious. There were three or four Ohio men here at our convention for Mr. McKinley.[62]

The managers for the various candidates assembled in St. Louis about June 7, although the convention would not formally begin until June 16. In spite of discouragement, Allison's friends still planned to put up his name. His lieutenants stole a march on the others by arranging for the posting of his pictures before any others were put up, thus pre-empting the best spots. The Iowa delegation was led by Colonel D. B. Henderson, with National Committeeman Albert B. Cummins, Senator John H. Gear, a member of the resolutions committee, and Congressman William P. Hepburn, a member of the credentials committee, in good position to serve Allison's cause.

The editor of the Waterloo *Courier* admitted on June 8 that for weeks "it has been apparent" that nothing but an earthquake could stop McKinley. If by a miracle something should happen to him, then Allison would have a chance. The Iowans tried to keep up a brave front, however, an effort that reached its climax with a banner headline on page one of the Council Bluffs *Nonpareil* on June 12: "Bright for Allison." But the real news was to be found on an inside page, where Senator Gear was reported as saying that Allison had a chance if McKinley were not nominated on the first ballot. More ominous was the report that the Allison Club of Dubuque had decided to give up the trip to St. Louis. On the 15th the Council Bluffs paper announced that the special trains chartered by the Allison boosters to go from Des Moines to St. Louis via the Wabash Railway had been cancelled.

Nevertheless, the drama was played out to the end as if it still had some meaning. All the avowed candidates went through with their set plans of nominating speeches: Allison was the first to be named, his sponsor being a political unknown by the name of John N. Baldwin of Council Bluffs, son of the famous Judge Caleb Baldwin. Reed was named by Henry Cabot Lodge; Morton by Chauncey Depew, Allison's nemesis of 1888; and McKinley by Joseph B. Foraker.

Baldwin, an attorney for the Union Pacific Railway and probably General Dodge's choice for this assignment, was a man of ample girth though not a rival to his father's heroic proportions; his large and pontifical voice dwelt on Allison's virtues by indirection. Most of his speech consisted of an invocation of the memory of James G. Blaine and a long quotation from Blaine's letter to Garfield recommending Allison for a place in the Cabinet: "Then comes Allison. He is true, kind, reasonable, fair, honest, and good. He is methodical, industrious, and intelligent — and would be a splendid man to sail along with smoothly and successfully." [63] But it was too late to derive any benefit from a claim on James G. Blaine's blessing, even if genuine, and this one was not. Baldwin's home town paper, the *Nonpareil*, ruefully reported on the 19th: "The speech elicited very little enthusiasm, although it was applauded at some points."

Only one ballot was necessary for a verdict: Clarkson's strategy of pledging the most second-choice votes was never given a chance to work. McKinley's vote was $661\frac{1}{2}$; Reed's, $84\frac{1}{2}$; Quay's, $61\frac{1}{2}$; Morton's, 58; while Allison brought up the rear with $35\frac{1}{2}$ made up of 26 from Iowa, 3 from Texas, 3 from Utah, one each from Arizona, Oklahoma, and the District of Columbia, and one-half a vote from Louisiana. [64] Reed had secured most of his votes from his native New England, but Morton and Quay could not even garner all of their own state votes. McKinley received all that remained. Small wonder that Albert B. Cummins wrote to Clarkson, who was prevented from attending the convention, probably by illness:

I regret very much that you were not at St. Louis, although the proceedings of the convention could not have been a source of much pleasure to you or to any of Allison's friends. I think now, as I have thought for twenty or thirty days past, that it would have been better if Allison had withdrawn. While the delegates from Iowa were absolutely loyal to him, and had no disposition whatever to get into the bandwagon, it yet seemed to me that to receive so small a vote would be humiliating to a man who had twice before been a candidate, and who had occupied so eminent a position in the affairs of the United States during the last twenty years.[65]

The real drama of the convention had been staged in connection with the fight over the adoption of a gold plank in the platform, with Senator Henry Cabot Lodge one of the foremost proponents of this plank, and Senator Henry Moore Teller of Colorado its chief opponent. Teller's efforts to keep the plank out of the platform led to his bolt from the party in which he was followed by approximately one hundred Silver Republicans. Lodge then secured the usual innocuous clause calling for international bimetallism.[66]

When interviewed, Allison ignored his own defeat but commented at length on the platform:

The platform is a fair reflex of the will and judgment of the Republican party, and of great numbers not hitherto members of it. . . . The financial plank leaves no doubt as to its meaning and purpose. It pledges the party to the existing standard of gold until an international agreement is secured; it opposes free coinage of silver by the United States alone; it favors true bimetallism through international agreement between the leading commercial nations, the only way it can be accomplished; it promises the necessary legislation and administrative action to maintain the parity in value of all our currency or money standard. The platform is equally explicit as regards the policy of protection, and other topics of national interest.[67]

Thus ended any dreams that William Boyd Allison might ever have had about the presidency. If nothing else, his age was against him. It was very likely that McKinley would be elected in 1896; he would then be the candidate again in 1900. Forced to wait until 1904, Allison would then be seventy-five years of age, far beyond the life expectancy of the times and certainly too old for the office. His defeat was nothing to be ashamed of, however, and apparently he wasted not a second in grief or in remorse. Ironically, the presidential aspirations of another Iowan, the gifted Horace Boies,[68] were defeated in the same year by William Jennings Bryan, who swept to victory in the Democratic convention on the strength of his "Cross of Gold" speech. This was not Iowa's year. A race between two men from the same state would have been somewhat unique but probably lacking in "fireworks" from the principals. Fundamentally, the two men were very much alike in spite of Boies's endorsement of free silver. Each man was conservative by nature, but Boies was more willing to risk a positive judgment without regard to the consequences.

Republicans were soon given plenty of work to do if they were to save the country from that "dangerous radical," William Jennings Bryan. Allison contributed his full share of work to the campaign, speaking widely and helping to counteract the free silver views of the Silver Democrats and Silver Republicans. Earlier Allison had been content to describe the pamphlet, *Coin's Financial School* by W. H. Harvey, as a "cloudy book," [69] but he now had to use stronger language in this "battle of the standards." Probably neither before nor since has America come so close to the Marxian "class struggle" as in this campaign. A September check-up by Mark Hanna and the Republican national committee showed even rock-ribbed Iowa in danger, and a complement of special speakers was rushed into the state to save the day. Allison even urged, without success, that former President Harrison come to Dubuque for a speech.

In July, Senator Gear had written to Louis T. Michener: "Well, we are having and we are going to have, a regular 'monkey and parrot time.' We shall lose rafts of Republicans in Iowa, and possibly two or three congressmen; but we will gain, especially in the old portion of the state, a large number of Germans who left the party a few years ago, but will come back this year." [70] Gear's gloomy prophecy was not realized, however. After a campaign in which his managers resorted openly to such pressures as threats of closing factories if Bryan were elected, McKinley carried the state and the nation handily. Every one of the eleven Republican members of the "all-star" congressional delegation from Iowa was returned, some with handsome majorities. One eminent Iowan stated later that he had voted for McKinley on the money question after voting the Democratic ticket fifty-eight times previously. [71]

Allison received a warm letter of congratulations from Richard P. Clarkson for his part in helping to carry Iowa for McKinley, noting that Iowa had done better than Ohio. Allison was entitled to recognition from McKinley and the party, and it is good to record that he received it. It seems absolutely certain that McKinley either sounded him out for or definitely offered him the portfolio of the State Department. The possibility of such an offer was recorded in his diary by a contemporary, Charles G. Dawes, and it was later asserted categorically in the Memorial Resolutions offered by the Joint Committee of the General Assembly of Iowa in 1908.[72]

One of Allison's letters at the time gives pretty good proof that some sort of Cabinet offer was made to him. He wrote to his good friend General James H. Wilson in January of 1897: "I note what you say about Cabinet place. My situation is such that I could not afford to accept either the State or Treasury Department." In addition, there is a strong statement from Senator O. H. Platt of Connecticut, a man high in party circles and close to McKinley: "Confidentially, I will say to you I think Mr. McKinley did not indicate to Allison that he would be glad to have him take the Treasury, but did want him to become Secretary of State. Now the talk is that he will offer the Secretaryship of State to Mr. Sherman." [73]

One can readily believe that Allison would have had less interest in the State Department than in the Treasury. Certainly he had far less equipment for the position. With his defeat in 1896 and his presumable rejection of a place in the Cabinet, Allison could now philosophically content himself with his leadership in the Senate, assuredly his for life. Who was more fitted for the role of "elder statesman"?

☆ XVII ☆

Conservatives and Progressives: The Clashing Generations

THE DEFEAT OF ALLISON's presidential aspirations in 1896, followed by his refusal of a place in the Cabinet, truly marked a turning point in his career. Henceforth he would be a Senator "for life or good behavior"; no higher place was available, no lesser place would attract him. Sixty-seven years old, he had found his level; from now on there would be only the legislative routine. Outwardly, of course, there was no difference in his manner or policies. Observers in the Senate visitors' gallery could still see the same faithful and efficient leadership, quiet and unobtrusive, yet alert at all times. His position was further enhanced by formal elevation to the chairmanship of the Republican caucus when his long-time friend, John Sherman, resigned to accept the first place in McKinley's Cabinet,[1] the place that very likely might have been Allison's. He had again permitted a colleague to go upstairs into the President's official family, as in Windom's case, and had succeeded to one of that colleague's honors in the Senate.

Allison's emergence as party leader and elder statesman was made more noticeable by two somewhat fortuitous circumstances: the calling of a special session of Congress to consider a tariff bill to replace the botched-up Wilson-Gorman Act; and the illness of Nelson W. Aldrich, chairman of the Senate Committee on Finance. Allison, as the ranking member after Aldrich, fell heir to the leadership of this committee, so powerful in tariff making.[2] From this point in Allison's career, one can discern a little more clearly the drift toward those actions that made him known as a "Western man with Eastern principles."

The extraordinary session of the Fifty-fifth Congress, which met on March 15 and adjourned on July 24, 1897, was a strenuous one, almost defying complete and orderly description. The fights were over two great and inseparable issues: tariff reform and currency. The election of 1896 had definitely not guaranteed the triumph of gold monometallism, as so many people had easily concluded from the victory of McKinley. There was still a strong bloc of Silver Senators whose strength could not be ignored, and some kind of deal would have to be made. Since the Western Senators demanded free silver and tariff protection on wool, hides, and lead, the logical move for the protectionists was to try to wean some of these Westerners away from free silver or else to make concessions to them.

A far-flung plan, really a plot, was thought up whereby the tariff advocates sent Colorado's Senator Edward O. Wolcott, who was ready to desert the free silver cause, to Europe as a negotiator to secure an agreement on international bimetallism in return for tariff concessions from the United States. The Western Senator carried out his part, well knowing that his desertion of free silver would probably end his political career, but the strategy ran aground when the rank-and-file Senators from the West refused to vote for the tariff concessions that Wolcott had optimistically advanced to the French as bait.[3]

The House then quickly passed a tariff bill named after Nelson Dingley of Maine and sent it to the Senate. In the midst of the furious Senate debates and cloakroom negotiations that followed, Aldrich's illness removed him from Washington's inhospitable climate, and Allison took over the leadership. Eventually a tariff bill, the highest yet enacted, was put together in the Senate and passed by a vote of 38 to 28. The promises of concessions that Wolcott had made to the French were scornfully brushed aside by spokesmen for home interests. Senator William E. Chandler of New Hampshire, one of the few bona fide Republican bimetallists, exerted strong pressures on Allison and McKinley, but to no avail. "Both made assertions that they were entirely sympathetic and ready to do anything in their power, but either their promises were not entirely candid or their power did not extend very far"[4] is the verdict of Chandler's biographer. The Senate version of the Dingley Bill was now submitted to a joint conference committee that "completed the work in the familiar star chamber fashion." [5] The House passed the bill on July 19, the Senate on July 24, and the President signed it on the same day.[6]

It would be hard to say whether Allison's reputation was enhanced or harmed by his performance in this tariff fight. In general, he was both praised and blamed. Chandler was critical, saying that Allison's intentions were excellent but that he had "neither the knowledge of tariff matters nor the force of character of the Rhode Island senator." But Allison was very much in step with the great majority of his fellow Republicans in 1897. One has only to read the speeches of Iowa's greatest orator of this era, Robert G. Cousins of Tipton, to see the classic expression of a blind faith in the protective tariff and to sense what Allison would have been up against if he had tried to work for a reduced tariff.[7] James S. Clarkson, Jonathan P. Dolliver, Cyrenus Cole, and all the other party wheel horses were equally strong in their devotion to this shibboleth of Republicans (and Pennsylvania Democrats).

The tariff issue, so important in 1897, was pushed into the background in 1898 by outside events. For years America had been watching the growing seriousness of the plight of the Cubans under Spain's harsh rule. The sinking of the *Maine* on February 15, 1898, awoke the indifferent and the casual lookers on and converted many of them, temporarily at least, into firebrands,[8] while others retained their equanimity and opposed intervention as unnecessary and unjustified. Allison and most of his friends were definitely ranked on the side of the antiexpansionists, the isolationists of the day. Chief among these were Allison's colleague, John Henry Gear of Burlington, bitterly opposed to the annexation of Hawaii, a collateral issue of the Cuban question; Richard P. Clarkson of the *Register*; General Grenville M. Dodge; and, more notably and positively, Allison's great friend, Colonel David B. Henderson.[9]

The bluff, genial Colonel was outspoken in stating his position. On March 8, 1898, he delivered a brief but pointed speech on the subject in Congress, the heart of which is in this passage:

I have had letters from my people wanting us to take Cuba, to punish Spain. I simply write back that no international law makes the United States the regulator of the wrongs of the earth. God has written no motto on the banner of our country that demands of us the regulating of the wrongs of other countries to their people. We all sympathize with the liberty-loving and fighting Cubans, but they are citizens of another Government. So long as that question is before us, I follow the advice of Washington, recommending that we mind strictly our own business.[10]

The Chicago *Tribune* under Joseph Medill took sharp issue with Henderson, whereupon the Colonel sent a clipping of Medill's editorial to his close friend, Richard P. Clarkson, with instructions as to its use in the *Register*. He added in strict confidence a story from a friend to whom President McKinley had read the speech, "commenting on it and approving it. Of course this must not get into the papers, at least not in any way from me." [11]

However much Allison and other important leaders such as Aldrich, Hanna, Fairbanks, Eugene Hale, O. H. Platt, and Spooner in the Senate, and "Czar" Thomas B. Reed and Colonel Henderson in the House, opposed the decision to intervene, and however much President McKinley may have approved Henderson's nonintervention speech, the decision was made, the fateful step was taken,[12] and the United States found herself engaged in a war with Spain. No charges of treason have been leveled at the provocators of this war, but it is pretty well agreed that certain special groups and individuals, inflamed with "the martial spirit," led the country into an unnecessary conflict.[13]

Regardless of their opposition to the war, Allison and Henderson had to take a real interest in the conflict and help to support it. In his capacity as chairman of the Senate Appropriations Committee, Allison played a leading role in seeing to it that the necessities of war were provided. In addition, he had a personal interest due to the fact that his nephew and namesake, W. B. Allison, Jr., volunteered for service. The young man, who had been acting as assistant clerk of his uncle's committee, now was given the rank of captain and duty as an assistant adjutant general.[14]

The victory was soon won, and in August the President busied himself with the task of selecting a peace commission to represent the United States at the Paris Conference. Allison rejected a place on the commission which was offered to him.[15] What excuses he made to McKinley are not known, but among his friends a pretty story was later circulated that he preferred to stay in Washington and help in the fight for the confirmation of Richard P. Clarkson's son-in-law, Edward R. Meek of Fort Worth, as a federal judge for the Northern District of Texas.[16]

It seems never to have occurred to Jonathan Dolliver, who is the source of this story, that Allison owed a greater obligation to his country than to the Clarksons and the Meeks; very likely the point was exaggerated by Dolliver in his great-hearted manner. There may also have been other reasons for Allison's declination. For one thing, confirmation was by no means certain. Some would have opposed his appointment over the heads of members of the Foreign Relations Committee; the ultra-expansionists who regarded him as an inveterate compromiser might have objected.[17] Nothing in Allison's background especially fitted him for membership on the Commission; one thinks of the occasion in 1897 when McKinley wanted to appoint him as Secretary of State and wonders why the President so persistently thought of Allison for this kind of service. There is nothing anywhere else in the evidence to indicate that Allison was long or seriously considered for this assignment in Paris.

The Peace Commission had its troubles but finally signed a treaty with Spain, the terms providing for the relinquishment of Cuba and title to the Philippine Islands and to Puerto Rico as well, the United States to pay a round sum of twenty million dollars. The Treaty of Paris was signed on December 10, 1898; the fight for ratification began in January, 1899; the final vote came on February 6. Ardent imperialists, such as Henry Cabot Lodge and Nelson W. Aldrich, had converted most of the reluctant Republicans except the venerable Senator Hoar; and William Jennings Bryan, the titular Democratic leader, had convinced himself and about a dozen Democratic Senators that a vote for ratification was correct. According to his reasoning, this would close up the war and put the issue of imperialism before the people in the coming presidential election.[18] Allison gave his vote to the ratificationists.[19]

In fact, Allison now completely changed his attitude on the issue of imperialism. Once the war which he had opposed had been fought and won, he came out in favor of holding all the Philippines, then a moot question.[20] He became a good friend of that brilliant leader of the expansionist forces, the new Senator from Indiana, Albert J. Beveridge, who put himself under Allison's wing and in return received warm support for his efforts to interest the country in the new spirit. On arriving in Washington in 1899, Beveridge reported that he found the Senate dominated by a "marvelous combination" composed of Aldrich as manager, Allison as "conciliator and adjustor,"

Spooner as "floor leader and debater," and Platt as "designer and builder" — "The Four" as they have been called.

A friendship quickly developed between Allison and Beveridge; on one occasion, after Beveridge had made an impassioned speech pleading for rank imperialism in the Philippines, Allison was the first to shake his hand. A few months later Beveridge, while touring the Islands, wrote to Allison: "I trust you will keep in mind the matter of committeeships. I hope I have somewhat qualified myself for Foreign Relations. As I told you I am ready to sacrifice all other committees for that although I am earnestly desirous of Judiciary and Finance as well as Foreign Relations."

The ambitious Beveridge had to accept defeat on these aspirations, however, but he found solace in other recognition he received. On one occasion he sat in on the session of the Foreign Relations Committee while it drew up a statement of American policy; he must have looked on approvingly as Allison joined O. H. Platt, Lodge, and Cushman K. Davis in a declaration that the Philippine Islands were now territory belonging to the United States, that it was America's intention to "retain them as such" and to "establish and maintain such governmental control throughout the archipelago as the situation may demand." [21]

Beveridge's letter regarding committee assignments is only one indication of the prestige and power that Allison had acquired. John Sherman had been transferred to the Cabinet, and the eminent Senator Justin S. Morrill of Vermont, whose service in both houses totaled almost forty-four years, had died. The passing of this grand old man, who was Allison's friend and next door neighbor on Vermont Avenue, left Allison as the "Father of the Senate," [22] truly a Nestorian figure to whom both high and low appealed for advice and help. In addition to being chairman of the caucus, he was chairman of the steering committee and of the committe on committees. [23]

In April, 1899, word came that "Czar" Reed might retire from the Speakership and from Congress. Allison's faithful aide, Colonel David B. Henderson, immediately announced his intention to try for the place. [24] Richard Clarkson and the *Register* led the fight for the Henderson cause, ably aided by other Iowa newspapers, while Allison wrote to Aldrich in Henderson's behalf and, it is a safe guess, to many others. [25] The first stage of the struggle for support ended in June; [26] the formal vote did not take place until the beginning of the session

From L. A. Coolidge, *An Old-Fashioned Senator, Orville H. Platt*

"THE FOUR" OF THE SENATE IN CONFERENCE AT THE HOME OF
NELSON W. ALDRICH IN 1903

Left to right: Orville H. Platt, John C. Spooner, William B. Allison, Nelson W. Aldrich

ABOUT 1880

IN 1902

SENATOR WILLIAM BOYD ALLISON

of the Fifty-sixth Congress on December 4, 1899. Henderson's only serious rival was Joseph G. Cannon; fortunately for Henderson, Cannon was blocked by a fellow-Illinoisan, Albert J. Hopkins, but since neither Cannon nor Hopkins would defer to the other, Henderson's selection by the caucus was virtually assured.[27] One observer laconically recorded the event in his diary: "Went to the House where I saw Henderson elected Speaker." [28]

Before taking leave of the last year of the nineteenth century, where we find Allison and Henderson at the peak of their power, it is fitting that some notice should be taken of the death of Allison's rival of 1872 — James Harlan. The intervening years had had their moments of personal recognition for Harlan: membership on the commission to negotiate a settlement of the *Alabama* claims; keynote speeches and dedication addresses almost without number — any gracious honor could be his, so long as it was empty of political power. Beaten back in his aspirations for Governor in 1875 and for Senator in 1876, he had been a possible selection as the nominee for Governor in 1895 and again in 1897, in the late evening of his life. During the 1897 convention preliminaries, Albert B. Cummins wrote to a friend: "Look out for Harlan. I do not think it at all unlikely that he will be nominated. If he goes to Cedar Rapids and is in fair health and vigor, there will be a tremendous inclination to put him in." [29]

Cummins proved to be a poor prophet, however. The honor went to Leslie M. Shaw, the Denison banker (as it did again in 1899), and James Harlan trudged away from his last convention, unwept and unsung, totally forgotten by the party for which he had done so much in its founding years. The older party members could remember only the Cherokee Affair;[30] the younger ones probably ignored him. Two years later, on October 5, 1899, the first citizen of Mount Pleasant was dead.

For some time now — in fact ever since the "battle of the standards" in 1896 — the political scene had been fairly calm in Iowa. In 1899, however, the Allison "machine" — a machine that was all the more powerful for never calling itself a machine — faced a severe test. Allison's aged and mediocre colleague, John Henry Gear, was approaching the end of his term of office; the senatorial election would take place early in the forthcoming session of the legislature in 1900. A number of aspirants for the seat hoped that Gear would not make the race or that he could be beaten if he insisted in asking for re-election in spite of his age. Chief among these was Albert Baird Cummins, the brilliant Des Moines lawyer who still counted himself a loyal supporter of Allison, but who wanted to win Iowa's other seat in the Senate, whether Allison approved or not.

The prospect of a victory for the elegant reformer from Des Moines was not pleasing to the Allison leaders, whom Iowans of that day openly referred to as "The Regency." Besides the Senator himself, the "Regents" were Joseph W. Blythe of Burlington, chief counsel for the Burlington Railroad; his brother, James E. Blythe of Mason City; and Judge Nathaniel M. Hubbard of Cedar Rapids, counsel for the Chicago & North Western Railroad. James S. Clarkson still had a voice in their councils, even though he now lived in New York; so did Grenville M. Dodge; while men from Council Bluffs, Sioux City, and other places were called on as circumstances dictated.[31]

The seriousness with which the political leaders of that day regarded the Cummins threat is indicated in their letters. For example, Ret Clarkson complained about brother Richard's support of the Cummins candidacy instead of the Gear cause. Very patiently Richard explained to Ret that since the *Register* had supported Cummins six years earlier, it could not very well now reverse itself and support another candidate. As for Gear, Richard assured Ret of his gratitude for Gear's help in the Judge Meek matter, but insisted he could not desert Cummins for this reason alone. As for Allison, "All the Cummins men are Allison men, and The Register will be for Allison as long as he lives. . . . Allison has made both the State and the Nation greater. He ought to have been president in place of Ben Harrison, and if he had been, there would have been no second term for Cleveland." [32]

The Iowa election campaign for members of the legislature to meet in 1900 increased in heat if not light as the months went by. Cyrenus Cole, now part-owner and editor in his own right of the Cedar Rapids *Republican*, and a Cummins man in 1893-1894, tried to be neutral. He wrote to Allison of the difficulties created by Gear's age.[33] Earlier, the pro-Gear, anti-Cummins railroad spokesman, "Regent" Joseph W. Blythe, had tried hard to overcome Cole's neutrality.

I wish you could see your way clear to help us bring this fight to a finish now. It is approaching its last round, and if we could have a little active help from you, I feel sure that the end would be much hastened. I think you know that I do not want to unduly press this, and I recognize fully your situation and the obligations growing out of your personal relations with Mr. Cummins; but when, in your own time and in your way, you can see an opportunity to help us, we shall be very grateful.[34]

The entrenched power of the Allison wing of the party was not to be denied. On January 8, 1900, when the Twenty-eighth General Assembly began its sessions, the first test of power went against the Cummins people when their candidate for Speaker of the House was beaten, and at the senatorial caucus that night a Cummins spokesman asked that Cummins' name be withdrawn from consideration. Gear's nomination followed by acclamation. In the legislature, he won handily over the Democratic nominee, Fred E. White, by a vote of 111 to 32.[35] The verdict of the *Register* was that Cummins had made a fine showing, but that he had had against him "a railroad with millions backing the biggest 'boss' the state ever knew." [36] This reference to Joseph W. Blythe and the Burlington was not the reaction of a radical but the calm judgment of the editor of the state's largest and most influential Republican newspaper.

There is no escaping the conclusion that the determination to put up Senator Gear for re-election in this contest was a decision born of desperation. The bosses had wanted to prevent the election of Cummins at any price. Now if Gear should die, his replacement would be in the hands of Governor Leslie M. Shaw, who was friendly to the Allison-Blythe-Hubbard wing of the party.[37] At seventy-five Gear was too old and feeble to perform the duties of the office, even if he might be granted a few more years of life. In less than a month after the election, one of the bosses of Iowa, Judge Hubbard of the Regency, wrote Cyrenus Cole: "No Gear man can now vote for Cummins for Senator, if Senator Gear should die, — which I hope he will not." Then, facing reality, Hubbard added, "I greatly fear the crisis is close at hand, and that Senator Gear will not survive many days. This is for your eyes . . . and no other." [38]

With the Cummins threat apparently safely scotched, the Allison group could now turn its attention to other matters. It so happened that just at this time a move was on foot to give James S. Clarkson, for some years out of the political limelight,[39] a richly deserved reward for his long party service. This was to be the political plum of election as Secretary of the Senate, a prize that had been dangled before him in 1897. The matter seems to have been one that could have been managed easily enough by such leaders as Allison, Aldrich, and many others who were indebted to Clarkson. Just why the plan fell through can not be fully determined, but the important point for this story is that Clarkson blamed Allison as one of a small group that failed to stand by him when the chips were down.[40] Clarkson wrote a powerful letter of denunciation to Cyrenus Cole, blaming three Senators who withheld their aid because he would not pledge his support to certain interests, and blaming another Senator "whom I had supposed to be my friend for 30 years" for withholding his voice in caucus and also holding back four proxies that he carried in his pocket.[41] This could have been no other than Allison, who protested his innocence to Clarkson: "I am deeply pained to hear . . . that you blame your truest and best friends, and among them myself. . . . Some scoundrel must have told you untruths, as many untruths were told during the controversy."[42] Apparently Clarkson was overly sensitive in this case and really defeated himself by abruptly withdrawing his name because he could not have the undivided vote of all the Republican Senators.

Thus the year 1900 had opened with trouble for Allison over the senatorship and the Clarkson appointment. Hardly had these problems been solved when a difficult decision faced Allison. There was no doubt about the renomination of McKinley that year, but the second place on the ticket was available because of the death of Vice President Garret A. Hobart in November, 1899. The one person who could dare to dispute with the President over the choice for a running mate was Marcus Alonzo Hanna, now a Senator in his own right. Hanna wanted Cornelius N. Bliss for the spot, but McKinley was not enthusastic about him. Allison and many others were considered, among them John D. Long, John Hay, Elihu Root, and Charles W. Fairbanks. Allison refused the place outright, suggested Jonathan Dolliver, and worked hard for him. But Boss Platt of New York wanted to get rid of Governor Theodore Roosevelt and was able to secure his nomination, even though Roosevelt did not want the honor.[43]

The McKinley-Roosevelt ticket for 1900 had hardly been decided upon when in July, 1900, the long expected death of Senator Gear occurred, and Governor Leslie M. Shaw promptly obliged the Allison forces by appointing Dolliver to the vacant seat.[44] There could be no objection to the Fort Dodge man on the score of ability, character, and industry; the only resentment would be in the Cummins ranks. Well might Cummins have said that the Allisonians had been able to eat their cake and have it too. By using Gear in the election a few months earlier they had been able to forestall Cummins from the chance of victory in an open, competitive race, where the people's choice could at least be indirectly asserted. Now Gear was dead, as expected; the "ins" could extend their control by appointing a man who had never run for the office instead of one who had twice put up a good fight. Little wonder if the affair rankled in Cummins' heart and if deep resolves were made as to plans and methods to be used in future contests. As yet, however, Cummins made no open moves; on the surface he remained loyal to Allison and the party.

The presidential election of 1900 was a routine affair. The ticket of McKinley and Roosevelt swept over Bryan's second try for the White House, this time with imperialism the chief issue rather than free silver. McKinley's vote ran higher than in 1896, and America settled down to enjoy a spell of prosperity and peace. There had been a full recovery from the depression brought on by the Panic of 1893; prices were generally higher due to a larger supply of gold made available by discoveries of new fields and to the cyanide process of refining; the gold standard had been adopted officially; agriculture was prosperous for the first time since 1865.

The first few months of the new McKinley term were uneventful, the inauguration in March being followed by the long summer vacation, but the calm was rudely shattered on September 6 by a bullet from the gun of the anarchist, Leon Czolgosz. The President lingered between life and death for a week, but the end came on September 14. The assassin, who had accomplished nothing for his cause, made possible the elevation of Theodore Roosevelt to the presidency, the youngest and one of the most dynamic men ever to hold that office.

The new President, mindful of his accidental succession, did not immediately launch a drive for personal control. Shrewd politician that he was, he recognized the power of the party organization and its agents in Congress, and he gladly worked with it. As a student of government and politics, and as Governor of New York, he had learned that a chief executive must be a chief legislator as well, if he is to be a successful and memorable President. The only way for him to get a legislative program adopted would be through tactful cooperation with Congress. His meteoric and fortuitous rise to the top had not yet allowed him to build up a great nationwide popular following to which he could appeal or an organization devoted to him personally.

In turning to Congress, the youthful, vigorous Roosevelt met Iowans in almost every important and strategic post. In the Senate, of course, there was Allison, member of "The Four," the totally unofficial group that had acquired a power so great that even a President had to consult them if senatorial action were desired.[45] In addition to Allison, there were Aldrich of Rhode Island, Orville H. Platt of Connecticut, and John Coit Spooner of Wisconsin, all chairmen or members of important committees.[46] Close to "The Four" and sometimes more powerful with regard to specific matters and causes were Henry Cabot Lodge of Massachusetts and Eugene Hale of Maine, both good friends of Allison. And then there was the new junior Senator from Iowa, Dolliver, who regarded Allison with filial devotion and who soon became a favorite with Roosevelt.

In the House Roosevelt found Allison's faithful friend Henderson as Speaker, heading an Iowa delegation of eleven Republicans who were virtually under Allison's orders because of their regard for him and their partial dependence on his favor. Four of them were chairmen of important committees: John A. T. Hull, Military Affairs; William P. Hepburn, Interstate and Foreign Commerce; John F. Lacey, Public Lands; and Robert G. Cousins, Expenditures in the Treasury Department. In addition, all of the delegation held high ranking assignments on these and other committees.[47]

But the political calm in Iowa and in the nation was soon to be broken. The year 1901 can be classified as one of the most important years in Iowa politics and, in a negative sense, one of the most important in Allison's career. In this year came the first triumph of his rival, Albert Baird Cummins, and the first definite and formal division of Iowa Republicans into Conservative (Standpat) and Progressive factions.

This split had been in the making for several years. In some ways, Progressivism was akin to the Liberal Republicanism of 1872 and the Mugwumpery in the Republican ranks in 1884. More directly, it was a descendant of the Populist movement of the 1890's. It is possible to list a number of criteria that set off the Progressives from the Standpatters, but such a list is of value only if one remembers that very few men even approached wholehearted adherence to every point in the catalog. There were many shades of belief, and while the labels were most often applied to Republicans, there were actually the same distinctions among the Democrats.

Progressives wanted tariff reform downward and they wanted reciprocity; they wanted legislation to curb the great business interests, especially to guard against the formation of trusts with monopolistic power; they wanted regulation of the railroads, the grain elevator companies, the insurance companies, the meat-packing companies, the stock market ("Wall Street"); they wanted reforms to wipe out "the shame of the cities," and they wanted more democracy in state government, hence their support of the direct primary, the initiative and referendum, and the recall. Standpatters opposed some or all of these objectives, in varying degrees.[48]

The "Big Three" in the Standpat-Progressive struggle in Iowa, and close to the top in national politics, were Allison, Cummins, and Dolliver. There was almost nothing of the doctrinaire about these men. The "Standpatter" Allison was not a champion of the rights of any privileged class; the "Progressive" Cummins was not the champion of an oppressed lower class, much less of a proletariat. Dolliver, nominally a Standpatter, was actually a Progressive at heart, but for years he remained loyal to Allison out of personal gratitude for Allison's political assistance and out of sheer affection for the grand old man who treated him like a son. As for wealth, Allison was a professional politician whose small fortune consisted of his inheritance from his second wife and the profits from investments in safe stocks. Dolliver had little money besides his income as a member of Congress and his fees as a public speaker. Cummins was one of the leading lawyers of the state and probably had earned far more money than Allison had ever collected as a member of Congress. He was known as a man of elegant tastes and discriminating judgment, and he moved in the highest ranks of Iowa business and society. As associates and supporters, he could number such men as F. M. Hubbell of Des Moines, banker, real estate baron, insurance company owner and executive; [49] Fred L. Maytag, wealthy manufacturer of Newton; [50] John H. Hartman, newspaper publisher of Waterloo; A. B. Funk, publisher of the Spirit Lake Beacon; and Thomas A. Way, banker and farm land magnate of Iowa and Minnesota.

Cummins bowled over all opposition in the state convention held at Cedar Rapids in August. He openly asserted that Joe Blythe and N. M. Hubbard had challenged him and that he had accepted the challenge; he wanted the convention to decide between them. The result was a resounding victory for Cummins, his 860½ votes more

than double the 369½ for James H. Trewin and the 359 for W. F.
Harriman, his chief rivals. When Cummins returned to Des Moines
after the convention, the reception was fit for a conquering hero. The
Grant Club, made up of the pillars of the party, and the Cummins
Convention Club met his train; he was taken to the Grant Club House
in a procession, riding in F. M. Hubbell's carriage with Governor
Leslie M. Shaw as a fellow passenger. And surely no one wrote a more
gratifying letter to him than Senator William Boyd Allison:

Allow me to extend to you my hearty congratulations upon your nomination
yesterday. I wish to cooperate with you in the campaign. I have planned to
be absent from the state about three weeks leaving [Dubuque] on Saturday.
I will take an early occasion after my return to see you and consult with you
as to organization of the work. By that time the committee will be in working
order. Your nomination will be well received in the state and I have no doubt
you will receive a large majority when the votes are counted.[51]

The convention that had nominated Cummins had also taken a
significant step in the writing of its platform. The tariff plank,
written by George Evan Roberts, soon came to enjoy national fame.
Indeed, this convention had builded better than it knew. The tariff
plank asserted in clear though not revolutionary language "the sovereignty of the people over all corporations and aggregations of capital and the right residing in the people to enforce such regulations,
restrictions or prohibitions upon corporate management as will
protect the individual and society from abuse of the power which
great combinations of capital wield." It then concluded: "We favor
such amendments of the interstate commerce act as will more fully
carry out its prohibition of discrimination in rate making and any
modifications of the tariff schedules that may be required to prevent
their affording a shelter to monopoly." The whole plank was adopted
as proposed by Roberts without objection or debate in the resolutions
committee and by the unanimous vote of the full convention. This
was the tariff revision proposal that gained fame and attention under
the name of the "Iowa Idea"; [52] actually, the other clauses came nearer
to realization and are worthy of more attention. Roberts gave Walter
Wellman, a famous correspondent of the era, credit for the title.

The large majority for Cummins that Allison had predicted was
realized. The Democrats helped to insure Republican victory by
breaking up into factions, one led by Thomas J. Phillips, the winner
of the nomination for Governor; the other by the brilliant young

lawyer, Horace J. Stiger of Toledo. Richard Clarkson reported to his brother that "the Cummins political juggernaut is as relentless as the juggernaut of ancient times," and that Cummins was still a candidate for the United States Senate.[53]

But the Cummins juggernaut, however relentless, was not powerful enough to roll over the Allison machine. Both Allison and Dolliver were up for re-election in 1902. Allison's campaign for re-election was conducted by his friends. James S. Clarkson, finding the capacity to forgive and forget Allison's treatment of him and the grace to serve his political ambitions, offered to write an article for the *Register*, favoring the re-election of Allison by the unanimous action of the legislature. Ret's brother accepted the offer promptly and with approval, adding his belief that the Davenport *Democrat* and other Democratic papers generally would see the justice of "non-partisan recognition of a man who has never been offensive in his partisanship." [54] The article appeared in the *Register* on Tuesday, December 10, 1901, under the title "Allison and Iowa — Noblesse Oblige." On reading it one would never know that there had been any difficult moments in the relationships of these two men. The essay consisted of a sober review of the record that Allison had compiled, and then gave reasons why the state could honor herself by honoring Allison with the compliment of a unanimous vote.

Despite Ret's bold and eloquent plea for a nonpartisan vote for Allison, the Democrats did not cooperate. They put up a distinguished Clinton publisher-editor whose public career, like Allison's, ran all the way back to pre-Civil War days — Judge E. H. Thayer. Against Dolliver, running for the remainder of Gear's term, the Democrats nominated John J. Seerley of Burlington. Party lines held fast, and each Republican received 119 votes; each Democrat, 20.[55] In his acceptance speech Dolliver endorsed the ideas on the tariff adopted at the previous state convention of his party and boldly asserted that the Dingley Tariff of 1897 was already unnecessary on many items, on some, absurd. [56] Allison, having already returned to Washington, was not present to make an acceptance speech at this, his last election by the General Assembly.

Just before the close of the year 1901 Allison had assisted in securing the Secretaryship of the Treasury for ex-Governor Leslie M. Shaw, the Denison banker who had gone into politics largely in order to fight what he considered the dangerous monetary policies of Bryan.

Shaw had favorably impressed Roosevelt with his sound-money speeches during the campaign of 1900; when, through Allison and Henderson, Shaw was asked to become Secretary, he accepted.[57]

As Cyrenus Cole has noted, this was "the golden age" of Iowa's strength in Washington; surely never before and perhaps never since has the state possessed so much influence in American government. Now, in addition to her power in Congress, two of Iowa's men, Tama Jim Wilson and Leslie M. Shaw, were in the President's official family. To these should be added George E. Roberts as Director of the Mint, and Maurice D. O'Connell as Solicitor of the Treasury, giving Fort Dodge two of the highest places in the government just short of the Cabinet itself. Several Iowans were also in the diplomatic service.

And now at long last something was done for James S. Clarkson, and Allison, along with Dolliver, had a hand in it. On April 12, 1902, Dolliver wrote that he and Allison had fixed it up with Senator T. C. Platt of New York to secure the post of Surveyor of the Port of New York City for Clarkson. Dolliver required three pages to give Ret the necessary assurances that this time there would be no slip-up, no shortage of a virtual unanimity in the vote. Two days later he wrote again, addressing Ret as "Dear General" in memory of the days when Clarkson was First Assistant Postmaster General, and assured him of success.[58] The appointment was confirmed on April 17, 1902, and at last the tension between Allison and Clarkson could cease. Not only that, Clarkson would now be in an excellent "listening post," where he could be of great service to Allison, Dolliver, and Shaw. As a reactivated member of the high councils of the Republican party, he could also be of real service to President Roosevelt.[59]

During the remainder of the year things happened which showed that a new day had arrived in Iowa politics. Governor Cummins saw to it that the 1902 platform served his purposes. In urging one of his trusted lieutenants, Nathan E. Kendall of Albia, to seek a place on the platform committee of the state convention of 1902, he wrote: "I would like to see a platform written as you can write it, expressing the progressive ideas of this generation. I do not want to have anything said that is not fundamentally sound or which goes beyond our expressions of last year." [60] The Cummins program was carried out completely. The platform of 1901 was reaffirmed, even to the point of repeating the clause that held that the tariff must not be allowed to serve as a shelter to monopolies.[61]

A second sign of the passing of the old order was the sale of the Des Moines *Register* by Richard P. Clarkson. The principal purchaser was George E. Roberts, a good Allisonian but a man with a forward look, as his authorship of the "Iowa Idea" shows. The retirement of the Clarksons from the *Register* was the significant thing. The details of the negotiations were handled on the Eastern end by Ret and Senator Dolliver.[62]

But the most dramatic act, marking 1902 as a watershed in Iowa political history, was one that threw the Allison wing of the party into the greatest confusion. It so happened that in September of 1902 President Roosevelt had summoned Allison, Aldrich, Spooner, Hanna, and Lodge to his summer home at Oyster Bay for a secretive but not secret conference on party policy;[63] in a larger sense the object was to reach an agreement on a division of power between the President and the leaders of the Senate.

In spite of poor health, Allison had left Iowa, where the congressional campaign was in full swing, and where his good friend David B. Henderson was engaged in a bitter fight for re-election, and had gone to Oyster Bay. Imagine the consternation among the party leaders at this meeting when Allison received a telegram from Henderson on September 16:

Being satisfied that I am not in harmony with many of our party who believe that free trade in whole or in part [is the] remedy [for] the trust evil I have withdrawn from the congressional race.[64]

Roosevelt, Allison, officers of the Republican national committee, and others sent urgent wires to the bluff old soldier, urging him to reconsider. These pleas disturbed him, Henderson confessed to Allison in a long telegram the next day, but he was adamant in his decision not to run. He gave Allison many reasons: his inability to swallow "free trade" as a medicine to "cure the trusts"; the drain on his savings — "everybody is bleeding me"; the charges that he was a drunkard; complaints from Waterloo — "at my age, and holding my position, I ought to be exempt from the dirty mud slinging of Waterloo Republicans, and have no disposition to longer submit to it." He asked Allison to "take pains" to explain to all concerned: "I could spend all my time straightening out Republicans. . . . I have neither the time nor the strength for such work. Can fight Democrats and Populists, but not the other class." [65]

Evidently Henderson had come to his decision suddenly, after

Allison had left for the East. "I wanted you [the] last few days very much," he wrote, "but you had gone when I returned from Waterloo." Allison was greatly distressed, but Henderson would not change his mind. His explanations to Allison, in the long telegram, were not made public; for some strange reason, Allison even denied having heard from his distressed colleague. From that day to this a certain amount of mystery has hung over the episode.[66]

This mystery was deepened and compounded when one of Henderson's closest friends, Cyrenus Cole, later wrote such words as these: "In 1902 . . . [Henderson] announced unexpectedly that he would not be a candidate for renomination. . . . His own explanation was that he wanted to practice law in New York to provide better for his family. He had other and more personal reasons which have never been written into history. Nor will I write them into it now. It is too late."[67] Perhaps there were personal reasons known only to Cole and other intimate friends; even so, the act can be stripped of some of its mystery. To begin with, Cole's premise is incorrect: Henderson did not announce that he would not be a candidate for renomination, with all that that implies. He had already been renominated by his district and had made plans for his campaign when suddenly, on September 16, he announced his withdrawal.

A bitter campaign was being waged against the man who was Allison's first lieutenant and who had been a party leader since the 1860's. Such a man might well feel justified in turning with disgust from the game of politics with the remark, "Let the new light shine."[68] This fight on Henderson, which began with an attack on his czaristic tactics as Speaker, was really due to his position on the tariff. The criticism began as early as February, 1902; perhaps it encouraged the Cummins crowd to think they could replace him. O. B. Courtright was mentioned as a rival. Henderson's friends retaliated by arranging to hold the district nominating convention in May, instead of in July or August as was customary. Courtright withdrew in a huff, and Henderson won the nomination. But the criticism continued, and in mid-July, Allison wrote to Richard Clarkson: "I agree with you, however, as to the importance of making a clear, plain declaration of the Republican view on the tariff. This is important in view of the fact that Iowa's declaration will be looked to with interest because of the interest taken in our Speaker."[69] The state convention of the party, meeting on July 30, made no direct reference to Henderson's policies, but it did adopt a tariff plank that he could accept with only slight enthusiasm. As noted above, the plank was the work of the Cummins people; it endorsed protection in principle but favored such changes as might become advisable, inveighed against tariffs used to shelter monopolies, and frankly endorsed reciprocity.

Another natural assumption could be that Henderson's decision was due to anger at not being included among the guests at the conference at Oyster Bay. Henderson, as Speaker of the House, might well have thought himself entitled to inclusion in such a conference on legislative policy. There is surely some significance in the fact that he chose the day of the Oyster Bay meeting to send the telegram to Allison.

The best explanation, however, is that Speaker Henderson was the first victim of the "Cummins juggernaut," even if by indirect means only. Early in September, Governor Cummins had assured Henderson that his friends were not refusing to support him, but this assurance was not altogether truthful, inasmuch as the Governor was at the same time openly and confidently leading the opposing faction of the party. In June he had explained the split in the Iowa party to President Roosevelt in a letter dealing with a patronage problem:

Republicans of Iowa act so unitedly after conventions that you have had no opportunity to know the character of the fight that went on last year and which is still in progress. It will not harm the party and its majorities will grow but there are two grand divisions in our ranks, and I hope I am not egotistical when I say that I lead the larger one. Notwithstanding the action of the delegation, the division of which I speak is entitled to recognition. Our boys do not want it to be understood that the national administration is against them. Knowing you as well as I do I feel sure that if you were in Iowa you would be the leader of the men who are now following me. Having these things in mind, it seems to me that the delegation ought not to complain if you insist upon a reasonable division of the patronage.[70]

In the light of this letter, it would seem to be impossible for Cummins to carry on the kind of factional fight that he so well describes and at the same time have his "boys" give support to Henderson, the No. 2 man in the other faction. As a matter of fact, Henderson discovered that the Cummins group in the Third District was continuing to criticize his tariff views; he could not forget that this faction thought once of putting up a candidate against him. These blows to his pride were too much for a man of his seniority and prestige. It should be added that this psychological situation was worsened by a naturally choleric temper, aggravated by suffering due to his ill-fitting artifical limb. His decision to withdraw followed. In reply to a wire from Richard Clarkson, urging the Speaker to reconsider, Henderson replied: " Thanks for your kind hearted telegram, but I have got tired of the growing politics that are dominating Iowa, and tired of the personal abuse coming from republican sources. I have worked hard enough to entitle me to decent treatment considering the position that I hold." [71]

The exact reactions of the Allison group can be seen from a letter written the day after Henderson's withdrawal, from the very center of their circle, by James S. Clarkson to M. S. Quay:

> The only thing for Henderson who has acted in a moment of passion or pique, to do is to allow the Convention to meet again and renominate him and accept, calling that a new vote of confidence. The Republican Congressional Committee has telegraphed him as a Committee, so has Hanna as Chairman of the National Republican Committee, and in this action Allison, Lodge, Spooner and Aldrich joined. We are bringing great pressure to bear on Henderson today. His sudden freak has caused the National Republican Committee a great deal of anxious concern.[72]

The words "Henderson who has acted in a moment of passion or pique" were written by a man who had known Henderson like a brother for over thirty years. But the district convention did not renominate the self-exiled hero. Instead, a distinguished lawyer and jurist from Clarion, Judge Benjamin P. Birdsall, was chosen. Governor Cummins wrote to the victor: "To tell you the truth, confidentially, I did not expect the convention to do so wise a thing. I believe that you will not only make a better representative in Congress than Colonel Henderson would have made, but that you will be elected by a much larger majority than he could have received." [73] Lese majeste! Small wonder that Allison & Co. fought this man so hard and came to distrust him, because be it remembered that all the while Cummins was putting up an appearance of friendship with the Allisonians. A few days later the Governor wrote to a protégé: "Henderson, instead of hurting us, as he intended to do, has killed himself. Everything is going well, and the 'Iowa Idea' is gathering adherents every day." [74]

The fight between the Cummins Progressives and the Allison Standpatters grew warmer as the new year went along. While Allison did not take an open stand against Cummins, indeed ostensibly was on the best of terms with him, as much could not be said for many others who could be thought of as Allisonians. For example, in March, 1903, Secretary of the Treasury Leslie M. Shaw, Cummins' predecessor as Governor and a man at the opposite pole of thought from him, wrote to James S. Clarkson, now something of an interpreter of Western political movements to the Republican leaders in the East, urging him to solicit contributions to assist in the Iowa fight. "They had better contribute fifty or a hundred thousand this year than a half a million next. A bucket of water today will quench an incipient fire that a well-organized fire department cannot extinguish if allowed to get under way." [75]

About a month later a secret meeting was held in Chicago between the two factions of the party at which Allison, Joseph W. Blythe, and Cummins came to an agreement about the wording of the platform to be drawn up at the forthcoming state convention. Leslie M. Shaw, not actually present at the conference, which ran from morning until far into the night, stood by and received the details which he passed on to Ret Clarkson. The main object on both sides was not a good tariff plank but political advantage. Shaw and others thought that Cummins had fallen into a trap that would finish him in Iowa politics. If he accepted the national platform, which was in conflict with the state document, he would stultify himself; if not, he would lose caste both in and out of the state. Shaw added that there was to be no open fight on Cummins, but that Captain John A. T. Hull had already served notice that he would need financial help to hold his congressional seat in 1904 against the Cummins man, Judge S. F. Prouty, a "rampant tariff revisionist." Shaw wanted Clarkson to raise some money for the anti-Cummins cause. Clarkson responded that "The sooner such a man is retired from leadership in the party, much the better for the party." [76]

Well might they have decided not to wage an open fight against Cummins. He had reached a stage in the growth of his power where he could negotiate as an equal with Allison or Allison's strongest lieutenants. His views on the Chicago meeting with Allison and his resulting demands were set forth in a letter to the conservative George D. Perkins, editor and publisher of the Sioux City *Journal*, in which he insisted that the Chicago agreement be lived up to. Cummins wrote to Allison in exactly the same vein, closing with the words: "It is of the highest importance that you and I know precisely what we will stand for in the convention." [77]

In the light of these letters the words of George E. Roberts in his historical account of the "Iowa Idea" become understandable, although not completely candid in failing to reveal the pressure from Cummins. As Roberts puts it, early in 1903, even before the next state convention had been called, conferences of "recognized leaders" were held to agree on the tariff and trust resolutions to be adopted. The result of the conference was a general understanding that Senator Allison, after communicating with representative men from various parts of the state, should submit a declaration, "the general purport of which was agreed to with the language subject to his revision." Senator Allison agreed to serve as a medium for the disagreeing forces to compose their differences, rather than as an arbitrator.[78]

The Republicans of Iowa held their state convention in Des Moines on July 1, 1903, and adopted this tariff and trusts plank as drawn up by Allison:

We reiterate our faith in the historic principles of protection. Under its influence our country, foremost in the bounties of nature, has become foremost in production. It has enabled laborers to successfully insist upon good wages and induced capital to engage in production with reasonable hope of fair reward. Its vindication is found in the history of its success and the rapidity with which our natural resources have been developed and our industrial independence secured, and we heartily renew our pledge to maintain it. The tariff rates enacted to carry this policy into effect should be just, fair, and impartial, equally opposed to foreign control and domestic monopoly, to sectional discrimination and individual favoritism, and must, from time to time be changed to meet the varying conditions incident to the progress of our industries and their changing relations in our foreign and domestic commerce. Duties that are too low should be increased and duties that are too high should be reduced. We endorse the policy of reciprocity as the natural complement of protection. Reciprocity between nations is trade for mutual advantage and both sides must give and take. We approve the treaty with Cuba, recently ratified, as conferring substantial benefits upon both countries, and urge that the remaining steps, necessary to make it effective, be promptly taken.

On this plank George E. Roberts commented that the reciprocity portion was more favorable to the policy contained in the "Iowa Idea" and that the other portions contained all of the previous statements, but the wording was more acceptable to those who regretted the seeming admission that the tariff did afford shelter to monopoly.[79] Thus again, Allison had sucessfully played the role of a compromiser.

After an acrimonious campaign, in which Cummins received some

Historical Dept., Des Moines

ALBERT BAIRD CUMMINS

Mrs. Harry R. Beddow, Dubuque

SENATOR ALLISON IN 1907

The Funeral Cortege Leaving the Allison Home in Dubuque

August 8, 1908

blows from the Standpatters as well as from the Democrats, who were conceded by Cummins to have an excellent candidate, he was able to report triumphantly to his friend, Charles G. Dawes of Chicago: "I cannot help but be a little proud of the fact that I was originally elected and now re-elected by a plurality which is larger by twenty thousand than any governor of Iowa ever received." He also wrote to Allison: "I appreciate deeply your efficient assistance in bringing about so harmonious a campaign." [80]

Meanwhile, the *Register and Leader*, as the *Iowa State Register* had been rechristened, had been going through another shift in ownership. For various reasons, mainly inability to give enough time and personal direction to make the paper function as he knew it should, George E. Roberts was eager to dispose of his recent investment. This was known to some as early as July, 1903. Naturally, each political faction was eager to get control of the paper, the greatest single journalistic force in the state, but had to wait some time before the matter was determined. "I want very much to see the paper continue in friendly hands or fall into still more friendly hands," Cummins wrote to his friend Thomas A. Way, "but there are some things I cannot do even to secure that potent influence." [81] On November 2, 1903, the principal stockholder, Samuel Strauss, disposed of his holdings to Harvey Ingham (the editor whom Roberts had brought in from Algona), A. B. Funk of Spirit Lake, James A. Smith of Osage, and F. L. Maytag of Newton; Roberts continued as president. If this arrangement had held up, the Cummins wing would have been amply served by the paper, but by November 7 the deal was off, for personal reasons; the new stockholders were Harvey Ingham and Gardner Cowles, the latter a long-time associate of Ingham at Algona. Roberts still continued as president.

Regarding this announcement, Cummins wrote to Thomas A. Way:

I feel just as badly about it as anyone can, but I am accustomed to these things and take them philosophically. I feel sure that when it becomes necessary, our boys will meet the emergency with the same courage and zeal that they have always displayed. Immediately after Funk, Smith and Maytag went out and Cowles came in, Harvey Ingham came to my office and spent an hour or two with me, giving me every detail of the trouble and assuring me that the attitude of the paper towards me would not change. I think he is honest in his intention, but you and I know that Cowles will be the dominant spirit. He has one half the stock of the paper, and no other man has more than one-sixth, and aside from that he is the strongest character now connected with the paper. I intend to have a talk with Senator Maytag on Monday or Tuesday along the line of protection, and I will let you know what the outcome is.[82]

Cummins' uncertainty about Cowles's attitude was soon removed, however. The *Register and Leader* almost immediately showed its friendliness; one editorial by Harvey Ingham so staunchly and ably defended the Governor's program that Cummins wrote to him that he thought the editorial "would do more to put the present controversy upon its proper basis than anything that has yet appeared." [83] Allison had lost his most powerful editorial voice in Iowa.

For a time, after Cummins' re-election, Iowa politics was quiet. The Republican national convention of 1904 did the natural thing, indeed the only possible thing: it nominated Roosevelt for the presidency in his own right. For Vice President the choice was Charles K. Fairbanks; about the only real excitement of the convention was furnished by the keynote speech of Representative Robert G. Cousins of Tipton, Iowa, whose selection as speaker came about through the good offices of Allison. Cousins was an orator of the old school, a true spellbinder when before a cheering partisan audience. There was not much reward for those who analyzed the content of his speeches; they consisted mostly of praise for the Republican party and gratitude for the blessings of the protective tariff, which he held to be the source of America's wealth and strength.[84]

Allison took some part in the various campaigns of 1904, but his activity was curtailed by a noticeable decline in his health. John A. Kasson, now an elder statesman and far above the party strife of the past, wrote from his home in Washington to Ora Williams, reporter for the *Register and Leader*, to tip him off. "I am grieved to hear bad news of Allison's health." [85] For years Allison had been conserving his strength by declining all but the most necessary trips and speeches. Because of this, President Roosevelt had hesitated to ask him to come to the Oyster Bay conference in 1902. His principal trouble was an enlargement of the prostate which necessitated painful treatments twice daily.[86]

In general, the election of 1904 went off with a pretty fair division of the spoils between the two factions in Iowa. Roosevelt, in whom both sides claimed a share, was an easy winner; the entire Republican congressional slate won, with the Standpatters definitely able to claim a majority of the eleven men in the delegation, led by Captain John A. T. Hull, whose first victory dated back to 1890.

A feature of the election was the final ratification of the amendment to the state constitution providing for biennial state elections and for the holding of the sessions of the legislature in January of the odd-numbered instead of the even-numbered years. Senators Allison and Dolliver both strongly supported this amendment, which won by a margin of 23,000.[87] Heretofore the Governor, the Lieutenant Governor, a judge of the supreme court, and the superintendent of public instruction, along with the members of the General Assembly, had been elected in the odd-numbered years, the other state officers and members of Congress in the even-numbered. It is hard to imagine any intelligent person voting against the proposal that might well be termed "an amendment to save the nerves and energies of politicians." Now they would be freed from the necessity of doing annual battle for some office or other.

For two years the Iowa political scene remained fairly calm, and Allison could concentrate his energies on his work in the Senate. In 1906 he was saddened by the death of his long-time friend and political lieutenant, Colonel Henderson. Their acquaintance had begun in September, 1861, when Colonel William B. Allison had mustered the young student into the Union army. "Our friendship was uninterrupted during his whole career from his entry into the military service until his death," said Allison.[88] The grand old soldier and perfect exemplifier of the Civil War veteran in politics had been stricken with paralysis followed by blindness. For months he had lingered in Mercy Hospital in Dubuque, but at last, on February 25, 1906, he was released from his suffering. Unfortunately, Allison was not among those who were able to attend the funeral ceremonies at Dubuque; chronic illness now forced him to conserve his energy to the utmost,[89] and a hard trip to Iowa in the dead of winter would probably have been suicidal.

A few days after the funeral of his old friend, Senator Allison celebrated his seventy-seventh birthday, and the *Register and Leader* pointed out that he would also mark another anniversary on March 4 — his forty-third year in Congress, with the exception of the two-year interim between his service in the House and his elevation to the Senate. "Still Hale and Hearty" read the caption over his current picture in the paper.[90] Unhappily, this was not completely true.

☆ XVIII ☆

Allison and Roosevelt

ONE OF THE PLEASANTER aspects of the Allison story is the warm personal relationship that developed between the youthful President Roosevelt and the aging Nestor of the Senate. It almost seems as if a playful trick of Fate had brought together this dynamic Chief Executive and the shuffling semi-invalid [1] who commanded the confidence of so many colleagues and who was known as a genius at the art of compromise. Allison was a budding politician with several conventions behind him when Roosevelt was born in 1858; now the young man was in the seat to which Allison had aspired and which a kindlier fortune might have given to him. Their friendship had begun almost immediately after Roosevelt's accession to power. Allison was the first of The Four to write to the new President, who replied warmly: "When do you come to Washington? I shall want to see you before I write my message, because there are two or three points upon which I do not desire to touch until after consultation with you." [2] It required no false humility on Roosevelt's part to treat Allison with respect and even affection; on his side, Allison could well cherish the warmth of Roosevelt's friendship and admire the boundless energy and the flair for success of the young President.

One of the first issues to face Roosevelt was that of reciprocity. The Dingley Tariff Act of 1897, in the making of which Allison had played so large a part, had provided for the appointment of a special commissioner for the negotiation of reciprocal trade agreements. McKinley's appointee had been none other than Allison's opponent in a

294

long-forgotten rivalry, John A. Kasson, now living in semi-retirement in Washington. That gentleman did his work well, and seventeen "Kasson Treaties" were ultimately negotiated.[3] These treaties, providing only the mildest sort of reciprocal exchanges, now had to run the gauntlet of the Senate, where the one implacable foe was Nelson W. Aldrich, Allison's close friend in The Four. The pacts were not ratified during the McKinley administration, which ostensibly favored them, and now Roosevelt proved to be indifferent.

Allison has been charged with being one of the group that helped Roosevelt to quash these proposals, [4] but he would never have accepted this indictment. As usual, he was careful about committing himself, but to his credit it must be said that he worked hard to let the treaties have their chance in open debate on the Senate floor. Aldrich, on the other hand, was in favor of killing them in committee. In October, 1901, some weeks before Roosevelt would send his first message to Congress, Allison made a fairly forthright speech at Tama, Iowa,[5] asserting his own attitude which he repeated in a letter to Roosevelt.

It seems to me that the Dingley law having specially provided for reciprocity treaties, and the President [McKinley] having acted upon Section 4 of that law and negotiated these treaties under it, that it is the duty of the Senate to take them up and act upon them. If in [the] view of the Senate they are not satisfactory, they can be amended or rejected. It seems to me that good faith to other nations requires this.[6]

Roosevelt forwarded Allison's letter to Aldrich, but the latter would not budge. Forced to choose, Roosevelt followed the Rhode Islander rather than the Iowan, and thus the Kasson Treaties were put away, never to be resurrected.

In what might be called the formative years of the Roosevelt era, the President cautiously felt his way into an ambitious program. During the summer of 1902 a tremendous tension built up over such issues as reciprocity, the tariff in its other aspects, and a strike among the anthracite coal miners which was countered by an intransigent and wholly unreasonable attitude among the mine owners. On September 16 the President held what was supposed to be a secret meeting at his summer home at Oyster Bay with Senators Aldrich, Allison, Hanna, Spooner, and Lodge. The conference was called, if one may judge by the events that followed, for the purpose of fixing upon an administration policy agreeable to The Four and to the master politician and chairman of the Republican national committee, Senator

Mark Hanna.[7] Only Platt of The Four was unable to attend; perhaps Lodge was there to help his close friend, the President, as he fenced with the leaders of the Senate. (This was the meeting, incidentally, that Henderson surprised with his telegram of resignation.)

During Roosevelt's first term he seemed quite willing to divide power, allowing The Four to dominate the field of domestic legislation in return for clear rights of leadership in foreign affairs. These were the years of speaking softly and carrying a big stick, according to the Rooseveltian formula; of the assertion of supremacy in the Caribbean and the evolution of the Roosevelt corollary to the Monroe Doctrine; of the substitution of Panama for Nicaragua as the route for an isthmian canal connecting the Atlantic and the Pacific.

With these policies Allison was not greatly concerned. Of all The Four, he was the least prepared by training or natural interest for playing a major part in the making of foreign policy. This, plus the factor of his constantly declining health, would account sufficiently for his general acquiescence in the Roosevelt program. He made no protest against the aggressive nationalism which Roosevelt preached or the doubtful ethics employed. The highhanded tactics in acquiring the Panama site by means of conspiracy, for example, drew no comment from Allison, and as chairman of the Appropriations Committee he helped to supply the necessary money by speeding the passage of the supply bills. As has been well said, the Nicaraguan route was available, and "working together, Roosevelt and Hay with Hanna, Spooner, Cullom, and Aldrich, could have chosen it or could have secured the Panama route honorably." [8] To this list the name of Allison might well have been added. Instead, one can only say that he and his clerks toiled away in the committee room and kept the machinery oiled with the necessary financial lubricants.

After the endorsement furnished by the 1904 election, Roosevelt turned more boldly toward the field of domestic legislation. Up to this point he had acted as a referee between the Standpatters and Progressives, a role he now continued but with definite leanings toward the Progressive point of view. He was uncertain in his own mind whether he was a "conservative radical" or a "radical conservative." [9] Much the same could be said about Allison within the limits of Iowa politics. Although usually thought of as a Conservative, he had, so far, steered his course between the Cummins and anti-Cummins factions. His Tama speech of 1901 was a declaration of intention to listen to Iowa more and Aldrich less; and he had helped to make the Iowa tariff plank of 1903 acceptable to both factions.

The issue that would bring forth a clearer declaration of attitude from both men was not long in showing up. There was a growing demand for legislation that would give the Interstate Commerce Commission power to regulate more effectively the great carriers and to eliminate abuses which had grown up over the years. Especially sought after was the power to regulate the railroad rate structure. The original Interstate Commerce Act of 1887 had been deliberately drawn up as a weak and ineffective measure, more designed to hush the voices of the "radicals" of that day than to provide real control. The Elkins Rebate Act of 1903 was admittedly a failure.[10] From 1904 on President Roosevelt had talked and written of the need for a new attack on the general problem.

When the Fifty-eighth Congress met in December, 1904, for its short session, nearly every member of the House Committee on Interstate and Foreign Commerce had his own idea of a proper bill for meeting the situation, and after some weeks of public hearings a number of bills were ready for introduction. The principal ones were the Cooper-Quarles Bill, the Esch Bill, the Townsend Bill, and one named after Iowa's own William Peters Hepburn of Clarinda, the chairman of the committee and a long-time student of the problem. It was no secret that the Hepburn Bill had been drawn up with the assistance of President Roosevelt, Attorney General William H. Moody, and many spokesmen for the railroads, notably the Burlington counsel, Joseph W. Blythe, who soon turned against the bill he had helped to prepare.[11] The Hepburn Bill was "vulnerable" from the moment it became known that the Burlington attorney was behind it. Hepburn's residence in Clarinda, a town whose economic existence depended almost wholly on the C. B. & Q., was too apparent to be missed by the critics. Chief among the opponents of the bill was Governor Cummins, whose voice was heard all the way to Washington. One of his talking points was that the new "court of transportation" provided for in the bill would require the appointment of many new judges. To a friend Cummins wrote of the bill that "the good is so inseparably connected with the bad that it cannot be made to meet the requirements of the hour. It is difficult for me to believe that it was intended as a solution of the problem." He had a good point when he noted that under the law the railroads had the right of appeal but not the shippers.[12]

This first Hepburn Bill was sidetracked, with the author's approval, and he gave his support to the passage of the combined bills of Esch and Townsend, a result that was achieved by a vote of 326 to 17, indicating either a phenomenal degree of approval or a desire to pass the problem on to the Senate. That body did nothing more than to set up an investigating commission that required many months for its researches,[13] which were not completed when Congress adjourned in March. Allison took advantage of this respite for another trip to Europe.[14]

The year 1905 was truly memorable for the revelations of malpractices in the life insurance business as brought out by a searching inquiry made under the direction of Charles Evans Hughes.[15] By the end of the year any informed observer knew that Congress would have to take some action to curb those whom Roosevelt characterized as "malefactors of great wealth." The only question was whether the action would be taken by the federal and state governments, with the advice and assistance of the business interests, or without and in spite of those interests. Not only had the insurance scandals in New York been exposed, but others as well. The Pennsylvania Railroad coal car scandal, the Atchison rebates, and the publicity methods used by the railroads had "brought public opinion to the boiling point on the transportation question." [16] These sickening disclosures opened the eyes of the people to the need for action, and thus a definitely new spirit was abroad in the land as 1906 opened.

Against this new spirit, the Standpatters had to fight without the benefit of many good troopers of the past. David B. Henderson was no longer on hand. Matthew Quay, the very symbol of rock-ribbed Pennsylvania Republicanism, had died in 1904; Allison's congenial partner in The Four, Orville H. Platt of Connecticut, had passed away in 1905; "Fighting Bob" La Follette had taken the place of Joseph V. Quarles in the Senate; and La Follette's antithesis, John Coit Spooner, was soon to refuse to make the fight for re-election, actually resigning his seat in 1907. Allison and Aldrich remained, but Allison and Aldrich were not as compatible as formerly. Jonathan P. Dolliver, Allison's junior partner, worked with the Standpatters only out of personal loyalty to Allison. Albert J. Beveridge of Indiana was beginning to lead the way toward the victory for the direct primary system and the inheritance tax.[17]

Worst of all for the Standpatters, President Roosevelt, in his annual message to Congress on December 5, 1905, showed that he was in full sympathy with the new spirit. He asserted that there must be a grant of power to an agency that could decide upon reasonable maximum railroad rates, subject to review by the courts. Evils such as passes, cuts in passenger rates, and fictitious damages (damage claims paid so as to serve as a discrimination in favor of certain shippers) must be outlawed. Only rate agreements that were favorable to the public must be allowed, if such agreements were to be made between railroads. Other points minor in nature were also advanced.

Shortly after the Christmas recess Congressman Hepburn of Iowa was ready with a new bill cast in the form of amendments to the Interstate Commerce Act of 1887. This "second" Hepburn Bill empowered the Interstate Commerce Commission, among other things, to establish maximum freight rates subject to court review. After study it went through his Committee on Interstate and Foreign Commerce and was rewritten as a new bill. After this bill had been debated in Committee, still another version, the third, was introduced and became the Hepburn Act of history.[18]

Now ensued a most involved and dramatic legislative battle.[19] The possibility that the Chief Executive may be the Chief Legislator as well was never more clearly demonstrated than in the fight for legislation that would put teeth into the Interstate Commerce Act of 1887 and bring the railroads under effective regulation. President Roosevelt virtually took over the management of the fight to put the Hepburn Bill through Congress, so much so that it might well be called the "Roosevelt Bill."[20] He was the one who, more than anyone else, fought for a remedial act, using every resource and never relenting until a measure of relief had been enacted. In waging this fight Roosevelt called on Allison to be his captain in the Senate, a great honor, perhaps, but a heavy responsibility as well for a man of Allison's years. His colleague, Dolliver, now a favorite with Roosevelt, would be an able assistant.

There was never much doubt that the bill would go through the House. The hard fight would take place in the Senate, where Nelson W. Aldrich was commander of the forces opposed to the bill. What a spectacle this afforded! What a puzzle for those who must have their history in solid black and white! Aldrich, one type of Republican, opposed Roosevelt, also a Republican, but one who was much inclined to experimentalism; Aldrich, an unashamed believer in a system of government that put Business at the top, opposed to a man who could say that he was trying to save Business by saving it from itself.

Aldrich's tactic was to delay and postpone, apparently in the hope that something would happen to weaken or kill the whole effort. For this reason he favored reporting the bill from committee in an unamended form, thus depriving Dolliver, who was also a member of the committee, of any chance to make capital for the bill or himself by influencing the committee to amend the bill as he desired. In getting the bill out of committee, Aldrich also secured the passage of a motion to allow each committee member the right to propose amendments from the floor. Thus the battleground would be the Senate floor, where Aldrich had many powerful allies, and not the committee room, where Dolliver had more friends than Aldrich. At the same time Aldrich took advantage of the desire of the Democrats to share in the credit for the reform bill by craftily arranging for one of their members, Benjamin M. Tillman, to be the floor leader of the fight for the bill. Tillman, a brilliant but radical and eccentric Senator from South Carolina, known to his day and to history as "Pitchfork Ben," was a bitter personal enemy of Roosevelt. The two men had not spoken for years, and now Tillman was to be the floor leader for the President's bill! But Roosevelt was equal to this emergency; he arranged to communicate with Tillman through the good offices of ex-Senator William E. Chandler of New Hampshire.[21]

The matter dragged on from January to May, 1906, by which time the principal obstacle seemed to be the inability to agree on the powers of the courts to review the rulings of the Interstate Commerce Commission. Should they be broad or narrow? This seemed to be the impassable road block. Aldrich and his allies, the "railroad Senators," wanted to keep the traditional broad powers. In this way the orders of the Commission might be subjected to endless litigation and delay, and the railroads could gain their point by indirection. Attorney General Moody drafted an amendment affirming the right of the railroads to ask for a court review of the Commission's decisions. Senator Philander C. Knox of Pennsylvania rejected this and offered one asserting the right of the courts to pass on the "lawfulness" of the orders of the Commission. Moody, as Roosevelt's adviser, in turn rejected this on grounds of vagueness and the prospect it offered of endless litigation. Senator Chester I. Long of Kansas presented an amendment which, if adopted, would have ruled out any judicial review of the facts of a case whatsoever, since the court could only determine whether, on any given order, the Commission had exceeded its power or violated the constitutional rights of the carrier. Roosevelt endorsed this,[22] but now Senator Joseph W. Bailey of Texas and his wing rose up to oppose it, because it seemed to be giving too much power to the administrative agency. Bailey countered with an amendment concerning the injunction power, one depriving the courts of the authority to issue temporary writs suspending rate orders.

Roosevelt and Allison, fearing that Aldrich might go along with the Bailey suggestions, quickly countered with an amendment thought up by Spooner, the expert constitutional lawyer, which would force the roads to put into escrow, pending a decision, whatever amount was in dispute if the roads had secured a suspension of the rates. This would protect all parties, but at the same time it would prevent mere delaying tactics by the roads; they could not afford to put millions of dollars in escrow unless they were really sincere in their requests for a review.

The next move was made by the Democrats, who caucused and decided not to go along with Bailey and Tillman, their own men. Roosevelt then had two choices: to come up with something more extreme or to return to the simpler provisions of the original Hepburn Bill supplemented with acceptable amendments. He chose the latter course and embarked upon it, but only with the help of William Boyd Allison as his principal agent in interviewing Senators for his cause. Allison performed efficient and valiant service, as Roosevelt acknowledged.[23] Not only that, he offered and carried through, partly because of the magic of his name and the trust and esteem in which he was held, the key amendment that insured passage of the bill.

The debate had been brought to the point where passage absolutely depended on some agreement as to the powers of the courts to review the orders of the Interstate Commerce Commission. How far could Congress go in limiting or defining the judicial power? There were two obvious courses of action: ignore the matter and let the courts decide for themselves when future suits would necessitate construction of the statute; or define the power in precise terms. The railroad spokesmen would not agree to the former, and those who favored regulation could not object to the latter. What was needed was a formula that would please the Standpatters and enable enough others to vote for it to insure passage. This formula was brought forth by

Allison, but, due to illness, his good friend Cullom acted as his agent in putting it before the Senate. It was long and technical; the separate points were adopted one by one after a lengthy and serious debate, lofty in tone. By its principal provisions, the circuit courts were given power to "enjoin, set aside, annul or suspend" the orders of the Commission; the latter must be given five days' notice to allow time for the preparation of a protest; the hearing must then go before a three-judge court.[24]

Although this is known as the "Allison Amendment," a moot question is the identity of the real author. The chances are that this piece of legislation, like most, was the work of a whole battery of lawyers and transportation experts. Let him who doubts this read the *Congressional Record*, 59th Congress, 1st Session, containing the brilliant and highly involved debate that followed between Aldrich, Tillman, Bailey, Charles W. Fulton of Oregon, Augustus O. Bacon of Georgia, and other able constitutional lawyers.

Yet a considerable controversy has arisen over the question of authorship. Aldrich's biographer has claimed for him and the "astute lawyers" behind him the major share of the credit. The "amendments" should be named after Aldrich, he writes; "it is fanciful to call them the 'Allison Amendments' [*sic*]." Later, a story was told that Allison had not heard of "his" amendment until he was asked by reporters as he was boarding a train to explain his brain child.[25] But more important than these *ex post facto* assertions is the fact that Allison himself greeted the first public announcement of the clauses bearing his name with a denial of paternity!

How could this happen? The chronology is as follows: the "Allison" amendment was first publicly announced on May 4, not by Allison but by President Roosevelt, who called in the reporters and told them he had accepted the Allison formula. The next day it was reported that the Iowa Senator had disclaimed the full authorship; he had merely suggested it; Senator Charles W. Fulton of Oregon was the principal author. The next few days were complicated by Allison's illness. He attended the Senate on the morning of the 8th but remained in his room in the afternoon, hence the role of Senator Cullom as his agent and spokesman. Allison reappeared in the Senate on May 11, looking well. In the days that followed he took a full part in the running debate and ably defended his proposals, item by item, winning special praise from Senator Dolliver for his common-sense explanations, unclouded by the intricacies of constitutional law.[26] As in the case of the amendments to the Bland Bill of a long departed day, Allison did not claim sole authorship but warmly defended the proposals that now bore his name.

The key question that naturally suggests itself is: what happened between the 5th, when Allison's denial was reported, and the 8th, when Cullom introduced his amendment for him? The natural assumption would be that somebody went to Allison and persuaded him to let the President use his name because of the weight that it would carry with doubtful members and with the public. This charge has been made by one student of the period, but it cannot be so; the origins of the amendment go back of these dates.[27]

President Roosevelt is his own best defendant in this case. Almost a month earlier, he had written to Senator Knute Nelson of Minnesota, outlining the strategy to be used. He clearly alluded to "Allison's amendment," also to the partnership of Roosevelt and Allison in working for the bill, and counseled breaking up the amendment into two parts. This would seem to prove that Allison had at least heard of his amendment before the reporters made it known to him. More importantly, Roosevelt wrote to Allison on May 5:

I am informed by ex-Senator Chandler that Senator Dolliver denies today on your authority, that the so-called "Allison amendment" is yours. This is the amendment which you brought to me the other day. I told you that the amendment was absolutely unobjectionable, and in my judgment no one who chose to exercise an intelligent judgment could in good faith object to it, because it leaves the Hepburn bill, as regards the court review, absolutely unchanged. . . .

I write this because I do not wish there to be any misunderstanding. I expressed my hearty acquiescence in the amendment when you presented it to me, and I remain heartily acquiescent in it.[28]

In a letter written a few days later to one Edward Payson Bacon, the President strongly defended the Allison amendment; [29] perhaps he did so in letters to others. Some six days later he wrote Allison, giving a long summary of the history of the fight for the Hepburn Bill to date. One vital sentence reads as follows: "Shortly after this you in company with Senator Cullom called upon me with the amendment which is now commonly called the Allison amendment." [30] Years later Roosevelt wrote: "Finally both sides reluctantly agreed to accept the so-called Allison amendment which did not, as a matter of fact, work any change in the bill at all. The amendment was drawn by

Attorney-General Moody after consultation with the Inter-State Commerce Commission, and was forwarded by me to Senator Dolliver; it was accepted, and the bill became law." [31]

Allison in a certain mood might very well have denied authorship, either in disgust at seeing himself so handily used by the aggressive Roosevelt or in honest deference to the fact that the President had had so large a part in the construction not only of the amendment but of the entire bill. Allison had been Roosevelt's agent to work the cloak-rooms and persuade the doubtful members on this bill. All of these comments seem to indicate that there was without doubt an "Allison Amendment," whether or not the title is an accurate one. If it is reasonable to call the "Hepburn" bill a "Roosevelt" bill, then by the same logic it is reasonable to call the "Allison" amendment the "Roosevelt" amendment.

By way of final judgment in the light of the above evidence, it seems that one may well agree with the conclusion: "The authorship of the amendment . . . remains obscure. Whoever wrote it, Allison guided it." [32] Perhaps this is honor enough. Certainly it is difficult to think of any other Senator in that session who could have served the President so well and at the same time retained the confidence of all the other members of the body and at last secured the necessary votes for the key clause of the bill. Every deliberative body needs a genius of this sort; fortunate is the group that possesses a William Boyd Allison. This trait moved W. R. Boyd, the Cedar Rapids publisher who knew him so well, to emphasize Senator Hoar's verdict: Allison has a genius for attaining the unattainable. [33]

Who won in this battle of wits and politics between the President and the Senator from Rhode Island? A variety of opinions have been expressed. An argument can be and has been made in favor of a complete victory for Aldrich. This argument cites debates to show that the "narrow-review" people blunderingly admitted their defeat. Another point of view sees a victory for Roosevelt, who got just what he wanted: a bill that did not specifically state the terms of review but left this question to the courts themselves. This is what the Allison measure provided. [34] Still another claim has been made that the amendment was brought about by a "combination of the con-servatives and the waverers; it was the final outcome of the maneuvers of Aldrich; it was so worded as to allow the progressives, by sophisti-cated arguments, to save their faces; and it entirely defeated the primary purpose of the bill to which the President apparently had been committed." [35]

The verdict might well be left to neutral observers of a later date. By one it is seen as a divided victory; the "reformers" won in so far as they prevented the railroads from turning the courts into a delaying agency. The Commission was now to be a "really competent administrative board" as long as it stayed within the Constitution. Secondly, the burden of proof was now put upon the railroads, not the Commission. The railroads won on one point, however; any rate or any practice that was complained of was left in force until a decision had been made.[36] The "Allison Amendment" was "extremely vague" in phraseology in the opinion of one eminent authority, who finds that the courts "virtually sustained" the constitutional arguments of the proponents of "narrow review" and the validity of the Commission principle. In other words, the courts upheld the ideas contained in the amendment attributed to Senator Long of Kansas.[37]

Allison's work was not done when he presented the saving amendment and secured its passage. As part of the furious maneuvering that had made up the fight, the President had deserted the coalition he had made with Senators Tillman and Bailey. Several days later Tillman good-naturedly confessed to the Senate that he had been "taken in" when he agreed to play his part. In the course of his remarks he asserted that the President had accused Senators Knox, Foraker, and Spooner of chicanery. When Roosevelt heard of this he impetuously called the remark "a deliberate and unqualified falsehood." Both Tillman and Chandler produced evidence to prove the point; then Roosevelt compounded the trouble by saying that Tillman had initiated the use of Chandler as an agent in the negotiations. Now it was the turn of Chandler and Tillman to call the President a liar. Roosevelt retaliated by imputing double-dealings to Senator Bailey of Texas. The Texan now joined the game of name-calling by accusing Roosevelt of being "an unqualified, deliberate, and malicious liar." [38] At this point Roosevelt again used Allison's reputation as the "grand old man" of the Senate. He wrote Allison a long letter, giving a full history of the whole episode; the letter was released to the newspapers, and Allison accommodated Roosevelt by having it inserted in the *Congressional Record*.[39] All in all, it seems clear that the President again had relied on Allison as his "front," and that the Iowa Senator had played the role faithfully and well to the end.

The passage of the Hepburn Act was in part a concession to the forces that were demanding reform. For years a spirit of unrest had been growing, a spirit fed by a literature of exposure that was a feature of the time. Originating as far back as 1894 with the revelation of certain malpractices of the Standard Oil Company by Henry Demarest Lloyd, and continued by Ida M. Tarbell in the early 1900's, the popularity of this type of literature increased noticeably with the shocking disclosures made by Lincoln Steffens, Charles Edward Russell, Upton Sinclair, and others. In a soundly documented and unspectacular fashion, exposure was made of acts and practices that ran all the way from unethical procedures that were barely within the law to outright crime. Disregarding his own indebtedness to these writers for their aid to his reform program, President Roosevelt unfairly gave them the label of "muckrakers."

Up to 1906 the output of the muckrakers had been virtually impeccable in both taste and scholarship. Unfortunately, that year brought a change in this type of literature. A tendency toward sensationalism crept in, and by 1908 "muckraking" had degenerated into yellow-sheet journalism of the worst sort.[40]

The turning point might well be indentified with the appearance in William Randolph Hearst's *Cosmopolitan Magazine* of a series of articles by the well-known novelist, David Graham Phillips, entitled "The Treason of the Senate." [41] Nelson W. Aldrich, Stephen B. Elkins, Chauncey Depew, Boies Penrose, James Kean, Joseph B. Foraker, Joseph W. Bailey, John C. Spooner, Arthur P. Gorman, and many others, including Allison, were subjects of the muckraking pen of the Indiana author. Phillips was not a political reporter; he was a novelist and short-story writer who had been persuaded to undertake the assignment by Bailey Millard, the *Cosmopolitan's* editor, who wanted him because of his vitriolic pen. At the most only a few months were spent in gathering and writing up the material for the articles. In his search for material, Phillips was assisted by Gustavus Myers, later the author of *The History of Great American Fortunes*, and Harrison Phillips, a kinsman.[42]

The articles made no effort to present a balanced view of the careers of the subjects. In a sensational manner the author endeavored to demonstrate that Aldrich and Gorman were not honest leaders of the Senate, Republican and Democratic respectively, but merely corrupt politicians who had entered into a "merger" to act together in

the service of Big Business and themselves. Many other Senators had
joined in this conspiracy, according to Phillips, hence the "treason"
of the Senate, treason to the American people and to the principle of
representative government.

As for Allison, there is little that needs to be said, because Phillips
said so little about him. If Allison paid any attention to the article, he
must have smiled at the small space accorded to him in spite of his position as chairman of the Republican conference and of the steering committee, and his prominence in all the deliberations in the areas of
finance, appropriations, and interstate commerce. The principal
charges leveled against him were two: he was a millionaire (along with
Aldrich, Elkins, and others); and he had had a hand in some shady
railroad promotion in Iowa in the 1860's.

The first charge was a familiar one, entirely without basis; ever
since his early congressional years opponents and critics had harped
on Allison's "wealth." There was some good-natured joking among
his close friends about his "millions." No one would have been happier
than Allison to be a millionaire, but he had not even distantly approached that mark, in spite of all his good connections with railroad
presidents, bankers, politicians, and others who were on the inside of
big deals. He had played the market in a small way early in his public
career, along with General Dodge and James F. Wilson. He had received frequent tips from David A. Wells and Edward Atkinson, the
liberal economists and reformers. But had it not been for the legacy
from his second wife it is doubtful if Allison's holdings would have
totalled more than a few thousand dollars in cash and securities, his
modest home in Dubuque, and the small place in Washington that
he had shared with Mrs. Grimes until her death in 1890, and which he
had lately rented furnished to George E. Roberts to save himself the
upkeep.

As for the shady railroad dealings, it has been shown in this study
that he is subject to criticism for his close approach to the borderline
of propriety for his questionable services to John I. Blair in 1868-1869
and his subservience to Morris K. Jesup. Those actions were all a part
of the era of low standards in political and business morality. Like
many others, Allison had put this behind him. Phillips had nothing
to say of the railroad reforms then in progress and Allison's effective
part in them, not to mention his role in the passage of the first great
reform of 1887. The novelist turned muckraker should have had

more to say against Allison or he should have omitted him altogether
from his list of "traitors."

While Allison maintained his power and prestige in Washington,
trouble loomed on the Iowa political scene. His rule there was being
challenged more seriously than ever before, as the war between the
Standpatters and the Progressives grew in fury. Allison and Cummins
had not yet come to an open break in their personal relations, but
Cummins, now seeking a third nomination for the governorship, had
thrown off all pretense that he could ever make peace with the Blythe-
managed pro-railroad forces; on their side, they returned the compliment with interest.

Early in 1906 Cummins wrote to Robert M. La Follette, who had
just won election to the Senate in Wisconsin and who was the acknowledged leader of the Progressives:

> In this state we are in the midst of another struggle which bids fair to be a
> cyclone as compared with the zephyrs that have gone before. While I am
> more reluctant than it is possible for me to express to again lead the fight, it
> is more than probable that I will have to do it, or allow our forces to dis-
> integrate, and our movement for better things to be checked. All the rail-
> roads, and all the vicious, evil influences of politics will be arrayed against
> us.[43]

It soon became clear that the man who had been chosen to oppose
Cummins for the Republican gubernatorial nomination was George D.
Perkins, editor and publisher of the Sioux City *Journal*, a former
Harlanite who had long since made his way into the Allison camp, a
man who might well be described as an "enlightened conservative."
Cummins, who knew that the fight would be a hard one, felt justified in trying for a third consecutive term, the first man in Iowa
history to do this. "I believe Mr. Perkins' nomination and election
would be a complete surrender to the very worst elements in Iowa
politics," Cummins wrote to a friend. "I have no doubt that he is,
personally, an honest man, but I know that his candidacy is inspired
by Mr. Blythe, and that he must win, if he wins at all, through the
help of the combined and united railway strength."[44]

The struggle for delegates in the nominating convention went on
for months. Smith W. Brookhart, then in the early stages of his
colorful career, was one who received commendation from Cummins
for his good work in the pre-convention campaign: "You must be
omnipresent, for I hear of your work everywhere. I did not believe

it was possible for you or anyone to infuse such energy into the campaign as is now manifest in your part of the state." [45] Many other loyal and enthusiastic disciples carried the Cummins doctrine throughout the state, while the *Register and Leader* waged relentless war against Blythe and Perkins, especially the former.

It was in connection with his campaign for the third-term nomination that Cummins made the statement denying his intention to run against Allison for the Senate, a statement that was soon to become famous as the "Torbert Letter" which would rise to haunt him two years hence. The politics of the times dictated that Cummins must not antagonize those Allison supporters who were willing to go along with the new Progressive ideas while remaining personally loyal to Allison. This was the position occupied by Major W. H. Torbert, a friend and neighbor of the Senator since Allison's early years in Dubuque. Seemingly designed to reassure Major Torbert and others of similar position, the letter of April 19, 1906, was a clear expression of Cummins' current attitude toward Allison:

I note what you say with respect to Senator Allison. I am not a candidate for Senator Allison's place, nor have I ever suggested such a thing to mortal man. It is simply abominable, the way my enemies lie about me. I am a candidate for governor — nothing else — and it would be just as appropriate for me to deny that I was a candidate for President of the United States or appointment to some vacancy upon the Supreme Court of the United States as to deny a candidacy against Senator Allison. It is unmitigated rot, and should not deceive any man.[46]

The letter to Torbert, which was not made public at this time, probably contributed some strength to the Cummins cause in the Dubuque area, where Major Torbert could circulate its contents, but it could hardly have been a determining factor in the persuasion of delegates from the state as a whole. The bitterly fought campaign ended with an even more bitterly fought convention in which Cummins added another victory to his list by a vote of 933 to 603 for Perkins and 104 for S. W. Rathbun.[47] In all of these proceedings, Allison was publicly neutral, however much his usual allies took the side of Perkins.

Now the party must try to heal its self-inflicted wounds and to present as solid a front as possible to the voters. This proved to be an impossibility in spite of the appeals made by Cummins to Allison and Tama Jim Wilson for their meliorating influence. Taking note of

310 William Boyd Allison

Allison's poor health, Cummins offered to come to Dubuque and talk politics whenever Allison was sufficiently recovered to see him; he also suggested that Allison issue a statement in the form of a public letter instead of the customary speech opening the canvass to which his seniority entitled him. From Wilson, Cummins hoped for a speech or at least a letter.[48]

In spite of Cummins' best efforts at closing the breach in the party, he was not successful. In a rash of ticket-scratching, voters left the party in frightening numbers. Cummins' vote was 215,995, a bare fraction over 50 per cent of the total; his Democratic opponent, Claude R. Porter, received 196,123, and the four minor party candidates a total of 19,287. This left Cummins a dangerously small margin of 1,585 over his combined opposition. It is a safe speculation that there were many thrown-away Republican votes among those 19,287 ballots garnered by the minor parties, just as there had been in 1901 and 1903, when their returns were almost identical. In 1901 Cummins' share of the total had reached 58 per cent; in 1903, 57 per cent; now it had fallen to a bare 50 per cent. Well might a bitter Standpat Republican have wished that he had been able to bring himself to vote for a Democrat and thus cook the Cummins goose once and for all.

Cummins' victory enabled him to go ahead with efforts to secure enactment of the Progressive proposal, taken over from the Populists, for the popular election of United States Senators. It would have been completely natural for him to think that he might successfully take his senatorial case to the people, thus circumventing the Conservative majority in the legislature which had balked him on two occasions and which always threatened to do so as long as the railroads and other large business interests had political power. Of course there were other factors that helped to account for the growing support for the proposal. For one thing, the *Cosmopolitan* series on "The Treason of the Senate" had had its effect.[49] Popular election of Senators was one part of the growing creed of those who believed in the efficacy of direct elections as a cure for the current ills of representative government.

An earlier General Assembly had authorized a call for a national conference of Governors to consider a constitutional amendment providing for popular senatorial elections. Governor Cummins followed up his 1906 victory by issuing the call for this conference, to meet in Des Moines on December 5. Thirty delegates from eleven states actually attended, and many Governors sent encouraging messages; the result was the passage of a resolution strongly urging Congress to submit such an amendment.

Partly as a result of this, and certainly in furtherance of the Cummins-Progressive program for greater participation by the people in their own government, the General Assembly of 1907 passed a direct primary law providing for the nomination of state officers by party primaries and for the choice of a party senatorial candidate at the same election. This was the same type of legislation that Cummins had requested in his inaugural message.[50]

The workings of the direct primary law, as applied to senatorial elections, were intended to serve as a bypass of the old system of legislative elections until the national plan for direct elections could be secured by a constitutional amendment. Presumably, the party caucuses in the legislature would be required to name the candidate chosen by the voters in the primary, although there was no such stipulation in the law.

Meanwhile, the General Assembly had followed the old plan in the re-election of Senator Jonathan P. Dolliver on January 21, 1907, thus providing for the continuation of the teamwork between Allison and the junior Senator, now recognized as one of the most brilliant orators in the Senate. There had been some grumbling among the extreme Standpatters about Dolliver's liberalism and his inclinations toward Progressivism, but the only alternative was Cummins. Of course, they preferred to stand by Dolliver with his known allegiance to Allison. Bad feeling between Dolliver and Cummins, due to Dolliver's support of George D. Perkins in 1906, added fuel to these fires of intraparty conflict.[51]

An inventory of the political situation in both Iowa and the nation reveals the stalemate that had been reached in the fight between the factions. The challenges of the Progressives had been met by compromise; the formula of the "Iowa Idea" had been adopted as an answer to the tariff problem; railroad reform had become a reality; nationally, the exposures of the muckrakers had been followed up with beneficial results. Only the most reactionary could in good conscience object to the changes made to date. And yet a certain malaise lingered among the leaders.

Perhaps the "bankers' panic" of 1907 contributed to this feeling. "The country is in a very nervous condition," General Dodge wrote to Allison, "not for anything that has occurred [in Wall Street], or in my opinion, that will occur, but the attacks of the States, & the fear of what the President is going to do, & then the foolish talk of the railroad presidents about going into bankruptcy, 2c fares, etc. has created a disturbance in the country that is unnatural and uncalled for." [52] James S. Clarkson showed how far he had gone in imbibing the Rooseveltian doctrine of "malefactors of great wealth" by declaring in a letter to Louis T. Michener: "These are times to make the old-timers hold their breath. I can imagine how you feel about the attempt of the one per cent of Americans who have been seeking to make all the profit in this country and to lay the other ninety-nine per cent under tribute and slavery, attempting now to automobile the President off the track." [53] George E. Roberts, safely out of the battle after almost getting caught in the thick of it before selling the Des Moines *Register*, analyzed the public state of mind as follows: "There is more pleasure in the memories of Iowa politics of twenty years ago than in mixing in Iowa politics of the present. Jealousy, suspicion of public men, hatred & bitterness poison the air out there. I think there will be a fight on Allison if he lives & is a candidate for re-election. The state is fat with prosperity but strangely discontented." [54]

Truly a new day had come in Iowa senatorial politics. The era of easy Allison victories was a thing of the past. Now the aging leader was faced with a contest in which very conceivably he could be beaten. George Roberts, with true analytical skill, had put his finger on the trouble.

The issue was reform (Progressivism) versus maintenance of the status quo (Conservatism), but it would be fought in terms of persons and personalities. In the eyes of the people, "reform" and "Albert B. Cummins" were synonymous terms; the question was, would Allison lend his name to the Conservatives? George Roberts had said: "there will be a fight on Allison if he lives & is a candidate for re-election."

"If he lives." The date of his conjecture was April 4, 1907.

☆ XIX ☆

Exit in Triumph

WHEN THE FIFTY-NINTH Congress adjourned on March 4, 1907, Allison was only twenty-five days short of his seventy-eighth birthday. The time was rapidly approaching when a decision would have to be made as to his candidacy for a seventh term. Yet a positive action was difficult for him to take; either the state of his health or a disposition to assume that the office should naturally be his without a party contest seemed to hold him back. Perhaps it was a combination of both.

There is no doubt that Allison's health had declined, even if the critical stage had not yet been reached. Almost every letter to or from him makes some reference to his condition; his most devoted friends commented on it to each other. Shortly after adjournment General Dodge wrote to Allison that he had received a good report through Allison's nephew and urged him to come out to Council Bluffs for a visit, "if you feel able. . . . Perhaps you may not feel like leaving home with your troubles." Allison did not accept the invitation, but he responded: "I think you and I are both fortunate in being as well as we are, taking into acc't our advanced years. . . . My own health is very good now excepting my local trouble which seems to be improving. General health is good and I am able to do considerable work during the day." [1] In May, Thomas P. Cleaves, clerk of the Senate Appropriations Committee, wrote to Lee McNeely, Allison's private secretary: "I am extremely gratified to hear such a favorable report on the Senator's improvement and progress and sincerely hope he will . . .

313

fully regain his former excellent health." Probably no other people
on earth knew Allison as well as these two men, or were less inclined
to deceive each other with insincere optimism about his health.[2]

Although the Iowa primary election would not be held until June
of 1908, Allison's friends were already pressing him to make an announcement of his candidacy. As early as April, 1907, Congressman
Benjamin P. Birdsall wrote to Dolliver that Governor Cummins had
told him he expected to run for the Senate and was debating the date
of his formal announcement. Birdsall hoped that Allison would soon
make his own announcement, yea or nay; a negative decision, however
sincerely made on account of failing health, would appear to be a
surrender if made after Cummins' declaration.[3] This intervention
brought no response, however. Allison might be pardoned for a
certain apathy concerning an election that would not take place for
almost a year. It had been so long since he had had to make a contest
in a popular election that perhaps he did not realize the amount of
time needed to arouse public opinion. Moreover, he seemed to think
it beneath his dignity to scramble for the office so far in advance, and
it took considerable pressure from certain sources to extract a formal
announcement from him.

The spokesman of the "force Allison to announce" movement was
Ernest E. Hart, a prominent attorney of Council Bluffs and a member
of the Republican national committee. Hart talked with Allison in
Chicago and later confirmed their conversation in a series of letters,
the first on June 22. He had reported to some of the Allison backers
in Iowa, Hart wrote, and "they are still more insistent than before I
left [for Chicago] on definite information as to your being a candidate." Admitting that it was humiliating for Allison to have to
make an announcement so early, Hart added that it was generally assumed in Iowa that Cummins would announce for the senatorship,
and if Allison did not make a formal announcement it would give
the opposition a chance to say that he considered the senatorial place
as his private property. "In fact, my dear Senator," Hart continued,
"I have some doubts as to whether or not you realize the state of
mind which these ardent advocates of the Governor get into. It
seems a species of insanity."

As to organization and procedure, Hart suggested a manager who
was "quick and alert, and one of large acquaintance in the state. The
clerical work of course could be taken care of by such a bright young

man as your secretary, and others whom he could call about him." Hart then recommended that Allison make his announcement through the Associated Press. "Your long experience however in political matters will enable you to see more clearly than I can the best course to be pursued." Allison replied to this appeal: "I wish of course so far as I can, to meet the wishes of yourself and the friends you name, but it seems to me that a public proclamation from me is not necessary, at least at the present time." [4]

Not satisfied with this prospect of delay, Hart again insisted on a definite announcement. He reported that a Cummins enthusiast, H. W. Byers of Harlan, had recently been in Council Bluffs and had left the impression that a "systematic and strenuous campaign of opposition" would be conducted by the Cummins forces. Then, as his closing argument, Hart quoted a letter just received from Joseph W. Blythe, the recognized leader of the Standpat wing of the party in Iowa, urging an explicit announcement. "I do not think that ought to be postponed," Blythe had written, "or that it ought to be left entirely for Mr. Allison to decide." In spite of this strong letter, Allison still stubbornly refused to announce, replying on July 11: "I do not feel that at this time I should make public confirmation of my candidacy." [5]

The Senator was not entirely inactive, however, and there was not the least doubt that he intended to run. He and the "bright young man" who served as his secretary were going ahead on their own to solicit from all the Republican members of the Iowa delegation in Congress lists of voters and other data on the Republicans in their respective districts. Several of them replied favorably; one sent a list in which every name was marked "C" or "P" for Conservative or Progressive. [6]

More important, Allison arranged for his junior colleague, Jonathan P. Dolliver, to make a speech in his behalf. On August 23 Allison wrote Dolliver the first of many letters in which he furnished ammunition for Dolliver's use. This particular letter reviewed Allison's position on the Hepburn Act and compared it favorably to a stand taken by Secretary of War William Howard Taft. [7]

At last, on August 26, 1907, Allison made the long awaited announcement, in an interview with reporters:

Senator Allison in response to an inquiry as to his candidacy for re-election to the Senate, said: "The Associated Press is authorized to announce that I

will be a candidate before the primaries for the Republican nomination . . .
to succeed myself. I have invariably so indicated to friends when spoken to
on the subject & supposed it was generally understood throughout the state
that I was a candidate for re-election, but it having been intimated in certain
quarters that there was some doubt on the subject, & that probably I would
not again be a candidate, I feel that justice to all requires this definite
statement." [8]

So now the fat was in the fire. General Dodge followed up at once
with urgent advice that Allison's physical stamina should be exhibited.
"It would be well for you to attend some function away from home,
the State Fair or some such gathering. An object lesson does more than
anything else and it would stop the prattle of those who pretend you
are not well." Dodge added that he had seen Ret Clarkson, who had
sent assurances of readiness to help. Although in better health than
he had been for the last two years, Allison did not follow Dodge's
advice to appear at functions "away from home." Rather, he remained in Dubuque during the fall months, made a number of public
speeches, and received visitors. In late September members of the
Inland Waterways Commission, en route to Keokuk by boat to meet
President Roosevelt, stopped at Dubuque and called on the Senator,
all reporting that they were delighted to find him in such good health.[9]

Ernest E. Hart quickly organized an Allison Club in Council Bluffs;
soon there would be five hundred members, he wrote. "Many of the
people who were for Mr. Cummins for governor are against him on
this proposition. By this I mean people of standing and influence. The
net result will be [that] a great body of voters in this section will
follow such leadership." [10]

In Washington, Ret Clarkson and Dodge met for luncheon and
talked over what they could do for Allison. Perkins of the Sioux City
Journal had sent a reporter to Clarkson for an interview, but Ret,
because of his official position, hesitated to give it to him until he had
consulted President Roosevelt. The President "will not allow me
to go to political conventions nor to write for the press on public
matters," Ret reported to Allison, "because he says whatever I say
would be taken as having been done by his direction." However, Ret
felt sure that Roosevelt would not interfere in the requested interview, because of his "fervent friendship & . . . complete trust" in
Allison. "I can't understand how any man in Iowa can have an
ambition so vaulting as to think that he can get the Iowa people to
send him to the Senate in your place," Clarkson continued. He assured

Allison that he would "go back to the tap-roots & call attention to the great service you have rendered to Iowa, as well as to the nation, & shall try to ring the old bells of lifelong friendship loudly enough to call up the conscience of Iowa, if it needs reviving." This might be called the classic statement of the feelings of the pro-Allisonians at that time. Illinois had just re-elected Shelby M. Cullom, "of similar age," Clarkson continued, and "Iowa cannot afford to demean itself by not re-electing you." Nor, he concluded, could Iowa ignore the claims of the nation to "the great service from you which it has been receiving for so many years." Ret had struck the keynote; the Allison papers throughout the campaign played upon the emotions of the voters, with sentimental stories of Iowa's "Grand Old Man" and with quotations from his colleagues in Congress as to the high position he held among them.[11]

Since the governorship was also up for election in 1908, Allison and Dolliver for a time thought it would be good strategy to get Congressman Gilbert N. Haugen of Northwood to run for that office.[12] As a banker and large landowner, Haugen might have proved to be a magnet for Conservative votes if his name could have been coupled with Allison's on the ticket. This idea was soon given up, however, when it was discovered that Beryl F. Carroll of Bloomfield was already well out in front as a Conservative candidate. A Carroll-Haugen contest would merely have enhanced the chances of the Progressive candidate, Lieutenant Governor Warren Garst.[13]

For the record, it might be added that James S. Clarkson sent his advice, as requested by General Dodge, but his suggestions reveal that he was still living in the era of post-Civil War politics.[14] In a campaign plan of eleven points, not one showed a full awareness of the appeal of the reforming zeal of the Progressives. The only point Ret offered applicable to the twentieth century was that stress should be laid on Allison as one of the creators of the protective tariff system, and this was a point not upheld by sound history and lacking popular appeal compared to the "Iowa Idea." Moreover, it ran counter to the current belief that the tariff was in need of revision downward.

Of more importance, historically, was Clarkson's effort to persuade Roosevelt that during his anticipated visit to Iowa he should use his good offices to secure Governor Cummins' withdrawal from the race. Actually, Cummins had not yet formally announced his candidacy, but there was no doubt that he would be a candidate. If

Cummins were to make it known that he would not contest Allison's claims on the office, he would simply be deferring "his just ambition and would put the whole State back of him when his time shall have come," Clarkson wrote to Roosevelt. "You are sure to be consulted on this in Iowa, and I believe you can bring about that which . . . will be best for Cummins as for Allison, and far away best for the State and the nation." [15] But President Roosevelt preferred the role of neutral in this contest and very cleverly managed to avoid offense to either side.

In October the Allison campaign began to take on more drive. First, Allison put himself on record as a party regular by publicly announcing that if in the coming primary in June, 1908, the voters should express "preference for another," he would abide loyally by the result.[16] This statement was probably elicited by the fact that many Republicans claimed that the actions of the voters would not be binding on the members of the General Assembly, some even threatening to support the Democratic candidate, should their choice for Senator not be chosen in the primary. To scotch this movement, Allison, and later Cummins, both asserted that they meant to accept the results of the primary.

Far more important is the beginning of a new series of letters, continuing those begun in August, which reveal the details of a well thought out plan for firing the opening gun in Allison's campaign. Briefly stated, the plan called for a dinner and public meeting in Council Bluffs at which Jonathan Dolliver would deliver an address in praise of Allison.

On October 8 Allison wrote to Dolliver, giving him a memorandum on certain legislation involving the war with Spain and the policy in Cuba and the Philippines, all of which had been considered in appropriation bills and which he had helped to forward. He continued:

I have communicated with the Council Bluffs people and I have no doubt they will extend to you an invitation to address the Club early in November. I think it is of the utmost importance that you should do this and of course what you say there will be widely disseminated. I cannot express to you my appreciation of the service this will be to me to have this address made as you propose.[17]

Dolliver's reply reveals the spirit behind his service to Allison: "I will make the speech as smooth as possible and will let you see it before I fire it off. I will make [it] short so that we can circulate it through the Press and in pamphlet form. I wish I could make [it] equal to my affection for you and your claims on the good will of the people of Iowa." [18] In reply Allison suggested that he make "a special appeal to the young men of Iowa in my behalf. So many of them are not personally acquainted with me who are personally acquainted with you, & an appeal from you, a young man to the young men, I think would be greatly appreciated." [19]

The invitation from Council Bluffs to Dolliver was soon forthcoming, exactly as Allison had assured him. Charles M. Harl of that city sent Allison a copy of the letter that had been sent to Dolliver, adding: "As you are aware, the first Allison Club organized for your re-election was the Pottawattamie County Allison Club. We felt by reason of his position as a junior senator from Iowa, his great ability, his familiarity with your candidacy that an address from him would be of great value not only locally but throughout the state." [20] General Dodge at once corroborated this information. [21]

Allison took his cues promptly and wrote to Harl: "I have no doubt Sen. Dolliver will accept the invitation and that he will be glad to respond favorably. . . . I especially appreciate your willingness to accept the presidency of the Club and I am sure it is wise to enter upon the campaign in the spirit expressed by you in your letter to Sen. Dolliver. I am sure that this method of conducting a campaign will have a tendency to promote harmony in the Republican party, which is very much needed if we are to maintain the ascendancy of the party in this state." [22]

Still trying to help Dolliver in making the best possible case, Allison sent him more data, this time about the rate bill, a topic which earlier he had been willing to leave to Dolliver's own familiarity with the facts. "I suggest that you look over the letter of the President to me, found on Page 7098, Congressional Record, of date of May 15, 1906, relating to the rate bill, if you shall discuss that. . . . It may not be wise to use this, but I merely call your attention to it that you may think of it." [23]

In reply, Dolliver asked Allison about the use of Cummins' letter to W. H. Torbert in 1906 — the letter in which Cummins disclaimed any intention of running for the Senate against Allison. Allison's reply is worth noting in full because it reveals his disinclination to make use of this controversial document.

Since receiving yours respecting the letter written by Gov. Cummins I have thought the matter over carefully and have also ascertained as near as I

could the feeling of the person to whom the letter was written, respecting
the publication of the letter. It was written under such circumstances and in
such way as that I think the person to whom it was written wants himself
at the proper time to make it public and make it public here in this city and
the arguments used in favor of this method have so much weight with me
that I think it is better for you not to insert it in your speech at Council Bluffs,
and I think it would weaken the speech and lead to personalities that may
not be agreeable in any way. You know what the Governor said to you and
I have no doubt many others could testify likewise, but this particular letter
has surrounding it certain circumstances that make it important that it
should be published here.[24]

   Allison's last letter of counsel to Dolliver before the big Council
Bluffs meeting was concerned mainly with publicity methods. He
suggested that copies of the speech should be sent to the Fort Dodge
Messenger (Dolliver's home town paper, owned by George E. Roberts)
and copies run off as proofs and sent to the daily papers of Iowa. In
addition, a "skilled shorthand reporter" should take the speech down
"as you are likely to put some things into it that will not be from your
written speech." Allison offered to take care of this latter detail by
writing to Judge Walter I. Smith of Council Bluffs. "I think arrangements will surely have to be made to have it printed in pamphlet
form and widely circulated," he concluded.[25]

   At last the big day arrived. The *Nonpareil* of November 25, 1907,
carried a picture of Allison on the first page and an account of the
meeting to be held that evening. A special point was made that
ladies would be welcome. The same paper for the next day was almost
an "Allison special." "ALL HONOR ALLISON" was the banner headline; "Large Audience Hears Senator Dolliver's Eulogy of Colleague's Work" was the next headline below, followed by the statement that an audience of more than one thousand heard Dolliver as
he spoke for more than two hours. An inside page carried a picture
of Dolliver and a complete text of his speech. The Dubuque *Times-
Journal* had a lead story on the event, as did the Des Moines *Register
and Leader*, now an out-and-out Cummins paper. The latter said:
"In a notable address tonight, United States Senator J. P. Dolliver
made an eloquent plea to the citizens of Iowa to give his distinguished
colleague, William B. Allison, a re-election to his seat in the Senate,"
and added that a large crowd was there from all over the state, actually
more than his backers had expected. This paper reprinted Dolliver's
text in full but without comment.[26]

Harl's report to Allison was ecstatic.

The members of the Club here had very high expectations with reference to the character of the meeting, but they were all surpassed. . . . No such tribute has ever before been paid to any citizen of Iowa. . . . The speech of Sen. Dolliver left absolutely nothing to be desired. Lofty in its tone, eloquent in its expression and uncompromising in its attitude, it was a speech which read in cold type will have a profound influence throughout the state and yet it loses much when separated from Dolliver's great personality.

Allison's reply was a simple but complete and sincere expression of his gratitude to Harl and the Pottawattamie Allison Club for what they had done.[27]

An examination of Dolliver's speech,[28] which "in cold type" certainly does lose much "when separated from Dolliver's great personality," reveals that Dolliver used a portion of the Torbert Letter, in spite of Allison's advice to the contrary. Two months before the Dolliver speech, he and Cummins had corresponded on the meaning of this letter. Cummins had made the first move, prompted by rumors coming to him that Dolliver had said that the Governor had promised not to run against Allison. Cummins patiently explained that he had once told Dolliver himself that he did not expect to run against Allison and that he had been assured by both Allison and Dolliver that Allison would not be likely to run again because his working days were over. Now, wrote Cummins, he felt free to run because obviously Allison was in poor health, could not do the work called for, and that the men who were pressing Allison to run were doing so only to control the office and somehow keep Cummins from attaining it. It was not too late yet for Allison to withdraw with honor, Cummins concluded.[29]

Dolliver's answer was a long restatement of various understandings that he had received from Cummins as to the postponement of his candidacy until Allison had voluntarily withdrawn from the race. He reminded the Governor that they had talked about his senatorial ambitions just before Christmas of 1906, while both were in Chicago, and that Cummins had then assured him that "if when the time came [Allison] presented himself for re-election, you would under no circumstances antagonize him." Allison himself should be the judge as to his ability to perform the duties of the office, wrote Dolliver, and he appealed to Cummins to let Allison have the office, to which he was wedded, without a contest.[30] Cummins' refusal to comply with this idea had led Dolliver to bring the subject, if not the name, of the Torbert Letter into his Council Bluffs speech.

There was considerable difficulty in arriving at the exact meaning of the words that Cummins had used in his letter to Major Torbert. Indicative of the passionate feelings aroused by the contest is the fact that this letter became one of the great talking points of the whole campaign, completely overshadowing the basic issues between Conservatism and Progressivism. Throughout the campaign the Allison headquarters used letterheads with the Torbert Letter printed on the back; it was also featured in the widely circulated pamphlet containing Dolliver's Council Bluffs speech.

One result of Dolliver's use of the letter was to force the hand of Governor Cummins, who had not yet made a formal announcement of his candidacy. On December 4 he denied that he had ever promised never to run against Allison, and offered to give $1,000 to charity if anyone could prove that he had. At last, on December 16, the *Register and Leader* published the long awaited formal declaration of Cummins' intention to contest the nomination with Senator Allison.[31]

In the meantime, Torbert himself had had some misgivings about the use that had been made of the letter by Dolliver. On December 11 he had called in his lawyers, prepared a letter to Dolliver which would "fully and fairly present the case"; two days later he sent an additional letter to Dolliver, making it clear that Dolliver had used only a portion of the original letter from Cummins.[32]

In January, 1908, Governor Cummins, writing "off the record," explained his version of the letter to A. B. Funk, perhaps his closest political ally, making a complete statement about the Torbert Letter and a frank declaration of his political ambitions:

The letter simply stated to Torbert the argument that we were making everywhere; namely that I was not a candidate for the Senate, not a candidate for the Allison succession, but was a candidate for Governor, and nothing else; and I called to his attention that it would be as inappropriate for me to publicly pledge myself against a candidacy for the Allison succession as it would be to pledge myself against any other candidacy to arise in the future. The letter was not used to bring me any support in Dubuque County. It did not change, by a hair's breadth, the character of the campaign made against me. I believe that I have as keen a sense of honor as any living man, but I marvel over and over again how any honest man could torture this letter into a pledge that I would never be a candidate against Allison, or into any attempt to deceive.

You know, and I know, that it would be little short of a crime against good government to re-elect Senator Allison. His working days are over, and you have too high and true a perception of public duty to believe that, in these times especially, a Senator should be elected simply to allow him to die in office. I started out in public life with the ambition to be Senator and I feel that this is the only opportunity that remains for me. If I fail now, it is very unlikely that I will ever again be a candidate for public office. I feel sure of winning, and I know the temper of the people of Iowa as well as any man can know it.[33]

The sentence, "The letter was not used to bring me any support in Dubuque County," raises the question as to whether Cummins was referring to the *intention* of the letter or to the *result*. The intention had almost certainly been to exert some degree of influence on Major Torbert and his friends — otherwise the letter is meaningless.

Twelve years later (1920), after he had enjoyed years of success in the Senate and could certainly afford to tell the truth, Cummins wrote to Cyrenus Cole, giving essentially the same explanation. Denying that he had ever had any discussion of the matter with Senator Allison or had ever made any bargain with Senator Dolliver, he explained that he had told Dolliver he would not be a candidate if Allison intended to run and "somewhere along about that time I wrote Torbert to substantially the same effect." Cummins further asserted that Dolliver "at a later time" assured him that Allison would not run, for "reasons with which you are perfectly familiar and which need not be mentioned"; that these reasons were known to hundreds and that he was "never more astonished" than when he learned later that Allison had changed his mind, or "some one had changed it for him"; and that he learned after Allison's death and his own election the "whole inside story" of the conference where it was "determined that Allison would be a candidate," information which he did not intend to publish now as it was "ancient history" and not "very creditable to several of the men who were at the meeting." [34]

Four years after this letter to Cole, Cummins received a "Memorandum" from Smith D. Fry, a distinguished Washington journalist, purporting to give the full story of 1907-1908. According to Fry, Dolliver had told him at "Christmas time," 1906, that Allison had decided not to run. (This certainly conflicts with Dolliver's letter to Cummins in 1907.) Fry visited Allison and asked for a comment. Admitting that his kidneys were affected, Allison told Fry that he would abide by his doctor's decision as to whether he should quit or not. "I've run down from 203 pounds to 181 pounds," he said, "and you know that's not my fighting weight." Fry's next point was that Allison sent Dolliver to Cummins in January of 1907 to tell the Governor that he would not be a candidate in 1908, although the Senator refused to let Fry publish this story at the time. A few months later, in April, 1907, Allison changed his mind and decided to run. Fry closed his memorandum with a story that weakens his whole account, in which the dates "1907" and "1908" are completely confused. He claimed that because of Allison's emaciated appearance he did not dare return to Iowa before the election, and for that reason Congress stayed in session arguing over a battleship bill for forty extra days. It is true that Congress did not adjourn until May 30, 1908, but the naval appropriation bill was passed on May 12. The main reason for the long session was not Allison's political chances at home but a protracted debate over the currency bill which eventually became the Aldrich-Vreeland Act.[35]

Whatever rationalizations Cummins may have made later, in 1908 he entered into the campaign for Allison's seat with vigor. He asked his supporters for a campaign pitched upon a high plane and asserted that he wanted election on his merits as a fighter for good government. Yet he endorsed an editorial in the Odebolt *Chronicle* as "altogether the best presentation of the case" that had appeared. The points made by the *Chronicle* were several: Allison's extreme age and his well-known disease would make it impossible for him to live through another term. Even if in the prime of life, he should not be re-elected because he was a follower, not a leader. He had never been associated with any reform. His closest friends were Aldrich, Hale, and Foraker, all notorious servants of the great corporations. Allison never protested against the "system" whereby the Senate bosses blocked reforms by invoking senatorial courtesy against good appointees; never protested against the smothering of good legislation such as the pure food bills which were buried for fifteen years. He was supported by the very forces which in Iowa opposed the primary law, the maximum freight rate law, and the 2-cent law. Allison was not corrupt; his vote could not be bought — but he was conservative by nature, careful and cautious, always consulted his personal interests rather than the country's good; permitted wrongs by others when his interference would bring retaliation; refused to take the initiative unless his own future was involved. Most of the sins of omission and commission by the Senate were partly his responsibility. He was still unchanged in any way. He and Aldrich and Hale and Lodge controlled the committee appointments, and thus they could block the reporting of any corporation control laws or any good farm legislation. "He belongs to a past generation and clings to old things." [36]

These were hard blows but the stuff of which politics is made. Meanwhile Allison's friends were not idle. Professional writers, such as Julian Richards of Waterloo and Washington, and the regular party workers who ran the Des Moines headquarters harped on Allison's great prestige, his long devotion to duty, and the debt of gratitude that Iowa owed him. George E. Roberts wrote an extended eulogy of "Allison's Life Work." As much capital as possible was made out of Allison's Civil War activities, his committee memberships in the House and Senate, and his interest in the old soldiers, Mississippi River improvements, transcontinental railroads, the farmers' welfare, and educational advantages for Negroes. The charges that he was in critically poor health were met by official denials or by simple assertions that he was fully ready to carry the load of his duties. Privately, there were many confessions of his sufferings and disability mixed up with occasional assertions from trustworthy sources that his health was much better than it had been, presumably in 1906, although no dates were mentioned. In June of 1907, Ernest E. Hart of Council Bluffs, who had just returned from a visit to Allison at Dubuque, reported him in excellent health and spirits, "just as strong and vigorous as he was before his illness last year." [37]

A series of letters from John T. Adams to Dolliver not only reveals the capably managed details of the Allison campaign but also the flair for the game of politics possessed by this "local Mark Hanna." Adams, a lumber and milling magnate of Dubuque, wrote to Dolliver that he had accepted the chairmanship of the Allison campaign because no one else seemed willing to take the job. Adams was highly successful both in the recruitment of speakers and the procurement of finances. "This is really the most fun I ever had," Adams wrote early in 1908. "The Governor is thoroughly beaten already . . . there will not be any part of his machine left large enough for a post mortem." [38]

The Republicans of Iowa held their annual state convention in Des Moines in March, 1908. The senatorship was in no way an item on the agenda of the meeting, but nevertheless the partisans of both men maintained official headquarters at the Hotel Savery and fiercely contended for the favor of the delegates, most of whom were leaders in their respective localities and able to command many votes therein. The Allison headquarters were in Parlors A and D and were staffed by Adams and a local committee under ex-Adjutant General Melvin H. Byers. The Cummins workers were A. B. Funk, H. W. Byers, James A. Smith of Osage, and Emory H. English.[39]

A leading Cummins paper prophesied that the convention would "name four delegates at large to the national convention, instruct for Taft, eulogize Senator Allison, and adopt a platform calling for a revision of the tariff." [40] The first two points of the prophecy were completely fulfilled; on the last the convention exceeded expectations and actually favored the tariff revision plan then known as the "Ohio Idea." On the third point, the convention did not stop at the mere eulogizing of Allison, but adopted a plank asking for his re-election.

Resolved, That we favor the retention of Senator William B. Allison in his place; that we do this because he has brought great distinction to the state, because he has served the whole party of the whole country, with singular fidelity and ability, because of his present commanding position in the senate and in the councils of the nation, and because he has strength in all situations and in all emergencies. He is recognized as the master legislative architect of his time. The nation, almost without regard to party, admonished the people of Iowa of its interest in this great statesman. Therefore, we stand for his re-election, the continuation of his wise counsel, and the retention of his services to the country at large.

This plank was not adopted without a hard fight, however. The vote in the resolutions committee was split, 7 to 4 in favor of the pro-Allison plank; in the convention as a whole the vote was 678 to 510.[41] Major John F. Lacey of Oskaloosa, George D. Perkins of Sioux City, and Congressman B. P. Birdsall of Clarion spoke in favor of Allison; while State Senator Thomas Cheshire of Des Moines led the Cummins forces in their unsuccessful effort to defeat the resolution.[42]

The endorsement of the Ohio Idea on tariff revision was a victory for the Cummins forces, and one suspects that anti-Cummins men accepted this as a relatively unimportant matter, a mere statement of an idea, in order to get on to their victory in the kind of politics that professional politicians understand best, the politics of naming men for office. By instructing for William Howard Taft for President and by endorsing William Boyd Allison for Senator, the Conservatives had won a victory that any man in the street could understand. The protest of the Cummins men that the whole thing was outside the realm of proper convention action gave them little satisfaction. One of them, John W. Hartman of the Waterloo *Courier*, commented: "Turning to the matter of minor consideration, matters pertaining to mere men, the convention performed ignobly. It usurped prerogatives to which it was not entitled. It is open to just and severe criticism for endorsing Senator Allison. It is not believed the Senator himself would approve of such behaviour." [43] The *Butler County Tribune* quoted Senator Cheshire as saying that the convention action was an effort to "repudiate the primary system and return to the caucus," to which Major Lacey retorted, "If we are not here to endorse Senator Allison, what are we here for?" [44]

The heat of the campaign now increased. The Waterloo *Courier* asserted that Iowa had taken a national lead in reform because of the inspiration of Cummins and that he now had a perfect right to aspire to the Senate. Joseph W. Blythe, who had been saluted at the convention, became the bogey man of the Progressives. "Is not the same Joseph W. Blythe the Morgan, the Hill, the Harriman of the state of Iowa? . . . Would not the return of the standpatters to control in the state, mean domination by Blythe and the railroad interests the same as they did dominate for years?" [45] Cummins justified his race in 1906 for a third term as Governor, a sore point with many voters, as necessary to block the control of the state by Blythe and his associates. "I know there were and are a great many honest men among them, but they do not make themselves felt, and I know and you know that for years the little coterie of men of which he was the center were able to prevent any legislation which they did not favor." As for Allison, "every corporate interest that is to be regulated by the law, both in the state and out of it, is exerting all its influence for the retention of Senator Allison. Every railroad company in the state, and all their managers and general attorneys, are moving heaven and earth to defeat me." [46]

One of the less attractive features of the Cummins campaign was the use of Allison's last photograph, taken in 1907. According to the Des Moines *Tribune*, the Cummins campaign committee "doctored" the photograph to make the Senator look even older than he was. Both pictures appeared on the front page of the *Tribune* on May 27, 1908, under an angry heading: "Infamous Outrage." The paper accused the Cummins headquarters staff of handing out the fake picture and of circulating it through the state. The Allison managers were, meanwhile, using a picture taken about 1902 in their literature.

The Allison forces fought back furiously. Two Allison papers made an effort to show that the Senator was a true friend of labor. The Council Bluffs *Nonpareil* had an article claiming that Allison was the first Congressman to work for an eight-hour bill, citing April, 1866, as the time of this action; the Cedar Rapids *Evening Times* reprinted an editorial from *The Labor Leader*, the recognized labor paper of the state, in which a good word was said for Allison, and several instances cited in which he had voted or worked in favor of labor. Among these were the amendment to appropriate $150,000 for investigation of mine explosions and safety appliances; $10,000 for the relief of Pembroke Banton of Waterloo, who had been injured in Panama; and a child labor bill for the District of Columbia. Allison was also credited with being one of the authors of the safety appliance (car coupler) act of 1895, a supporter of the employers' liability act, and in favor of the eight-hour law for workers in the District of Columbia.[47]

While his campaign managers fought the good fight in Iowa, Allison had returned to Washington for the first session of the Sixtieth Congress, which convened on December 2, 1907. There, while charges and accusations flew back and forth at home, he resumed his regular legislative routine. On May 29, 1908, one day before adjournment, he answered his last roll call in Congress,[48] and he and his secretary returned to Iowa for the election. Plans had been laid for him to return later to Johns Hopkins University Hospital for an operation for the removal of his prostate gland. Just before the hour of adjournment on May 30, Vice President Fairbanks announced the appointment of the National Monetary Commission, established by the Aldrich-Vreeland Act, to carry out a sweeping investigation of the currency problem. Allison was naturally one of the members, along with Aldrich, Hale, Knox, Teller, Bailey, and others. This was the last honor William Boyd Allison would receive from the body he had served so long.[49]

One of the most eloquent pleas made for Allison before the election was by Irving H. Hart, the brilliant young editor of the small but influential Clarksville paper, the *Butler County Tribune*. This sheet had formerly been one of the strongest supporters of Cummins, but in May, 1908, it came under new ownership and the editorial supervision of Hart. Completely reversing the policy of the previous editor overnight, Hart delivered telling blows in favor of Allison. Asserting, mistakenly, that Allison and General Baker of Minnesota were the only survivors of the first Republican national convention,[50] the plea was made that if Allison were pushed aside for age alone, it would be to say that Iowa had "no sentiment for the past, no care for the present, and no lofty hopes for the future."[51] The Council Bluffs *Nonpareil* of June 1 closed the campaign by saying that "Allison is Stronger" and that the recent session of Congress had given him more prestige than ever; he was now "more than ever able to serve the state and nation." A large picture accompanied the article, and mention was made that Allison had stopped over in Chicago on his way back to Iowa.

While in Chicago, Allison stayed at the Auditorium Annex, where the Republicans were already gathering for the national convention. A reporter talked to the "Nestor of the Senate," who appeared to be in the "best of health and spirits" and in an optimistic frame of mind. The tariff must be revised, he told the reporter, and recommended that a special session of Congress be called immediately after the election to deal with the problem.[52]

The eventful election on June 2 proved to be a great victory for Allison and the Conservatives. His total vote was 105,891 compared with 95,256 amassed by Cummins. Not only that, B. F. Carroll of Bloomfield won out over Warren Garst of Coon Rapids for the governorship by a vote of 88,834 to 63,737; John G. Hamilton, the prohibitionist, received 29,292 votes. Nine of the eleven Republican nominees for Congress — Charles A. Kennedy, Albert F. Dawson (Allison's former secretary), Charles E. Pickett, Gilbert Haugen, James W. Good, John A. T. Hull, W. P. Hepburn, Walter I. Smith, and Elbert H. Hubbard — were considered Standpatters; Nathan E. Kendall of Albia and Frank P. Woods of Estherville were the only Progressives who were victorious.

This was the only state-wide popular election Allison ever participated in, and it was an intraparty affair. Even so, there was great satisfaction in the victory. It was at least a partial answer to those who had said Allison could not win in an appeal to the rank and file. An analysis of the vote, county by county, shows an interesting pattern.[53] Allison's greatest strength was in the southern half of the state, where he lost only six counties. Of these, only Polk County, Cummins' home, had an appreciably large vote against Allison. A possible explanation is that the influence of the four great railroad systems in that region had a lot to do with the result. The Burlington, Blythe's own line; the Rock Island from Davenport to Council Bluffs; the North Western, the line of the late Judge N. M. Hubbard; and the Milwaukee, all traverse the southern half of the state. Undoubtedly there were other factors: the influence of strong newspapers, effective work by local leaders, the power of tradition. To many voters, Allison had become a well-beloved figure in whom they took great pride, and the Allison campaign managers and editors had played up this theme to great effect. In the northern part of the state Allison carried only fifteen counties, and only two of these were in the northwestern quarter; the other thirteen were in the eastern counties which had been settled much earlier.

As soon as the results of the election were known, the spotlight swung away from Allison and came to rest on his valiant aide, Jonathan Dolliver. With the Republican national convention only a few days away, Dolliver's name was freely mentioned as a possibility for the second place on the ticket, even occasionally for the first place. But this interest in the Fort Dodge man did not have an unmixed motivation. On the part of some it was a sincere compliment: Jonathan Prentiss Dolliver was their idea of a man well suited for a place on the national ticket.[54] On the part of others, however, it was a supposedly clever move, readily transparent to the Allisonians, to remove Dolliver from his senatorship, thus opening a new avenue for Cummins to reach the Senate. The Cummins forces denounced the Standpatters for selfishly blocking Dolliver's chances.[56]

But with all such matters Allison was little concerned. He did not attend the national convention, but it was reported that he had written to Dolliver concerning the vice-presidency, although his message was not made public.[57] Nor did Allison attend the Iowa Republican convention in Waterloo which soon followed. No doubt he was pleased at the reports of harmony which emanated from the meeting.[58]

The old man was entitled to a period of peace and rest, now that his own victory in the primary was out of the way. The manipulation of conventions, the drudgery of political campaigns, the allocation of patronage — these things could now be left to the younger men. From the obscurity and the disappointment of a defeated can-

The Register and Leader.

THE IOWA STATE FAIR
AUGUST 20-28
REDUCED RATES
ON ALL RAILROADS

THE IOWA STATE FAIR
AUGUST 20-28
REDUCED RATES
ON ALL RAILROADS

VOL. 59—NO. 34.　　DES MOINES, IOWA, WEDNESDAY MORNING, AUGUST 5, 1908.—TWELVE PAGES.　　TWO CENTS. On TRAINS FIVE CENTS.

SENATOR WILLIAM BOYD ALLISON DIES; HEAT HASTENS DEATH OF DISTINGUISHED IOWA STATESMAN

SENATOR ALLISON DIES IN DUBUQUE; HEAT A SURPRISE

Ravages of Disease Kills Noted Iowa Statesman at Age of 79 Years.

OPPRESSIVE HEAT CAUSE Of SUDDEN COLLAPSE

Had Been Unconscious Since Last Saturday— Served Longest Term.

CONDITION PITIFUL IN THE PAST MONTH

Son of Affliction Cause of Excruciating Pain Including Coma.

ZEPPELIN AIRSHIP IN RECORD FLIGHT

WONDER OF THE AGE OCCUPIES VALLEY OF THE RHINE

THOUSANDS WATCH FLIGHT

FASTEST TIME MADE WAS 42 AN HOUR 57 MILES PER HOUR

One Man Weeps On Sight of Ship— No Serious Accident Befalls On Entire Course.

A STATE'S FRIEND AND A NATION'S COUNSELOR HAS GONE.

ALLISON'S DEATH IS A GREAT SHOCK

WASHINGTON HAD NOT BEEN PREPARED FOR IT.

HELD IN HIGHEST ESTEEM FOR YEARS.

HEAD OF APPROPRIATIONS COMMITTEE FOR YEARS.

Senator's Counsel in Matters of Party Welfare of Paramount Importance —Funeral Plans.

CUMMINS INTENDS TO NAME SENATOR

WILL FILL ALLISON VACANCY BY APPOINTMENT.

WILL THEN BE A CANDIDATE ED.

CONTEST TRANSFERRED TO THE LEGISLATIVE CAUCUS.

Much Speculation Immediately Follows as to the Probable Succession to Seat in Senate.

SHOCK IN DES MOINES

News of Senator Allison's Death Totally Unexpected.

didate for county office in Ohio to the official leadership of the majority in the Senate; from being a leg-man for others to turning down Cabinet offers and vice-presidential feelers, and being twice a presidential possibility — these memories could fill his mind as he leisurely contemplated his return to Congress in December.

When his close friends visited him they found him physically run down but mentally alert and highly pleased over his primary victory. He unaffectedly referred to the President as "Theodore" and shrewdly prophesied that in four years Roosevelt might ask Taft to step aside.[59] But time was growing short.

Before long, bad news came from Dubuque. Allison's secretary, Lee McNeely, on his return from the Chicago convention noticed a critical worsening of the Senator's condition.[60] Others also saw the change,[61] and McNeely passed some of Allison's appointment matters over to Senator Dolliver.[62] In order to escape the intense heat of Dubuque, Allison was taken out to the farm home of Mrs. Fannie Stout O'Donnell, daughter of his long-time friend, H. L. Stout. Rumors spread fast throughout the state. On July 29 Governor Cummins wrote to one of his followers: "I believe that the chances are that the Senatorial matter will be again considered, because the reports I have from Dubuque indicate that Senator Allison is very feeble." [63]

His reports were correct. Hope was abandoned for prolonging the invalid's life, and on August 1 he was brought back to the familiar surroundings of his home on Locust Street. This gesture of love was of no avail, however. The poor man had lost his mental faculties and was in a coma most of the time. Surgery had long ago been ruled out as a means of relief. The end came at 1:33 on Tuesday afternoon, August 4, 1908.

A few days later two old men sat together at lunch in Washington — James S. Clarkson and Grenville M. Dodge. The General was so moved he could hardly speak of his old friend. It remained for the more articulate Clarkson, in a letter to Al Swalm, to write almost an epitaph for William Boyd Allison:

Our beloved Iowa is nearly an orphan these days, and an unhappy one at that. The death of Allison, although we knew that it might come at any minute, was still a great shock to us all. He had lived so long and been powerful so long and we had all turned to him whenever we needed help . . . and now that he is gone it seems as though we had lost a point of the compass.[64]

Bibliography:
Manuscript Collections

THE WILLIAM BOYD ALLISON Papers, located at the *Iowa State Department of History and Archives* at Des Moines, are contained in some 550 boxes, each holding approximately 200 letters. The papers include only a few scattered items dated before 1870, but they become richer in numbers and content as Allison's career developed and he became a famous national figure. This collection was preserved through the intercession of General Grenville M. Dodge.

Other collections of papers at Des Moines which added much to the Allison story are: the extensive Grenville M. Dodge Papers, the Samuel J. Kirkwood Correspondence, the James S. Clarkson Papers (supplemented by a larger collection in the Library of Congress), the Albert Baird Cummins Papers, and the William Penn Clarke, John A. T. Hull, and John A. Kasson collections. The papers of James Harlan have apparently been lost; therefore, his role in this story is obtained from letters to and from him found in these and other collections. The same applies to the papers of James F. Wilson, a few of which have recently been located in the Fairfield Public Library and not yet made available. At the *State Historical Society of Iowa* at Iowa City, the papers of Jonathan P. Dolliver were the most valuable. Other collections consulted there were the Cyrus Clay Carpenter Papers, the Cyrenus Cole Papers, and the Albert F. Dawson Scrapbooks.

Small collections in private hands in Iowa are: the David B. Henderson Papers, owned by Mr. Donald M. Peaslee of Laurens; the

I. M. Fisher Papers, owned by Mr. Irving H. Hart of Cedar Falls; the F. E. Bissell Scrapbook, owned by Mr. F. E. Bissell of Dubuque; and the R. P. Clarkson Scrapbook, owned by Elizabeth Clarkson Zwart (Mrs. Donald Metcalf) of Des Moines.

Of great value and interest are the letters of Charles E. Perkins, some in the Burlington Archives at the Newberry Library in Chicago, and some in the possession of *Richard C. Overton, Manchester, Vermont.*

Many other collections of manuscripts have yielded information, although not all in the quantity of those mentioned above. *Library of Congress*: the papers of Nelson W. Aldrich (unrestricted portion), Benjamin Helm Bristow, Andrew Carnegie, Grover Cleveland, William M. Evarts, Hamilton Fish, James A. Garfield, Benjamin Harrison, Andrew Johnson, Robert T. Lincoln, William McKinley, Louis T. Michener, Justin S. Morrill, Whitelaw Reid, Theodore Roosevelt, Edwin M. Stanton, Elihu Washburne, and James H. Wilson. *Illinois State Historical Library, Springfield*: the papers of Lyman Trumbull, Horace White, and Joseph G. Cannon. *Massachusetts Historical Society, Boston*: Edward Atkinson Papers. *Princeton University*: William Worth Belknap Papers. *New York Public Library*: Levi P. Morton Papers. *Hayes Memorial Library, Fremont, Ohio*: Rutherford B. Hayes Papers. *Newberry Library, Chicago*: Burlington and Illinois Central Papers, and the Orville E. Babcock Papers. *State Historical Society of Wisconsin, Madison*: Luman H. Weller Papers. *University of Chicago*: Stephen A. Douglas Papers. *Yale University Library*: Chauncey M. Depew Papers. *West Virginia University, Morgantown*: Stephen B. Elkins Papers.

Footnotes

CHAPTER I — THE OHIO YEARS

[1] For this genealogical information, I have used the Dubuque *Daily Times*, Jan. 7, 1884, containing an obituary of John Allison; data supplied to me by Attorney J. Thomas Mitchell of Bellefonte, Pa., June 26, 1950, and by Mrs. Emma B. Hawley of the Western Reserve Historical Society Library, Cleveland, Ohio; and Ben: Perley Poore, a typewritten manuscript biography in Box 1, *William Boyd Allison Papers* (Iowa State Dept. of History and Archives, Des Moines), the basis for an article published in *The Magazine of Western History*, 6:65-85 (May, 1887). Poore, a Washington journalist, was a personal friend of Allison's. (This manuscript will hereafter be referred to as Poore MS.) Mrs. Allison's tombstone was seen and noted by me on a personal tour of Perry Township, April 27, 1947, in company with Mr. Ed. M. Dunner, a venerable citizen of Rowsburg familiar with the Allison family history.

[2] The author made a personal visit to the old Allison homestead on April 27, 1947.

[3] Data supplied by Fred H. Allison, Belmond, Iowa, a grandnephew of William B. Allison.

[4] H. S. Knapp, *A History of the Pioneer and Modern Times of Ashland County* (Philadelphia, 1863), 428-9. The dates of his commissions are given as March 1, 1830; March 1, 1833; March 25, 1836; March 19, 1839. Also see biography of Allison by Jeannette P. Nichols in *Dictionary of American Biography*, 1:220-22 (hereafter listed as *DAB*).

[5] Many years later a friend of Allison's boyhood days wrote to him: "The early teachings we received when boys in the homes of our good parents and from the pulpit of Old Mount Hope Meeting House, laid the foundations for what you are as a statesman and for what I am as a minister of the Lord Jesus Christ." Rev. David A. Cunningham to Allison, Feb. 27, 1884, Box 37, *Allison Papers*. Cunningham was at the time pastor of the First Presbyterian Church, Wheeling, W. Va.

[6] Ohio is fortunate in its possession of scholars who have produced a magnificent six-volume work edited by Carl Wittke, *The History of the State of Ohio* (Columbus, 1940-1944). Of this series, Vol. III, *The Passing of the Frontier, 1825-1850* (1941) by Francis P. Weisenburger, and Vol. IV, *The Civil War Era, 1850-1873* (1944) by Eugene H. Roseboom are excellent background for the years of the Allison family residence in Ohio. A briefer work is Roseboom and Weisenburger, *A History of Ohio* (New York, 1934; 2nd ed., Columbus, 1953).

[7] Weisenburger, *Passing of the Frontier*, 10. See Works Progress Administration, *The Ohio Guide* (New York, 1940), for evidence of the carryover of the New England influence

335

to the present day. Also see Harlan Hatcher, *The Western Reserve* (Indianapolis, 1949); Stewart H. Holbrook, *The Yankee Exodus* (New York, 1950); Rexford Newcomb, *Architecture of the Old Northwest Territory* (Chicago, 1950).

[8] Weisenburger, *Passing of the Frontier*, 81.

[9] *Ibid.*, 53; Robert E. Chaddock, *Ohio Before 1850: A Study of the Early Influence of Pennsylvania and Southern Populations in Ohio* (New York, 1908), 31-4; *History of Wayne County, Ohio* (2 vols., Indianapolis, 1910), 1:108.

[10] William Warren Sweet, *Religion on the American Frontier*: Vol. II, *The Presbyterians, 1783-1840* (New York, 1936), 21-2, discusses this point. See also Charles A. Hanna, *The Scotch-Irish* (2 vols., New York, 1902); William L. Fisk, Jr., "The Scotch-Irish in Central Ohio," *Ohio State Archaeological and Historical Quarterly*, 57:111-25 (April, 1948).

[11] Weisenburger, *Passing of the Frontier*, 53-4; Arthur S. Link, *Wilson: The Road to the White House* (Princeton, 1947), 1.

[12] The *Allison Papers* have only a few scattered items before 1870.

[13] Allison to C. A. Carlisle, Sept. 14, 1906, Box 13, *ibid.*, expresses his regret at his inability to attend a cornerstone-laying ceremony of the South Bend, Indiana, Y. M. C. A., named in honor of the Studebaker brothers. He tells Carlisle that he knew them well as boys. See *DAB*, 18:180-81, for Studebaker biography.

[14] Ashland (Ohio) *Times*, Oct. 13, 1897.

[15] Sweet, *Religion on the American Frontier*, 2:9.

[16] Henry Howe, *Historical Collections of Ohio* . . . (2 vols., Cincinnati, 1902), 2:841. The sentence, "He lived on a farm, and walked into Wooster every day to school," suggests that he boarded with relatives or friends.

[17] Campaign Biography, Des Moines *Iowa State Register*, Feb. 9, 1896. (This newspaper, to which frequent reference will be made, will be listed hereafter as Des Moines *Register*.) E. A. Smith, *Allegheny, A Century of Education* (Meadville, Pa., 1916), 446; letter to the author from C. S. Miller, director of Alumni Relations, July 9, 1945.

[18] This paragraph based on Smith, *Allegheny, passim*. On Kingsley as a theological controversialist, see *DAB*, 10:410-11; on Stebbins, see *ibid.*, 17:550-51.

[19] Donald G. Tewksbury, *The Founding of American Colleges and Universities Before the Civil War* (New York, 1932), 70-71, 71n, 109; Smith, *Allegheny*, 140, Chap. 3.

[20] Smith, *Allegheny*, 137.

[21] Sadie A. Cook to Allison, Jan. 5, 1886, Box 37, *Allison Papers*.

[22] Cunningham to Allison, Feb. 27, 1884, Box 37, *ibid.*

[23] See Carroll Cutler, *A History of Western Reserve College* (Cleveland, 1876); Helen Kitzmiller, *One Hundred Years of Western Reserve* (Hudson, 1926).

[24] G. H. Barnes, *The Antislavery Impulse* (New York, 1933); G. H. Barnes and D. L. Dumond (eds.), *The Weld-Grimké Letters* (New York, 1934); Sweet, *Religion on the American Frontier*: Vol. III, *The Congregationalists*; G. G. Atkins and F. L. Fagley, *History of American Congregationalism* (Boston, 1942); Robert S. Fletcher, *A History of Oberlin College* (2 vols., Oberlin, 1943); Frederick W. Waite, *A History of Western Reserve College. The Hudson Era* (Cleveland, 1941); C. Bruce Staiger, "Abolitionism and the Presbyterian Schism of 1837-1838," *Mississippi Valley Historical Review*, 36:391-414 (December, 1949).

[25] Allison became a pewholder in the Second Presbyterian Church at Dubuque but never a full-fledged member. Rev. Gaylord Couchman to the author, Oct. 21, 1947.

[26] John R. Commons, "Horace Greeley and the Working Class Origins of the Republican Party," *Political Science Quarterly*, 24:468-88 (September, 1909); W. E. Binkley, *American Political Parties: Their Natural History* (New York, 1943), Chaps. 8 and 9. Binkley makes many references to the religious backgrounds and their eventual effects on the Republican party.

27 James W. Grimes to Salmon P. Chase, Oct. 3, 1854, quoted in William Salter, *The Life of James W. Grimes* . . . (New York, 1876), 54.

28 Cleveland *Plain Dealer*, Dec. 3, 1856, quoted in Roseboom, *Civil War Era*, 323.

29 There is a possibility that he studied for some time with a lawyer named Eugene Pardee. Allison received a letter from a close friend, N. E. Dawson of Burlington, Sept. 19, 1894, saying he had met Pardee's son, who claimed this honor for his father. If so, Allison was studying with a leader of the Wooster bar and a staunch antislavery man. See Ben Douglas, *History of the Lawyers of Wayne County, Ohio* (Wooster, Ohio, 1900), 256-7.

30 Obituary notice of Matthew Allison in the Dubuque *Times*, Apr. 17, 1874.

31 Judge Lyman R. Critchfield, Wooster, Ohio, to the author, Aug. 7, 1947.

32 Poore MS, *Allison Papers*. The name of Jennings as clerk of courts was furnished to the author through the kindness of C. O. McGuire, clerk of courts, Ashland, Ohio, Sept. 10, 1947.

33 The advertisements of these three law partnerships can be followed in the columns of the Ashland *Times* and the Ashland *Union*, 1853 to 1857. In 1870 Allison received this letter from Smith: "I am still trudging along — practicing law. You see my boy stands in the place [partner] where you once did. Turning to our old Book Record of cases, I read thus — 'Here commences the Record of Smith & Allison copartnership of business dating from Sept. 15, 1851.' " J. W. Smith to Allison, Nov. 3, 1870, Box 2, *Allison Papers*. Another bit of testimony is found in the following letter from Mrs. Henry Wallace, wife of the first Henry Wallace of Iowa, mother of Henry C., and grandmother of Henry A. Wallace: "The 'spirit' moves me to write you and I obey, hoping you will pardon the liberty as we are natives of the same State of Ohio, and same County; while a little school-girl at College I was under the care of 'Mrs. Bolivar Kellogg' with whose husband you studied law, and my honored Father (Col. Cantwell) often spoke of you as a rising man also my uncle Dr. Cantwell who met you in Dubuque several years ago, therefore because of this — your having been an honor to both our native and adopted State — I write you." Mrs. Henry Wallace to Allison, Sept. 20, 1887, Box 41, *Allison Papers*.

34 Robert W. Shultz, Secretary, Ashland Lodge, No. 151, F. & A. M., Ashland, Ohio, to the author, July 27, Aug. 18, 1948.

35 Howe, *Historical Collections of Ohio*, 1:252.

36 George William Hill, *History of Ashland County, Ohio* (Ashland, 1880), 149, and unnumbered page opposite.

37 Commons, "Horace Greeley and the Working Class Origins of the Republican Party," 469. See also Binkley, *American Political Parties*, Chaps. 8-9; William Starr Myers, *The Republican Party: A History* (New York, 1928); Jeter A. Isely, *Horace Greeley and the Republican Party, 1853-1861* . . . (Princeton, 1947); A. W. Crandall, *The Early History of the Republican Party, 1854-1856* (Boston, 1930); Francis Curtis, *The Republican Party* . . . (2 vols., New York, 1904); Glyndon G. Van Deusen, *Thurlow Weed: Wizard of the Lobby* (New York, 1947); James A. Rawley, *Edwin D. Morgan, 1811-1883* (New York, 1955); Allan Nevins, *Ordeal of the Union* (2 vols., New York, 1947), 2:398-404, 466-70.

38 Albert Bushnell Hart, *Salmon Portland Chase* (Boston, 1899), 112ff., 132-3; Roseboom, *Civil War Era*, 279.

39 Binkley, *American Political Parties*, 207-208; Albert J. Beveridge, *Abraham Lincoln, 1808-1858* (2 vols., Boston, 1928), 2:184-96.

40 Philip Kinsley, *The Chicago Tribune: Its First Hundred Years* (New York, 1943), for a reference to this religious influence on Joseph Medill, an Ohioan before he went to Chicago to join the *Tribune*. This instance is cited as a reminder that the religious impulse was not confined to the clergy.

41 Commons, "Horace Greeley and the Working Class Origins of the Republican Party"; Barnes, *Antislavery Impulse*, 197; Philip S. Foner, *Business and Slavery: The New York Merchants and the Irrepressible Conflict* (Chapel Hill, N. C., 1941), *passim*, especially Chap. 17; A. M. Schlesinger, Jr., *The Age of Jackson* (Boston, 1945). Lloyd Lewis, *It Takes All*

Kinds (New York, 1948), 168-9, makes the point very strongly. A Chicago meeting, addressed by James H. Lane, was held on "a Saturday night when the workingmen would be free, and the sailors in from the lakes and the longshoremen up from the docks, and the farmers across from the field. For, make no mistake about it, the Republican Party was a radical, almost a New Deal party in 1856. It was the masses attacking the classes."

[42] Binkley, *American Political Parties*, 207. Also see the judicious remarks by James G. Randall, *Lincoln the President: Springfield to Gettysburg* (2 vols., New York, 1945), 1:82-3n.

[43] Ashland *Times*, May 11, 1854. The "J. B. Allison" has not been identified. Perhaps "W. B." was intended. Alexander Allison was a cousin of William B. Allison.

[44] Robert B. Warden, *An Account of the Private Life and Public Services of Salmon Portland Chase* (Cincinnati, 1874), 345; Hart, *Chase*, 152-4; *DAB*, 4:29; Eugene H. Roseboom, "Salmon P. Chase and the Know Nothings," *Mississippi Valley Historical Review*, 25:335-50 (December, 1938).

[45] Ashland *Union*, July 9, Oct. 15, 1856; Stilson Hutchins in the Dubuque *Herald*, Oct. 1, 1862. In Iowa, William Penn Clarke and James Thorington were important members of the Know-Nothing party. See Vol. I of the *William Penn Clarke Correspondence* (Iowa State Dept. of History and Archives, Des Moines).

[46] Ashland *Times*, July 13, 1854. Allison was on the committee on resolutions at the county convention that elected him a delegate to the state convention.

[47] Roseboom, *Civil War Era*, 284-5.

[48] *Ibid.*, 303.

[49] John Sherman, *Recollections of Forty Years in the House, Senate and Cabinet* (2 vols., Chicago, 1895), 1:105; Joseph P. Smith (ed.), *History of the Republican Party in Ohio* (2 vols., Chicago, 1898), 1:33, 35.

[50] See R. A. Billington, *The Protestant Crusade* (New York, 1938); Harry J. Carman and Reinhard Luthin, "Some Aspects of the Know Nothing Movement Reconsidered," *South Atlantic Quarterly*, 39:213-34 (April, 1940); Binkley, *American Political Parties*, 209-210; Roseboom, "Salmon P. Chase and the Know Nothings," 335-50.

[51] New York *Semi-Weekly Tribune*, Feb. 22, 1856; *Proceedings of the Republican National Convention . . . 1856*, 73-6.

[52] Crandall, *Early History of the Republican Party*, 28-9.

[53] New York *Semi-Weekly Tribune*, Feb. 22, 26, 1856.

[54] *Ibid.*, Feb. 22, 1856; New York *Daily Times*, Feb. 26, 1856.

[55] New York *Semi-Weekly Tribune*, Feb. 26, 1856; Crandall, *Early History of the Republican Party*, 141.

[56] Crandall, *Early History of the Republican Party*, 179-81.

[57] Ashland *Union*, July 9, 1856.

[58] *Ibid.*, Aug. 20, 1856.

[59] Ashland *Times*, Aug. 21, 28, 1856. A letter to the author from Judge William T. Devor of Ashland describes Kenny as a vivacious, convivial, energetic, and altogether likeable Irishman who enjoyed a wide popularity and left a legend of good fellowship behind him. He was elected a state senator from his county in 1861.

[60] George H. Porter, *Ohio Politics During the Civil War Period* (New York, 1911), 18, 26, and map facing 26.

[61] See *The Biographical Directory of the American Congress, 1774-1927* (Washington, 1928), for data on these men.

[62] Poore MS., *Allison Papers*.

[63] For a discussion of this phase of history see the essay by William O. Lynch, "The Advance into the Middle West," in Jeannette P. Nichols and James G. Randall (eds.), *Democracy in the Middle West, 1840-1940* (New York, 1941). See also Stephen Vincent Benet, *Westward Star* (New York, 1943).

CHAPTER II — FROM BUCKEYE TO HAWKEYE

[1] Poore MS., *Allison Papers.*

[2] "The Campaign Biography of 1896," Des Moines *Register*, Feb. 9, 1896.

[3] William J. Petersen, *Iowa, The Rivers of Her Valleys* (Iowa City, 1941), 42-3; Marquis Childs, "River Town," *Harper's Magazine* (November, 1932), reprinted in John T. Flanagan, *America is West* (Minneapolis, 1945).

[4] Franklin Oldt (ed.), *History of Dubuque County, Iowa* . . . (Chicago, n. d.), 337-9.

[5] See "The Campaign Biography of 1896."

[6] M. M. Hoffmann, *Antique Dubuque, 1673-1833* (Dubuque, 1930), *passim.*

[7] F. I. Herriott, "Whence Came the Pioneers of Iowa?" *Annals of Iowa* (third series), 7:464 (July, 1906). See also William J. Petersen, "Population Advance to the Upper Mississippi Valley, 1830-1860," *Iowa Journal of History and Politics*, 32:335-6 (October, 1934), for a tabular study of the nativity of the Iowa population in 1860, which shows Ohio far ahead of any other state.

[8] W. W. Hamilton of Dubuque to Kirkwood, Apr. 29, 1859, on the need to solicit the German vote: "Germans are as thick as bees up here." *Samuel J. Kirkwood Correspondence* (Iowa State Dept. of History and Archives, Des Moines).

[9] Oldt (ed.), *History of Dubuque County*, 107, quoting the Dubuque *Express and Herald*, Apr. 12, 1855; *ibid.*, 117, quoting same paper for Feb. 4, 1857.

[10] Isley, *Horace Greeley and the Republican Party*, 216, referring to and quoting from the New York *Daily Tribune*, Feb. 20, 1857.

[11] Oldt (ed.), *History of Dubuque County*, 340.

[12] *Ibid.*, 635, and *passim*. The *Stephen A. Douglas Papers* (University of Chicago) contain no important letters from Samuels. This is difficult to explain, because Iowa was not yet the Democratic cipher that it came to be. See David S. Sparks, "The Decline of the Democratic Party in Iowa, 1850-1860," *Iowa Journal of History*, 53:1-30 (January, 1955).

[13] *The History of Dubuque County, Iowa* . . . (Chicago, 1880), 778-9; and oral statement by Miss Martha Baker, Dubuque, Iowa, to the author.

[14] Oldt (ed.), *History of Dubuque County*, 337-8. Azro B. F. Hildreth in Charles City *Intelligencer*, May 27, 1869. On Samuels as an orator, see Owen Peterson, "Ben Samuels in the Democratic National Convention of 1860," *Iowa Journal of History*, 50:225-38 (July, 1952).

[15] For example, see Allison to Kirkwood, Apr. 7, 1861, No. 356, *Kirkwood Correspondence*, where Allison writes: "I have never had any sympathy with Cooley & that class of malcontents here. I have been an humble instrument in thwarting many of their schemes."

[16] The election was held Jan. 3, 1859. The Iowa State Bank was a frontier financial institution of that day, modeled after those set up by Ohio and Indiana. A central office or parent bank served as headquarters for a system of functioning branch banks. A maximum of thirty branches was allowed for the whole state. See Howard H. Preston, *A History of Banking in Iowa* (Iowa City, 1922), 85.

[17] Allison was listed in a contemporary city directory as a "boarder."

[18] Box 1, *Allison Papers.*

[19] 68 *U. S. Reports* (1 Wallace), 175. In this case before the Supreme Court he was associated with a prominent attorney from Des Moines, S. V. White, who later became a businessman in New York City. For sketch of White, see *DAB*, 20:119-20. The temptation is to believe that White did most of the legal work on the case while Allison supplied the footwork in Washington. On the case of Gelpcke *v.* The City of Dubuque, see Charles Fairman, *Mr. Justice Miller and the Supreme Court, 1862-1890* (Cambridge, Mass., 1939), 213-21; Ethan P. Allen, "Gelpcke *v.* The City of Dubuque," *Iowa Journal of History and Politics*, 28:177-93 (April, 1930).

[20] Louis Pelzer, "The Origin and Organization of the Republican Party in Iowa," *Iowa*

Journal of History and Politics, 4:487-525 (October, 1906); David S. Sparks, "The Birth of the Republican Party in Iowa, 1854-1856," *ibid.*, 54:1-34 (January, 1956).

21 The political situation in Dubuque will be discussed in detail below.

22 Salter, *Grimes*, a work that stands up remarkably well; *DAB*, 7:631-2.

23 Pelzer, "Origin and Organization of the Republican Party in Iowa," 489, says the Free Soilers withdrew their nomination of Simeon Waters and endorsed Grimes. Recently a claim has been made on behalf of Crawfordsville as the real birthplace of the Republican party. Actually, a very good argument can be made for Crawfordsville if one allows for the spirit of the convention rather than the use of the word "Republican." For a contrary view, see Emory H. English, "Iowa Republicans Organized in 1856," *Annals of Iowa* (third series), 32:43-6 (July, 1953).

24 Crandall, *Early History of the Republican Party*, 22.

25 Grimes to Chase, Oct. 3, 1854, quoted in Salter, *Grimes*, 54.

26 H. W. Lathrop, *The Life and Times of Samuel J. Kirkwood* . . . (Iowa City, 1893), 42; Sparks, "Birth of the Republican Party in Iowa," 6-7.

27 Pelzer, "Origin and Organization of the Republican Party in Iowa," 490.

28 Isely, *Greeley and the Republican Party*, 97-8, quoting the New York *Daily Tribune*, Aug. 23, 1854.

29 Grimes to Chase, Apr. 8, 1855, quoted in Salter, *Grimes*, 68. See Reinhard H. Luthin, "Salmon P. Chase's Political Career Before the Civil War," *Mississippi Valley Historical Review*, 29:517-40 (March, 1943).

30 Grimes to Chase, Oct. 14, 1855, in Salter, *Grimes*, 78.

31 Pelzer, "Origin and Organization of the Republican Party in Iowa," 498-9.

32 Obituary of James F. Wilson, Fairfield *Daily Ledger*, Apr. 23, 1895. Also see sketch in *DAB*, 20:331-3.

33 See comment on Harlan in a letter by John Y. Stone of Glenwood, Iowa, to Grenville M. Dodge, Jan. 31, 1871, Box 18, *Grenville M. Dodge Papers* (Iowa State Dept. of History and Archives, Des Moines).

34 Nathaniel M. Hubbard to Kirkwood, Nov. 11, 1865, No. 1056, *Kirkwood Correspondence*. Sparks, "The Birth of the Republican Party in Iowa," 22, points out that although Kirkwood had left the Democratic party in 1854, "he did not find a new party to his liking until 1855." This was after he came to Iowa.

35 Crandall, *Early History of the Republican Party*, 166.

36 Oldt (ed.), *History of Dubuque County*, 338-9.

37 J. Fred Myers to Allison, Jan. 19, 1888, Box 264, *Allison Papers*.

38 William Vandever to Kirkwood, May 19, 1859, No. 87, Box 1, *Kirkwood Correspondence*. "I think that the delegation from Dubuque may be counted among your friends." Vandever was at the time one of Iowa's two Representatives in Congress.

39 Ira J. Alder to Allison, May 14, 1888, Box 41, *Allison Papers*. Alder was an attorney in Iowa City.

40 *Proceedings of the First Three Republican National Conventions of 1856, 1860, 1864* (Minneapolis, 1892), 110.

41 Des Moines *Register*, Jan. 19, 20, 1869; F. I. Herriott, "Iowa and the First Nomination of Abraham Lincoln," *Annals of Iowa* (third series), 8:81-115, 186-220, 444-66 (July, October, 1907; July, 1908); 9:186-228 (October, 1909), deals exhaustively with many aspects of the campaign of 1860 and has pictures of 29 of the Iowa delegates.

42 Petersen, "Population Advance to the Upper Mississippi Valley, 1830-1860," 335.

43 Ora Williams. The list was published in a syndicated news story. See Cedar Falls *Daily Record*, Dec. 8, 1945.

44 Grenville M. Dodge, "Personal Biography" (typewritten MS), *Dodge Papers*.

45 Dan Elbert Clark, *Samuel Jordan Kirkwood* (Iowa City, 1917), *passim*; Lathrop, *Kirkwood*, *passim*.

46 There are unsupported statements that Kirkwood and Allison knew each other as boys. This could not be, because Kirkwood was sixteen years older than Allison. One good authority says that they knew each other in Ohio before coming to Iowa. This was very likely. See George O. Seilhamer, *Leslie's History of the Republican Party* (2 vols., New York, n. d.), 2:8.

47 The loss or destruction of most of his papers might account for the reluctance of writers to tackle the subject. See sketch in *DAB*, 20:331-3; Earle D. Ross, "James F. Wilson, Legalistic Free-Soiler," *Annals of Iowa* (third series), 32:365-75 (July, 1954). *The Biographical Directory of the American Congress, 1774-1949* (Washington, 1950), 2028, corrects many errors that were in the entry on Wilson in the 1928 edition of that work.

48 John E. Briggs, *William Peters Hepburn* (Iowa City, 1919), *passim*; *DAB*, 8:568-9.

49 George Frazee, "Clark Dunham," *Annals of Iowa* (third series), 4:209-218 (October, 1899); Benjamin F. Gue, *History of Iowa . . .* (4 vols., New York, 1903), 4:82.

50 *DAB*, 4:619-20. Harry J. Carman and Reinhard Luthin, *Lincoln and the Patronage* (New York, 1943), 156, erroneously credits him to Illinois.

51 The following letter from Loughridge to Kirkwood is an example of the "old Ohio tie" at work: ". . . saying nothing about feelings of friendship, on account of old associations, on nothing but purely political considerations I could advocate your nomination. But when I unite with these considerations, feelings of personal friendship founded on a long and pleasant acquaintance and friendship, I shall certainly favor your nomination and will do what I can to secure it." Loughridge to Kirkwood, May 15, 1859, No. 77, Box 1, *Kirkwood Correspondence*.

52 Edward Younger, *John A. Kasson: Politics and Diplomacy from Lincoln to McKinley* (Iowa City, 1955), *passim*.

53 Kasson to Kirkwood, July 18, 1859, No. 137, Box 1, *Kirkwood Correspondence*.

54 J. C. Savery to Kirkwood, July 3, Nov. 26, 1859, *ibid*.

55 Younger, *Kasson*, 105.

56 *Proceedings . . . First Three Republican Conventions*, 170.

57 This summary follows the account given in Herriott, "Iowa and the First Nomination of Lincoln," 81-115, 186-220.

58 William E. Baringer, *Lincoln's Rise to Power* (Boston, 1937), 224.

59 James S. Clarkson to Louis T. Michener, May 19, 1915, *Louis T. Michener Papers* (Library of Congress).

60 Carl Sandburg, *Abraham Lincoln, The Prairie Years and the War Years* (New York, 1954), 173-4. Cartter was later appointed Chief Justice of the District of Columbia, *ibid.*, 715. See also Roseboom, *Civil War Era*, 362-3.

61 Murat Halstead, *The Caucuses of 1860 . . .* (Columbus, 1860). The Halstead account is reprinted in Paul Angle (ed.), *The Lincoln Reader* (New Brunswick, 1947), 265-76.

62 P. Orman Ray, *The Convention That Nominated Lincoln . . .* (Chicago, 1916), 32-3.

63 See Poore MS., *Allison Papers*.

64 Dubuque *Weekly Times*, May 24, 1860.

65 Oldt (ed.), *History of Dubuque County*, 346.

66 William J. Petersen, *Steamboating on the Upper Mississippi . . .* (Iowa City, 1937), 295, citing the Dubuque *Herald*, May 22, 23, 31, 1860.

CHAPTER III — ALLISON JOINS "DODGE & CO."

[1] See David S. Sparks, "The Birth of the Republican Party in Iowa, 1848 to 1860" (typewritten Ph.D. thesis, University of Chicago, 1951).

[2] In 1896 Jacob Rich, perhaps Allison's closest friend, wrote a letter defending the character of the second Mrs. Allison and in the course of the letter referred to the fact that the first Mrs. Allison had died in 1860 of a "pulmonary affection." See Jacob Rich to William Ripley, March 29, 1896, *R. P. Clarkson Scrapbook* (in the possession of Mrs. Elizabeth Clarkson Zwart Metcalf, Des Moines). The mystery of the silence surrounding the death of the first Mrs. Allison is provocative of speculation. A simple headstone in the family plot in Linwood Cemetery, Dubuque, is her only memorial.

[3] See Roy F. Nichols, *The Disruption of American Democracy* (New York, 1948), 303-305; George Fort Milton, *The Eve of Conflict: Stephen A. Douglas and the Needless War* (Boston, 1934), 437-8, 444, 447; Halstead, *Caucuses of 1860*, 16, 55-6, for references to Samuels' part in 1860. The Charleston (South Carolina) *Mercury*, Apr. 30, May 1, 1860, refers specifically to Samuels' speech. This paper was kindly checked for me by David Allen Turner. See also Peterson, "Ben Samuels in the Democratic Convention of 1860," 232-4.

[4] Allison to Kirkwood, Apr. 7, 1861, No. 356, Box 1, *Kirkwood Correspondence*. As to Crane, he played the role of Allison's Man Friday for many years to come. His reward was an appointment as postmaster at Dubuque during the Benjamin Harrison administration.

[5] Allison to William Penn Clarke, Aug. 26, 1860, Vol. II, *Clarke Papers*. The punctuation in this letter illustrates Allison's inability to make proper use of commas and periods. The comma after "locality" should be a period. This is the earliest-dated letter from Allison's own pen that has been found.

[6] Dubuque was included in the itinerary of Seward's tour of the Northwest that was designed to win the vote of that region for Lincoln. The tour is described in Theodore C. Blegen (ed.), "Campaigning with Seward in 1860," *Minnesota History*, 8:150-71 (June, 1927); also in Blegen, *Grass Roots History* (Minneapolis, 1947), 232ff.

[7] A circular which was sent to Governor Kirkwood is preserved in the *Kirkwood Correspondence*.

[8] George W. Jones to J. S. Black, Attorney General of the United States, Aug. 18, 1860, re John F. Duncombe, General Records Office, Dept. of Justice, Appointment Papers, Iowa (National Archives). See John C. Parish, *George Wallace Jones* (Iowa City, 1912), 42-4, 189-205, for evidence of the feud between Jones and Douglas.

[9] Herbert M. Hoxie to Grenville M. Dodge, Nov. 25, 1860, Box 1, *Dodge Papers*.

[10] Hoxie to Dodge, Nov. 16, 1860, Jan. 5, 1861, *ibid*. These and other letters discussing politics and business run from October, 1860, to April, 1861, in Boxes 1 and 2, *ibid*. Also see Younger, *Kasson*, 116.

[11] Allison to Clarke, Dec. 16, 1860, Vol. II, *Clarke Papers*. To make good sense out of the last sentence of the first paragraph, it is necessary to shift the comma after "course" by putting it after "urged."

[12] Sandburg, *Lincoln*, 94-104, deals with Lincoln's one term in Congress, 1847-1849.

[13] General Records Office, Dept. of Justice (RG60), Appointment Papers, W. H. F. Gurley (National Archives).

[14] For Dillon, see Clyde E. Jacobs, *Law Writers and the Courts: The Influence of Thomas M. Cooley, Christopher G. Tiedeman, John F. Dillon Upon American Constitutional Law* (Berkeley, Calif., 1954).

[15] See footnote 13.

[16] Timothy Davis to Bates, Feb. 7, 1861, re Allison, General Records Office, Dept. of Justice (RG60), Appointment Papers (National Archives). Actually, Allison may have had at least two other recommenders. The Davis letter is marked "3" on the back, indicating two preceding letters from other sources, according to the system used in filing these letters.

However, the "Abstract," a final summary of the credentials, lists only the one for Allison and fourteen for Gurley. Grimes, Harlan, Vandever, and Curtis signed one letter as the Iowa delegation to Congress.

17 This description is based on material found in the *Dodge Papers*. Younger, *Kasson*, 110-12, has an excellent summary of Dodge's life.

18 Dodge Personal Biography, 1:33-4, *Dodge Papers*; C. H. Eldridge to Allison, Feb. 4, 1884, *Allison Papers*. J. R. Perkins, *Trails, Rails and War: The Life of General G. M. Dodge* (Indianapolis, 1929), 64 (hereafter referred to as Perkins, *Dodge*), refers to Gurley as "Curley." For a description of Washington as a city, a habitat, and a center of government in 1861, see Margaret Leech, *Reveille in Washington, 1860-1865* (New York, 1941).

19 Dodge Personal Biography, 1:438-41, *Dodge Papers*, consists of a report given by Allison to N. E. Dawson, March 11, 1888. Dawson, an Iowa journalist, was gathering historical materials for General Dodge at the time.

20 Allison to Kirkwood, March 24, 1861, No. 347, Box 1, *Kirkwood Correspondence*.

21 Sherman, *Recollections of Forty Years*, 1:233-4. A facsimile copy of the letter is reproduced, facing p. 234. Just why this particular letter was chosen for illustration is hard to discover. Both Vernom Cooper, "The Public Career of William Boyd Allison" (typewritten Ph.D. thesis, State University of Iowa, 1927), and Jeannette P. Nichols in her biography of Allison in *DAB*, 1:220-22, refer to Allison's defeat for "District Attorney" as a cause of his leaving Ohio, whereas his race there had been for "Prosecuting Attorney." The timing of the letter to Sherman as well as the terminology clearly indicate that the reference was to the more recent case.

22 See Allison to Kirkwood, March 24, 1861, *Kirkwood Correspondence*, cited in footnote 20.

23 F. E. Bissell to Kirkwood, March 26, 1861, No. 353, *ibid*.

24 See Fairman, *Mr. Justice Miller and the Supreme Court*, 40-52.

25 Allison to Kirkwood, Apr. 7, 1861, No. 356, Box 1, *ibid*.

26 Allison to Dodge, telegram, Apr. 2, 1861, Box 2, *Dodge Papers*.

27 Allison to Baldwin & Dodge, Apr. 9, 1861, *ibid*.

CHAPTER IV — ALLISON AND THE CIVIL WAR

1 *History of Dubuque County*, 416.

2 Dubuque *Times*, Apr. 21, 1861.

3 Hoxie to Dodge, Apr. 16, 1861, Box 2, *Dodge Papers*.

4 Allison to Dodge, Apr. 19, 1861, *ibid*.

5 Hoxie to Dodge, Apr. 20, 1861, *ibid*.

6 See Kirkwood to Dodge, May 25, 1861, and Simon Cameron, Secretary of War, to Dodge, June 17, 1861, *ibid*.

7 *Laws of Iowa, 1861* (Extra Session), Chaps. 17, 22; Cyril B. Upham, "Historical Survey of the Militia in Iowa, 1838-1865," *Iowa Journal of History and Politics*, 17:393 (July, 1919).

8 Allison's commission was dated June 29, 1861. *Report of the Adjutant General . . . of Iowa . . . 1863* (2 vols., Des Moines, 1863), 1:1.

9 See Oldt (ed.), *History of Dubuque County*, 268-9. Box 470, *Allison Papers*, contains receipts for passes issued by Allison. Davenport *Gazette*, Aug. 19, 20, 1861; S. H. M. Byers, *Iowa in War Times* (Des Moines, 1888), 59-60.

10 Quoted in Oldt (ed.), *History of Dubuque County*, 271.

11 Sanders to Allison, n. d. [1887], Box 13, *Allison Papers*. For Sanders, see Gue, *History of Iowa*, 4:230-31.

[12] The David B. Henderson story as given here is reconstructed from the *Henderson Papers*, kindly loaned to me by his grandson, Don M. Peaslee, Laurens, Iowa; statement by Allison in tribute to Henderson, Dubuque *Times*, Feb. 27, 1906, at the time of Henderson's death. See also Seilhamer, *Leslie's History of the Republican Party*, 2:12-16.

[13] Kenneth M. Stampp, *And the War Came* (Baton Rouge, La., 1950), 287-93.

[14] Congressman William S. Holman of Indiana, a tough-minded Democrat, succeeded in forcing the House of Representatives to go on record in reaffirmation of the Crittenden Resolution that the war was a war to preserve the Union. See Randall, *Lincoln, the President*, 2:225; *Congressional Globe*, 37 Cong., 2 Sess., 15.

[15] Democratic politics can be followed in Olynthus B. Clark, *The Politics of Iowa During the Civil War and Reconstruction* (Iowa City, 1911), 74-83, 111-14, 120, 174-5. A new study of this subject is badly needed.

[16] See Clark, *Politics of Iowa During Civil War and Reconstruction*, 123-6; many letters in the *Dodge Papers* and the *Kirkwood Correspondence* refer to this subject. For a comparable situation in another state, see Richard N. Current, *Old Thad Stevens* (Madison, Wisc., 1942), Chap. IX, entitled "Peace — or the Party?"

[17] For the platform, see Herbert S. Fairall, *Manual of Iowa Politics* (Iowa City, 1884), 57-8.

[18] Randall, *Lincoln, the President*, 2:204.

[19] Paul S. Peirce, "Congressional Districting in Iowa," *Iowa Journal of History and Politics*, 1:339-43 (July, 1903).

[20] Earl B. Delzell, "William Boyd Allison, an Iowa Statesman and Mason," *Grand Lodge Bulletin* (Cedar Rapids, Iowa), 32:No. 8 (October, 1931).

[21] Allison to Kirkwood, June 10, 1862, Box 1, No. 515, *Kirkwood Correspondence*.

[22] On Shubael P. Adams, see Oldt (ed.), *History of Dubuque County*, 773.

[23] "Allison the Statesman," an interview with Allison by Frank G. Carpenter, June 11, 1895. Clipping in *R. P. Clarkson Scrapbook*.

[24] Charles City *Intelligencer*, June 26, July 3, 7, 31, 1862.

[25] Independence *Buchanan County Guardian*, Aug. 12, 1862.

[26] *Idem*. Also see Charles City *Intelligencer*, Aug. 14, 1862; Davenport *Gazette*, Aug. 9, 1862.

[27] Independence *Buchanan County Guardian*, Aug. 12, 1862.

[28] Dubuque *Herald*, Aug. 8, 1862.

[29] M. M. Hoffmann, *The Church Founders of the Northwest, Loras and Cretin and Other Captains of Christ* (Milwaukee, 1937), 318-19.

[30] D. A. Mahony to Kirkwood, Apr. 30, 1861, Box 7, *Kirkwood Correspondence*. The appointees criticized were D. N. Cooley, whom Allison would soon replace, much to Mahony's ultimate sorrow, and Captain Francis J. Herron, who soon went into active service and became a major general at the age of twenty-five.

[31] This summary of the life of Dennis A. Mahony is my own synthesis based on a considerable study of many sources.

[32] Jacob Rich in the Independence *Buchanan County Guardian*, June 11, 1861. George D. Perkins in the Cedar Falls *Gazette*, May 31, 1861, said that if Mahony lived in the South he would be a real secessionist.

[33] Some prominent War Democrats were: W. W. Belknap of Keokuk, John M. Corse, Cyrus Bussey, M. M. Crocker, J. A. Williamson, George Tichenor, C. C. Cole, Judge E. H. Thayer, several of whom later became Republicans. For a balanced treatment of the charges of "treason," see William F. Zornow, "Treason as a Campaign Issue in the Re-election of Lincoln," *Abraham Lincoln Quarterly*, 5:348-63 (June, 1949). Also, see Robert Rutland, "The Copperheads of Iowa: A Re-examination," *Iowa Journal of History*, 52:1-30 (January, 1954).

[34] D. A. Mahony, *The Prisoner of State* (New York, 1863), *passim*; Wood Gray, *The Hidden Civil War: The Story of the Copperheads* (New York, 1942), 88; John A. Marshall, *American Bastile* . . . (Philadelphia, 1874), 403-416; Davenport *Gazette*, Aug. 15, 1862; Independence *Buchanan County Guardian*, Aug. 19, 1862. Robert S. Harper, *Lincoln and the Press* (New York, 1951), 150, errs in accepting the statement of Franc B. Wilkie, *Pen and Powder* (Boston, 1888), 9-10, that Mahony had been nominated prior to his incarceration. In fact, Harper contradicts his own statement made two paragraphs previously, where he says that Wilkie carried the news of Mahony's nomination to him in the prison at Washington.

[35] Mahony, *Prisoner of State*, 392-4.

[36] Davenport *Gazette*, Aug. 15, 20, 1862; Iowa City *Republican*, Aug. 27, 1862.

[37] Gray, *Hidden Civil War*, 97; Henry Clyde Hubbart, *The Older Middle West, 1840-1880* . . . (New York, 1936), 184.

[38] Gue, *History of Iowa*, 2:86.

[39] Mahony to Kirkwood, Aug. 15, 1862, Nos. 547, 548, Box 7, *Kirkwood Correspondence*. Earlier, on Jan. 13, Mahony had written to Kirkwood that he was sending him the *Herald*, saying that he feared Kirkwood had permitted his mind to become prejudiced against him, but he hoped to continue on good terms, politics apart.

[40] Independence *Buchanan County Guardian*, Aug. 19, 1862. The Iowa City *Republican*, Aug. 27, 1862, was much more outspoken: "Dennis A. Mahony, Dubuque's unenvied treason monger, has been arrested by the U. S. Marshall [*sic*] for Iowa, on a charge of discouraging enlistments. His arrest was demanded by the highest considerations known to the country. Any man in a loyal portion of the country, who will so write and speak and act as to give aid and comfort to the sworn and banded enemies of the Union, and thus increase the hazards of life and limb of the Union men who have volunteered themselves to their country, deserves not only to be arrested but deserves the fate of a traitor. . . . His pestilent course has been arrested, and other miserable copyists and lick spittels of Mahony will do well to take warning from his example."

[41] Fairfield *Weekly Ledger*, Aug. 21, 1862. Gray, *Hidden Civil War*, 88, refers to Sheward as "Dana." All other sources use "David." See also Hubbart, *Older Middle West*, 185; Randall, *Lincoln, the President*, 2:232. Mahony, *Prisoner of State, passim*, gives many details about others who were arrested and imprisoned.

[42] See Fairfield *Weekly Ledger*, Apr. 21, 1862, and succeeding issues for references to Negus. See Oldt (ed.), *History of Dubuque County*, 144, for Hutchins.

[43] See Leech, *Reveille in Washington*, Chap. 8; Marshall, *American Bastile*, 403-416.

[44] Dubuque *Herald*, Aug. 23, 1862.

[45] *Ibid.*, Aug. 22, 1862.

[46] Iowa City *Republican*, Aug. 27, 1862; Fairfield *Weekly Ledger*, Sept. 4, 1862.

[47] Cedar Falls *Gazette*, Aug. 29, 1862.

[48] Dubuque *Herald*, Sept. 24, 1862.

[49] *Ibid.*, Sept. 24, Oct. 1, 1862. The "dark-lantern party" is a veiled reference to the American, or Know-Nothing, party.

[50] Davenport *Gazette*, Oct. 29, 1862; Josiah Henry Benton, *Voting in the Field* . . . (Boston, 1915), 51-2; Fairfield *Weekly Ledger*, Oct. 23, 1862.

[51] Independence *Buchanan County Guardian*, Dec. 2, 1862. Most of Mahony's votes had come from Dubuque County voters who expressed themselves then as on many later occasions as believers in his views and his character. A few days after the election, Mahony was given his release from Old Capitol Prison on the ground that his health was being impaired, since he was suffering from an incipient paralysis, a rather phenomenal diagnosis in the light of Mahony's subsequent career of seventeen active years. Gray, *Hidden Civil War*, 184, 220, dismisses Mahony and Henry Clay Dean, Iowa's other great Copperhead leader, all too lightly. Mahony received the most complete endorsement of his fellow-citizens, who

elected him to the office of sheriff in 1863 and 1865. In later years he was a trusted citizen and fearless leader of the people, and incidentally, a frequent correspondent of Allison's, apparently on very cordial terms. He appeared as a stalwart Greenbacker in a Detroit convention, and he announced his support of Hayes in 1876. He died in 1879.

[52] Allison made the claim in the interview with Frank G. Carpenter noted in footnote 23. On the claim for Dillon, see Thomas Withrow to Dodge, Aug. 12, 1863, Box 5, *Dodge Papers*.

[53] Benton, *Voting in the Field*, 47-52.

[54] Oldt (ed.), *History of Dubuque County*, 290, 292-3. The prominent Republican leaders referred to were: F. E. Bissell, P. H. Conger, William B. Allison, O. P. Shiras, Shubael P. Adams, and B. F. Blocklinger. All except Blocklinger were later men of some prominence in Iowa politics.

[55] George M. Titus, "The Battle for Biennial Elections," *Annals of Iowa* (third series), 29:163-75 (January, 1948), tells from personal experience the story of the conditions and attitudes that prevailed during the days of annual elections.

[56] Two observers reported to Dodge on the convention. See Herbert M. Hoxie to Dodge, July 1, 1863; M. M. Crocker to Dodge, July 2, 1863, Box 5, *Dodge Papers*.

CHAPTER V — ALLISON JOINS THE RADICALS

[1] "Linkensale" (Lurton D. Ingersoll) in the Muscatine *Journal*, reprinted in Cedar Falls *Gazette*, Jan. 15, 1864.

[2] A. Lawrence Lowell, "The Influence of Party upon Legislation in England and America," *Annual Report, American Historical Association* (1901), is a profound statistical study of the votes of the Thirty-eighth Congress, also the Twenty-ninth, Fifty-fifth, and Fifty-sixth. Also, see Frederick W. Moore, "Representation in the National Congress from the Seceding States, 1861-65," *American Historical Review*, 2:461 (April, 1897).

[3] For literature on the Thirty-eighth Congress and its members, see James G. Blaine, *Twenty Years of Congress: From Lincoln to Garfield* . . . (2 vols., Norwich, Conn., 1884-1886); George S. Boutwell, *Reminiscences of Sixty Years* . . . (2 vols., New York, 1902), 2:1-16; Younger, *Kasson*, 157-76.

[4] *Biographical Directory of the American Congress, 1774-1949* (Washington, 1950), 274. Curtis resigned on August 4; Wilson filled the vacancy and took his seat on Dec. 2, 1861.

[5] Younger, *Kasson*, Chap. IX; Edward Younger, "John A. Kasson and the Beginnings of the Universal Postal Union, 1863, 1867," *Annals of Iowa* (third series), 28:3-27 (July, 1946); DAB, 10:260-61.

[6] Kasson to Dodge, Jan. 10, 1860, *Dodge Papers*; William E. Smith, *The Francis Preston Blair Family in Politics* (2 vols., New York, 1933); Younger, *Kasson*, 100.

[7] Hoxie to Dodge, Apr. 5, Dec. 6, 1864, Boxes 6, 8, *Dodge Papers*.

[8] For Price and Hubbard, see Gue, *History of Iowa*, 4:137, 216-17. See also Charles E. Payne, *Josiah Bushnell Grinnell* (Iowa City, 1938), *passim*. Louella M. Wright, *Peter Melendy* . . . (Iowa City, 1943), is a study of one of Grinnell's colleagues in railroad promotion and a partner in frustration.

[9] Poore (ed.), *Congressional Directory* . . . *1869*, 110-11. This is the first *Directory* in the form that we know it.

[10] Quoted in Salter, *Grimes*, 388-9.

[11] Judge Jedediah Brown of Fort Atkinson, Iowa, to Azro B. F. Hildreth, Apr. 14, 1867, cited in Charles Aldrich, *The Life and Times of Azro B. F. Hildreth* . . . (Des Moines, 1891), 399; Rich to Kirkwood, Nov. 22, 1865, No. 1081, *Kirkwood Correspondence*.

[12] Harlan's biographer makes no mention of his status as a minister. See Johnson Brigham, *James Harlan* (Iowa City, 1913). Aaron W. Haines, *The Makers of Iowa Methodism* . . . (Cincinnati, 1900), 78-81, stresses Harlan's lay leadership in the church.

13 This statement is based on evidence found in a letter from John Y. Stone, Glenwood, Iowa, to Dodge, Jan. 31, 1871, Box 18, *Dodge Papers.*

14 His daughter married Robert Todd Lincoln in 1868.

15 R. R. Russel, *Improvement of Communication with the Pacific Coast as a Factor in American Politics, 1783-1864* (Cedar Rapids, 1948), has many allusions to Harlan's activity in sponsoring railway legislation.

16 *Cong. Globe*, 38 Cong., 1 Sess., 18.

17 *Ibid.*, 44.

18 *Ibid.*, 44-5.

19 *Ibid.*, 281. Also see Wright, *Melendy*, 215-23.

20 *Cong. Globe*, 38 Cong., 1 Sess., 1344, 1559, 1886; 13 *U. S. Statutes at Large*, 72.

21 Allison to Hildreth, May 5, 1864, in Aldrich, *Hildreth*, 380.

22 Even as late as 1907-1908, when Allison was making his last race for office and was being pushed mightily by Albert B. Cummins for the Republican nomination for Senator, he used this item. See Box 362, *Allison Papers.*

23 *Cong. Globe*, 38 Cong., 1 Sess., 706; Hoxie to Dodge, Feb. 27, 1864, Box 6, *Dodge Papers.*

24 Dwight Agnew, "The Rock Island Railroad in Iowa," *Iowa Journal of History*, 52:207 (July, 1954).

25 *Cong. Globe*, 38 Cong., 1 Sess., 3244.

26 James Daniel Richardson, *A Compilation of the Messages and Papers of the Presidents, 1780-1891* (Washington, 1896-1899), 6:179, 191.

27 Benjamin F. Shambaugh (ed.), *The Messages and Proclamations of the Governors of Iowa* (7 vols., Iowa City, 1903-1905), 2:353; 3:28.

28 Randall, *Lincoln, the President*, 2:204-205. Also see definition of "Radical Republican" as given in *The Dictionary of American History* (5 vols., New York, 1940), 4:395; T. Harry Williams, *Lincoln and the Radicals* (Madison, Wisc., 1941), *passim.* William F. Zornow, *Lincoln & The Party Divided* (Norman, Okla., 1954), 15, calls the Radicals by a new name, "Unconditionals," which he attributes to usage of the times in some states.

29 Randall, *Lincoln, the President*, 2:207-211. Lyman Trumbull later became a Conservative Republican.

30 It is necessary to take exception to the unsupported statement by Randall in his *Lincoln, the President*, 2:217, that Grimes and Harlan should be grouped with Cowan of Pennsylvania, Browning of Illinois, Collamer of Vermont, Henderson of Missouri, and Doolittle of Wisconsin as Conservative Republicans. Proof of their Radicalism will be given here as the story of 1864-1865 unfolds. Harlan was pro-Lincoln for personal reasons if none other, but he was not with the Conservatives. Grimes gradually drew apart from the Radicals and became highly critical of their politics and actions, during 1866-1871. It is an interesting speculation that he might have become a Liberal Republican in 1872 and possibly a Democrat later if more years and better health had been granted him. Compare the actual career of Lyman Trumbull of Illinois with this speculative thought about Grimes.

31 Specific citation will be given below.

32 *Cong. Globe*, 38 Cong., 1 Sess., 519, 2113-17.

33 N. C. Deering to Hildreth, May 5, 1864, quoted in Aldrich, *Hildreth*, 381. It is easy to believe that Deering was asking this question at Allison's suggestion.

34 Williams, *Lincoln and the Radicals*, 306-333, summarizes a mass of evidence on this subject, covering the years 1863-1864. So does Zornow, *Lincoln & the Party Divided*, *passim.*

35 Peter Melendy, letter to Cedar Falls *Gazette*, June 17, 1864.

36 Jacob Rich to Kirkwood, June 27, 1864, *Kirkwood Correspondence.*

[37] On the plot to force Lincoln's resignation from the ticket, see Zornow, *Lincoln & the Party Divided*, 110-18; Benjamin P. Thomas, *Abraham Lincoln* (New York, 1952), 441-4. I must acknowledge an error in a statement about Allison's attitude toward President Lincoln made in my article entitled "William B. Allison's First Term in Congress, 1863-1865," *Iowa Journal of History*, 50:342 (October, 1952). My statement, based on a letter from Allison to Secretary of War E. M. Stanton, in the *Edwin M. Stanton Papers* (Library of Congress), dated Aug. 11, and with the year "1864" penciled in, quoted Allison as writing of Lincoln as "the obstinate and unjust man who holds the executive power of the Nation." This letter was actually written August 11, 1867, and it referred not to Lincoln but to President Johnson. The error came about through uncritical acceptance of the date "1864." The error was discovered and kindly called to my attention by Mr. Benjamin P. Thomas.

[38] Charles City *Intelligencer*, Sept. 1, 1864.

[39] Allison to Kirkwood, Sept. 2, 1864, No. 949, Box 2, *Kirkwood Correspondence*.

[40] Oldt (ed.), *History of Dubuque County*, 308, quotes the Dubuque *Herald* to the effect that Allison secured a substitute for $150. As to a promise to volunteer, nothing has been discovered. Allison was seriously ill for several months in 1861-1862, due to exposure in connection with his duties as special aide to the Governor.

[41] Winfred A. Harbison (ed.), "Zachariah Chandler's Part in the Re-election of Abraham Lincoln," *Mississippi Valley Historical Review*, 22:267-76 (September, 1935).

[42] Dubuque *Times*, Apr. 14, 21, 1865.

[43] See A. W. Dunn, "Senator Allison's Recollections of Public Men," *American Review of Reviews*, May, 1909.

[44] The resignation from the Senate was effective May 17, 1865. Shelby M. Cullom, *Fifty Years of Public Service* (Chicago, 1911), 135, says Harlan's appointment was due to the intercession of Bishop Matthew Simpson of the Methodist Episcopal Church. Robert D. Clark, *The Life of Matthew Simpson* (New York, 1956), 229, gives documentary proof for the same statement. Harlan had been a student at Indiana Asbury (now DePauw) University at the time that Simpson had been president. See *ibid.*, 92-4; Brigham, *Harlan*, 17, 30, 33, 36. Carman and Luthin, *Lincoln and the Patronage*, 311, say that Elijah Sells, auditor of the Treasury Department, gave "powerful backing" to Harlan. They also say that President Lincoln conferred with Governor Yates and Senator Trumbull of Illinois "and others" regarding Harlan. They further point out that Harlan had come to have very close relations with the President: at the second inaugural he was Mrs. Lincoln's escort; Harlan's daughter, Mary, was often escorted by Robert Todd Lincoln (whom she later married); Harlan was at Lincoln's side when he made his last public address from the White House on April 11, 1865. Elijah Sells, an Iowan and a prominent Methodist, either for help now or because of past friendship, was rewarded by Harlan with an appointment as Superintendent of Indian Affairs in the Southern Agency.

[45] See Dubuque *Times*, March 12, 17, 21, 1865.

[46] For a detailed account of this senatorial contest, see Sage, "William B. Allison and Iowa Senatorial Politics, 1865-1870."

[47] Henderson to Kirkwood, Dec. 12, 1865, No. 1121, *Kirkwood Correspondence*.

[48] Rich to Kirkwood, March 12, 1865, No. 958, *ibid.* Concerning Rich, see George E. Roberts, "The Career of Jacob Rich," *Iowa Journal of History and Politics*, 13:165-74 (April, 1915). Aldrich, *Hildreth*, 394; Hildreth to Kirkwood, Apr. 1, 1865, No. 961, *Kirkwood Correspondence*.

[49] Rich to Kirkwood, Apr. 4, 1865, No. 964, *Kirkwood Correspondence*. A short excerpt from this letter is given in Clark, *Kirkwood*, 307.

[50] Stone to Kirkwood, June 2, 1865, No. 979, *Kirkwood Correspondence*.

[51] Howard K. Beale, *The Critical Year, A Study of Andrew Johnson and Reconstruction* (New York, 1930), 64, 99-106, analyzes Harlan's dubious ethics in remaining as a member of Johnson's official family long after a difference of viewpoint had developed. Beale's inter-

pretation of Harlan is strengthened by a consideration of the Iowa senatorial politics involved in his actions.

52 Harlan to Kirkwood, July 18, 1865, No. 995, *Kirkwood Correspondence.*

53 Rich to Kirkwood, Sept. 3, 1865, No. 1014; Grimes to Kirkwood, Sept. 27, 1865, *ibid.*

54 Allison to Kirkwood, Nov. 4, 1865, No. 2477, *ibid.*; Clark, *Simpson*, 257-8.

55 Grimes to Kirkwood, Oct. 4, 12, 28, Dec. 2, 1865; Jan. 2, 7, 1866, *Kirkwood Correspondence.* All of these letters are printed in "Letters of James W. Grimes," *Annals of Iowa* (third series), 22:469-503, 556-88 (October, 1941, January, 1942). The editing of the published letters is inadequate, especially as to the spelling of names. For fuller quotations from these letters, see Sage, "William B. Allison and Iowa Senatorial Politics, 1865-1870," 107-110.

56 Statement to the author by Edward Younger. See also his *Kasson*, 177-200.

57 Caleb Baldwin to N. P. Dodge, Jan. 11, 1866, *Dodge Papers.*

58 Cedar Falls *Gazette*, Jan. 19, 1866; Clark, *History of Senatorial Elections in Iowa*, 142.

CHAPTER VI — POLITICS, LEGISLATION, AND BUSINESS

1 *Cong. Globe*, 39 Cong., 1 Sess., 21-2.

2 George Alfred Townsend, *Washington Outside and Inside* (Hartford, Conn., 1873), 149-59, 478. On Townsend, see *DAB*, 18:616-17. For "moral collapse" see Allan Nevins, *The Emergence of Modern America, 1865-1878* (New York, 1927), Chap. VII.

3 Platt Smith to Allison, Jan. 5, 1866, 8 D8.16, Vol. 2, *Illinois Central Papers* (Newberry Library, Chicago).

4 Smith to Allison, Feb. 2, 1866, *ibid.*

5 Smith to Oakes Ames, March 13, 1866, *ibid.*

6 *Cong. Globe*, 39 Cong., 1 Sess., 3811.

7 *Ibid.*, 2320-21.

8 *Ibid.*, 1297-8.

9 *Ibid.*, 3517.

10 *Ibid.*, 2480; Allison to Edward Atkinson, May 20 [1866], *Edward Atkinson Papers* (Massachusetts Historical Society, Boston). A search for the letters from Allison in this collection was made for me by Mr. Stephen T. Riley, Curator, who also made arrangements for their photostatic reproduction. The author wishes to express his gratitude to Mr. Riley for this kindness.

11 Allison to Atkinson, Nov. 27, 1867; Oct. 14, 29, 1869, *Atkinson Papers*. For Atkinson, see *DAB*, 1:406-407; Harold F. Williamson, *Edward Atkinson: The Biography of an American Liberal, 1827-1905* (Boston, 1934). On Wells, see note 32 below.

12 *Cong. Globe*, 39 Cong., 1 Sess., 2680.

13 *Ibid.*, 3633-7, 3657.

14 *Ibid.*, 3142, 3164-6.

15 *Ibid.*, 1456-63.

16 *Ibid.*, 3063-4.

17 *Ibid.*, 1367, 1861, 2545, 3849-50.

18 Charles City *Intelligencer*, Aug. 16, 30, 1866; Chicago *Tribune*, quoted in Dubuque *Times*, July 31, 1866; Dubuque *Times*, Aug. 24, 1866; Dubuque *Herald*, Aug. 23, 24, 1866.

19 Dubuque *Times*, Aug. 28, 1866.

20 Dubuque *Herald*, Aug. 19, 1866.

21 *Ibid.*, Sept. 14, 1866.

22 *Ibid.*, Sept. 2, 1866.

[23] *Ibid.*, Sept. 6, 1866.

[24] See Dubuque *Times*, issues during Sept. and Oct., 1866.

[25] Younger, *Kasson*, 199-206.

[26] Payne, *Grinnell*, 231. See also Cyrenus Cole, *A History of the People of Iowa* (Cedar Rapids, 1921), 380, and his *Iowa Through the Years* (Iowa City, 1940), 315, where this error is repeated. Oskaloosa *Herald*, June 14, 1866, tells of the convention; the succeeding weekly issue tells of Rousseau's attack. L. F. Parker, "Josiah Bushnell Grinnell," *Annals of Iowa* (third series), 2:249-59 (January, 1896), refers to the Rousseau assault on Grinnell but does not relate it to the loss of the nomination. Parker was Grinnell's floor manager at the convention. Allison joined in the oratorical attack on Rousseau and helped to close up the case by demanding that Speaker Schuyler Colfax execute the order of the House and deliver a reprimand to Rousseau. *Cong. Globe*, 39 Cong., 1 Sess., 4014-17.

[27] Oskaloosa *Herald*, June 14, 1866.

[28] Cullom, *Fifty Years of Public Service*, 128-9.

[29] *Cong. Globe*, 39 Cong., 2 Sess., 1180-82.

[30] *Ibid.*, 1215, 1733.

[31] *Ibid.*, 1660-61.

[32] *Ibid.*, 1656-8; F. W. Taussig, *The Tariff History of the United States* (7th ed., New York, 1923), 175-8; Fred B. Joyner, *David Ames Wells, Champion of Free Trade* (Cedar Rapids, 1939), 51-6. Both Taussig and Joyner point out that Wells was not yet a free trader but merely a tariff reformer. In his vote against suspension of the rules, Allison was joined by Kasson and James F. Wilson; he was opposed by Grinnell and Price; Hubbard did not vote. Allison to Atkinson, Mar. 8, 1867, *Atkinson Papers*.

[33] Dodge Personal Biography, 4:1141, *Dodge Papers*.

[34] *Ibid.*, 1148; Rich to William Ripley, Aug. 9, 1897, *R. P. Clarkson Scrapbook*. Another indication of Allison's proximity to the family is found in a letter from Grimes to his wife, Apr. 16, 1866. In a casual way he writes: "Allison and I went to hear Mr. Hale preach." Salter, *Grimes*, 291.

[35] Dodge Personal Biography, 4:1139, 1158, *Dodge Papers*.

[36] Salter, *Grimes*, 337-57.

[37] Dodge to Horace White, Oct. 22, 1913, *Horace White Papers* (Illinois State Hist. Society, Springfield).

[38] Testimony before the Poland Committee, "Poland Report," *House Report No. 77*, 42 Cong., 3 Sess., 304-308.

[39] Dubuque *Herald*, Sept. 4, 1868. It will be recalled that the party had been badly divided in 1866.

[40] Charles City *Intelligencer*, Aug. 20, 1868.

[41] Allison to Atkinson, Nov. 9, 1868, *Atkinson Papers*.

[42] Gaillard Hunt, *Isaac, Elihu, and Cadwallader Washburne* (New York, 1925), 241-2; there are many letters in the *Washburne Papers* (Library of Congress) attesting to the friendship between Allison and Washburne.

[43] Allison's association with these men is also indicated in many letters in Box 5, *Allison Papers*.

[44] *James R. Sheffield Autobiographical Memoir*, in the possession of Frederick Sheffield, New York City, who kindly made it available to me. The recommendation for the managership of the Cooke interests came from Allison's colleague and fellow committee member on Ways and Means, General Robert C. Schenck of Ohio. Cooke had offered the place to John Sherman, who declined; then to Schenck, who accepted but resigned in order to accept the appointment as Minister to England; he recommended Allison. Cooke begged Schuyler Colfax to take the place temporarily, saying he knew nothing of Allison. Colfax

refused; the place later went to ex-Senator Benjamin F. Wade. See Ellis P. Oberholtzer, *Jay Cooke, Financier of the Civil War* (2 vols., Philadelphia, 1907), 2:231.

45 Neither man ever denied that he had used his influence to get the route changed. *Cong. Globe*, 40 Cong., 3 Sess., 1466-7.

46 Townsend, *Washington Outside and Inside*, 437, 491-2. Wilson later exultingly reported to Dodge that he had complained to Horace White, editor of the *Tribune*, and that Townsend's contract which would soon expire would not be renewed.

CHAPTER VII — A TIME OF DECISION

1 Tichenor to Dodge, Apr. 14, 1869, Box 16, *Dodge Papers*.

2 Wilson left only a few papers, which are still not available to researchers. Therefore, letters to him often have to be interpreted from his replies found in other collections. A few Wilson papers have recently been discovered in the Fairfield Public Library.

3 James F. Wilson to Dodge, Apr. 22, 1869, Box 16, *Dodge Papers*.

4 *DAB*, 20:331-3. Current, *Old Thad Stevens*, facing p. 289, has a Mathew Brady photograph of Wilson and the other members of the Board of Managers for the House in the trial of President Andrew Johnson.

5 Cedar Falls *Gazette*, Apr. 23, 1869, reprint from the Chicago *Post*.

6 Jacob Rich to Kirkwood, May 10, 1869, *Kirkwood Correspondence*. See Wright to Kirkwood, Apr. 16, 1865, No. 967, *ibid*. Samuel Merrill had been elected to succeed Stone as Governor in 1867 and was renominated for a second term in 1869. Gue, *History of Iowa*, 4:187-8.

7 Tichenor to Dodge, May 13, 1869, Box 16, *Dodge Papers*.

8 Tichenor to Dodge, May 19, 1869, Dodge Personal Biography, 4:1177, *ibid*. Frank W. Palmer, editor of the Des Moines *Register*, had been elected to Congress to succeed Dodge in 1868. Gue, *History of Iowa*, 4:207.

9 Tichenor to Dodge, Sept. 28, 1869, Box 16, *Dodge Papers*.

10 Independence *Bulletin*, quoted in Cedar Falls *Gazette*, Sept. 10, 1869.

11 *DAB*, 20:551-2.

12 Allison to Atkinson, Dec., n. d., 1869, *Atkinson Papers*; Allison to Dodge, Dec. 16, 1869, Box 16, *Dodge Papers*.

13 Allison to Dodge, Dec. 26, 1869, Box 16, *Allison Papers*.

14 Dan Elbert Clark, *History of Senatorial Elections in Iowa* (Iowa City, 1912), 149.

15 *Idem*.

16 Cedar Falls *Gazette*, Jan. 14, 21, 1870.

17 Dubuque *Herald*, Jan. 6, 1870.

18 *Idem*.

19 *Ibid*., Jan. 16, 1870.

20 "A Friend" to Allison, Dec. 14, 1870, Box 219, *Allison Papers*. The letter was sent from Fort Dodge.

21 Dubuque *Herald*, Jan. 19, 1870.

22 Dodge Personal Biography, 4:1192-4, *Dodge Papers*.

23 For example, see Wilson to Allison, Nov. 29, 1870, Box 219, *Allison Papers*.

24 F. W. Palmer to Dodge, Feb. 8, 11, 1870, Box 17, *Dodge Papers*.

25 Tichenor to Dodge, Feb. 10, 12, 1870, *ibid*.; Younger, *Kasson*, 229-37.

26 A. M. May, Waukon, to Allison, March 21, 1870; W. N. Burdick, Cresco, to Allison, June 10, 1870, Box 219, *Allison Papers*.

27 Tichenor to Dodge, June 20, 1870, Box 19, *Dodge Papers*.

[28] Caleb Baldwin to Allison, June 23, 1870, Box 219, *Allison Papers.*

[29] Mildred Throne (comp.), "Iowans in Congress, 1847-1953," *Iowa Journal of History,* 51:338 (October, 1953); Peirce, "Congressional Districting in Iowa," 339-53.

[30] Cedar Falls *Gazette,* Aug. 26, 1870.

[31] Perkins, *Dodge,* 245-6.

[32] *Cong. Globe,* 41 Cong., 2 Sess., 1262, 4665; 3 Sess., 922-4, 1614; Dodge to Mrs. Dodge, Feb. 12, 1871, *Dodge Papers;* Homer H. Field and Joseph R. Reid, *History of Pottawattamie County, Iowa* (2 vols., Chicago, 1907), 1:59-60.

[33] Henry C. Lea to Allison, June 11, 1870, Box 219, *Allison Papers.*

[34] See *Cong. Globe,* 41 Cong., 2 Sess., Appendix, 190-98 for Allison's remarks; Taussig, *Tariff History,* 178n.

[35] R. A. Babbage to Allison, Dec. 2, 3, 1870, Box 2, *Allison Papers.*

[36] Morris K. Jesup to Allison, Dec. 6, 14, 1870, *ibid.*

[37] White to Dodge, Nov. 18, 1870, Box 17, *Dodge Papers;* White to Allison, Dec. 18, 1870, Box 13, *Allison Papers.*

CHAPTER VIII — THE MANTLE OF GRIMES

[1] Rich to Allison, Dec. 14, 1870, Box 2, *Allison Papers.*

[2] O. P. Shiras to Allison, Dec. 15, 1870, Box 219, *ibid.*

[3] See Mary R. Dearing, *Veterans in Politics: The Story of the G. A. R.* (Baton Rouge, La., 1952), especially pp. 80-218 for the definitive history of the G. A. R.'s activities at this time. Also, see Wallace E. Davies, *Patriotism on Parade . . .* (Cambridge, Mass., 1955), Chap. IX.

[4] F. W. Palmer to Dodge, Jan. 4, 1871; Tichenor to Dodge, Jan. 9, 1871; Allison to Dodge, Jan. 14, 1871, Box 18, *Dodge Papers.*

[5] Leland L. Sage, "The Clarksons of Indiana and Iowa," *Indiana Magazine of History,* 50:429-46 (December, 1954); Gue, *History of Iowa,* 4:53-5; George Mills, "The Fighting Clarksons," *The Palimpsest,* 30:283-9 (September, 1949).

[6] Tichenor to Dodge, Jan. 7, 1871, Box 18, *Dodge Papers.*

[7] See Allison to Dodge, Jan. 14, 1871; Tichenor to Dodge, Jan. 18, 25, 1871; Carpenter to Dodge, Jan. 31, 1871, *ibid.;* Tichenor to Carpenter, Apr. 5, 1871, *Cyrus Clay Carpenter Papers* (Iowa State Historical Society, Iowa City). For the entire story in its full setting, see Mildred Throne, "Electing an Iowa Governor, 1871: Cyrus Clay Carpenter," *Iowa Journal of History,* 48:335-70 (October, 1950).

[8] The entire transaction is traceable in a series of letters from Stone to Dodge, Jan. 14, 21, 28, 31, Apr. 3, 5, 1871, and Allison to Dodge, Apr. 8, 1871, Box 18, *Dodge Papers.*

[9] For Harlan's speech, see *Cong. Globe,* 42 Cong., 1 Sess., Appendix, 62-7. Allison himself recognized the political value of Harlan's speech and praised it to Dodge. Allison to Dodge, Apr. 8, 1871, *Dodge Papers.* Brigham, *Harlan,* 252-9, praises Harlan's speech but does not say that the treaty Grant wanted was never obtained. Charles C. Tansill, *The United States and Santo Domingo, 1798-1873* (Baltimore, 1938), 459-60, calls Harlan's speech "an able and cogent defense of the actions of President Grant" but also points out that Harlan "could be adroit as well as direct." The fullest treatment of the Santo Domingo episode, aside from Tansill's monograph, is to be found in Allan Nevins, *Hamilton Fish: The Inner History of the Grant Administration* (New York, 1936), 316ff.; C. M. Fuess, *Carl Schurz* (New York, 1932), 163-6, 173-5; Samuel F. Bemis, *A Diplomatic History of the United States* (New York, 1950), 400-404. The form "San Domingo" was in vogue at the time rather than the modern "Santo Domingo."

[10] Wilson to Dodge, Apr. 20, 1871, Box 18, *Dodge Papers;* Wilson to Allison, Apr. 10, 1871, Box 2, *Allison Papers.*

11 Harlan to Dodge, May 27, 1871, Box 19, *Dodge Papers*. Brigham, *Harlan*, 262-3, completely omits the element of Dodge's role in the senatorial politics of 1871-1872.

12 Independence *Buchanan County Guardian*, Aug. 25, 1863.

13 *DAB*, 1:220-22.

14 Brigham, *Harlan*, 260-62; Jefferson *Bee*, June 30, 1871; Dubuque *Times*, June 22, 1871; Iowa City *State Press*, July 5, 1871; Burlington *Weekly Hawk-Eye*, July 6, 1871; Fort Dodge *Iowa Northwest*, July 6, 1871.

15 Waterloo *Iowa State Reporter*, July 12, 26, 1871; William Warren Sweet, "The Methodist Episcopal Church and Reconstruction," *Transactions*, Illinois State Historical Society, 20:83-94 (1914); Willard R. Smith, *Schuyler Colfax, The Changing Fortunes of a Political Idol* (Indianapolis, 1952), 283-5; Ralph E. Morrow, "Northern Methodism in the South During Reconstruction," *Mississippi Valley Historical Review*, 41:197-218 (September, 1954); Clark, *Simpson, passim*.

16 The first story of the Cherokee land sale known to this writer was one that appeared in the Iowa City *State Press*, Oct. 10, 1866. See also the Dubuque *Times*, Nov. 6, 1866; a full copy of Harlan's letter of defense, addressed to D. N. Cooley, appeared in the Nov. 9, 1866, issue. The story appeared spasmodically after this time; eventually a sizeable literature grew up. The latest and probably most authentic discussion is by Paul W. Gates, *Fifty Million Acres: Conflicts over Kansas Land Policy, 1854-1890* (Ithaca, N. Y., 1954), 153ff. See also Lula Lemmon Brown, *Cherokee Neutral Lands Controversy* (Pittsburg, Kans., 1930); James G. Randall (ed.), *The Diary of Orville Hickman Browning, Vol. II, 1865-1881* (*Collections*, Illinois State Historical Library, Vol. 22, 1933), 219, 239.

17 For data on Henry Van Ness Boynton and a picture, see C. Vann Woodward, *Reunion and Reaction: The Compromise of 1877 and the End of Reconstruction* (Boston, 1951), 29, and facing 34. "Gath" wrote: "The Indian business of the country in its worst form, buying goods, making agencies, intriguing for Indian trust funds, land treaties, etc., has long been handled by a Senator from Iowa and one from Kansas, Harlan and Pomeroy." Townsend, *Washington Outside and Inside*, 534.

18 "Harlan is in Washington trying to cover up the developments in the Cherokee lands cases. I suppose he will do it although if exposed it would alone defeat him. You should have someone look into this." Dodge to Allison, Nov. 7, 1871, Box 219, *Allison Papers*. Harlan could not "cover up," so he tried to explain away the charges. His letters were printed in the Burlington *Hawk-Eye*, Des Moines *Register*, Sioux City *Journal*, Cedar Falls *Gazette*, and, be it said to its credit, the Dubuque *Times*, an Allison paper.

19 Hawkins Taylor to Allison, Dec. 15, 1871, Box 220, *Allison Papers*. Ironically, John Allison, the Register of the Treasury, had been assisted in getting his position by Harlan. See Harlan to Secretary of the Treasury, May 13, 1861, Box 45, *Robert Todd Lincoln Papers* (Library of Congress).

20 Hawkins Taylor to Allison, Dec. 15, 1871, Box 220, *Allison Papers*; Fred Meyers of Denison to Kirkwood, Oct. 29, 1875, Box 4, *Kirkwood Correspondence*; Meyers to Allison, Nov. 29, 1875, Box 25, *Allison Papers*.

21 Cyrenus Cole, *I Remember, I Remember: A Book of Recollections* (Iowa City, 1936), 138-9; Brigham, *Harlan*, 262-3, errs grievously in saying that the *Register* deserted from the Harlan cause on the day before the General Assembly met.

22 Harlan to Hildreth, Feb. 7, 1872, quoted in Aldrich, *Hildreth*, 410-11. See also Mills, "The Fighting Clarksons," 283. A long study of the *Clarkson Papers* and a careful consideration of the dates involved in the *Register's* change of attitude show that it is both easy to exaggerate the influence of the *Register* of that time and to garble the story of the rift in the Clarkson family. Ret was in his "freshman" year as editor; Des Moines did not have the influence then that it later acquired. The all-important legislative elections had been held in October; the *Register's* switch came on December 13. How many legislative votes could the *Register* change between December 13 and January 10? On January 24, 1909, the *Register* published a letter from Ret to the then editor, Harvey Ingham, complaining of a recent assertion that the *Register* of 1871-1872 had been neutral. Ret wrote

that the *Register* had "led and practically originated the fight for Allison," a preposterous claim which all the evidence refutes, and which the writer in the *Register*, presumably Ingham, disproves by citing the editorial of December 13, 1871, as the first to favor Allison.

23 Charles E. Perkins to Allison, May 28, 1881, Perkins Letterbook No. 5, *Richard C. Overton Collection* (Perkins letters are in possession of Richard C. Overton, RFD, Manchester Depot, Vermont).

24 Allison to Kirkwood, Nov. 27, 1871, Box 4, *Kirkwood Correspondence.*

25 Rich to Kirkwood, Dec. 17, 1871, *ibid.*

26 Kirkwood to Allison, Dec. 22, 1871, Box 220, *Allison Papers.*

27 Tichenor to Allison, Dec. 22, 1871, *ibid.*; Clarkson to Dodge, Feb. 1, 1872, Box 19, *Dodge Papers.*

28 George D. Perkins in Sioux City *Journal*, Jan. 1, 1875, quoted in Clark, *History of Senatorial Elections in Iowa*, 169; S. W. Rathbun, editor, in correspondence to his paper, the Marion *Weekly Register*, Jan. 12, 1872.

29 Brigham, *Harlan*, 264.

30 Rathbun in Marion *Weekly Register*, Jan. 12, 1872.

31 Carpenter Diary, Jan. 7, 1872, *Carpenter Papers.*

32 Al Swalm to his partner, quoted in Jefferson *Bee*, Jan. 12, 1872.

33 This account based principally on L. F. Andrews, "Allison's First Notable Fight for the Senate," Des Moines *Register and Leader*, March 1, 1908; Clark, *History of Senatorial Elections in Iowa*, 166-7; John P. Irish, "Des Moines Letter," Iowa City *Press*, Jan. 10, 17, 1872. The author wishes to make special acknowledgment to Miss Mildred Throne in calling the Irish letters to his attention.

34 Carpenter Diary, Jan. 10, 1872, *Carpenter Papers.*

35 Waterloo *Iowa State Reporter*, Jan. 24, 1872.

36 Allison to Garfield, Jan. 20, 1872, *James A. Garfield Papers* (Library of Congress).

37 Allison to Dodge, Jan. 24, 1872, Box 19, *Dodge Papers.*

38 Horace Porter to Dodge, Jan. 26, 1872, Box 19, *ibid.*

39 Harlan to Hildreth, Feb. 7, 1872, in Aldrich, *Hildreth*, 410-11.

40 See Palmer to Dodge, Jan. 18, 1872, Box 19, *Dodge Papers*: "The fight for Allison and Ret was made splendidly."

41 Burlington *Hawk-Eye*, Jan. 14, 1872.

42 The latter charge was one that would have to wait until 1908 for an answer.

43 Sioux City *Weekly Journal*, Jan. 18, 1872.

44 *House Journal, 1872*, 87-8.

45 Carpenter Diary, Jan. 18, 19, 1872, *Carpenter Papers.*

46 James McDill of Afton, Iowa, to Lyman Trumbull, Jan. 19, 1872, Vol. 73, *Lyman Trumbull Papers* (Library of Congress). This letter is cited in Earle D. Ross, *The Liberal Republican Movement* (New York, 1919), 51.

47 *The Nation*, 14:34 (Jan. 18, 1872).

48 Dodge Records, 1:438-41, *Dodge Papers.* The interview was conducted on March 11, 1888, by N. E. Dawson, a former newspaperman with the Burlington *Hawk-Eye.*

49 Dodge Records, 8:299-305, *Dodge Papers.*

50 Waterloo *Iowa State Reporter*, Jan. 24, 1872.

51 Tichenor to Dodge, Feb. 1, 1872, Box 19, *Dodge Papers*; Hoxie to Dodge, Mar. 17, 1872, *ibid.*

52 Burlington *Weekly Hawk-Eye*, Feb. 1, 1872. This item appears in Fred E. Haynes, *Third Party Movements Since the Civil War* . . . (Iowa City, 1916), 23. The Burlington editor appears to forget that his favorite was also a "railroad Senator."

53 Nevins, *The Emergence of Modern America, 1865-1878,* 163-4.

54 Allison to Dodge, Feb. 1, 1872, Box 19, *Dodge Papers.*

55 Salter, *Grimes,* 388-9. Allison's preoccupation with business matters in New York is attested by his letters written from the Brevoort House to Whitelaw Reid in February, March, April, 1872, *Reid Papers.*

CHAPTER IX — ELECTIONS AND SCANDALS

1 John A. Joyce to Allison, Dec. 2, 8, 1870, Box 219, *Allison Papers.*

2 Ross, *Liberal Republican Movement, passim; DAB,* 20:104-105; Kinsley, *Chicago Tribune,* 2:147; Royal Cortissoz, *The Life of Whitelaw Reid* (2 vols., New York, 1921); Joyner, *David Ames Wells;* Williamson, *Atkinson;* Glyndon G. Van Deusen, *Horace Greeley, Nineteenth-Century Crusader* (Philadelphia, 1953), 400-421.

3 This list is based on newspaper articles of the era and on statements occurring in the correspondence of Jacob Rich, James F. Wilson, S. J. Kirkwood, G. M. Dodge, Allison, and others. The Mount Pleasant *Henry County Press* was an ably edited Liberal Republican journal. See Mildred Throne, "The Liberal Republican Party in Iowa, 1872," *Iowa Journal of History,* 53:121-52 (April, 1955).

4 Cortissoz, *Reid,* 1:208. Allison had written to Reid about business matters and had given him a favorable though not glowing report on the Liberal Republican movement in Iowa. Allison to Reid, April 4, 1872, *Whitelaw Reid Papers* (Library of Congress).

5 See Helen Nicolay, *Lincoln's Secretary* (New York, 1949), 255, 267, for evidence of her father's belief in Harlan's influence with Grant.

6 McDill to Trumbull, Jan. 19, 1872, Vol. 73, *Trumbull Papers.*

7 Townsend, *Washington Outside and Inside,* 231.

8 *The North American Review,* 115:407 (October, 1872); Van Deusen, *Greeley,* 400-407.

9 Hoxie to Dodge, Mar. 17, 1872; Allison to Dodge, Mar. 30, 1872, Box 19, *Dodge Papers;* Carpenter Diary, Mar. 27, 1872, *Carpenter Papers.*

10 Wilson to Dodge, Apr. 2, 1872, *Dodge Papers.*

11 Dodge to Allison, Apr. 11, 1872, Box 220, *Allison Papers.*

12 William B. Hesseltine, *Ulysses S. Grant* (New York, 1935), 276-7, 277n.; *Proceedings of the National Union Republican Convention . . . 1872* (Washington, 1872), 44-54; Carpenter Diary, June 4, 1872, *Carpenter Papers.*

13 *The Nation,* Sept. 26, 1872. Ross says the Liberals could not profit because "too many groundless charges were afloat and the *Sun* in particular had 'cried wolf' too often to have the public very deeply impressed with news from that source." Ross, *Liberal Republican Movement,* 162-3.

14 *DAB,* 15:33-4.

15 Fred H. Harrington, *Fighting Politician, Major General N. P. Banks* (Philadelphia, 1948).

16 *DAB,* 12:2-3.

17 James Ford Rhodes, *History of the United States from the Compromise of 1850 to the McKinley-Bryan Campaign of 1896* (8 vols., New York, 1928), 7:66.

18 Rhodes could not have known this, but in 1877 Wilson wrote to Hayes, recommending McCrary for Attorney General, using these words: "a very able lawyer and a very pure man. . . . I selected him to be my successor in 1869 . . . because I knew his worth and intellectual power." Wilson to R. B. Hayes, Feb. 7, 1877, *Rutherford B. Hayes Papers* (Hayes Memorial Library, Fremont, Ohio). This note was kindly supplied to me by Mr. Watt P. Marchman, curator.

19 Dennis T. Lynch, *The Wild Seventies* (New York, 1941), 221-4, definitely accepts the idea of the guilt of the accused and says that no one knew how many other members

were involved because the friendly committee did not probe too deeply. Gustavus Myers, *History of the Great American Fortunes* (3 vols., Chicago, 1910), 2:359-66, tells the whole story.

[20] J. B. Crawford, *The Crédit Mobilier of America* (Boston, 1880), *passim*.

[21] This fact emerges from a critical reading of John Debo Galloway, *The First Transcontinental Railroad: Central Pacific, Union Pacific* (New York, 1950), 185-6; Perkins, *Dodge*, 176ff.

[22] Dodge to Wilson, Mar. 25, May 10, 1873, Dodge Letterbook, Box 382; Dodge to Allison, Apr. 5, 1873, *Dodge Papers*. The defense of Dodge in Perkins, *Dodge*, 264-85, seems to be an example of special pleading.

[23] "The Poland Report." The technical reference is *H. R. No. 77*, 42 Cong., 3 Sess., 289-93, 304-308, 356-7, 462.

[24] The sequence of events in Allison's election to the Senate, as given in *DAB*, 1:220-22, is inaccurate.

[25] Burlington *Hawk-Eye*, for example.

[26] *Cong. Record*, 43 Cong., Special Sess., 1:1. Blair Bolles, *Tyrant from Illinois: Uncle Joe Cannon's Experiment with Personal Power* (New York, 1951), 147, errs in saying that Cannon and Allison took their oaths of office on the same day. The House did not meet until December.

[27] Richard Hofstadter, *The American Political Tradition and the Men Who Made It* (New York, 1948), 171.

[28] William B. Parker, *The Life and Public Services of Justin Smith Morrill* (Boston, 1924), 221; letters from Morrill to Allison in *Allison Papers*, and Allison's letters to Morrill in the *Justin S. Morrill Papers* (Library of Congress).

[29] *Cong. Record*, 43 Cong., Special Sess., 1:48.

[30] Blaine, *Twenty Years of Congress*, 2:539.

[31] Burlington *Hawk-Eye*, June 6, 1873.

[32] Council Bluffs *Nonpareil*, Aug. 6, 1908, cited Dr. Salter's pride in the fact that he had performed the wedding ceremonies for three Iowa Senators: Grimes, Allison, Gear.

[33] James R. Sheffield to Allison, Feb. 21, 1886, quoting Miss Mollie Garfield, Box 39, *Allison Papers*.

[34] *History of Dubuque County*, 622ff.

[35] A long series of letters from Stout to Allison may be found in Box 2, *Allison Papers*. Allison's answers are not available but are indicated in Stout's replies.

[36] *Cong. Record*, 43 Cong., 1 Sess., 56, 57, 482.

[37] See the correspondence in Boxes 2, 220, *Allison Papers*; for data on the Court Division Bill, see 22 *U. S. Statutes at Large*, 172 (July 20, 1882).

[38] *Cong. Record*, 43 Cong., 1 Sess., 5273.

[39] *Senate Report 453*, 43 Cong., 1 Sess., pts. 1, 2.

[40] Ellis P. Oberholtzer, *A History of the United States Since the Civil War* (5 vols., New York, 1922), 3:136.

[41] *DAB*, 17:77-8.

[42] *E. g.*, Shepherd to Allison, June 1, 1874, Box 222, *Allison Papers*.

[43] *Senate Report 453*, 43 Cong., 1 Sess.

[44] A. F. MacDonald, *State and Local Government in the United States* (New York, 1955), 203.

[45] The literature on "agrarian radicalism" is vast. The summary here is based on the following articles: Mildred Throne, "The Grange in Iowa, 1868-1875," *Iowa Journal of History*, 47:289-324 (October, 1949); "The Anti-Monopoly Party in Iowa, 1873-1874,"

ibid., 52:289-326 (October, 1954); and "The Repeal of the Iowa Granger Law, 1878," *ibid.*, 51:97-130 (April, 1953). See also Earl S. Beard, "The Background of State Railroad Regulation in Iowa," *ibid.*, 51:1-36 (January, 1953).

[46] Ross attributes Ainsworth's success to the Liberal Republican influence. See Ross, *Liberal Republican Movement*, 210-13; also see Fred E. Haynes, *James Baird Weaver* (Iowa City, 1919), 172.

[47] Samuel Merrill to Allison, March 23, 1874, and Kirkwood to Allison, Apr. 24, 1875, Box 222, *Allison Papers*.

[48] *Cong. Record*, 43 Cong., 1 Sess., 1765-6.

[49] *Ibid.*, 43 Cong., 2 Sess., 208, 319, 459.

[50] 20 *U. S. Statutes at Large*, 87. Also see James A. Barnes, *Wealth of the American People* (New York, 1949), 455-6; Fred A. Shannon, *America's Economic Growth* (New York, 1940), 399-400.

[51] See John A. Joyce, *A Checkered Life* (Chicago, 1883), Chap. IV and ff.

[52] John McDonald, *Secrets of the Great Whiskey Ring . . .* (Chicago, 1880), *passim*. A thorough explanation of the techniques used by the members of the Ring is given in Townsend, *Washington Outside and Inside*, 242-5.

[53] See John A. Joyce to Allison, Oct. 25, 1873, Box 224; Mrs. John A. Joyce to Allison, May 21, Dec. 2, 1875, *Allison Papers*.

[54] New York *Times*, Dec. 20, 1877; New York *Tribune*, Dec. 20, 1877; Joyce, *A Checkered Life*, 297.

[55] After Babcock's resignation he was soon given an appointment as an engineer in the Fifth Lighthouse District. See Oberholtzer, *History of the United States*, 3:343.

[56] Horace Porter to Dodge, Jan. 26, 1872, Box 19, *Dodge Papers*.

[57] Wright to Kirkwood, Feb. 14, 1875, Box 4, *Kirkwood Correspondence*.

[58] Wilson to Kirkwood, Jan. 4, 1875; Allison to Kirkwood, 3 telegrams, n. d., and one letter, Jan. 8, 1875, *ibid.*

[59] Rich to Kirkwood, Apr. 16, 1875, *ibid.*

[60] The entire episode has been summarized in Leland Sage, "Weaver in Allison's Way," *Annals of Iowa* (third series), 31:485-507 (January, 1953).

[61] Joseph Morgan to Cyrenus Cole, Aug. 29, 1935, *Cyrenus Cole Papers* (State Historical Society of Iowa, Iowa City).

[62] R. S. Finkbine to Kirkwood, July 1, 1875, Box 4, *Kirkwood Correspondence*.

[63] Swalm to Allison, July 20, 1875, Box 25, *Allison Papers*; Swalm to Clarkson, Oct. 28, 1875, *James S. Clarkson Papers* (Library of Congress); J. Fred Meyers to Kirkwood, Oct. 28, 1875, Box 4, *Kirkwood Correspondence*.

[64] Kirkwood to Clarkson, Nov. 6, 1875, *Clarkson Papers* (Library of Congress).

[65] McCrary to Clarkson, Nov. 19, 1875, *ibid.*

[66] "Undreamed of" unless this cryptic allusion of Dec. 29, 1873, has some meaning: "Have you made any headway with Belknap in the Post Tradership matter?" Tichenor to Allison, Box 220, *Allison Papers*. Belknap had been under fire since 1872 for corruption in his Department, but the charges had been ignored by President Grant and his advisers. See Oberholtzer, *History of the United States*, 3:165.

[67] Henderson to Allison, Dec. 23, 1875, Box 224, *Allison Papers*.

[68] This account is based on P. H. Sheridan to Belknap, Apr. 1, 1875; Belknap to Allison, Apr. 3, 4, May 5, July 11, 1875; D. A. Wells to Allison, June 7, 20, July 9, 1875; Al Swalm to Allison, July 20, 1875; Box 25, *Allison Papers*; Allison to E. P. Smith, Commissioner of Indian Affairs, Sept. 21, 1875, Box 223, *ibid.*; Fort Dodge *Messenger*, July 29, 1875; Oberholtzer, *History of the United States*, 3:397-8; Stanley Vestal, *Warpath and Council Fire . . . 1851-1891* (New York, 1948), 205-208.

[69] Brigham, *Harlan*, 286-8; Cole, *Iowa Through the Years*, 346; Harlan to Allison, Nov.

23, 1875, Box 224, *Allison Papers*; draft copy of letter from Allison to Harlan, Dec. 16, 1875, Box 223, *ibid.*

[70] Harlan to Carpenter, Dec. 25, 1875, *Carpenter Papers.*

[71] Rich to Allison, Jan. 14, 1876, Box 226, *Allison Papers.* "Cooley is completely crushed, but takes it all good humoredly," added Rich with reference to Cooley's championship of Harlan against the Allison candidate.

[72] Wilson to Allison, Jan. 14, 1876, Box 227, *ibid.*

[73] James A. Garfield Diary, March 2, 1876, *Garfield Papers.* Perhaps the rumors of suicide account for the statement that is frequently met that Belknap ended his life at this time. E. g., see Roy Meredith, *Mr. Lincoln's Camera Man: Mathew B. Brady* (New York, 1946), 219.

[74] "Trial of William W. Belknap," *Cong. Record*, 44 Cong., 1 Sess., Vol. IV, Part 7.

[75] See *William Worth Belknap Papers* (Princeton University). For further light on Belknap's finances, a very pertinent topic here, see Philip D. Jordan, "The Domestic Finances of Secretary of War W. W. Belknap," *Iowa Journal of History*, 52:193-202 (July, 1954).

[76] Gue, *History of Iowa*, 4:17-18.

CHAPTER X — ALLISON AND SILVER

[1] Harry Barnard, *Rutherford B. Hayes and His America* (Indianapolis, 1954), 277.

[2] Kirkwood to Allison, Apr. 17, May 5, 1876, Box 226, *Allison Papers.*

[3] Clarkson to Allison, May 29, June 4, 1876, *ibid.*

[4] Wilson to Allison, June 5, 9, 1876, *ibid.*

[5] Allison to Hayes, June 17, 1876, *Hayes Papers.* (Copy kindly furnished by Mr. Watt P. Marchman, curator.) Kirkwood to Allison, June 19, 1876, Box 227, *Allison Papers.*

[6] Wilson to Kirkwood, June 23, 1876, Box 227, *Allison Papers.*

[7] Clarence H. Cramer, *Royal Bob: The Life of Robert G. Ingersoll* (Indianapolis, 1952), 80-81, supports this idea.

[8] Anderson to Allison, Nov. 29, 1876, Box 225, *Allison Papers.*

[9] H. C. Leighton to Allison, Dec. 18, 1876, Box 226, *ibid.* See also Ora Williams, "Iowa and the Making of a President," *Annals of Iowa* (third series), 32:507-514 (January, 1955).

[10] Kirkwood to Allison, Jan. 2, 1877, Box 229, *Allison Papers.*

[11] *Cong. Record*, 44 Cong., 2 Sess., 713-14.

[12] *Ibid.*, 91-4; Joseph F. Wall, *Henry Watterson, Reconstructed Rebel* (New York, 1956), 153.

[13] *Cong. Record*, 44 Cong., 2 Sess., 913, 1050; Woodward, *Reunion and Reaction*, 150-54.

[14] Wilson to Allison, Jan. 23, 1877, Box 231; Swalm to Allison, Jan. 24, 1877, Box 230; Burlington Board of Trade Resolutions, Box 225; Kirkwood to Allison, Jan. 24, 1877, Box 229, *Allison Papers.*

[15] See Dunn, "Senator Allison's Recollections of Public Men."

[16] The brilliant historical sleuthing of C. Vann Woodward in his *Reunion and Reaction* has now revealed the full story of the Compromise of 1877.

[17] Wilson to Hayes, Feb. 7, 12, 1877, *Hayes Papers.*

[18] *Cong. Record*, 44 Cong., 2 Sess., 2068.

[19] Wilson to Allison, Apr. 10, 1877, Box 231, *Allison Papers.*

[20] Wilson to Allison, Oct. 31, 1877, Box 231, *ibid.* Interestingly enough, as recently as 1955 certain liberal groups referred to this same John Marshall Harlan in language quite different from Wilson's; to them he was "Man of the Year 1896," an "iconoclast" and

"dissenter" who had maintained 59 years earlier that "The Constitution is not Color-blind!" *Saturday Review*, Nov. 12, 1955, p. 27. See also, Loren P. Beth, "Justice Harlan and the Uses of Dissent," *American Political Science Review*, 49:1085-1104 (December, 1955).

[21] The letters pro and con the Pro Rata Bill can be found in Boxes 227-230, *Allison Papers*.

[22] Perkins to Allison, June 16, Aug. 19, Nov. 3 [1877], Box 230, *ibid.*; Throne, "The Repeal of the Iowa Granger Law, 1878," 97-130. See pp. 109, 112, 129 for references to the role of M. C. Woodruff.

[23] *Allison Papers*, especially Boxes 227-230.

[24] Des Moines *Register*, Dec. 14, 21, 1877.

[25] Clark, *History of Senatorial Elections in Iowa*, 180-86; Dubuque *Weekly Times*, Jan. 16, 1878; Davenport *Gazette*, Jan. 17, 1878.

[26] *Iowa House Journal, 1878*, 39-40; *Senate Journal, 1878*, 30.

[27] Clement Studebaker to Allison, Jan. 20, 1878, Box 231, *Allison Papers*.

[28] *DAB*, 2:335-6; *Cong. Record*, 45 Cong., 1 (Special) Sess., 241.

[29] *Cong. Record*, 45 Cong., 1 (Special) Sess., 581; New York *Times*, Nov. 22, 1877.

[30] Jeannette P. Nichols, "Bland-Allison Act," *Dictionary of American History* (5 vols., New York, 1940), 1:198. Oberholtzer, *History of the United States*, 4:30-31, charges that "Allison's principles were lightly held" and that he listened to a "plea" to amend the bill. Sherman himself strongly implies that it was his conversations with Allison and his letter of December 10 that caused Allison to modify the bill. See Sherman, *Recollections of Forty Years*, 2:620-21.

[31] Sherman to Allison, Dec. 10, 1877, quoted in Sherman, *Recollections of Forty Years*, 2:620-21.

[32] Poore MS, Box 1, *Allison Papers*.

[33] *Cong. Record*, 45 Cong., 2 Sess., 173-5. His arguments were later held up to ridicule by J. Laurence Laughlin, *The History of Bimetallism in the United States* (3rd ed., New York, 1896), 228, note 2.

[34] *Cong. Record*, 45 Cong., 2 Sess., 47, 87-94, 549-64. The motion was carried by a vote of 42 to 20 in spite of a letter of denunciation of its provisions from Secretary John Sherman.

[35] Davenport *Gazette*, Feb. 6, 1878. Allison had given an interview to the Chicago *Tribune*, and it was to his remarks therein that the *Gazette* was alluding.

[36] *Cong. Record*, 45 Cong., 2 Sess., 1055-1112.

[37] Des Moines *Register*, Feb. 22, 1878.

[38] Carpenter to Allison, March 4, 1878, Box 27, *Allison Papers*.

[39] *Cong. Record*, 45 Cong., 2 Sess., 1285.

[40] *Ibid.*, 1410.

[41] *Ibid.*, 1418-20.

[42] Des Moines *Register*, Feb. 22, March 1, 8, 1878; *Harper's Weekly*, March 16, 1878, p. 206; Garfield Diary, Feb. 28, 1878, *Garfield Papers*.

[43] Perkins to Allison, Feb. 9, 1878, Perkins Letterbook No. 4, *Overton Collection*; Jesup to Allison, Feb. 13, 1878, Box 5, *Allison Papers*.

[44] Shannon, *America's Economic Growth*, 402-403.

CHAPTER XI — A GARFIELD REPUBLICAN

[1] Mark D. Hirsch, *William C. Whitney: Modern Warwick* (New York, 1948), 322.

[2] L. F. Randolph, Treasurer of Illinois Central Railroad, to Allison, Dec. 4, 1879, Box 5, *Allison Papers*.

[3] R. E. Graves to Allison, March 5, 1878, Box 5, *ibid.*

[4] Graves to Allison, Dec. 18, 1878, *ibid.*

[5] Graves to Allison, Dec. 19, 1878; H. L. Stout to Allison, Dec. 19, 1878, Apr. 11, 1879, *ibid.*

[6] Charles E. Perkins to Allison, Apr. 2, 1879, Perkins Letterbook No. 4, *Overton Collection.*

[7] C. H. Booth to Allison, March 28, Apr. 4, 1879, Box 5, *Allison Papers*; Irving H. Hart, *History of Butler County, Iowa* . . . (2 vols., Chicago, 1914), 1:424-6.

[8] Allison to Sherman, Nov. 10, 1878, *Hayes Papers.*

[9] Years later an unfriendly newspaper, the Clinton *Age,* accused Allison of being a free silver man in 1878. This Allison indignantly denied in a letter to a good friend and supporter: "Whatever may be said of my weakness on the money question I never was for free silver." Allison to Cyrenus Cole, Aug. 22, n. d., but obviously some time after Cole went to Cedar Rapids as an editor-publisher in 1898, *Cole Papers.*

[10] Allison to Hayes, Nov. 22, 1878, *Hayes Papers*; Allison to Hamilton Fish, June 28, 1878, Vol. 121, *Hamilton Fish Correspondence* (Library of Congress).

[11] Wilson to Clarkson, Jan. 9, 1880, *James S. Clarkson Papers* (Iowa State Dept. of History and Archives, Des Moines); Dodge to Wilson, Apr. 12, 1880, Dodge Letterbook, No. 386, *Dodge Papers.*

[12] Allison to Garfield, Jan. 7, 1880, *Garfield Papers*; *Proceedings of the Republican National Convention . . . 1880* (Chicago, 1881); *DAB,* 7:145-50; Robert G. Caldwell, *James A. Garfield, Party Chieftain* (New York, 1931), 278-91; David S. Muzzey, *James G. Blaine, Political Idol of Other Days* (New York, 1934), 158-72.

[13] Allison to Garfield, June 1, 1880, *Garfield Papers.* The date is surely in error. Allison to Garfield, June 25, 1880, *ibid.* The uneasiness about the chairmanship which Allison refers to was due to the fact that the national committee had no regular chairman; the campaign was directed by Stephen W. Dorsey, Secretary of the Republican national committee. See *DAB,* 5:387.

[14] Theodore C. Smith, *Life and Letters of James Abram Garfield* (2 vols., New Haven, 1925), 2:1034, quoting from Garfield diary.

[15] Allison to Garfield, Oct. 4, 1880, *Garfield Papers*; Allison to Reid, Oct. 4, 1880, *Reid Papers.*

[16] Allison to Garfield, Nov. 3, 1880, *ibid.* Allison was on the best of terms with Dorsey and a stockholder in a Dorsey-owned silver mine in Leadville, Colorado. See Dorsey to Allison, Feb. 9, 1880, Box 13, *Allison Papers*; Memorandum by William Windom, June 17, 1880, Box 6, *ibid.*

[17] Allison to Garfield, telegram, Nov. 3, 1880, *Allison Papers.*

[18] Caldwell, *Garfield,* 312.

[19] Smith, *Garfield,* Vol. 2, Chap. 27, "Cabinet-making," has provided a long and masterful refutation of those who claim influence for Blaine over Garfield. He cites the following as in error: Sherman, *Recollections of Forty Years,* 2:807; Gail Hamilton, *Biography of James G. Blaine* (Norwich, Conn., 1895), 486-503; Rhodes, *History of the United States,* 8:142; Edward Stanwood, *James Gillespie Blaine* (Boston, 1905), 238. Surely a distinguished list! Caldwell, *Garfield,* 313-31, by inference, and Muzzey, *Blaine,* 182-3, also refute the claims for Blaine. The discovery of new data makes it possible to add light to the story as given by Smith, Caldwell, and Muzzey.

[20] Clarkson to Kirkwood, Dec. 6, 1880, Box 5, No. 2153, *Kirkwood Correspondence.*

[21] Garfield to Allison, Dec. 18, 1880, *Garfield Papers.*

[22] Allison and others to Garfield, Dec. 16, 1880, *ibid.* James B. Weaver and E. H. Gillette as Greenbackers would, of course, not sign. There is no apparent explanation why the other members of the Iowa delegation — N. C. Deering and C. C. Carpenter — did not sign.

[23] This reconstruction is based on Blaine's letter as given in part by Smith, *Garfield,*

2:1060-61, and Hamilton, *Blaine*, 495-6. Each author seems to have chosen those parts of the letter which suited his or her thesis. Smith was trying to minimize Blaine's influence, Gail Hamilton (Blaine's niece, Mary Abigail Dodge, who wrote under the pen name of Gail Hamilton) to magnify it.

24 Smith, *Garfield*, 2:1061.

25 *Ibid.*, 2:1061-2.

26 This account follows Smith closely.

27 Smith, *Garfield*, 2:1062, 1072-94; Robert McElroy, *Levi P. Morton: Banker, Diplomat, Statesman* (New York, 1930), 118-28; *DAB*, 6:486-7.

28 Material on Windom is scarce, but it perhaps is of some significance to read that in 1883 certain forces in Minnesota thought the same way about Windom's return to the Senate. They were forced to vote for Dwight M. Sabin, a man of a questionable record as an employer of prison labor, "but many legislators would have voted for a less agreeable man than Sabin, if they could thus have been assured of Windom's retirement to private life." Frank H. Heck, *The Civil War Veteran in Minnesota Life and Politics* (Oxford, Ohio, 1941), 119.

29 Smith, *Garfield*, 2:1078-9.

30 Box 377, *Allison Papers*.

31 Box 6, *ibid.*, includes a bill from Dr. Mitchell for $45 for services rendered.

32 Davenport *Weekly Gazette*, Oct. 19, 1881.

33 Henderson to Allison, Jan. 17, 26, 1881, Box 238, *Allison Papers*.

34 Allison to Garfield, Jan. 22, 23, 1881, *Garfield Papers*.

35 Rich to Kirkwood, Feb. 20, 1881, Box 5, No. 2180, *Kirkwood Correspondence*.

36 Muzzey, *Blaine*, 183n.

37 Garfield to Allison, Feb. 28, 1881, *Garfield Papers*.

38 Allison to Garfield, March 1, 1881, *ibid.*

39 John A. Kasson puts the Treasury first in importance and adds the Interior and Post Office Departments as "the other powerful agencies." Kasson to Garfield, Nov. 11, 1880, *ibid.* This item was supplied through the kindness of Edward Younger, biographer of Kasson.

40 Allison to Garfield, March 1, 1881, *ibid.*

41 Garfield Diary, March 1, 1881, *ibid.*

42 Garfield Diary, March 2, 1881, *ibid.*

43 Whitelaw Reid to Elizabeth Mills, March 1, 1881, quoted in Cortissoz, *Reid*, 2:54.

44 Allison to Garfield, March 2, 1881, *Garfield Papers*.

45 On James, see *DAB*, 9:589.

46 Smith, *Garfield*, 2:1092-4.

47 Considering all the data given above, it is not possible to agree fully with Muzzey, *Blaine*, 182-3, when he says: "Furthermore, Garfield opposed Blaine's persistent recommendations of William B. Allison for the Treasury until the eleventh hour."

48 Allison to Garfield, March 2, 1881, *Garfield Papers*.

49 *Sheffield Memoir*. For a brief summary of the career of James Rockwell Sheffield, see *Who Was Who in America* (2 vols., Chicago, 1942, 1950), 1:1112. Also see Elting E. Morison (ed.), *The Letters of Theodore Roosevelt* (8 vols., Cambridge, Mass., 1951-1954), 2:1034.

50 *Harper's Weekly*, March 19, 1881, p. 180.

51 Cortissoz, *Reid*, 2:56.

52 *Cong. Record*, 47 Cong., Special Session of Senate, 2-3.

53 Allison to Garfield, March 5, 1881, *Garfield Papers*.

54 *The Nation*, March 10, 1881, p. 159; *Harper's Weekly*, March 26, 1881, p. 194. John

A. Kasson had a low opinion of Garfield — "an oratorical schoolboy" — and all his Cabinet. Windom he called "a well-disposed country man who will not spill his milk pail — till somebody jostles him." Kasson to his sister, June 5, 1881, *Wead Collection* (Hartford, Conn.). This item was given to me by Edward Younger. See his *Kasson*, 306.

[55] This was the 53rd Congress. Senator G. G. Vest of Missouri was the chairman of the Appropriations Committee during that term. The Republicans had control of the Senate in every term of Congress in the post-Civil War period with the exception of the 46th (1879-1881) and the 53rd, until the Democratic sweep of 1912. In the 47th Congress they needed the vote of the President of the Senate to break a tie.

[56] Caldwell, *Garfield*, 330.

[57] *DAB*, 16:28-9; George F. Howe, *Chester A. Arthur, A Quarter Century of Machine Politics* (New York, 1934), 139.

[58] Caldwell, *Garfield*, 343.

[59] Howe, *Arthur*, 142.

[60] Caldwell, *Garfield*, 345; Donald Barr Chidsey, *Gentleman from New York, A Life of Roscoe Conkling* (New Haven, 1935), 334-6.

[61] Smith, *Garfield*, 2:1081-2.

[62] Caldwell, *Garfield*, 346.

[63] Allison to Garfield, March 27, 1881, *Garfield Papers*.

[64] Selig Adler, "The Senatorial Career of George Franklin Edmunds, 1866-1891" (Ph. D. thesis, University of Illinois, 1936, used by permission of the author). Chidsey, *Conkling*, Chap. 30, note 10, cites Joseph G. Cannon's testimony on the personal motivations that operated in this *cause célèbre*.

[65] Oberholtzer, *History of the United States*, 4:114.

CHAPTER XII — IOWA POLITICS, 1881-1882

[1] Wilson to Allison, March 7, 1881, Box 240, *Allison Papers*; Wilson to Kirkwood, March 7, 1881, Box 5, No. 2210, *Kirkwood Correspondence*. Governor Gear had planned to give Allison's seat to Henderson, if Allison had gone into the Cabinet. See Wilson to Allison, March 23, 1881, Box 240, *Allison Papers*. Gear awarded Kirkwood's vacant seat to an able man from southern Iowa, James W. McDill of Afton, a former Congressman and member of the Iowa Board of Railroad Commissioners. McDill's appointment would run until the next meeting of the General Assembly.

[2] Jacob Rich to Kirkwood, March 3, 1881, *Kirkwood Correspondence*.

[3] Wilson to Allison, March 11, 1881, Box 240, *Allison Papers*.

[4] Wilson to Allison, March 18, 1881, *ibid*.

[5] Wilson to Allison, March 23, 1881, *ibid*.

[6] Wilson to Allison, March 26, 1881, *ibid*.

[7] Wilson to Allison, Apr. 4, 1881; Clarkson to Allison, Apr. 8, 1881, Box 238, *ibid*.

[8] Wilson to Allison, Apr. 8, 1881, Box 240, *ibid*.

[9] Des Moines *Register*, May 26, 27, 1881.

[10] Charles E. Perkins to Allison, May 28, 1881, Perkins Letterbook No. 5, *Overton Collection*.

[11] See Clark, *History of Senatorial Elections in Iowa*, 196-7, for quotations of Kirkwood to Rich, Oct. 31, 1881, and Kirkwood to E. R. Kirk, Oct. 20, 1881, from *Letterbooks of Samuel J. Kirkwood* (State Historical Society of Iowa, Iowa City). Clark, *History of Senatorial Elections in Iowa*, 195-9, gives many quotations from the Des Moines *Register*, showing its warm support of Kirkwood.

[12] David Brant, "Iowa Political Sketches," Cedar Rapids *Republican*, March 12, 1926.

13 Rich to Kirkwood, March 23, 1881, Box 5, No. 2213, *Kirkwood Correspondence.*

14 Henderson to I. M. Fisher, May 16, 1881, *I. M. Fisher Papers* (in possession of Irving H. Hart, Cedar Falls, Iowa, who kindly made the Henderson letters in this collection available to me).

15 Des Moines *Register,* June 30, 1881; Davenport *Weekly Gazette,* July 6, 1881.

16 Dubuque *Times,* Aug. 12, 1883. Box 377 of the *Allison Papers* contains many letters that amply demonstrate the state of hysteria from which Mrs. Allison suffered. It was just about this time that Dr. Sigmund Freud and his associates first identified hysteria as a disease of the nervous system. See Ernest Jones, *The Life and Work of Sigmund Freud* (2 vols., New York, 1953, 1955), 1:221ff. See also Walter Bromberg, *Man Above Humanity: A History of Psychotherapy* (Philadelphia, 1954), 152-5.

17 Des Moines *Register,* Jan. 11, 1882; Wilson to Allison, Jan. 12, 1882, Box 244, *Allison Papers;* Clark, *History of Senatorial Elections in Iowa,* 199.

18 How far off was the Iowa City editor who wrote that Kirkwood had "yielded to the entreaties of the late Chief Magistrate to become one of his advisers"? Iowa City *Republican,* quoted in Clark, *History of Senatorial Elections in Iowa,* 194.

19 Henry Villard to Allison, Apr. 18, 1882, Box 244, *Allison Papers.*

20 Allison to Mrs. Allison, July 18, 1882, Box 377, *ibid.*

21 Telegram, Frank Hatton to Senator James W. McDill, n. d., 1882, Box 242, *Allison Papers;* Sam Clark to Allison, June 6, 1882, Box 241, *ibid.*

22 Telegrams Runnells to Allison, Feb. 1, June n. d., 1882, and letter, Feb. 14, 1882, Box 243, *ibid.*

23 Henderson to Allison, Apr. 12, 24, 1882, and telegrams, May 5, June 19, 1882, Box 242, *ibid.; Cong. Record,* 47 Cong., 1 Sess., 3480, 4773, 6021, 6024, 6431.

24 Dubuque *Times,* Aug. 5, 1882.

25 Wilson to Allison, June 30, 1882, Box 244, *Allison Papers,* is only one of many on this subject.

26 P. J. Quigley to Allison, May 30, 1882, Box 343, *ibid.*

27 Everett P. Wheeler, *Sixty Years of American Life: Taylor to Roosevelt, 1850 to 1910* (New York, 1917), 271-6; Dan Elbert Clark, "History of Liquor Legislation in Iowa," *Iowa Journal of History and Politics,* 6:525 (October, 1908).

28 Cedar Falls *Gazette,* Apr. 21, June 23, 1882; Henderson to Allison, July 2, 1882, Box 242, *Allison Papers;* Walker Blaine to James G. Blaine, Aug. 8, 1882, quoted in Hamilton, *Blaine,* 614.

29 Henderson to I. M. Fisher, Oct. 27, 1882, *Fisher Papers.*

30 Throne (comp.), "Iowans in Congress," 342-4.

31 Teller to Kirkwood, Dec. 5, 1882, Box 5, No. 2318, *Kirkwood Correspondence.*

32 Kirkwood to Allison, Dec. 19, 1882, Box 242, *Allison Papers.*

33 Allison to Mrs. Allison, Sept. 10, 1882, Box 377, *ibid.*

CHAPTER XIII — A MAN OF INFLUENCE

1 Clark, "History of Liquor Legislation in Iowa," 503-608, gives the best outline of this topic. The item about John F. Duncombe was found in two letters from Maurice D. O'Connell to Clarkson, Feb. 17, 26, 1883, *Clarkson Papers* (Des Moines). O'Connell happened to meet Duncombe on the train; Duncombe volunteered his belief that the prohibition case was weak on a certain point; O'Connell passed this information on to Clarkson, who then secured Duncombe's assent to serve if invited by Wilson.

2 Fairall, *Manual of Iowa Politics,* 9.

3 Albert R. Anderson to Allison, Jan. 22, 1883, Box 244, *Allison Papers.* A few days

later Anderson wrote that the Republican party must support prohibition and the river counties must concede this to the rest of the party. Feb. 13, 1883, *ibid.*

4 Allison to Kirkwood, May 16, 1883, Box 5, No. 2329, *Kirkwood Correspondence.*

5 Cedar Falls *Gazette*, June 29, 1883.

6 Allison to Kirkwood, July 11, 1883, Box 5, No. 2340, *Kirkwood Correspondence.*

7 All these letters are in Box 5, *ibid.*

8 Cedar Falls *Gazette*, Aug. 17, 1883.

9 Dubuque *Times*, Aug. 13, 1883. What was meant by "gossamers" is obscure. From the newspaper story, it would seem to mean some sort of openwork sewing bag.

10 *Ibid.*, Aug. 16, 1883.

11 J. K. Graves to Kirkwood, Aug. 26, 1883, Box 5, No. 2350, *Kirkwood Correspondence.*

12 Mrs. Grimes's letter and one from Mrs. J. S. Morrill are in Box 377, *Allison Papers*; one from Mrs. Aylett R. Cotton is in Box 34, *ibid.* Cole, *I Remember, I Remember*, 232.

13 J. S. Morrill to Allison, Aug. 22, 1883, Box 32, Item 8050, *Morrill Papers.*

14 Allison to Morrill, Aug. 27, 1883, Item 8054, *ibid.*

15 A copy of the will is in Box 1, *Allison Papers.* Senator Morrill's testimony that "for the last year Mrs. Allison had appeared so bright and happy that we had in our family dismissed all apprehension as to her future" becomes very important in support of her right to make a will. See Box 377, *Allison Papers*, for letters from Mrs. Grimes; Box 8 for letters from Bowd Nealley, Bangor, Maine, thanking Allison for his promptness in sending out checks to the heirs.

16 Dubuque *Times*, quoted in Cedar Falls *Gazette*, Aug. 31, 1883.

17 J. K. Graves to Kirkwood, Aug. 31, 1883, Box 5, No. 2353, *Kirkwood Correspondence.*

18 Allison to Kirkwood, May 17, 1883, No. 2330, *ibid.*

19 Allison to Kirkwood, June 7, 1883, No. 2331, *ibid.*

20 The *Register* article was reprinted in the Cedar Falls *Gazette*, Sept. 21, 1883.

21 *Ibid.*, Oct. 19, 1883.

22 T. J. Burns, Casey, Iowa, to Allison, Oct. 12, 1883, Box 244, *Allison Papers.*

23 Allison to Kirkwood, Dec. 17, 1883, Box 5, No. 2363, *Kirkwood Correspondence.*

24 Dubuque *Daily Herald*, Jan. 6, 1884; Dubuque *Times*, Jan. 8, 1884.

25 Clark, *History of Senatorial Elections in Iowa*, 205-207; Des Moines *Register*, Jan. 23, 1884; Edward Younger, Kasson's biographer, to the author, Sept. 13, 1955.

26 Rich to Allison, Jan. 24, 1884, Box 249, *Allison Papers*; Des Moines *Register*, Jan. 24, 1884.

27 Rich to Allison, May 15, 1884, Box 249, *Allison Papers.*

28 Chicago *Tribune*, March 22, 1888; Cedar Falls *Gazette*, June 13, 1884; Des Moines *Register*, June 12, 1884.

29 John S. Runnells to Allison, June 29, 1884, Box 249, *Allison Papers.*

30 Williamson, *Atkinson*, 138.

31 Chester L. Barrows, *William M. Evarts* (Chapel Hill, N. C., 1941), 443.

32 Box 8, *Allison Papers*, has the letters from Crane and Bradley. In addition, the author has received personal testimony from Miss Martha Baker of Dubuque, who knew Allison, Crane, and Bradley well.

33 Cullom, *Fifty Years of Public Life*, 314. Perkins had written to Allison, Dec. 15, 1882, Box 243, *Allison Papers*, suggesting a commission to study the railroad problem and report its recommendations to Congress. He invited Allison to introduce the appropriate enabling resolution, suggesting William Windom, Carl Schurz, Judge Thomas M. Cooley of Michigan, Amasa Stone of Cleveland, Francis A. Walker, the economist, Henry Hitchcock of Missouri, and a leading merchant of Philadelphia, Baltimore, or Louisville as members of the commission. Allison's reply to this letter has not been found.

34 *DAB*, 11:6-7; J. Brooke Workman, "Governor William Larrabee and Railroad Reform in Iowa" (M. A. thesis, Iowa State Teachers College, Cedar Falls, Iowa, 1955).

35 Shambaugh (ed.), *Messages and Proclamations*, 6:5-31.

36 The conference report is printed in the *Cong. Record*, 49 Cong., 2 Sess., 171-3.

37 James R. Sheffield to Allison, Feb. 15, 1886, Box 39, *Allison Papers*.

38 Clark, *Kirkwood*, 374-8; Throne (comp.), "Iowans in Congress," 342-5.

39 Henderson to Kirkwood, Sept. 18, 1886, *Kirkwood Correspondence*.

40 Briggs, *Hepburn*, 138, 308, also note 433 on p. 424.

41 Brant, "Iowa Political Sketches," Iowa City *Republican*, Jan. 10, 1918. These sketches, which ran for some time during 1917-1918, have been reprinted in the *Iowa Journal of History*, 53:175-83, 341-66 (April, October, 1955).

42 Throne (comp.), "Iowans in Congress," 346-52 *passim*.

43 Harrison to Allison, Sept. 28, 1886, and Allison to Harrison, Sept. 30, 1886, Vol. 27, Nos. 5589, 5593, *Benjamin Harrison Papers* (Library of Congress). These letters were kindly furnished to me by the Rev. Harry J. Sievers, S. J., Harrison's latest biographer.

44 Cullom, *Fifty Years of Public Life*, 321-2; Rhodes, *History of the United States*, 8:290; *Cong. Record*, 49 Cong., 2 Sess., 633, 881, 1435.

45 Des Moines *Register*, Aug. 16, 17, 25, 1887.

46 In 1885 Larrabee had beaten Whiting, 175,605 to 168,619; in 1887 he beat T. J. Anderson, 169,595 to 153,706, but M. J. Cain, the Union Labor party candidate, polled 14,283 votes. If the Democrats and Union Labor men had not split their votes, Larrabee's margin would have been the pencil-slim 169,595 to 167,989.

47 Perkins to Clarkson, Nov. 26, 1887, *Overton Collection*.

48 Chicago *Tribune*, Jan. 6, 1888, correspondence from Des Moines. These words have the "ring" of Ret Clarkson, who frequently acted as correspondent for the *Tribune*.

49 *Cong. Record*, 50 Cong., 1 Sess., 16.

CHAPTER XIV — THE GREAT PRIZE ELUDES ALLISON

1 For example, see Sidney Hyman, *The American President* (New York, 1954), 139-50; Dennis W. Brogan, *Politics in America* (New York, 1954), 193-234.

2 See note 15, below.

3 Clarkson to Allison, Apr. 1, 1887, Box 42, *Allison Papers*.

4 Ben: Perley Poore to Allison, Apr. 20, 1887, Box 8, *ibid*. See *The Magazine of Western History*, 6:65-85 (May, 1887). A copy of one of the draft manuscripts for the article is preserved in Box 1, *Allison Papers*.

5 W. F. King to Allison, May 21, 1887, Box 13, *Allison Papers*; Cedar Rapids *Inter-Iowa*, June 23, 1887. A letter from S. H. Bauman of Mt. Vernon, Iowa, May 27, 1887, invited Allison to stay in his home during his visit to Cornell, Box 39, *Allison Papers*.

6 John Springer, "Charles Ashmead Schaeffer," *Iowa Historical Record*, 15:499-540 (July, 1899), indicates that Allison was sought in order to lend the prestige of his presence, now enhanced by his presidential aspirations, to the occasion, which "was a ceremonial of great and unusual dignity."

7 Iowa City *Republican*, June 23, 1887; William Boyd Allison, "The Strength of Our Government," published as a pamphlet by the State University of Iowa, 1887. An analysis of the Senator's speech reveals that it is utterly lacking in originality; the student of political philosophy might discern that Allison's Radical Republicanism of the 1860's had not diminished by 1887.

8 Des Moines *Register*, Aug. 16, 17, 25, 1887.

9 *Iowa Historical Record*, 3:576 (October, 1887).

[10] Sanders to Allison, n. d. [1887], Box 13, *Allison Papers.*

[11] Blaine to Whitelaw Reid, Oct. 11, 1887, quoted in Cortissoz, *Reid,* 2:113; Blaine to Patrick Ford, Jan. n. d., 1888, quoted in Hamilton, *Blaine,* 603-604. Blaine also wrote a withdrawal letter to B. F. Jones, Jan. 25, 1888. Muzzey, *Blaine,* 367-8, calls this the "Florence Letter" and says it was written after the letter to Ford.

[12] Allan Nevins, *Grover Cleveland, A Study in Courage* (New York, 1932), 395-6.

[13] Muzzey, *Blaine,* 370; Cortissoz, *Reid,* 2:113; Hamilton, *Blaine,* 603-604.

[14] Chicago *Inter-Ocean,* June 22, 1887.

[15] Edward A. White, "The Republican Party in National Politics, 1888-1891" (Ph. D. thesis, University of Wisconsin, 1941).

[16] Jeannette P. Nichols, "Contradictory Trends in Middle Western Democracy, 1865-1900," in Nichols and Randall (eds.), *Democracy in the Middle West, 1840-1940,* 84; also see Sherman, *Recollections of Forty Years, passim,* but especially 2:1022-40; *DAB,* 17:84-8.

[17] See Harry J. Sievers, S. J., *Benjamin Harrison, Fighting Hoosier* (Chicago, 1952), 179-87; *DAB,* 8:331-5; *Harper's Weekly,* Apr. 14, 1888, cover page picture and article on p. 267. Harrison did not carry a solid delegation to Chicago. Crumpacker and others were for Gresham. R. C. Buley, "The Campaign of 1888 in Indiana," *Indiana Magazine of History,* 10:34 (July, 1914).

[18] *DAB,* 7:607-609; Martha Gresham, *Life of Walter Quintin Gresham, 1832-1895* (2 vols., Chicago, 1919); *Harper's Weekly,* March 31, 1888, cover page picture and article on pp. 226-7.

[19] Clarkson to Elkins, May 18, 1888, *Stephen B. Elkins Papers* (West Virginia University, Morgantown). In addition to his Western strength, Gresham was favored by Henry Cabot Lodge. See John A. Garraty, *Henry Cabot Lodge* (New York, 1953), 103.

[20] Charles R. Williams (ed.), *Diary and Letters of R. B. Hayes* (5 vols., Columbus, 1922-1926), 2:392.

[21] William C. Dodge, Washington, D. C., to Allison, June 1, 1888, Box 261, *Allison Papers.*

[22] Sam M. Clark to Allison, Jan. 11, 1888, Box 260, *ibid.*

[23] The inaugural address is printed in the *Iowa Senate Journal, 1888,* 54-65, and in Shambaugh (ed.), *Messages and Proclamations,* 6:86-107 (Part dealing with railroads, pp. 92-107). The message is in *ibid.,* 6:32-85 (railroads, 73-6).

[24] For Republican platform, see Des Moines *Register,* Aug. 25, 1887; for Democratic platform, see Fayette *Fayette County Union,* Sept. 20, 1887.

[25] See Workman, "Governor William Larrabee of Iowa and Railroad Reform."

[26] Des Moines *Register,* Jan. 13, 1888.

[27] Clarkson to Allison, Jan. 13, 1888, Box 260, *Allison Papers.*

[28] Charles E. Perkins to Allison, Jan. 17, 1888, Box 264, *ibid.* There are many letters from Larrabee to Perkins in the *Burlington Papers* (Newberry Library, Chicago).

[29] Perkins to Allison, Feb. 17, 1888, Box 264, *Allison Papers.*

[30] The personal papers of Governor Larrabee have been destroyed (letter to author from Frederick Larrabee), so it is difficult if not impossible to ascertain his feelings on this matter. See Clarkson to Allison, June 8, 1888, Box 260, *Allison Papers.*

[31] Dr. Charles Beardsley to Allison, Jan. 31, 1888, Box 41, *ibid.* One wonders about Beardsley's private thoughts as he recalled the days of 1871-1872 when on behalf of Harlan he denounced Allison. Had he really changed his mind about Allison — or is this just politics?

[32] Gordon F. Hostettler, "Jonathan Prentiss Dolliver: The Formative Years," *Iowa Journal of History,* 49:42 (January, 1951).

[33] Dolliver's pledge to Allison, Feb. 19, 1888, Box 261, *Allison Papers.* On Dolliver as an orator, see Hostettler, "Jonathan Prentiss Dolliver, The Formative Years," 23-50, also his

Ph. D. thesis, "Oratorical Career of Jonathan Prentiss Dolliver" (State University of Iowa, 1947).

[34] This account of the convention is based on the Chicago *Inter-Ocean*, March 22, 1888, which contains the speech as quoted; the Chicago *Tribune*, March 22, 1888; Jacob Rich to Allison, March 22, 1888, Box 264, *Allison Papers*.

[35] Clarkson to Dolliver, Apr. 19, 1888, *Jonathan P. Dolliver Papers* (State Historical Society of Iowa, Iowa City).

[36] Elkins to Harrison, May 2, 1888, Box 29, *Harrison Papers*.

[37] Chicago *Inter-Ocean*, Feb. 14, 1888.

[38] Hamilton, *Blaine*, 604.

[39] James M. Tyner to Harrison, Feb. 20, 1888, Book 28, *Harrison Papers*.

[40] Elkins to Michener, Apr. 7, 1888, *Michener Papers*. These papers were obtained for the Library of Congress by the alertness of Albert T. Volwiler, and they are used by his kind permission.

[41] Elkins to Harrison, May 2, 1888, Book 29, *Harrison Papers*. O. D. Lambert, *Stephen Benton Elkins, American Foursquare* (Pittsburgh, 1955), 114-21, is lamentably brief in his analysis of the presidential politics of 1888.

[42] Clarkson to Michener, May 19, 1915, *Michener Papers*.

[43] R. C. Kerens to Russell Harrison, May 10, 1888, *Harrison Papers*.

[44] Clarkson to Henderson, May 28, 1888, Box 42; Henderson to Clarkson, May 29, 1888, Box 43, *Allison Papers*.

[45] Edward A. White, "A Woman Promotes the Presidential Candidacy of Senator Allison, 1888," *Iowa Journal of History*, 48:224 (July, 1950).

[46] This description is based largely on articles in the Iowa City *Republican*, June 15, 16, 20, 23, 1888; see also George M. Christian to Allison, May 11, 1888, Box 42, *Allison Papers*.

[47] Ira J. Alder to Allison, June 13, 1888, Box 43; Kirkwood to Allison, May 14, 1888, Box 41, *Allison Papers*.

[48] W. B. Allison, Jr., to Allison, May 23, 1888, Box 41, *ibid*.

[49] Eleanor Medill Patterson to Allison, n. d., Box 377, *ibid*.

[50] Nina L. Gillett to Allison, June 1, 1888, Box 42, *ibid*.

[51] See White, "A Woman Promotes the Presidential Candidacy of Senator Allison, 1888," 221-46. This is my own appraisal of Mrs. Hicks-Lord, based on a careful study of her letters in Boxes 263 and 43 of the *Allison Papers*, and allusions to her in the correspondence of Allison and Clarkson. Mrs. Hicks-Lord was of English extraction, and it seems valid to assume that she added her family name by hyphen after the death of her husband, Henry H. Hicks of Ohio. One comes upon her name in the newspapers of the period, and she is casually mentioned in Madeleine B. Stern, *Purple Passage, The Life of Mrs. Frank Leslie* (Norman, Okla., 1953), 123.

[52] Council Bluffs *Nonpareil*, June 16, 20, 1888; Des Moines *Register*, June 16, 17, 18, 19, 20, 1888; Chicago *Inter-Ocean*, June 16, 1888. The *Register* of June 16 carried the biography; so did the *Inter-Ocean* of the same date. Concerning the election to the Grand Lodge of Iowa, A. F. & A. M., see Box 1, *Allison Papers*; also Delzell, "William Boyd Allison, An Iowa Statesman and Mason." In Box 1 of *Allison Papers* there is a certificate of Allison's election to the Grand Lodge of Iowa, F. & A. M., in "recognition of his interests in the library."

[53] *Laws of Iowa, 1888*, Chaps. 28, 29.

[54] Clarkson to Allison, June 8, 1888, Box 260, *Allison Papers*.

[55] Perkins to Allison, June 13, 1888, Box 44, *ibid*. A copy of the letter is in the Perkins Letterbook No. 8, *Overton Collection*. Perkins to John Murray Forbes, June 13, 16, 1888, *ibid*.

[56] R. Root to Allison, n. d., Box 264, *Allison Papers*.

57 Chicago *Inter-Ocean*, June 22, 1888.

58 The obscure Mr. Bosworth had been a small town judge, assistant attorney general of Rhode Island, and for two unconnected terms a member of the General Assembly. He died on February 10, 1899, at which time he was serving as an associate justice of the Rhode Island supreme court. Providence *Journal*, Feb. 11, 1899. These facts were very kindly obtained for me by Miss Helen Kurtz of the Brown University Library. As to Aldrich's attitude, see N. W. Stephenson, *Nelson W. Aldrich* (New York, 1930), 434, note 8.

59 *Official Proceedings of the Republican National Convention . . . 1888* (Minneapolis, 1903), 159-60.

60 *Ibid.*, 168.

61 George Frisbie Hoar, *Autobiography of Seventy Years* (2 vols., New York, 1903), 1:411-13.

62 The *Tribune* was for Gresham as its first choice, Allison second. Eleanor Medill Patterson to Allison, n. d., Box 377, *Allison Papers*.

63 Chauncey Depew, *My Memories of Eighty Years* (New York, 1922).

64 Cyrenus Cole to Depew, Sept. 12, 1922, *Chauncey M. Depew Papers* (Yale University Library, New Haven, Conn.). This and the following letter from Depew were kindly furnished to me by Dr. C. Joseph Bernardo, whose doctoral thesis at Georgetown University (1949) dealt with the convention of 1888. Cole, in his autobiography, *I Remember, I Remember*, 167, gives an account of his request to Depew and a few brief extracts from Depew's reply.

65 Clarkson to Allison, June 22, 1888, Box 260, *Allison Papers*.

66 Dubuque *Daily Times*, June 23, 1888, clipping in Scrapbook of F. E. Bissell of Dubuque.

67 Dispatch from Cedar Rapids, June 24, 1888, in Chicago *Inter-Ocean*, June 25, 1888.

68 Des Moines *Register*, June 24, 1888.

69 Elliott F. Shepard to Harrison, June 23, 1888, Book 29, *Harrison Papers*. Shepard was publisher of the New York *Mail and Express*.

70 Stephenson, *Aldrich*, 71-2, and notes on p. 434; Charles Edward Russell, *Blaine of Maine, His Life and Times* (New York, 1931), 410.

71 See Barker to Harrison, June 30, 1888, Book 31, *Harrison Papers*.

72 White, "The Republican Party in National Politics, 1888-1891," 38, who cites "Remarks of 'a gentleman . . . who had a good deal to do with the nomination of Harrison,' Albany, Dec. 26, 1888, in New York Herald, Dec. 27, 1888."

73 Henderson to Allison, June 25, 1888, Box 262, *Allison Papers*.

74 Hamilton, *Blaine*, 607; *Proceedings of the Republican National Convention . . . 1888*, 186-7.

75 Muzzey, *Blaine*, 379.

76 John Sherman to Harrison, June 30, 1888, Book 32, *Harrison Papers*.

77 Chicago *Inter-Ocean*, June 26, 1888, almost gives the impression that Henderson was the manager of the Iowa delegation.

78 Clarkson to Michener, Apr. 19, May 19, 1915, *Michener Papers*.

79 Perkins to Allison, June 25, 1888, Box 264, *Allison Papers*.

80 Elliott F. Shepard to Harrison, June 25, 1888, Book 29, *Harrison Papers*.

81 Louis J. Lang (ed.), *The Autobiography of T. C. Platt* (New York, 1910), 218-19.

82 Harrison to Blaine, June 30, 1888, quoted in Hamilton, *Blaine*, 646.

83 Allison to Harrison, June 26, 1888, Book 29, *Harrison Papers*.

84 Harrison to Allison, June 28, 1888, Box 42, *Allison Papers*.

85 Chicago *Inter-Ocean*, June 26, 1888.

CHAPTER XV — A PARTY WHEEL HORSE

[1] *Cong. Record*, 50 Cong., 1 Sess., 6660. Hayes, Weaver, and Albert R. Anderson voted for the bill; the eight true Republicans against it. On Mills, see *DAB*, 13:14-15.

[2] See Allison to Harrison, July 3, 1888, Book 32, *Harrison Papers*.

[3] See especially *Harper's Weekly*, July 21, Aug. 11, 1888.

[4] John Sherman to Harrison, July 13, 1888, Book 34, *Harrison Papers*; G. M. Dodge to Allison, July 16, 1888, Box 261, *Allison Papers*.

[5] *Cong. Record*, 50 Cong., 1 Sess., 9109. The date was Oct. 3. On Oct. 4, Aldrich brought up the bill and made the first major speech. *Ibid.*, 9167-93. Some writers call the Senate substitute the "Allison Bill," some the "Aldrich Bill."

[6] *Harper's Weekly*, Oct. 13, 1888; Nevins, *Cleveland*, 388-94.

[7] Gardner Cowles, Algona, Iowa, to Allison, Oct. 5, 1888, Box 42, *Allison Papers*.

[8] Maurice D. O'Connell to Allison, Oct. 6, 1888, Box 264, *ibid*.

[9] *Cong. Record*, 50 Cong., 1 Sess., 9283-91.

[10] Blaine to Allison, telegram, Oct. 15, 1888; Butler to Allison, Oct. 10, 1888, Box 41; Clarkson to Allison, Oct. 10, 1888, Box 42, *Allison Papers*.

[11] Harrison to Allison, Oct. 9, 1888, Box 42, *ibid*.

[12] *Cong. Record*, 50 Cong., 1 Sess., 9613-14.

[13] Hiscock to Harrison, July 7, 12, 1888, Books 32, 33, *Harrison Papers*. Senator William E. Chandler generously reported to Harrison: "Allison, Hiscock and Aldrich are doing a difficult task with great industry, discretion and ability." Book 34, *ibid*. On Aldrich's part, see Stephenson, *Aldrich*, 73-4.

[14] Clarkson to Harrison, July 25, 1888, Book 35, *Harrison Papers*; Joseph Medill to Allison, Sept. 23, 1888, cited in Horace S. Merrill, *Bourbon Democracy of the Middle West, 1865-1896* (Baton Rouge, 1953), 199.

[15] Buley, "Campaign of 1888 in Indiana," 53.

[16] J. E. Clark, Clarinda, Iowa, to Allison, Nov. 8, 1888, Box 9, *Allison Papers*. Weaver was defeated by John F. Lacey of Oskaloosa; Anderson, by James P. Flick of Bedford.

[17] Clarkson to Harrison, June 30, 1888, Book 31, *Harrison Papers*; Clarkson to Allison, July 9, 1888, Box 260, *Allison Papers*.

[18] White, "Republican Party in National Politics, 1888-1891," 172ff., deals effectively with this topic, largely on the basis of the *Michener Papers and the Allison Papers*. Michener explains that he did not want to carry out the distasteful assignment of arranging for Quay's election, but did so at Harrison's insistence. The problem was to find a chairman agreeable to Morton and the New York interests. See memorandum on "Organization of National Committee in 1888," *Michener Papers*. Clarkson found his worst fears realized; he would do all the work and Quay would get all the credit.

[19] Letters of Mrs. Hicks-Lord to Allison and Clarkson, Boxes 42-43, *Allison Papers*. Clarkson had the misfortune to fall and sprain his ankle severely. This, in addition to his chronic rheumatism, gave the poor man a bad summer.

[20] Harrison to Allison, Nov. 13, 1888, *ibid*.

[21] J. Fred Meyers, Denison, Iowa, to Allison, Dec. 8, 1888, *ibid*.

[22] Maurice D. O'Connell to Allison, Dec. 9, 1888, *ibid*.

[23] Dolliver to Allison, Dec. 28, 1888, Box 261, *ibid*. Dolliver's allusion is backed up by one made a few days later by E. B. Nealley, Mrs. Allison's relative in Bangor, Maine. Nealley to Allison, Jan. 7, 1889, Box 9, *ibid*.

[24] *Harper's Weekly*, Jan. 15, 1889.

[25] Clarkson to Allison, Jan. 25, 1889, *Clarkson Papers* (Library of Congress).

[26] Joseph H. Manley to Michener, Jan. 29, 1888, *Michener Papers*.

27 Chicago *Tribune*, Jan. 29, 1889.

28 *Harper's Weekly*, Feb. 9, 1889 (correspondence dated Feb. 1).

29 Harrison to Blaine, Feb. 1, 1889, Book 64, *Harrison Papers*. The letter may also be found in A. T. Volwiler (ed.), *Correspondence Between Harrison and Blaine, 1882-1893* (Philadelphia, 1940), 50-51.

30 Harrison to Allison, Feb. 4, 1889, Book 64, *Harrison Papers*. The copy as found here seems to be in the handwriting of E. W. Halford, Harrison's secretary. Allison's letter of declination has not been found.

31 George William Curtis was not at all enthusiastic about Windom's qualities. See *Harper's Weekly*, March 16, 1889.

32 "W. E. M." to Clarkson, telegram, Box 4; Dodge to Clarkson, Jan. 31, 1889, Box 5, *Clarkson Papers* (Library of Congress).

33 J. K. Graves to Clarkson, Feb. 2, 1889, *Clarkson Papers* (Des Moines). The letter to Harrison is in Book 64, *Harrison Papers*. A Harrison adviser wrote, unbeknownst to Clarkson, in advocacy of Windom "if Allison wont have it or you wont have Allison," but added, "This ought not to interfere with anything you might feel inclined to do for Iowa or Clarkson." Henry W. Blair, Senator from Maryland, to Harrison, Feb. 4, 1889, *ibid.*

34 Perkins to Clarkson, March 18, 1889, Perkins Letterbook No. 8, *Overton Collection*.

35 Allison received dozens of letters from the faithful warning him about Larrabee's activity and potentialities. See letters from R. Root, W. F. Sapp, Edgar Pickett, Box 270, *Allison Papers*.

36 All in Box 270, *ibid.*

37 Allison to Harrison, Sept. 8, 1889, Book 86, *Harrison Papers*. This letter was very kindly furnished to me by the Rev. Harry J. Sievers, S. J.

38 See Jean B. Kern, "The Political Career of Horace Boies," *Iowa Journal of History*, 47:215-46 (July, 1949).

39 *Iowa House Journal, 1890*, 168. Clark, *History of Senatorial Elections in Iowa*, Chap. XVI, makes the election of Allison appear all too easy. Gue, *History of Iowa*, 3:161, gives a misleading account of this contest. He says that Larrabee took no part in it, whereas Larrabee and "Larrabeeans" worked hard in the 1889 campaign. Gue further says that "many" legislators voted for Larrabee in spite of his official silence. The vote was 8 out of a total of 150. It is of interest that Bestow, the only Democrat who ever amassed a threatening vote against Allison, was a man of only average fame within the state. He happened to be the one who received his party's token vote at the time of its greatest post-Civil War strength.

40 Brant's reminiscent article on the 1889 election of Allison appeared in the Iowa City *Republican*, July 19, 1917, and in the Cedar Rapids *Republican*, March 7, 1926. It was also reprinted in the *Iowa Journal of History*, 53:175-83 (April, 1955).

41 Clark, *History of Senatorial Elections in Iowa*, 216-21; Clarkson to E. W. Halford, March 4, 1890, Book 100, *Harrison Papers*. Jacob Rich sent a stream of letters to Allison giving reports on the situation. See Boxes 264, 280, *Allison Papers*. He kept hands off, so he said, but used his letters as opportunities to pepper Allison with requests for favorable tariff provisions on linseed, linseed oil, and poppy oil. He was at this time president of a large Dubuque linseed oil mill company.

42 Fred W. Wellborn, "The Influence of the Silver-Republican Senators, 1889-1891," *Mississippi Valley Historical Review*, 14:462-80 (March, 1928).

43 *Ibid.*, 465.

44 Allison to Kirkwood, June 30, 1890, Box 6, No. 2463, *Kirkwood Correspondence*.

45 *Cong. Record*, 51 Cong., 1 Sess., 5814, 6183, 6503.

46 26 U. S. *Statutes at Large*, 289.

[47] Quoted in Garraty, *Lodge*, 112.

[48] *Cong. Record*, 51 Cong., 1 Sess., 5990.

[49] See Jonathan P. Dolliver's speech at Council Bluffs, Nov. 25, 1907, as printed in the Council Bluffs *Nonpareil*, Nov. 26, 1907, and later reprinted in pamphlet form and distributed as a campaign document in 1908.

[50] Arthur Cecil Bining, *The Rise of American Economic Life* (New York, 1943), 72, 366; Festus P. Summers, *William L. Wilson and Tariff Reform* (New Brunswick, 1953), 108-109.

[51] Arthur Wallace Dunn, *From Harrison to Harding* (2 vols., New York, 1922), 1:44-5. Also see Hamilton, *Blaine*, 682-91.

[52] Rhodes, *History of the United States*, 8:350, does not mention Allison but credits Senator Nelson W. Aldrich with most of the leadership that put across the McKinley Bill. Many years later, Allison, apparently with great pride, credited John H. Gear of Burlington with the provisions for extension of the sugar bounty to the beet sugar product for this country. He did not bother to explain that Iowa was a large producer of beet sugar.

[53] The vote, distributed by district, was as follows:

District	Republican	Democratic
First	16,388	17,459
Second	11,738	20,748
Third	19,689	19,491
Fourth	16,023	17,972
Fifth	17,860	18,153
Sixth	16,572	17,092
Seventh	16,821	14,276
Eighth	19,003	18,887
Ninth	17,322	18,605
Tenth	18,395	17,084
Eleventh	15,972	15,065
	185,783	194,832

[54] E. H. Wicklin to Weller, Nov. 7, 1890, *Luman H. Weller Papers* (State Historical Society of Wisconsin, Madison, Wisc.).

[55] Bowd Nealley to Allison, Feb. 10, 1891, Box 9, *Allison Papers*.

[56] See Vincent P. De Santis, "Benjamin Harrison and the Republican Party in the South, 1889-1893," *Indiana Magazine of History*, 51:284-5 (December, 1955).

[57] Clarkson to Michener, May 29, 1890, *Michener Papers*.

[58] J. S. Clarkson to R. P. Clarkson, Jan. 24, 1891; Allison to R. P. Clarkson, Jan. 27, 1891, *R. P. Clarkson Scrapbook*.

[59] Wellborn, "Influence of the Silver-Republican Senators, 1889-1891," 472-80; Garraty, *Lodge*, 117-21; Stephenson, *Aldrich*, 88-90; W. A. Robinson, *Thomas B. Reed, Parliamentarian* (New York, 1930), 235-40; John R. Lambert, *Arthur Pue Gorman* (Baton Rouge, La., 1953), 147-66.

[60] White, "Republican Party in National Politics, 1888-1891," presents this point extremely well.

[61] Thomas C. Cochran and William Miller, *The Age of Enterprise* (New York, 1942), 163-4.

[62] Stephenson, *Aldrich*, 40-64, 97-8; *DAB*, 1:151-8, especially 153.

[63] *DAB*, 17:465-6 (Spooner); 8:102-104 (Hale); 8:421-2 (Hawley); 15:2-4 (Platt); 12:143-5 (McMillan); L. A. Coolidge, *An Old-Fashioned Senator, Orville H. Platt* (New York, 1910).

CHAPTER XVI — ALLISON FINDS HIS LEVEL

[1] For Cummins, see *DAB*, 4:597-9.

[2] John F. Lacey to Allison, Sept. 2, 1891, Box 284, *Allison Papers*.

[3] S. Monahan to Allison, Nov. 6, 1891, *ibid*.

[4] D. B. Henderson to R. P. Clarkson, Nov. 22, 1891, *R. P. Clarkson Scrapbook*.

[5] George H. Knoles, *The Presidential Campaign and Election of 1892* (Stanford, Calif., 1942), 34-7; Donald M. Dozer, "Benjamin Harrison and the Presidential Campaign of 1892," *American Historical Review*, 54:49-52 (October, 1948); Hamilton, *Blaine*, 698-9. John M. Blum, *The Republican Roosevelt* (Cambridge, Mass., 1954), 14, errs in saying that Harrison's renomination owed much to Clarkson. See several letters in the *Michener Papers*, especially Clarkson to Michener, May 19, 1915.

[6] B. F. Gue to R. P. Clarkson, March 15, 1891, *R. P. Clarkson Scrapbook*.

[7] "Iowans in Gotham," Des Moines *Register*, Feb. 28, 1892.

[8] Washington *Post*, Feb. 22, 1892, carried part of the interview. Frank Hatton, the former Iowan and former Postmaster General under Arthur, now publisher of the Washington *Post*, wrote to Mrs. Clarkson, evidently in reply to a complaint, explaining that the article was a news story, not an editorial, and therefore out of his province. Hatton to Mrs. Anna H. Clarkson, March 8, 1892, *Clarkson Papers* (Library of Congress).

[9] Clarkson to Allison, Feb. 26, 1892, Box 285, *Allison Papers*. Herbert Gibbons, *John Wanamaker* (2 vols., New York, 1926), deals very ineffectively with the Wanamaker-Clarkson relations.

[10] Mrs. Clarkson to Allison, March 7, 1892, Box 285, *Allison Papers*.

[11] Telegram, Mrs. Clarkson to Allison, March 12, 1892, *ibid*.

[12] Dozer, "Benjamin Harrison and the Campaign of 1892," 65.

[13] Clarkson to Allison, four telegrams, June 5, 1892, Box 285, *Allison Papers*.

[14] Dolliver to Clarkson, June 9, 1892, *Clarkson Papers* (Library of Congress); Everett Walters, *Joseph Benson Foraker, An Uncompromising Republican* (Columbus, 1948), 106.

[15] Allison to Morton, June 25, 1892, *Levi P. Morton Papers* (New York Public Library). Photostatic copies of all Allison and Clarkson letters were furnished through the kindness of Robert W. Hill, Keeper of the Manuscripts.

[16] Clarkson to Morton, Sept. 28, 1892, *ibid*. Also see McElroy, *Levi P. Morton*, 197-202, where it is made plain that one who opposed Morton was Boss Tom Platt. No other individual is singled out. Cortissoz, *Reid*, 2:178, conveniently ignores the story of Reid's nomination.

[17] Herman C. Nixon, "The Populist Movement in Iowa," *Iowa Journal of History and Politics*, 24:3-107 (January, 1926), especially pp. 61-2; John D. Hicks, *The Populist Revolt* (Minneapolis, 1931), 229-36.

[18] Clarkson to Morton, Sept. 28, 1892, *Morton Papers*.

[19] The Aldrich report was published as *Senate Report 1004*, 52 Cong., 1 Sess.

[20] Briggs, *Hepburn*, 165.

[21] C. Vann Woodward, *Tom Watson, Agrarian Rebel* (New York, 1938), 278-82; *Weller Papers*; James C. Olson, *History of Nebraska* (Lincoln, 1955), 238; Hicks, *Populist Revolt*, 236ff.; Nixon, "Populist Movement in Iowa," 62-5.

[22] Oberholtzer, *History of the United States*, 5:242.

[23] See Henry B. Russell, *International Monetary Conference* (New York, 1895), 376-408.

[24] Allison to R. P. Clarkson, Jan. 27, 1893, *R. P. Clarkson Scrapbook*.

[25] See Shannon, *America's Economic Growth*, 406.

[26] P. E. Studebaker to Allison, Feb. 1, 1893; Perkins to Allison, July 14, 1893, Box 292, *Allison Papers*.

[27] James S. Clarkson, "The Party of Lincoln, Grant and Blaine," a speech delivered at Louisville, Ky., May 10, 1893. Manuscript in *Clarkson Papers* (Library of Congress).

[28] Higgins to Allison, June 13, 1893, Box 291, *Allison Papers*.

[29] *Harper's Weekly*, Aug. 26, 1893, p. 806. Excellent pen and ink drawings of these men were given on p. 808.

[30] James A. Barnes, *John G. Carlisle, Financial Statesman* (New York, 1931), Chap. XII; Lambert, *Gorman*, Chap. IX.

[31] *Cong. Record*, 53 Cong., 1 Sess., 2957ff.

[32] Nevins, *Cleveland*, 507, citing the New York *Evening Post*, June 24, 1908.

[33] Cited in *ibid.*, 608; and Arthur F. Beringause, *Brooks Adams* (New York, 1955), 113; Joseph Benson Foraker, *Notes of a Busy Life* (2 vols., Cincinnati, 1916), 1:471.

[34] Hirsch, *Whitney*, 475-7.

[35] *Harper's Weekly*, July 14, 1895, p. 650. Strangely, Lodge's latest and best biographer, John A. Garraty, entirely omits 1894 and 1895 from his study.

[36] See Summers, *Wilson and Tariff Reform*, especially Chaps. X and XI.

[37] *Cong. Record*, 53 Cong., 2 Sess., 1796-7.

[38] Lambert, *Gorman*, Chap. X.

[39] Wells to Allison, Feb. 18 [1894], Box 218, *Allison Papers*.

[40] *Cong. Record*, 53 Cong., 2 Sess., Appendix, Part I, 691-706. Thomas Updegraff, Representative from the Third Iowa District, assisted in the distribution. See Updegraff to Allison, May 2, 1894, Box 295, *Allison Papers*. Allan Nevins' comment is questionable: "Aldrich . . . Hoar. . . . These two were supported by Allison, a big rumbling fellow." *Cleveland*, 576. Allison was never a "big rumbling fellow."

[41] *Cong. Record*, 53 Cong., 2 Sess., 7136.

[42] Charles E. Perkins to Allison, May 9, 19, June 23, 1894, Box 295, *Allison Papers*.

[43] Gilbert B. Pray to Allison, Aug. 25, Sept. 30, Oct. 8, 1893, Box 292, *ibid.*

[44] Kern, "Political Career of Horace Boies," 215-46; Cole, *I Remember, I Remember*, 192ff.

[45] Charles E. Perkins to Allison, March 14, 1893, Perkins Letterbook No. 10, *Overton Collection*.

[46] A. B. Cummins to R. P. Clarkson, Jan. 29, 1894, *R. P. Clarkson Scrapbook*.

[47] H. J. Playter, Washington, Iowa, to Allison, Jan. 10, 1894, Box 295, *Allison Papers*.

[48] Clarkson to Allison, Oct. 15, 1894, Box 293; George M. Reynolds to Allison, Oct. 24, 1895, Box 295, *ibid.*

[49] A. B. Cummins to Allison, Apr. 5, 1894, and Allison to Cummins, Apr. 25, 1894, Box 295, *ibid.* Allison's letter was delayed, perhaps, by the illness and death of Mr. Brayton, his friend and the caretaker of his house in Dubuque. See E. B. Nealley, Bangor, Maine, to Allison, Apr. 19, 1894, Box 10, *ibid.*

[50] Washington *Post*, cartoon by Coffin, reprinted in Dubuque *Sunday Times*, July 28, 1895.

[51] John Hay to Henry Adams, Sept. 3, 1895, quoted in William R. Thayer, *The Life and Letters of John Hay* (2 vols., Boston, 1915), 2:124-6.

[52] Allison to Kasson, Nov. 24, 1895, *Wead Collection*. This letter was kindly furnished to me by Edward Younger.

[53] Chicago *Tribune*, Jan. 16, 1896; Des Moines *Register*, Jan. 22, 1896; Clark, *History of Senatorial Elections in Iowa*, 235-8.

[54] James S. Clarkson to Cole, Dec. 9, 20, 23, 1895, *Cole Papers*. This and other letters cited herein were furnished to me through the great kindness of Miss Mildred Throne.

[55] Des Moines *Register*, March 12, 1896. The Philadelphia *Press*, March 8, 1896, had a good story on Allison's prospects and the plans for launching the Allison candidacy at

this convention. This paper consistently gave Allison a "good press," as did the Chicago *Inter-Ocean*.

[56] Waterloo *Daily Courier*, Apr. 1, 1896.

[57] Elmer E. Ellis, *Henry M. Teller, Defender of the West* (Caldwell, Idaho, 1941), 243.

[58] Waterloo *Daily Courier*, Apr. 29, 1896.

[59] Allison to James H. Wilson, May 4, 1896, Box 2 (a), *James H. Wilson Papers* (Library of Congress).

[60] See Herbert Croly, *Marcus Alonzo Hanna, His Life and Work* (New York, 1919), 166-89; Thomas Beer, *Hanna* (New York, 1929), 135-66; Philip D. Jordan, *Ohio Comes of Age* (Vol. V of *A History of Ohio*), 206-212.

[61] Waterloo *Daily Courier*, May 5, 1896.

[62] Clarkson to Michener, Feb. 27, 1896, Box 2, *Michener Papers*; Gear to Harrison, May 4, 1896; Harrison to Gear, May 8, 1896, Vol. 165, *Harrison Papers*.

[63] Gue, *History of Iowa*, 4:13; Cedar Rapids *Gazette*, June 26, 1896.

[64] Charles Olcott, *The Life of William McKinley* (2 vols., Boston, 1916), 1:315.

[65] A. B. Cummins to J. S. Clarkson, June 20, 1896, Box 4, *Clarkson Papers* (Library of Congress). Cummins must have included 1892 along with 1888, although this is hardly fair to Allison.

[66] Garraty, *Lodge*, 166-72; Ellis, *Teller*.

[67] Waterloo *Daily Courier*, June 19, 1896.

[68] Kern, "Political Career of Horace Boies," 215-46.

[69] Allison to Kasson, Nov. 24, 1895, *Wead Collection*. Courtesy of Edward Younger.

[70] Gear to Michener, July 20, 1896, *Michener Papers*.

[71] T. S. Parvin to Kasson, Nov. 14, 1896, *John A. Kasson Papers* (State Dept. of History and Archives, Des Moines).

[72] Charles G. Dawes, *A Journal of the McKinley Years* (Chicago, 1950), 105; *Iowa Senate Journal, 1908*, 55.

[73] Allison to James H. Wilson, Jan. 18, 1897, Box 2 (a), *Wilson Papers*; O. H. Platt to John R. Buck, quoted in Coolidge, *Platt*, 505-506.

CHAPTER XVII — CONSERVATIVES AND PROGRESSIVES

[1] *DAB*, 1:220-22.

[2] Dunn, *From Harrison to Harding*, 1:223-4; Stephenson, *Aldrich*, 142.

[3] Stephenson, *Aldrich*, 140; Ellis, *Teller*, 249-50, describes Wolcott as a Clevelander, a friend of Mark Hanna, before moving to Colorado. His Eastern connections made it difficult for him to follow completely the free silver views of the Westerners.

[4] Leon B. Richardson, *William E. Chandler* (New York, 1940), 555-6.

[5] Oberholtzer, *History of the United States*, 5:462-3.

[6] *Cong. Record*, 55 Cong., 1 Sess., 2750, 2909, 2962; Summers, *Wilson and Tariff Reform*, 261. Also see Edward Nelson Dingley, *The Life and Times of Nelson Dingley, Jr.* (Kalamazoo, Mich., 1902), 433-4; Richardson, *Chandler*, 554ff.; Stephenson, *Aldrich*, Chap. X.

[7] Jacob Swisher, *Robert G. Cousins* (Iowa City, 1938), 50-63.

[8] Garraty, *Lodge*, 195-200; Richard W. Leopold, *Elihu Root and the Conservative Tradition* (Boston, 1954), 22.

[9] John H. Gear to Cyrenus Cole, Jan. 21, Feb. 10, 1898, *Cole Papers*; Des Moines *Register*, Jan., Feb., March, 1898, *passim*; Perkins, *Dodge*, 313.

[10] *Cong. Record*, 55 Cong., 2 Sess., 2618.

11 Chicago *Tribune*, March 10, 1898, clipping in *R. P. Clarkson Scrapbook*; D. B. Henderson to R. P. Clarkson, March 12, 1898, *ibid.*

12 *Cong. Record*, 55 Cong., 2 Sess., 4244, 4252, 4288.

13 See Julius W. Pratt, *The Expansionists of 1898* (Baltimore, 1936), Chaps. VI, VII; Thomas A. Bailey, *A Diplomatic History of the American People* (New York, 1950), Chap. XXX; Walter Millis, *The Martial Spirit* (Boston, 1931), *passim.*

14 F. B. Heitman (ed.), *Historical Register and Directory of the United States Army . . .* (2 vols., Washington, 1903), 1:160; *Obituary Records of Graduates, Yale University* (New Haven, 1939), 71. I am grateful to Miss Dorothy Harris of the Alumni Records Office for data on W. B. Allison, Jr.

15 Dawes, *Journal of the McKinley Years*, 168, entry for Aug. 16, 1898.

16 J. P. Dolliver to R. P. Clarkson, March 15, 1899, *R. P. Clarkson Scrapbook*. Biographical data on Judge Edward R. Meek was kindly secured for me by Charles W. Davidson, College of Law, State University of Iowa, to whom the author expresses sincere gratitude. It is a pleasure to add that Meek was confirmed and that he served thirty-eight years on the bench, retiring Jan. 1, 1936. He died April 10, 1939.

17 Richard W. Leopold, Northwestern University, to the author, March 18, 1950.

18 Bailey, *Diplomatic History of the American People*, 523; Garraty, *Lodge*, 201-202; W. Stull Holt, *Treaties Defeated by the American Senate* (Baltimore, 1933), 177; Ellis, *Teller*, 317.

19 Des Moines *Register*, Feb. 7, 1899.

20 Allison to Professor W. H. Norton, Cornell College, Aug. 24, 1898, *Allison Papers*; William B. Allison, "Congress and the Philippines," *The Independent*, 51:2930 (Nov. 2, 1899).

21 See Claude G. Bowers, *Beveridge and the Progressive Era* (Boston, 1932), 21, 122, 138, 289; Beveridge to Allison, June 5, 1899, Box 73, *Allison Papers*.

22 Clipping dated Dec. 31, 1898, Albert F. Dawson Scrapbook, *Dawson Papers* (State Historical Society of Iowa, Iowa City). Senator Morrill died on Dec. 28, 1898.

23 Des Moines *Register*, Dec. 6, 1899.

24 D. B. Henderson to R. P. Clarkson, Apr. 20, 1899, *R. P. Clarkson Scrapbook*.

25 Allison to Aldrich, May 11, 13, 1899, *Nelson W. Aldrich Papers* (Library of Congress).

26 Henderson to Kasson, June 11, 1899, *Kasson Papers*.

27 New York *Times*, Dec. 3, 5, 1899.

28 Dawes, *Journal of the McKinley Years*, 208; *Cong. Record*, 56 Cong., 1 Sess., 4-5. Henderson's official vote was 177; his Democratic rival, James D. Richardson of Illinois, received 153; minor candidates received 6 votes.

29 Cummins to S. D. Cook, July 30, 1897, *Albert Baird Cummins Papers* (State Dept. of History and Archives, Des Moines, Iowa).

30 W. R. Laughlin, College Springs, Iowa, to R. P. Clarkson, Aug. 9, 1897, *R. P. Clarkson Scrapbook*. Laughlin had lived in Kansas at the time of the Cherokee affair and had been sent to Washington as an agent for the settlers, so he says in his letter. For reference to his work, see Gates, *Fifty Million Acres*, 173-7.

31 Oral statements to the author by Emory H. English and Ora Williams; J. W. Blythe to Allison, Apr. 21, 1899, Box 73, *Allison Papers*; Blythe to Cyrenus Cole, June 27, 1899; N. M. Hubbard to Cole, March 28, 1900, *Cole Papers*.

32 R. P. Clarkson to J. S. Clarkson, March 2, 1899, Box 1, *Clarkson Papers* (Library of Congress).

33 Cole added: "When you come up again the old age argument will be raised. They are all protesting that they want you returned — I think that they will have their desire." Cyrenus Cole to Allison, Sept. 25, 1899, Box 73, *Allison Papers*; Cole, *I Remember, I Remember*, 284-5.

34 J. W. Blythe to Cole, June 27, 1899, *Cole Papers*.

[35] Clark, *History of Senatorial Elections in Iowa*, 239-45.

[36] Des Moines *Register*, Jan. 19, 1900. This passage has been widely quoted, *e. g.*, Haynes, *Third Party Movements*, 450.

[37] On Shaw, see *DAB*, 17:43-4.

[38] N. M. Hubbard to Cole, Feb. 3, 1900, *Cole Papers*.

[39] Blum, *The Republican Roosevelt*, 43, attributes Clarkson's obscurity during these years to Hanna. My own opinion is that after 1896 Ret tried to crash the business world in preference to the game of politics and journalism. In reading hundreds of his letters I have never come upon a complaint about Hanna — and Ret was a genius at complaining about his enemies and opponents who conspired to hold him back.

[40] This incident has never been described in public print. It is fully covered in a series of letters and telegrams in the *Clarkson Papers* (Library of Congress). The successful candidate was Charles G. Bennett of Brooklyn, New York, a member of the House in the 54th and 55th Congresses and an unsuccessful candidate for the 56th. See *Cong. Directory*, 57 Cong., 1 Sess. (3rd ed.), 194.

[41] Clarkson to Cole, n. d., *Cole Papers*.

[42] Allison to Clarkson, Feb. 4, 1900, *Clarkson Papers* (Library of Congress).

[43] Croly, *Hanna*, 309-318; Beer, *Hanna*, 223-7; Blum, *The Republican Roosevelt*, 21-2; G. Wallace Chessman, "Theodore Roosevelt Campaigns Against the Vice-Presidency," *The Historian*, 14:185 (Spring, 1952); Julian W. Richards, "Stories on Dolliver," *Waterloo Evening Courier*, Oct. 22, 1910. Roosevelt was placed in nomination by Lafayette Young of Iowa. See *Proceedings of the Republican National Convention . . . 1900*, 131-2. Bowd Nealley to Allison, Sept. 27, 1900, Box 11, *Allison Papers*, wrote: "We all watch your public life with interest and were greatly pleased at the promptness with which the scheme to bottle you up in the Vice Presidency was rejected. The Senator from Iowa has a longer head than Teddy."

[44] Clark, *History of Senatorial Elections in Iowa*, 246.

[45] Stephenson, *Aldrich*, 134.

[46] *Cong. Record*, 57 Cong., 1 Sess., 387-8.

[47] *Ibid.*, 242-5.

[48] Arthur S. Link, *American Epoch* (New York, 1955), 68-91; Eric F. Goldman, *Rendezvous with Destiny, A History of Modern American Reform* (New York, 1953), 75-83; George Mowry, *Roosevelt and the Progressive Movement* (Madison, Wisc., 1946), 10-11; Russel B. Nye, *Midwestern Progressive Politics* (East Lansing, Mich., 1951), 195ff. Kenneth W. Hechler, *Insurgency, Personalities and Politics of the Taft Era* (New York, 1940), 12, credits Judge Nathaniel M. Hubbard with the first use of the word "Insurgents" to describe the Progressives.

[49] George Mills, *The Little Man with the Long Shadow: The Life of Frederick M. Hubbell* (Des Moines, 1955).

[50] A. B. Funk, *Fred L. Maytag, A Biography* (Cedar Rapids, 1936).

[51] Allison to Cummins, Aug. 8, 1901, *Cummins Papers*.

[52] George E. Roberts, "The Origins of the 'Iowa Idea,'" *Iowa Journal of History and Politics*, 2:69-73 (January, 1904).

[53] R. P. Clarkson to J. S. Clarkson, Nov. 17, 1901, *Clarkson Papers* (Library of Congress).

[54] R. P. Clarkson to J. S. Clarkson, Nov. 24, 1901, *ibid.*

[55] Clark, *History of Senatorial Elections in Iowa*, 246-7.

[56] Roberts, "Origins of the 'Iowa Idea,'" 73-4.

[57] Cole, *Iowa Through the Years*, 433-4; *World Review*, 11:451 (Dec. 28, 1901). Also see H. H. Kohlsaat, *From McKinley to Harding* (New York, 1923), 123-4, who claims to have planted the idea in Roosevelt's mind as a means of heading off any Shaw boom for the

presidency in 1904. It is preposterous to think that Roosevelt would have feared Shaw to this extent.

58 J. P. Dolliver to J. S. Clarkson, Apr. 12, 1902, Box 1, *Clarkson Papers* (Library of Congress).

59 In Blum, *The Republican Roosevelt*, 43-8, the impression is given that President Roosevelt took the initiative in recruiting Clarkson for his "team" in New York. The evidence cited above would not uphold this interpretation.

60 Cummins to N. E. Kendall, June 7, 1902, *Cummins Papers.*

61 Roberts, "Origins of the 'Iowa Idea,'" 76-8.

62 This account of the sale is based on letters in the *Clarkson Papers*, some in the Library of Congress and some in the Iowa State Dept. of History and Archives at Des Moines.

63 The conference was revealed in the columns of the Des Moines *Register and Leader*, Sept. 17, 1902. Stephenson, *Aldrich*, 194, refers to the conference as a well-kept secret.

64 Henderson to Allison, Sept. 16, 1903, Box 346, *Allison Papers*; Stephenson, *Aldrich*, 454, note 53.

65 Henderson to Allison, Sept. 17, 1902, *Allison Papers.*

66 Willard Hoing, "Colonel David Bremner Henderson: Speaker of the House" (M. A. thesis, Iowa State Teachers College, 1956), devotes several pages to this subject.

67 Cole, *I Remember, I Remember*, 329-30. See also Stephenson, *Aldrich*, 191, 195, and 454, note 53.

68 This quotation was frequently attributed to Speaker Henderson in the press of the day. See Cedar Falls *Semi-Weekly Gazette*, Sept. 26, 1902; Des Moines *Register and Leader*, Sept. 22, 1902. Henderson's announcement was given to the Dubuque newspaper by Lee McNeely, who acted as his spokesman and press representative at the time. McNeely had been private secretary to Col. Henderson and a clerk in the House; he was soon to become secretary to Allison.

69 Allison to R. P. Clarkson, July 15, 1902, *R. P. Clarkson Scrapbook.*

70 Cummins to Henderson, Sept. 10, 1902; Cummins to Theodore Roosevelt, June 26, 1902, *Cummins Papers.*

71 Henderson to R. P. Clarkson, Sept. 17, 1902, *R. P. Clarkson Scrapbook.*

72 J. S. Clarkson to M. S. Quay, Sept. 17, 1902, *Clarkson Papers* (Library of Congress).

73 Cummins to B. P. Birdsall, Sept. 27, 1902, *Cummins Papers.*

74 Cummins to John Kemble, Oct. 2, 1902, *ibid.*

75 Leslie M. Shaw to J. S. Clarkson, March 26, 1903, *Clarkson Papers* (Library of Congress).

76 Shaw to Clarkson, Apr. 13, 1903; Clarkson to Shaw, Apr. 15, 1903, *Clarkson Papers* (Des Moines); Shaw to Clarkson, Apr. 16, 1903, *Clarkson Papers* (Library of Congress).

77 Cummins to George D. Perkins, Apr. 16, 1903; Cummins to Allison, Apr. 17, 1903, *Cummins Papers.*

78 Roberts, "Origins of the 'Iowa Idea,'" 78.

79 *Ibid.*, 78-9.

80 Cummins to Dawes, Nov. 5, 1903; Cummins to Allison, Nov. 9, 1903, *Cummins Papers.*

81 Cummins to Thomas A. Way, July 14, 1903, *ibid.*

82 Cummins to Way, Nov. 14, 1903, *ibid.*

83 Cummins to Harvey Ingham, Jan. 30, 1904, *ibid.*

84 Bowers, *Beveridge*, 205; Swisher, *Cousins, passim*; M. B. Smith, "A Theoretical Analysis of the Speeches of Robert Gordon Cousins" (Ph. D. thesis, University of Minnesota, 1952).

85 Kasson to Ora Williams, Oct. 4, 1904, Vol. 6, *Kasson Papers* (Des Moines).

86 Lee McNeely to the author; this fact was admitted in the obituary articles in August, 1908.

[87] Benj. F. Shambaugh, *The Constitutions of Iowa* (Iowa City, 1934), 291; Titus, "The Battle for Biennial Elections," 163-75.

[88] Dubuque *Daily Times*, Feb. 27, 1906.

[89] Correspondence by "Raymond" in the Chicago *Tribune*, reprinted in the Des Moines *Register and Leader*, July 4, 1906. "But last winter the Iowa senator began to break down physically."

[90] Des Moines *Register and Leader*, March 2, 3, 1906.

CHAPTER XVIII——ALLISON AND ROOSEVELT

[1] The description is from Miss Martha Baker of Dubuque. Miss Baker, a most remarkable nonagenarian of vivacious manner and clear memory, knew Allison well. As an intimate friend of his three nieces, the daughters of Matthew Allison, she saw him often over a long period of years. In her phrase, Allison never stepped out boldly but "shuffled along, in a timid manner." Miss Martha Baker to the author in personal conversation, August 1, 1954.

[2] Roosevelt to Allison, Sept. 27, 1901, *Allison Papers*; Stephenson, *Aldrich*, 174.

[3] Younger, *Kasson*, 364-79; J. Laurence Laughlin and Parker Willis, *Reciprocity* (New York, 1903), 302; Mary Jane Thierman, "John Adam Kasson: His Reciprocity Treaties and Their Fate" (M. A. thesis, Iowa State Teachers College, 1953).

[4] Stephenson, *History of the American People*, 2:434.

[5] Dubuque *Times*, Oct. 16, 1901. Allison made essentially the same speech in a number of Iowa towns.

[6] Allison to Roosevelt, Nov. 2, 1901, *Theodore Roosevelt Papers* (Library of Congress).

[7] Stephenson, *Aldrich*, 194-9.

[8] Tyler Dennett, *John Hay: From Poetry to Politics* (New York, 1933), 382-3.

[9] Blum, *The Republican Roosevelt*, 23; Des Moines *Register and Leader*, July 4, 1906.

[10] Lambert, *Elkins*, 261-6, analyzes the workings of the Elkins Act, 1903-1905, and quotes from President Roosevelt's annual message to Congress, December, 1905, asking for better legislation to secure regulation of rates, including the sentence: "It must include putting a complete stop to rebates in every shape and form." Richardson, *Messages and Papers of the Presidents*, 16:6976.

[11] Briggs, *Hepburn*, 252, 413, note 408; *Cong. Record*, 58 Cong., 3 Sess., 2198-9.

[12] Cummins to William Larrabee, Feb. 15, 1905; Cummins to H. L. Spencer, Jan. 28, 1905, *Cummins Papers*; Des Moines *Register and Leader*, Jan. 26, 1906, cited in Briggs, *Hepburn*, 406, note 360.

[13] *Cong. Record*, 58 Cong., 3 Sess., 2205-2206, 2227.

[14] Nicholas Murray Butler, *Across the Busy Years* (2 vols., New York, 1939-1940), 2:30.

[15] Merlo J. Pusey, *Charles Evans Hughes* (2 vols., New York, 1951), 1:140-68.

[16] Briggs, *Hepburn*, 262-3.

[17] Mowry, *Theodore Roosevelt and the Progressive Movement*, 25-6.

[18] Briggs, *Hepburn*, 265-6; *Cong. Record*, 59 Cong., 1 Sess., 577, 712; H. R. Bill No. 10,099, *ibid.*, 981, 1520; *House Committee Reports*, 59 Cong., 1 Sess., No. 591, pp. 1-2; H. R. Bill No. 11,488.

[19] See Stephenson, *Aldrich*, Chap. XIX; Richardson, *Chandler*, Chap. XXVIII; Francis B. Simkins, *Pitchfork Ben Tillman* (Baton Rouge, La., 1944), Chap. XXVIII; Sam Acheson, *Joe Bailey, The Last Democrat* (New York, 1932), 188-200; Henry F. Pringle, *Theodore Roosevelt, A Biography* (New York, 1931), 415-25; Morison (ed.), *Letters of Theodore Roosevelt*, Vols. IV, V, VI, *passim*, especially Vol. VI, Appendix II, 1558-71, for an essay by John M. Blum, "Theodore Roosevelt and the Hepburn Act: Toward an Orderly System of

Control." See also W. Z. Ripley, *Railroads: Rates and Regulations* (New York, 1912), 499-512; Alfred H. Kelley and Winfred A. Harbison, *The American Constitution: Its Origins and Its Development* (New York, 1948), 600ff.; J. W. Bryan, "Aspects of the Senatorial Debate Upon the Rate Bill," *American Law Review*, 41:801ff. (1907). Ray Stannard Baker, "The Railroad Rates, A Study in Commercial Autocracy," *McClure's*, 26:47-59 (November, 1905), provides excellent background for understanding the temper of the times which made some sort of action by Congress imperative.

20 Blum, "Theodore Roosevelt and the Hepburn Act," 1561, flatly asserts, "Roosevelt had constructed the Hepburn bill with practiced care." Blum has the most recent account of this great battle; my account follows his closely.

21 Blum, *ibid.*, 1564; Simkins, *Tillman*, 421-6; Richardson, *Chandler*, 659-61.

22 Roosevelt to Long, Jan. 31, May 5, 1906, Morison (ed.), *Letters of Theodore Roosevelt*, 5:142, 258.

23 Roosevelt to Senator Knute Nelson, Apr. 11, 1906; Roosevelt to Allison, Apr. 12, May 5, 10, 14, 1906, *ibid.*, 5:209, 210, 258, 261, 270.

24 The amendment was introduced on the afternoon of May 8, 1906; see *Cong. Record*, 59 Cong., 1 Sess., 6501. The analysis given here follows closely that found in Ripley, *Railroads: Rates and Regulations*, 501-507.

25 Stephenson, *Aldrich*, 310-11. Actually, there were seven parts to the proposal; the term "Allison Amendments" is justifiable. Jeannette P. Nichols, "Contradictory Trends in Middle Western Democracy, 1865-1900," in Nichols and Randall (eds.), *Democracy in the Middle West, 1840-1940*, 87-8. Allison's illness and frequent confinement to his rooms at the Portland Hotel throw some doubt on this story. Nothing has been discovered in the evidence to indicate that he left Washington during this period. See *Cong. Record*, 59 Cong., 1 Sess., *passim*, especially all pages recording the Senate debates, May 4-14, 1906.

26 Des Moines *Register and Leader*, May 5-15, 1906, not only has its own full coverage on this topic, but it ran copious quotations from leading newspapers in New York, Washington, St. Louis, and elsewhere. The *Register and Leader*, May 12, had a most amusing cartoon, showing Allison looking out of his front door in great surprise at a baby on his doorstep, labelled "Allison Amendment." The cartoon was captioned, "Mine?"

27 See footnote 25 above.

28 Roosevelt to Knute Nelson, Apr. 11, 1906, in Morison (ed.), *Letters of Theodore Roosevelt*, 5:209-210; Roosevelt to Allison, May 5, 1906, *ibid.*, 5:258-9.

29 Roosevelt to Edward Payson Bacon, May 8, 1906, *ibid.*, 5:260.

30 Roosevelt to Allison, May 14, 1906, *ibid.*, 5:270-72.

31 Theodore Roosevelt, *An Autobiography* (New York, 1914), 437.

32 Blum, "Theodore Roosevelt and the Hepburn Act," 1567, 1569.

33 See T. V. Smith, *The Legislative Way of Life* (Chicago, 1940), 68-96, and *Discipline for Democracy* (Chapel Hill, N. C., 1942), 93-116.

34 Stephenson, *Aldrich*, 309-313; Blum, "Theodore Roosevelt and the Hepburn Act," 1570-71; Allison to Dolliver, Aug. 23, 1907, Box 362, *Allison Papers*.

35 Richardson, *Chandler*, 664ff.

36 Ripley, *Railroads: Rates and Regulations*, 507-509.

37 Kelley and Harbison, *American Constitution*, 600-605.

38 Richardson, *Chandler*, 668-70; Simkins, *Tillman*, 437-9.

39 *Cong. Record*, 59 Cong., 1 Sess., 6886-7. This letter is cited in footnote 30 above.

40 On the general history of muckraking, see C. C. Regier, *The Era of the Muckrakers* (Chapel Hill, N. C., 1932), *passim*. Probably no two writers would agree exactly as to the date of the transformation from helpful, scholarly, scientific muckraking over to "yellow-sheet" sensationalism. Link, *American Epoch*, 76-7, strongly asserts the date to be 1906.

[41] *Cosmopolitan Magazine*, 41:627-32 (October, 1906). These articles were reprinted in book form by Academic Reprints, Stanford, Calif. [1953].

[42] Louis Filler, *Crusaders for American Liberalism* (New York, 1939), 203-216. The idea for such a series had originated with Charles Edward Russell in 1905 and rejected by *Everybody's* as too risky. Then Millard, who had been employed by Hearst to increase the circulation, came up with the same idea. *Ibid.*, 247. An admirable example of refutation of the Phillips attack is to be found in Lambert, *Gorman*, 363-73.

[43] Cummins to La Follette, Jan. 30, 1906, *Cummins Papers.*

[44] Cummins to E. C. Roach, Rock Rapids, Feb. 5, 1906, *ibid.*

[45] Cummins to Brookhart, March 19, 1906, *ibid.*

[46] Cummins to W. H. Torbert, Apr. 19, 1906, *ibid.* Also see Clark, *History of Senatorial Elections in Iowa*, 250-53, and Cyrenus Cole, *I Remember, I Remember*, 316-17. Cole reasons that Cummins, alarmed over the factional fight that had developed because he had come into the gubernatorial race for a third term after George D. Perkins had announced, made overtures to the Allison crowd.

[47] Des Moines *Register and Leader*, Aug. 2, 1906. The Cummins machine even invaded Dubuque. In May the Dubuque County convention voted unanimously to empower one Fred Kretschmer to name the delegation to the state convention. Kretschmer announced that he would select an unmixed Cummins slate. Allison leaders such as his former secretary, now postmaster, Joseph Morgan, were attacked openly as examples of the "machine bossism" of the past. An effort to drag Allison into the fight was made, but he sent word that he would not take sides. *Ibid.*, May 11, 1906.

[48] Cummins to Allison, Aug. 25, 1906; Cummins to James Wilson, Aug. 25, 1906 *Cummins Papers.*

[49] Link, *American Epoch*, 77: "Phillips combined truth, fiction, and outright prevarication; but his indictment of the business domination of the Senate added a powerful impetus to the movement for the direct election of senators."

[50] Clark, *History of Senatorial Elections in Iowa*, 248-50; *Laws of Iowa, 1907*, 51; *Senate Journal, 1907*, 57 (for Cummins' inaugural address); Emory H. English, "Evolution in Iowa Voting Practices," *Annals of Iowa* (third series), 19:249-89 (April, 1948), gives the background of the passage of the primary law of 1907 and adds comment as to its value.

[51] Clark, *History of Senatorial Elections in Iowa*, 247-8; Cummins to G. M. Curtis, Dec. 24, 1906, *Cummins Papers.*

[52] Dodge to Allison, Mar. 15, 1907, Box 362, *Allison Papers.*

[53] J. S. Clarkson to L. T. Michener, Apr. 6, 1907, Box 1, *Clarkson Papers* (Library of Congress).

[54] George E. Roberts to Clarkson, Apr. 4 [1907], *Clarkson Papers* (Des Moines).

CHAPTER XIX — EXIT IN TRIUMPH

[1] Dodge to Allison, Mar. 15, 1907, Box 362, *Allison Papers*; Allison to Dodge, Apr. 15, 1907, Box 363, *ibid.*

[2] Cleaves to McNeely, May 22, 1907, *ibid.* In a conversation on February 10, 1956, Mr. McNeely gave me almost exactly these same words. A lapse of nearly forty-nine years had not dimmed his memories or his opinions of 1907 concerning Allison's health.

[3] B. P. Birdsall to Dolliver, Apr. 9, 1907, *Dolliver Papers.*

[4] Ernest E. Hart to Allison, June 22, 1907, Box 363, *Allison Papers*; Allison to Hart, June 24, 1907, *ibid.* The "backers" Hart referred to were Judge Walter I. Smith, Victor Bender, and State Senator Charles G. Saunders, all of Council Bluffs.

⁵ Hart to Allison, June 26, 1907; Allison to Hart, July 11, 1907, *ibid.*

⁶ Assurances of assistance were received from Congressmen Haugen, Hull, Lacey, Kennedy, and Conner. Robert G. Cousins reported that all his contacts were through a few influential leaders. Boxes 363, 364, *ibid.*

⁷ Allison to Dolliver, Aug. 23, 1907, Box 362, *ibid.*

⁸ A copy of this announcement, written on United States Senate stationery is in *ibid.* It was generally published on Aug. 27, 1907. The next day Allison wrote to Congressman Hull, repeating the explanation for the announcement. Box 363, *ibid.*

⁹ Dodge to Allison, Aug. 27, 1907, Box 362, *ibid.*; Dubuque *Times-Journal*, Sept. 15, 29, 1907.

¹⁰ Hart to Allison, Aug. 30, 1907, Box 363, *ibid.*

¹¹ Clarkson to Allison, Aug. 31, 1907, Box 362, *ibid.* For a pro-Allison paper, see issues of Dubuque *Times-Journal* during campaign.

¹² Allison to Dolliver, Sept. 20, 1907; Dolliver to Allison, n. d., *Allison Papers.*

¹³ Emory H. English to the author, Dec. 30, 1954. Mr. English was editor of the Mason City *Daily Times* in 1907-1908, in Haugen's district, and close to all the political leaders of that day.

¹⁴ Clarkson to Dodge, Sept. 16, 1907, *Clarkson Papers* (Des Moines).

¹⁵ Clarkson to Theodore Roosevelt, Sept. 27, 1907, *ibid.*

¹⁶ Dubuque *Times-Journal*, Oct. 1, 1907.

¹⁷ Allison to Dolliver, Oct. 8, 1907, *Dolliver Papers.* A carbon copy is in Box 362, *Allison Papers.*

¹⁸ Dolliver to Allison, Oct. 10, 1907, *Allison Papers.*

¹⁹ Allison to Dolliver, Oct. 12, 1907, *ibid.*

²⁰ Charles M. Harl to Allison, Oct. 17, 1907, Box 363, *ibid.*

²¹ Dodge to Allison, Oct. 18, 1907, Box 362, *ibid.*

²² Allison to Harl, Oct. 19, 1907, Box 363, *ibid.*

²³ Allison to Dolliver, Oct. 23, 1907, *Dolliver Papers.*

²⁴ Allison to Dolliver, Nov. 4, 1907, *ibid.*

²⁵ Allison to Dolliver, Nov. 8, 1907, *ibid.*

²⁶ Council Bluffs *Nonpareil*, Nov. 25, 26, 1907; Dubuque *Times-Journal*, Nov. 26, 1907; Des Moines *Register and Leader*, Nov. 26, 1907, carrying dispatch from Council Bluffs dated Nov. 25, 1907.

²⁷ Harl to Allison, Nov. 26, 1907, Box 364, *Allison Papers.*

²⁸ See Hostettler, "The Oratorical Career of Jonathan P. Dolliver."

²⁹ Cummins to Dolliver, Sept. 12, 1907, *Dolliver Papers.*

³⁰ Dolliver to Cummins, Sept. 19, 1907, *ibid.*

³¹ Des Moines *Register and Leader*, Dec. 4, 16, 1907.

³² B. W. Lacy to Allison, Dec. 11, 13, 1907, Box 364, *Allison Papers*; Torbert to Dolliver, Dec. 11, 13, 1907, in Des Moines *Register and Leader*, Dec. 14, 1907.

³³ Cummins to A. B. Funk, Jan. 11, 1908, *Cummins Papers.*

³⁴ Cummins to Cyrenus Cole, Nov. 23, 1920, *Cole Papers.*

³⁵ The Fry Memorandum of July 5, 1924, was found in the *Cummins Papers* by Professor Ralph M. Sayre, who very generously placed it at my disposal. For Aldrich-Vreeland Act, see Stephenson, *Aldrich*, 325-30.

³⁶ Cummins to W. E. Hamilton, Jan. 11, 1908, *Cummins Papers*; Odebolt *Chronicle*, Jan. 9, 1908.

³⁷ The Roberts article is in the Dubuque *Times-Journal*, Mar. 19, 1908; the Hart interview, in the Council Bluffs *Nonpareil*, June 23, 1907. The *Allison Papers* for the period

are replete with declinations of invitations to various functions, always using a plea of illness and the necessity of conserving his strength. Even so good a friend as Leslie M. Shaw was turned down on a request for an introduction to a book of speeches. See Allison to Shaw, Feb. 8, 1908, Box 95, *Allison Papers.*

[38] John T. Adams to Dolliver, Feb. 7, March 2, 1908, *Dolliver Papers.* There are several other letters from Adams to Dolliver in this collection.

[39] Waterloo *Daily Courier*, March 17, 1908.

[40] *Ibid.*, March 18, 1908.

[41] *Idem.*

[42] Des Moines *Register and Leader*, March 19, 1908. This paper reports the vote as $673\frac{1}{2}$ to $510\frac{1}{2}$.

[43] Waterloo *Daily Courier*, March 20, 1908.

[44] Clarksville *Butler County Tribune*, March 26, 1908. The convention selected the following delegates-at-large to the national convention: George D. Perkins, Lafayette Young, Joe R. Lane, and Frank Simmons. See Des Moines *Register and Leader*, March 19, 1908.

[45] Waterloo *Daily Courier*, March 21, 1908.

[46] Cummins to G. W. Cowden, Apr. 24, 1908, *Cummins Papers.*

[47] Council Bluffs *Nonpareil*, May 20, 1908; Cedar Rapids *Evening Times*, June 1, 1908. The action of Congress in the Banton case helped to establish the principle of liability for injury incurred while in government service. See obituary of Pembroke Banton, Waterloo *Daily Courier*, Jan. 16, 1955.

[48] *Cong. Record*, 60 Cong., 1 Sess., 7184, shows Allison's last answer to a roll-call on May 29. The Senate went into an all-night session before adjournment on the 30th.

[49] Lee McNeely to the author, in conversation, Feb. 10, 1956. *Cong. Record*, 60 Cong., 1 Sess., 7274.

[50] Allison was not an official delegate to the Republican national convention of 1856.

[51] Clarksville *Butler County Tribune*, May 21, 1908.

[52] Des Moines *Register and Leader*, June 1, 1908.

[53] This analysis was originated by Professor Samuel Hays of the department of history, State University of Iowa, who very kindly made it available to me.

[54] Roosevelt to Benjamin Ide Wheeler, June 22, 1908, in *ibid.*, 6:1094; Taft to Charles Nagel, June 1, 1908, quoted in H. F. Pringle, *The Life and Times of William Howard Taft* (2 vols., New York, 1939), 1:354-5.

[55] Charles G. Saunders (June 4), Charles S. Vrooman (June 5), G. M. Dodge (June 5), Lafayette Young (June 5), I. S. Struble (June 4), James S. Clarkson (June 8), George E. Roberts (June 12), Maurice D. O'Connell (June 12), James E. Blythe (June 14), 1908, to Dolliver, *Dolliver Papers.* All these writers openly stressed the "fear of Cummins" motivation.

[56] Des Moines *Register and Leader* was the principal medium for this point of view. It first appeared in the issue of June 4, 1908, and followed in succeeding issues daily. Ding's cleverest cartoon appeared in the issue of June 13. It pictured Dolliver looking out a window at Roosevelt and Taft coming through the gate, Taft with a warrant entitled "Search for Vice Presidential Candidate." In the yard were three men labeled "Lafe" [Young], "Uncle George" [Roberts], and [John F.] "Lacey," busily posting the house with signs reading "Measles, Bubonic Plague, Mumps," etc. Lafe was shouting, "You mustn't come in here!" The caption of the cartoon was: "If there are any other reasons why Dolliver should be kept at home the Standpatters haven't thought of them yet."

[57] Des Moines *Register and Leader*, June 15, June 16-19, 1908. Allison made no attempt

to attend the Chicago convention but sent his secretary to represent his interests and to perform such favors as the distribution of his allotment of tickets.

58 Waterloo *Daily Courier*, June 24, 25, 1908; Briggs, *Hepburn*, 330-31.

59 Cole, *I Remember, I Remember*, 321-2.

60 Lee McNeely to the author, May 20, 1956.

61 "Bill" [W. P. Hepburn?] to Dolliver, June 20, 1908, *Dolliver Papers*: "My reports of Senator Allison's condition are discouraging but I hope he will recuperate in his home surroundings."

62 Lee McNeely to Dolliver, June 28, 1908, *ibid.* For example, the decision as to the nominee for the postmastership of Ottumwa.

63 Cummins to William Anderson of Jewell, Iowa, July 29, 1908, *Cummins Papers.*

64 Ret Clarkson to Al Swalm, Aug. 17, 1908, *Clarkson Papers* (Des Moines).

Index

Index